THE O'LEARY SERIES

INTRODUCTORY EDITION

Microsoft®
Access 2010:
A Case Approach

Timothy J. O'Leary

*Professor Emeritus,
Arizona State University*

Linda I. O'Leary

McGraw Hill

*Connect
Learn
Succeed*™

THE O'LEARY SERIES MICROSOFT® ACCESS 2010: A CASE APPROACH, INTRODUCTORY EDITION

Published by McGraw-Hill, a business unit of The McGraw-Hill Companies, Inc., 1221 Avenue of the Americas, New York, NY, 10020. Copyright © 2011 by The McGraw-Hill Companies, Inc. All rights reserved. No part of this publication may be reproduced or distributed in any form or by any means, or stored in a database or retrieval system, without the prior written consent of The McGraw-Hill Companies, Inc., including, but not limited to, in any network or other electronic storage or transmission, or broadcast for distance learning.

Some ancillaries, including electronic and print components, may not be available to customers outside the United States.

This book is printed on acid-free paper.

1 2 3 4 5 6 7 8 9 0 RMN/RMN 1 0 9 8 7 6 5 4 3 2 1 0

ISBN   978-0-07-733132-0
MHID   0-07-733132-X

Vice president/Editor in chief: *Elizabeth Haefele*
Vice president/Director of marketing: *John E. Biernat*
Senior sponsoring editor: *Scott Davidson*
Director of development: *Sarah Wood*
Developmental editor II: *Alaina Grayson*
Editorial coordinator: *Alan Palmer*
Marketing manager: *Tiffany Wendt*
Lead digital product manager: *Damian Moshak*
Digital developmental editor: *Kevin White*
Director, Editing/Design/Production: *Jess Ann Kosic*
Project manager: *Marlena Pechan*
Senior buyer: *Michael R. McCormick*
Senior designer: *Srdjan Savanovic*
Senior photo research coordinator: *Jeremy Cheshareck*
Media project manager: *Cathy L. Tepper*
Cover design: *Evan Modesto*
Interior design: *Laurie Entringer*
Typeface: *10/12 New Aster LT STD*
Compositor: *Laserwords Private Limited*
Printer: *R. R. Donnelley*
Cover credit: © Kjpargeter/Dreamstime.com
Credits: The credits section for this book begins on page ACC.1 and is considered an extension of the copyright page.

Library of Congress Cataloging-in-Publication Data

O'Leary, Timothy J., 1947-
    Microsoft Access 2010 : a case approach / Timothy J. O'Leary, Linda I. O'Leary. —
Introductory ed.
      p. cm. — (The O'Leary series)
    Includes index.
    ISBN-13: 978-0-07-733132-0 (alk. paper)
    ISBN-10: 0-07-733132-X (alk. paper)
    1. Microsoft Access. 2. Database management. I. O'Leary, Linda I. II. Title.
    QA76.9.D3O3874 2011
    005.75'65—dc22   2010029772

The Internet addresses listed in the text were accurate at the time of publication. The inclusion of a Web site does not indicate an endorsement by the authors or McGraw-Hill, and McGraw-Hill does not guarantee the accuracy of the information presented at these sites.

www.mhhe.com

Brief Contents

Introduction to
Microsoft Office 2010   IO.1

Lab 1: Creating a Database   AC1.1

Lab 2: Modifying and Filtering
a Table and Creating a Form   AC2.1

Lab 3: Querying Tables
and Creating Reports   AC3.1

Working Together 1:
Exporting Data   ACWT1.1

Command Summary   ACCS.1

Glossary of Key Terms   ACG.1

Index   ACI.1

Contents

INTRODUCTION TO MICROSOFT OFFICE 2010   IO.1

Objectives	IO.1
What Is Microsoft Office 2010?	IO.2
Word 2010	IO.2
Word 2010 Features	IO.2
Excel 2010	IO.5
Excel 2010 Features	IO.5
Access 2010	IO.7
Access 2010 Features	IO.7
PowerPoint 2010	IO.10
PowerPoint 2010 Features	IO.10
Instructional Conventions	IO.12
Commands	IO.12
File Names and Information to Type	IO.13
Common Office 2010 Features	IO.13
Common Interface Features	IO.14
Common Application Features	IO.28
Using Office Help	IO.60
Exiting an Office 2010 Application	IO.65
LAB REVIEW	IO.66
Key Terms	IO.66
Command Summary	IO.66
LAB EXERCISES	IO.68
Hands-On Exercises	IO.68
Step-by-Step	IO.68
On Your Own	IO.70

LAB 1 CREATING A DATABASE   AC1.1

Objectives	AC1.1
Case Study	AC1.2
Concept Preview	AC1.4
Designing a New Database	AC1.4
Planning the Club Database	AC1.5
Creating and Naming the Database File	AC1.6
Exploring the Access Window	AC1.9
Using the Navigation Pane	AC1.10
Creating a Table	AC1.10
Defining Table Fields	AC1.11
Entering Field Data	AC1.12
Changing Field Names	AC1.13
Defining Field Data Type	AC1.14
Using the Quick Add Feature	AC1.17

Using Field Models	*AC1.18*
Deleting a Field in Datasheet View	*AC1.21*

Modifying Field Properties — *AC1.22*
Switching Views	*AC1.22*
Setting Field Size	*AC1.24*
Changing Data Type	*AC1.26*
Editing Field Names	*AC1.27*
Defining a Field as a Primary Key	*AC1.28*
Entering Field Descriptions	*AC1.29*
Deleting a Field in Design View	*AC1.31*
Creating a Field in Design View	*AC1.31*
Creating an Attachment Field	*AC1.34*

Entering and Editing Records — *AC1.34*
Verifying Data Accuracy and Validity	*AC1.35*
Using AutoCorrect	*AC1.37*
Attaching Files to Records	*AC1.39*
Moving between Fields	*AC1.44*
Zooming a Field	*AC1.45*

Changing Column Width — *AC1.47*
Resizing a Column	*AC1.48*
Using Best Fit	*AC1.49*

Navigating among Records — *AC1.54*
Moving Using the Keyboard	*AC1.54*
Moving Using the Navigation Buttons	*AC1.55*
Moving to a Specific Record	*AC1.56*

Deleting Records — *AC1.57*

Creating a Table in Design View — *AC1.59*
Inserting a Field	*AC1.59*
Moving a Field	*AC1.61*
Copying Field Content	*AC1.64*

Creating Relationships — *AC1.65*
Closing Tables	*AC1.67*
Viewing Relationships	*AC1.67*
Defining Relationships	*AC1.69*
Opening Tables	*AC1.70*

Closing and Opening a Database — *AC1.72*
Closing a Database	*AC1.73*
Opening a Database	*AC1.73*

Setting Database and Object Properties — *AC1.75*
Documenting a Database	*AC1.76*
Documenting a Table Object	*AC1.77*

Previewing and Printing a Table — *AC1.78*
Previewing the Table	*AC1.78*
Printing a Table	*AC1.80*
Changing the Page Orientation and Margins	*AC1.80*

Exiting Access — *AC1.83*

FOCUS ON CAREERS — *AC1.83*

CONCEPT SUMMARY — *AC1.84*

LAB REVIEW — *AC1.86*
Key Terms	*AC1.86*
Command Summary	*AC1.87*

LAB EXERCISES — *AC1.90*
Screen Identification	*AC1.90*
Matching	*AC1.91*
True/False	*AC1.91*
Fill-In	*AC1.92*
Multiple Choice	*AC1.92*
Hands-On Exercises	*AC1.94*
Step-by-Step	*AC1.94*
On Your Own	*AC1.108*

LAB 2 — MODIFYING AND FILTERING A TABLE AND CREATING A FORM AC2.1

Objectives	*AC2.1*
Case Study	*AC2.2*
Concept Preview	*AC2.4*
Customizing Fields	*AC2.4*
Setting Display Formats	*AC2.6*
Setting Default Values	*AC2.7*
Defining Validation Rules	*AC2.10*
Hiding and Redisplaying Fields	*AC2.14*
Hiding Fields	*AC2.14*
Redisplaying Hidden Fields	*AC2.16*
Creating a Lookup Field	*AC2.17*
Using the Lookup Wizard	*AC2.18*
Searching for, Finding, and Replacing Data	*AC2.23*
Searching for Data	*AC2.23*
Finding Data	*AC2.25*
Replacing Data	*AC2.30*
Sorting Records	*AC2.32*
Sorting on a Single Field	*AC2.33*
Sorting on Multiple Fields	*AC2.34*
Formatting the Datasheet	*AC2.36*
Changing Background and Gridline Colors	*AC2.36*
Changing the Text Color	*AC2.39*
Filtering a Table	*AC2.40*
Using Filter by Selection	*AC2.41*
Removing and Deleting Filters	*AC2.42*
Filtering Using Common Filters	*AC2.43*
Filtering on Multiple Fields	*AC2.45*
Creating a Simple Form	*AC2.46*
Using the Form Tool	*AC2.47*
Using the Multiple Items Tool	*AC2.48*
Using the Form Wizard	*AC2.48*
Modifying a Form	*AC2.54*
Using Form Layout View	*AC2.54*
Moving Controls	*AC2.55*
Applying a Layout	*AC2.56*
Sizing and Moving Controls in a Layout	*AC2.58*
Splitting a Layout	*AC2.60*
Removing Rows from a Layout	*AC2.61*
Inserting, Merging, and Splitting Cells	*AC2.63*
Adding Existing Fields	*AC2.68*
Changing the Design Style	*AC2.69*
Using a Form	*AC2.71*
Navigating in Form View	*AC2.71*
Searching in Form View	*AC2.72*
Sorting and Filtering Data in a Form	*AC2.74*
Adding Records Using a Form	*AC2.75*
Organizing the Navigation Pane	*AC2.76*
Previewing and Printing a Form	*AC2.78*
Printing a Selected Record	*AC2.78*

Identifying Object Dependencies	AC2.79
FOCUS ON CAREERS	AC2.81
CONCEPT SUMMARY	AC2.82
LAB REVIEW	AC2.84
Key Terms	AC2.84
Command Summary	AC2.85
LAB EXERCISES	AC2.88
Matching	AC2.88
True/False	AC2.88
Fill-In	AC2.89
Multiple Choice	AC2.90
Hands-On Exercises	AC2.92
Step-by-Step	AC2.92
On Your Own	AC2.102

LAB 3 QUERYING TABLES AND CREATING REPORTS AC3.1

Objectives	AC3.1
Case Study	AC3.2
Concept Preview	AC3.4
Refining the Database Design	AC3.4
Evaluating Table Design	AC3.5
Creating a Table List Lookup Field	AC3.10
Deleting a Table	AC3.13
Defining and Modifying Relationships	AC3.13
Deleting Relationships	AC3.15
Editing Relationships to Enforce Referential Integrity	AC3.18
Creating a Query	AC3.19
Using the Query Wizard	AC3.20
Filtering a Query	AC3.23
Using Query Design View	AC3.25
Adding a Second Table to the Query	AC3.25
Adding Fields	AC3.27
Specifying Query Criteria	AC3.29
Hiding and Sorting Columns	AC3.32
Rearranging the Query Datasheet	AC3.34
Finding Unmatched Records	AC3.35
Finding Duplicate Records	AC3.39
Creating a Parameter Query	AC3.41
Displaying a Totals Row	AC3.45
Creating Reports	AC3.46
Using the Report Tool	AC3.47
Viewing the Report	AC3.48
Using the Report Wizard	AC3.50
Modifying the Report in Layout View	AC3.53
Changing the Report Theme	AC3.56
Modifying a Report in Design View	AC3.56
Formatting Controls	AC3.60
Deleting a Field	AC3.63
Sorting and Filtering Data in a Report	AC3.64
Preparing Reports for Printing	AC3.65
Modifying the Page Setup	AC3.65
Previewing and Printing Reports	AC3.67
Printing a Relationships Report	AC3.68
Compacting and Backing Up the Database	AC3.69
FOCUS ON CAREERS	AC3.71
CONCEPT SUMMARY	AC3.72
LAB REVIEW	AC3.74
Key Terms	AC3.74
Command Summary	AC3.75
LAB EXERCISES	AC3.78
Matching	AC3.78
True/False	AC3.78
Fill-In	AC3.79
Multiple Choice	AC3.80
Hands-On Exercises	AC3.82
Step-by-Step	AC3.82
On Your Own	AC3.88

WORKING TOGETHER 1: EXPORTING DATA ACWT1.1

Case Study	ACWT1.1
Exporting Data	ACWT1.1
Exporting to Excel 2010	ACWT1.2
Exporting to Word 2010	ACWT1.6
Copying a Query Object to Word 2010	ACWT1.7
Copying a Report	ACWT1.9
LAB REVIEW	ACWT1.13
Key Terms	ACWT1.13
Command Summary	ACWT1.13
LAB EXERCISES	ACWT1.14
Hands-On Exercises	ACWT1.14
Step-by-Step	ACWT1.14
Command Summary	ACCS.1
Introduction to Office Glossary	IOG.1
Access Glossary of Key Terms	ACG.1
Index	ACI.1

Acknowledgments

We would like to extend our thanks to the professors who took time out of their busy schedules to provide us with the feedback necessary to develop the 2010 Edition of this text. The following professors offered valuable suggestions on revising the text:

Joan Albright
Greenville Technical College

Wilma Andrews
Virginia Commonwealth University

Robert M. Benavides
Collin College

Kim Cannon
Greenville Technical College

Paulette Comet
The Community College of Baltimore County

Michael Dunklebarger
Alamance Community College

Joel English
Centura College

Deb Fells
Mesa Community College

Tatyana Feofilaktova
ASA Institute

Sue Furnas
Collin College

Debbie Grande
The Community College of Rhode Island

Rachelle Hall
Glendale Community College

Katherine Herbert
Montclair State University

Terri Holly
Indian River State College

Mark W. Huber
University of Georgia

Joyce Kessel
Western International University

Hal P. Kingsley
Trocaire College

Diane Lending
James Madison University

Dr. Mo Manouchehripour
The Art Institute of Dallas

Sue McCrory
Missouri State University

Gary McFall
Purdue University

Margaret M. Menna
The Community College of Rhode Island

Philip H. Nielson
Salt Lake Community College

Craig Piercy
University of Georgia

Mark Renslow
Globe University/Minnesota School of Business

Ann Rowlette
Liberty University

Chakra Pani Sharma
ASA Institute

Eric Weinstein
Suffolk County Community College

Sheryl Wright
College of the Mainland

Laurie Zouharis
Suffolk University

We would like to thank those who took the time to help us develop the manuscript and ensure accuracy through painstaking edits: Brenda Nielsen of Mesa Community College–Red Mountain, Stephen J. Adams of Cleveland State University, Candice Spangler of Columbus State Community College, and Kate Scalzi.

Finally, we would like to thank team members from McGraw-Hill, whose renewed commitment, direction, and support have infused the team with the excitement of a new project. Leading the team from McGraw-Hill are Tiffany Wendt, Marketing Manager; and Developmental Editor Alaina Grayson.

The production staff is headed by Marlena Pechan, Project Manager, whose planning and attention to detail have made it possible for us to successfully meet a very challenging schedule; Srdjan Savanovic, Designer; Michael McCormick, Production Supervisor; Kevin White, Digital Developmental Editor; Jeremy Cheshareck, Photo Researcher; and Becky Komro, copyeditor—team members on whom we can depend to do a great job.

Paula Gregory was influenced early on by her mother, who enrolled in computer classes at the local community college, using the first home computer released by Radio Shack—a TRS-80. Paula received her associate's degree with honors in 1990 at Yavapai College, majoring in computer science. In1991, she began teaching and helping students one-on-one with computers at Yavapai College, and went on to get her teaching certification in 1998. Since then, Paula has enjoyed teaching college students all about computers and Microsoft Office and Adobe products. MCAS-certified in Microsoft Word and Access, and ACA-certified in Adobe Photoshop, as well as an accomplished artist and writer, Paula enjoys combining all her skills to develop material that engages the audience and makes learning fun.

Preface

The 20th century brought us the dawn of the digital information age and unprecedented changes in information technology. There is no indication that this rapid rate of change will be slowing—it may even be increasing. As we begin the 21st century, computer literacy is undoubtedly becoming a prerequisite in whatever career you choose.

The goal of the O'Leary Series is to provide you with the necessary skills to efficiently use these applications. Equally important is the goal to provide a foundation for students to readily and easily learn to use future versions of this software. This series does this by providing detailed step-by-step instructions combined with careful selection and presentation of essential concepts.

Times are changing, technology is changing, and this text is changing too. As students of today, you are different from those of yesterday. You put much effort toward the things that interest you and the things that are relevant to you. Your efforts directed at learning application programs and exploring the Web seem, at times, limitless.

On the other hand, students often can be shortsighted, thinking that learning the skills to use the application is the only objective. The mission of the series is to build upon and extend this interest by not only teaching the specific application skills but by introducing the concepts that are common to all applications, providing students with the confidence, knowledge, and ability to easily learn the next generation of applications.

Instructor's Resource Center

The online **Instructor's Resource Center** contains access to a Computerized Test Bank, an Instructor's Manual, Solutions, and PowerPoint Presentation Slides. Features of the Instructor's Resource are described below.

- **Instructor's Manual** The Instructor's Manual, authored by the primary contributor, contains lab objectives, concepts, outlines, lecture notes, and command summaries. Also included are answers to all end-of-chapter material, tips for covering difficult materials, additional exercises, and a schedule showing how much time is required to cover text material.

- **Computerized Test Bank** The test bank, authored by the primary contributor, contains hundreds of multiple choice, true/false, and discussion questions. Each question will be accompanied by the correct answer, the level of learning difficulty, and corresponding page references. Our flexible EZ Test software allows you to easily generate custom exams.

- **PowerPoint Presentation Slides** The presentation slides, authored by the primary contributor, include lab objectives, concepts, outlines, text figures, and speaker's notes. Also included are bullets to illustrate key terms and FAQs.

Online Learning Center/Website

Found at **www.mhhe.com/oleary**, this site provides additional learning and instructional tools to enhance the comprehension of the text. The OLC/Website is divided into these three areas:

- **Information Center** Contains core information about the text, supplements, and the authors.

- **Instructor Center** Offers the aforementioned instructional materials, downloads, and other relevant links for professors.

- **Student Center** Contains data files, chapter competencies, chapter concepts, self-quizzes, additional Web links, and more.

Simnet Assessment for Office Applications

Simnet Assessment for Office Applications provides a way for you to test students' software skills in a simulated environment. Simnet is available for Microsoft Office 2010 and provides flexibility for you in your applications course by offering

Pretesting options
Post-testing options
Course placement testing
Diagnostic capabilities to reinforce skills
Web delivery of tests
Certification preparation exams
Learning verification reports

For more information on skills assessment software, please contact your local sales representative, or visit us at **www.mhhe.com**.

O'Leary Series

The O'Leary Application Series for Microsoft Office is available separately or packaged with *Computing Essentials*. The O'Leary Application Series offers a step-by-step case-based approach to learning computer applications and is available in both introductory and complete versions.

Computing Concepts

Computing Essentials 2012 offers a unique, visual orientation that gives students a basic understanding of computing concepts. *Computing Essentials* encourages "active" learning with exercises, explorations, visual illustrations, and screen shots. While combining the "active" learning style with current topics and technology, this text provides an accurate snapshot of computing trends. When bundled with software application lab manuals, students are given a complete representation of the fundamental issues surrounding the personal computing environment.

About the Authors

Tim and Linda O'Leary live in the American Southwest and spend much of their time engaging instructors and students in conversation about learning. In fact, they have been talking about learning for over 25 years. Something in those early conversations convinced them to write a book, to bring their interest in the learning process to the printed page. Today, they are as concerned as ever about learning, about technology, and about the challenges of presenting material in new ways, in terms of both content and method of delivery.

A powerful and creative team, Tim combines his 30 years of classroom teaching experience with Linda's background as a consultant and corporate trainer. Tim has taught courses at Stark Technical College in Canton, Ohio, and at Rochester Institute of Technology in upstate New York, and is currently a professor emeritus at Arizona State University in Tempe, Arizona. Linda offered her expertise at ASU for several years as an academic advisor. She also presented and developed materials for major corporations such as Motorola, Intel, Honeywell, and AT&T, as well as various community colleges in the Phoenix area.

Tim and Linda have talked to and taught numerous students, all of them with a desire to learn something about computers and applications that make their lives easier, more interesting, and more productive.

Each new edition of an O'Leary text, supplement, or learning aid has benefited from these students and their instructors who daily stand in front of them (or over their shoulders). The O'Leary Series is no exception.

Dedication

We dedicate this edition to our parents—Irene Perley Coats, Jean L. O'Leary, and Charles D. O'Leary—for all their support and love. We miss you.

Introduction to Microsoft Office 2010

Objectives

After completing the Introduction to Microsoft Office 2010, you should be able to:

1 Describe the Office 2010 applications.

2 Start an Office 2010 application.

3 Use the Ribbon, dialog boxes, and task panes.

4 Use menus, context menus, and shortcut keys.

5 Use Backstage view.

6 Open, close, and save files.

7 Navigate a document.

8 Enter, edit, and format text.

9 Select, copy, and move text.

10 Undo and redo changes.

11 Specify document properties.

12 Print a document.

13 Use Office 2010 Help.

14 Exit an Office 2010 application.

What Is Microsoft Office 2010?

Microsoft's Office 2010 is a comprehensive, integrated system of programs designed to solve a wide array of business needs. Although the programs can be used individually, they are designed to work together seamlessly, making it easy to connect people and organizations to information, business processes, and each other. The applications include tools used to create, discuss, communicate, and manage projects. If you share a lot of documents with other people, these features facilitate access to common documents. If you are away on business or do not have your PC with you, you can use Office 2010 Web applications, browser versions of Word, Excel, PowerPoint, and OneNote, to edit documents and collaborate with others.

Microsoft Office 2010 is packaged in several different combinations of programs or suites. The major programs and a brief description are provided in the following table.

Program	Description
Word 2010	Word processor program used to create text-based documents
Excel 2010	Spreadsheet program used to analyze numerical data
Access 2010	Database manager used to organize, manage, and display a database
PowerPoint 2010	Graphics presentation program used to create presentation materials
Outlook 2010	Desktop information manager and messaging client
InfoPath 2010	Used to create XML forms and documents
OneNote 2010	Note-taking and information organization tools
Publisher 2010	Tools to create and distribute publications for print, Web, and e-mail
Visio 2010	Diagramming and data visualization tools
SharePoint Designer 2010	Web site development and management for SharePoint servers
Project 2010	Project management tools

The four main components of Microsoft Office 2010—Word, Excel, Access, and PowerPoint—are the applications you will learn about in this series of labs. They are described in more detail in the following sections.

Word 2010

Word 2010 is a word processing software application whose purpose is to help you create text-based documents such as letters, memos, reports, e-mail messages, or any other type of correspondence. Word processors are one of the most flexible and widely used application software programs.

WORD 2010 FEATURES

The beauty of a word processor is that you can make changes or corrections as you are typing. Want to change a report from single spacing to double spacing? Alter the width of the margins? Delete some paragraphs and add others from yet another document? A word processor allows you to do all these things with ease.

Edit Content

Word 2010 excels in its ability to change or **edit** a document. Basic document editing involves correcting spelling, grammar, and sentence-structure errors and revising or updating existing text by inserting, deleting, and rearranging areas of text. For example, a document that lists prices can easily be updated to reflect new prices. A document that details procedures can be revised by deleting old procedures and inserting new ones. Many of these changes are made easily by cutting (removing) or copying (duplicating) selected text and then pasting (inserting) the cut or copied text in another location in the same or another document. Editing allows you to quickly revise a document, by changing only the parts that need to be modified.

To help you produce a perfect document, Word 2010 includes many additional editing support features. The AutoCorrect feature checks the spelling and grammar in a document as text is entered. Many common errors are corrected automatically for you. Others are identified and a correction suggested. A thesaurus can be used to display alternative words that have a meaning similar or opposite to a word you entered. The Find and Replace feature can be used to quickly locate specified text and replace it with other text throughout a document. In addition, Word 2010 includes a variety of tools that automate the process of many common tasks, such as creating tables, form letters, and columns.

Format Content

You also can easily control the appearance or **format** of the document. Perhaps the most noticeable formatting feature is the ability to apply different fonts (type styles and sizes) and text appearance changes such as bold, italics, and color to all or selected portions of the document. Additionally, you can add color shading behind individual pieces of text or entire paragraphs and pages to add emphasis. Other formatting features include changes to entire paragraphs, such as the line spacing and alignment of text between the margins. You also can format entire pages by displaying page numbers, changing margin settings, and applying backgrounds.

To make formatting even easier, Word 2010 includes Document Themes and Styles. Document Themes apply a consistent font, color, and line effect to an entire document. Styles apply the selected style design to a selection of text. Further, Word 2010 includes a variety of built-in preformatted content that helps you quickly produce modern-looking, professional documents. Among these are galleries of cover page designs, pull quotes, and header and footer designs. While selecting many of these design choices, a visual live preview is displayed, making it easy to see how the design would look in your document. In addition, you can select from a wide variety of templates to help you get started on creating many common types of documents such as flyers, calendars, faxes, newsletters, and memos.

Insert Illustrations

To further enhance your documents, you can insert many different types of graphic elements. These include drawing objects, SmartArt, charts, pictures, clip art, and screenshots. The drawing tools supplied with Word 2010 can be used to create your own drawings, or you can select from over 100 adjustable shapes and modify them to your needs. All drawings can be further enhanced with 3-D effects, shadows, colors, and textures. SmartArt graphics allow you to create a visual representation of your information. They include many different layouts such as a process or cycle that are designed to help you communicate an idea. Charts can be inserted to illustrate and compare data. Complex pictures can be inserted in documents by scanning your own, using supplied or purchased clip art, or downloading images from the World Wide Web. Additionally, you can produce fancy text effects using the WordArt tool. Finally, you can quickly capture and insert a picture, called a screenshot, from another application running on your computer into the current document.

Collaborate with Others

Group collaboration on projects is common in industry today. Word 2010 includes many features to help streamline how documents are developed and changed by group members. A discussion feature allows multiple people to insert remarks in the same document without having to route the document to each person or reconcile multiple reviewers' comments. You can easily consolidate all changes and comments from different reviewers in one simple step and accept or reject changes as needed.

Two documents you will produce in the first two Word 2010 labs, a letter and flyer, are shown here.

A letter containing a tabbed table, indented paragraphs, and text enhancements is quickly created using basic Word features

January 27, 2012

Dear Adventure Traveler:

Imagine camping under the stars in Africa, hiking and paddling your way through the rainforests of Costa Rica, or following in the footsteps of the ancient Inca as you backpack along the Inca trail to Machu Picchu. Turn these thoughts of adventure into memories you will cherish forever by joining Adventure Travel Tours on one of our four new adventure tours.

To tell you more about these exciting new adventu[...] area. These presentations will focus on the features and cu[...] of the places you will visit and activities you can participate [...] Plan to attend one of the following presentations:

Date	Time	Locati[...]
February 5	8:00 p.m.	Renaissan[...]
February 19	7:30 p.m.	Airport Pla[...]
March 8	8:00 p.m.	Crowne C[...]

In appreciation of your past patronage, we are ple[...] of the new tour packages. You must book the trip at least [...] this letter to qualify for the discount.

Our vacation tours are professionally developed s[...] everything in the price of your tour while giving you the be[...] these features:

➢ All accommodations and meals
➢ All entrance fees, excursions, transfers and tips
➢ Professional tour manager and local guides

We hope you will join us this year on another spec[...] Travel Tours each day is an adventure. For reservations, p[...] Travel Tours directly at 1-800-555-0004.

Be[...]

St[...]
Ad[...]

ADVENTURE TRAVEL TOURS

NEW ADVENTURES

Attention adventure travelers! Attend an Adventure Travel presentation to learn about some of the earth's greatest unspoiled habitats and find out how you can experience the adventure of a lifetime. This year Adventure Travel Tours is introducing four new tours that offer you a unique opportunity to combine many different outdoor activities while exploring the world.

Costa Rica Rivers and Rainforests

India Wildlife Adventure

Safari in Tanzania

Inca Trail to Machu Picchu

Presentation dates and times are January 5 at 7:00 p.m., February 3 at 7:30 p.m., and March 8 at 7:00 p.m. All presentations are held at convenient hotel locations. The hotels are located in downtown Los Angeles, in Santa Clara, and at the LAX airport.

Call Adventure Travel Tours at 1-800-555-0004 for presentation locations, a full color brochure, and itinerary information, costs, and trip dates. Student Name will gladly help with all of your questions.

A flyer incorporating many visual enhancements such as colored text, varied text styles, and graphic elements is both eye-catching and informative

Excel 2010

Excel 2010 is an electronic spreadsheet, or **worksheet**, that is used to organize, manipulate, and graph numeric data. Once used almost exclusively by accountants, worksheets are now widely used by nearly every profession. Nearly any job that uses rows and columns of numbers can be performed using an electronic spreadsheet. Once requiring hours of labor and/or costly accountants' fees, data analysis is now available almost instantly using electronic spreadsheets and has become a routine business procedure. This powerful business tool has revolutionized the business world. Typical uses include the creation of budgets and financial planning for both business and personal situations. Marketing professionals record and evaluate sales trends. Teachers record grades and calculate final grades. Personal trainers record the progress of their clients.

EXCEL 2010 FEATURES

Excel 2010 includes many features that not only help you create a well-designed worksheet, but one that produces accurate results. The features include the ability to quickly edit and format data, perform calculations, create charts, and print the spreadsheet. Using Excel 2010, you can quickly analyze and manage data and communicate your findings to others. The program not only makes it faster to create worksheets, but it also produces professional-appearing results.

Enter and Edit Data

The Microsoft Excel 2010 spreadsheet program uses a workbook file that contains one or more worksheets. Each worksheet can be used to organize different types of related information. The worksheet consists of rows and columns that create a grid of cells. You enter numeric data or descriptive text into a cell. These entries can then be erased, moved, copied, or edited.

Format Data

Like text in a Word document, the design and appearance of entries in a worksheet can be enhanced in many ways. For instance, you can change the font style and size and add special effects such as bold, italic, borders, boxes, drop shadows, and shading to selected cells. You also can use cell styles to quickly apply predefined combinations of these formats to selections. Additionally, you can select from different document themes, predefined combinations of colors, fonts, and effects, to give your workbooks a consistent, professional appearance.

Unlike the Word application, Excel includes many formatting features that are designed specifically for numeric data. For example, numeric entries can be displayed with commas, dollar signs, or a set number of decimal places. Special formatting, such as color bars, can be applied automatically to ranges of cells to emphasize data based on a set of criteria you establish and to highlight trends.

Analyze Data

The power of a spreadsheet application is its ability to perform calculations from very simple sums to the most complex financial and mathematical formulas. Formulas can be entered that perform calculations using data contained in specified cells. The results of the calculations are displayed in the cell containing the formula. Predefined formulas, called functions, can be used to quickly perform complex calculations such as calculating loan payments or statistical analysis of data.

Analysis of data in a spreadsheet once was too expensive and time-consuming. Now, using electronic worksheets, you can use what-if or sensitivity analysis by changing the values in selected cells and immediately observing the effect on related cells in the worksheet. Other analysis tools such as Solver and Scenarios allow you to see the effects of possible alternative courses of action to help forecast future outcomes.

Chart Data

Using Excel, you also can produce a visual display of numeric data in the form of graphs or charts. As the values in the worksheet change, charts referencing those values automatically adjust to reflect the changes. You also can enhance the appearance of a chart by using different type styles and sizes, adding three-dimensional effects, and including text and objects such as lines and arrows.

Two worksheets you will produce using Excel 2010 are shown below.

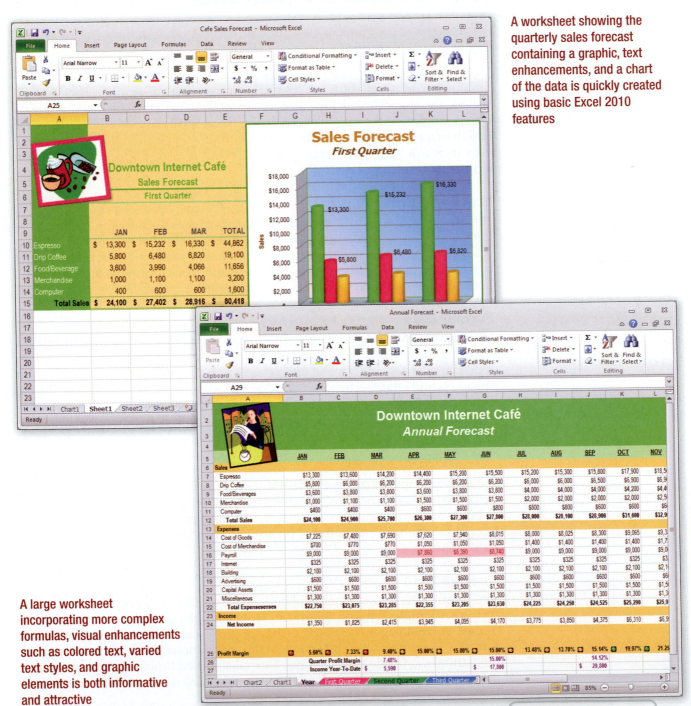

A worksheet showing the quarterly sales forecast containing a graphic, text enhancements, and a chart of the data is quickly created using basic Excel 2010 features

A large worksheet incorporating more complex formulas, visual enhancements such as colored text, varied text styles, and graphic elements is both informative and attractive

Access 2010 is a relational database management application that is used to create and analyze a database. A **database** is a collection of related data. **Tables** consist of columns (called **fields**) and rows (called **records**). Each row contains a record, which is all the information about one person, thing, or place. Each field is the smallest unit of information about a record.

In a relational database, the most widely used database structure, data is organized in linked tables. The tables are related or linked to one another by a common field. Relational databases allow you to create smaller and more manageable database tables, since you can combine and extract data between tables.

For example, a state's motor vehicle department database might have an address table. Each row (record) in the table would contain address information about one individual. Each column (field) would contain just one piece of information, for example, zip codes. The address table would be linked to other tables in the database by common fields. For example, the address table might be linked to a vehicle owner's table by name and linked to an outstanding citation table by license number (see example below).

Address Table

Name	License Number	Street Address	City	State	Zip
Aaron, Linda	FJ1987	10032 Park Lane	San Jose	CA	95127
Abar, John	D12372	1349 Oak St	Lakeville	CA	94128
Abell, Jack	LK3457	95874 State St	Stone	CA	95201

key fields linked

key fields linked

Owner's Table

Name	Plate Number
Abell, Jack	ABK241
Abrams, Sue	LMJ198
Abril, Pat	ZXA915

Outstanding Citation Table

License Number	Citation Code	Violation
T25476	00031	Speed
D98372	19001	Park
LK3457	89100	Speed

ACCESS 2010 FEATURES

Access 2010 is a powerful program with numerous easy-to-use features including the ability to quickly locate information; add, delete, modify, and sort records; analyze data; and produce professional-looking reports. Some of the basic Access 2010 features are described next.

Find Information

Once you enter data into the database table, you can quickly search the table to locate a specific record based on the data in a field. In a manual system, you can usually locate a record by knowing one key piece of information. For example, if the records are stored in a file cabinet alphabetically by last name, to quickly find a record, you must know the last name. In a computerized database, even if the records are sorted or organized by last name, you can still quickly locate a record using information in another field.

Add, Delete, and Modify Records

Using Access, it is also easy to add and delete records from the table. Once you locate a record, you can edit the contents of the fields to update the record or delete the record entirely from the table. You also can add new records to a table. When you enter a new record, it is automatically placed in the correct organizational location within the table. Creation of forms makes it easier to enter and edit data as well.

Sort and Filter Records

The capability to arrange or sort records in the table according to different fields can provide more meaningful information. You can organize records by name, department, pay, class, or any other category you need at a particular time. Sorting the records in different ways can provide information to different departments for different purposes.

Additionally, you can isolate and display a subset of records by specifying filter criteria. The criteria specify which records to display based on data in selected fields.

Analyze Data

Using Access, you can analyze the data in a table and perform calculations on different fields of data. Instead of pulling each record from a filing cabinet, recording the piece of data you want to use, and then performing the calculation on the recorded data, you can simply have the database program perform the calculation on all the values in the specified field. Additionally, you can ask questions or query the table to find only certain records that meet specific conditions to be used in the analysis. Information that was once costly and time-consuming to get is now quickly and readily available.

Generate Reports

Access includes many features that help you quickly produce reports ranging from simple listings to complex, professional-looking reports. You can create a simple report by asking for a listing of specified fields of data and restricting the listing to records meeting designated conditions. You can create a more complex professional report using the same restrictions or conditions as the simple report, but you can display the data in different layout styles, or with titles, headings, subtotals, or totals.

A database and a report that you will produce using Access 2010 are shown on the next page.

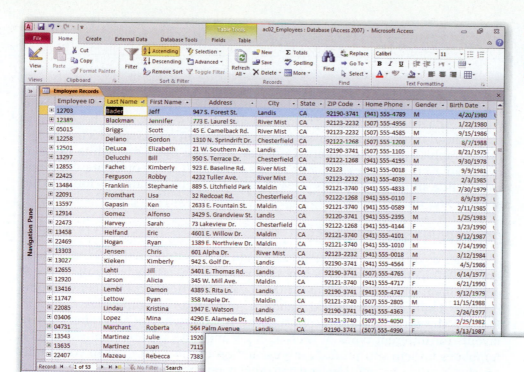

A relational database can be created and modified easily using basic Access 2010 features

A professional-looking report can be quickly generated from information contained in a database

PowerPoint 2010

PowerPoint 2010 is a graphics presentation program designed to help you produce a high-quality presentation that is both interesting to the audience and effective in its ability to convey your message. A presentation can be as simple as overhead transparencies or as sophisticated as an on-screen electronic display. Graphics presentation programs can produce black-and-white or color overhead transparencies, 35 mm slides, onscreen electronic presentations called **slide shows**, Web pages for Web use, and support materials for both the speaker and the audience.

POWERPOINT 2010 FEATURES

Although creating an effective presentation is a complicated process, Power-Point 2010 helps simplify this process by providing assistance in the content development phase, as well as in the layout and design phase. PowerPoint includes features such as text handling, outlining, graphing, drawing, animation, clip art, and multimedia support. In addition, the programs suggest layouts for different types of presentations and offer professionally designed templates to help you produce a presentation that is sure to keep your audience's attention. In addition, you can quickly produce the support materials to be used when making a presentation to an audience.

Develop, Enter, and Edit Content

The content development phase includes deciding on the topic of your presentation, the organization of the content, and the ultimate message you want to convey to the audience. As an aid in this phase, PowerPoint 2010 helps you organize your thoughts based on the type of presentation you are making by providing both content and design templates. Based on the type of presentation, such as selling a product or suggesting a strategy, the template provides guidance by suggesting content ideas and organizational tips. For example, if you are making a presentation on the progress of a sales campaign, the program would suggest that you enter text on the background of the sales campaign as the first page, called a **slide**; the current status of the campaign as the next slide; and accomplishments, schedule, issues and problems, and where you are heading on subsequent slides.

Design Layouts

The layout for each slide is the next important decision. Again, PowerPoint 2010 helps you by suggesting text layout features such as title placement, bullets, and columns. You also can incorporate graphs of data, tables, organizational charts, clip art, and other special text effects in the slides.

PowerPoint 2010 also includes professionally designed themes to further enhance the appearance of your slides. These themes include features that standardize the appearance of all the slides in your presentation. Professionally selected combinations of text and background colors, common typefaces and sizes, borders, and other art designs take the worry out of much of the design layout.

Deliver Presentations

After you have written and designed the slides, you can use the slides in an onscreen electronic presentation or a Web page for use on the Web. An onscreen presentation uses the computer to display the slides on an overhead projection screen. As you prepare this type of presentation, you can use the rehearsal feature that allows you to practice and time your presentation. The length of time to display each slide can be set and your entire presentation can be completed within the allotted time. A presentation also can be modified to display on a Web site and run using a Web browser. Finally, you can package the presentation to a CD for distribution.

A presentation that you will produce using PowerPoint 2010 is shown below.

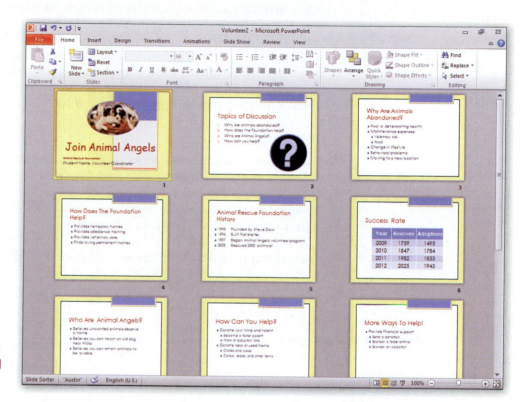

A presentation consists of a series of pages or "slides" presenting the information you want to convey in an organized and attractive manner

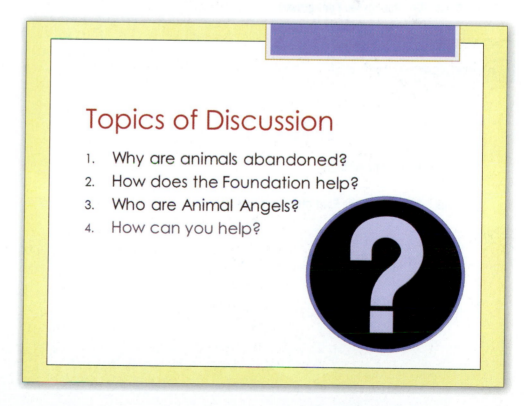

When running an on-screen presentation, each slide of the presentation is displayed full-screen on your computer monitor or projected onto a screen

Instructional Conventions

As you follow the directions in the following hands-on section and in the application labs, you need to know the instructional conventions that are used. Hands-on instructions you are to perform appear as a sequence of numbered steps. Within each step, a series of bullets identifies the specific actions that must be performed. Step numbering begins over within each topic heading throughout the lab.

Three types of marginal notes appear throughout the labs. Another Method notes provide alternate ways of performing the same command. Having Trouble? notes provide advice or cautions for steps that may cause problems. Additional Information notes provide more information about a topic.

COMMANDS

Commands that are initiated using a command button and the mouse appear following the word "Click." The icon (and the icon name if the icon does not include text) is displayed following "Click." If there is another way to perform the same action, it appears in an Another Method margin note when the action is first introduced as shown in Example A.

When a feature has already been covered and you are more familiar with using the application, commands will appear as shown in Example B.

Example A

1

- Select the list of four tours.

- Open the Home tab.

- Click **B** Bold in the Font group.

> **Another Method**
>
> The keyboard shortcut is [Ctrl] + B.

Example B

1

- Select the list of four tours.

- Click **B** Bold in the Font group of the Home tab.

OR

1

- Bold the list of four tours.

Sometimes, clicking on an icon opens a drop-down list or a menu of commands. Commands that are to be selected follow the word "Select" and appear in black text. You can select an item by pointing to it using the mouse or by moving to it using the directional keys. When an option is selected, it appears highlighted; however, the action is not carried out. Commands that you are to complete appear following the word "Choose." You can choose a command by clicking on it using the mouse or by pressing the [Enter] key once it is selected. Initially these commands will appear as in Example A. Choosing a command carries out the associated action. As you become more familiar with the application, commands will appear as shown in Example B.

Example A

1

- Click **A** ▾ Font Color in the Font group of the Home tab.

- Select Green.

- Choose Dark Blue.

Example B

1

- Click **A** ▾ Font Color and choose Dark Blue.

FILE NAMES AND INFORMATION TO TYPE

Plain blue text identifies file names you need to select or enter. Information you are asked to type appears in blue and bold. (See Example C.)

Example C

1

- Open the document wd01_Flyer.

- Type **Adventure Travel presents four new trips**

Common Office 2010 Features

Now that you know a little about each of the applications in Microsoft Office 2010, you will take a look at some of the features that are common to all Office 2010 applications. In this hands-on section you will learn to use the common interface and application features to allow you to get a feel for how Office 2010 works. Although Word 2010 will be used to demonstrate how the features work, only features that are common to all the Office applications will be addressed.

COMMON INTERFACE FEATURES

All the Office 2010 applications have a common **user interface**, a set of graphical elements that are designed to help you interact with the program and provide instructions as to the actions you want to perform. These features include the use of the Ribbon, Quick Access Toolbar, task panes, menus, dialog boxes, and the File tab.

Starting an Office 2010 Application

To demonstrate the common features, you will start the Word 2010 application. There are several ways to start an Office 2010 application. The two most common methods are by clicking the ● Start button to see a menu of available programs or by clicking a desktop shortcut for the program if it is available.

Additional Information

The procedure to start Excel, Access, and PowerPoint is the same as starting Word, except that you must select the appropriate program name or shortcut.

1

- Click ● Start to display the Start menu.

- Choose Microsoft Word 2010.

Having Trouble?

If you do not see the program name on the Start menu, select All Programs, choose Microsoft Office, and then choose Microsoft Word 2010.

OR

1

- Double-click the shortcut on the desktop.

2

- If necessary, click 🔲 Maximize in the title bar to maximize the window.

Your screen should be similar to Figure 1

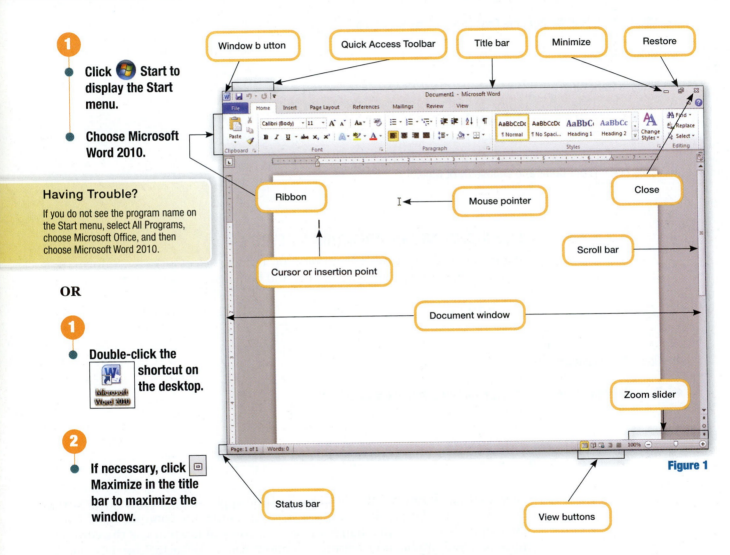

Figure 1

The Word 2010 program is started and displayed in a window on the desktop. All application windows display a title bar at the top of the window that includes the file name followed by the program name, in this case Microsoft Word. They also include the ▭ Minimize, ⬜ Restore Down, and ☒ Close buttons at the right end of the title bar. **Buttons** are graphical elements that perform the associated action when you click on them using the mouse. At the left end of the title bar is the W Window button. Clicking this button opens a menu of commands that allow you to size, move, and close the window just as the buttons on the right end of the title bar. To the right of the W Window button is the **Quick Access Toolbar** (QAT), which provides quick access to frequently used commands. By default, it includes the 🖫 Save, ↺ ▾ Undo, and ↻ Redo buttons, commands that Microsoft considers to be crucial. It is always available and is a customizable toolbar to which you can add your own favorite buttons.

Below the title bar is the **Ribbon**, which provides a centralized location of commands that are used to work in your document. The Ribbon has the same basic structure and is found in all Office 2010 applications. However, many of the commands found in the Ribbon vary with the specific applications. You will learn how to use the Ribbon shortly.

The large center area of the program window is the **document window** where open application files are displayed. When you first start Word 2010, a new blank Word document named Document1 (shown in the title bar) automatically opens, ready for you to start creating a new document. In Excel, a new, blank workbook named Book1 would be opened and in PowerPoint a new, blank presentation file named Presentation1 would be opened. In Access, however, a new blank database file is not opened automatically. Instead, you must create and name a new database file or open an existing database file.

The **cursor**, also called the **insertion point**, is the blinking vertical bar that marks your location in the document and indicates where text you type will appear. Across all Office applications, the mouse pointer appears as I I-beam when it is used to position the insertion point when entering text and as a ⍦ when it can be used to select items. There are many other mouse pointer shapes that are both common to and specific to the different applications.

On the right of the document window is a vertical scroll bar. A **scroll bar** is used with a mouse to bring additional information into view in a window. The vertical scroll bar is used to move up or down. A horizontal scroll bar is also displayed when needed and moves side to side in the window. The scroll bar is a common feature to all Windows and Office 2010 applications; however, it may not appear in all applications until needed.

At the bottom of the application window is another common feature called the **status bar**. It displays information about the open file and features that help you view the file. It displays different information depending upon the application you are using. For example, the Word status bar displays information about the number of pages and words in the document, whereas the Excel status bar displays the mode of operation and the count, average, and sum of values in selected cells. All Office 2010 applications include **View buttons** that are used to change how the information in the document window is displayed. The View buttons are different for each application. Finally, a **Zoom Slider**, located at the far right end of the status bar, is used to change the amount of information displayed in the document window by "zooming in" to get a close-up view or "zooming out" to see more of the document at a reduced view.

Displaying ScreenTips

You are probably wondering how you would know what action the different buttons perform. To help you identify buttons, the Office applications display ScreenTips when you point to them.

1 Point to the 📄 Save button in the Quick Access Toolbar.

Your screen should be similar to
Figure 2

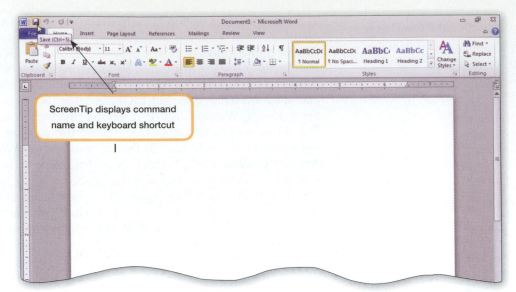

ScreenTip displays command name and keyboard shortcut

Figure 2

A **ScreenTip**, also called a **tooltip**, appears displaying the command name and the keyboard shortcut, Ctrl + S. A **keyboard shortcut** is a combination of keys that can be used to execute a command in place of clicking the button. In this case, if you hold down the Ctrl key while typing the letter S, you will access the command to save a file. ScreenTips also often include a brief description of the action a command performs.

Using Menus

Notice the small button ⏷ at the end of the Quick Access Toolbar. Clicking this button opens a menu of commands that perform tasks associated with the Quick Access Toolbar.

1 Point to the ⏷ button at the end of the Quick Access Toolbar to display the ScreenTip.

● Click ⏷ to open the menu.

Your screen should be similar to
Figure 3

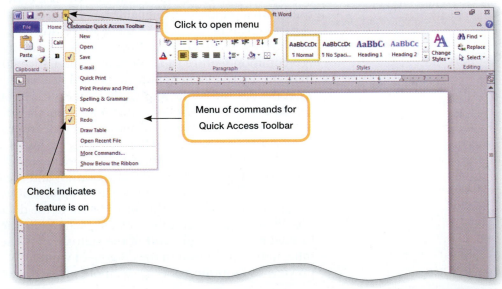

Click to open menu

Menu of commands for Quick Access Toolbar

Check indicates feature is on

Figure 3

The first 11 items in the menu allow you to quickly add a command button to or remove a command button from the Quick Access Toolbar. Those commands that are already displayed in the Quick Access Toolbar are preceded with a checkmark. The last two commands allow you to access other command features to customize the Quick Access Toolbar or change its location.

Once a menu is open, you can select a command from the menu by pointing to it. As you do the selected command appears highlighted. Like buttons, resting the mouse pointer over the menu command options will display a ScreenTip. Then to choose a selected command, you click on it. Choosing a command performs the action associated with the command or button. You will use several of these features next.

2

● **Point to the commands in the Quick Access Toolbar menu to select (highlight) them and see the ScreenTips.**

● **Click on the Open command to choose it and add it to the Quick Access Toolbar.**

Your screen should be similar to Figure 4

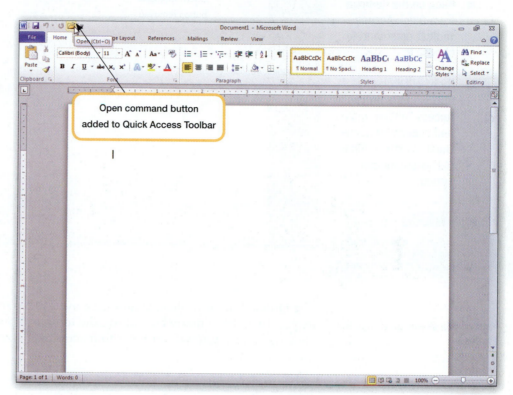

Open command button added to Quick Access Toolbar

Figure 4

The command button to open a document has been added to the Quick Access Toolbar. Next, you will remove this button and then you will change the location of the Quick Access Toolbar. Another way to access some commands is to use a context menu. A **context menu**, also called a **shortcut menu**, is opened by right-clicking on an item on the screen. This menu is context sensitive, meaning it displays only those commands relevant to the item or screen location. For example, right-clicking on the Quick Access Toolbar will display the commands associated with using the Quick Access Toolbar and the Ribbon. You will use this method to remove the Open button and move the Quick Access Toolbar.

3

- Point to the 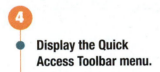 Open button on the Quick Access Toolbar and right-click.

- Click on the Remove from Quick Access Toolbar command to choose it.

- Right-click on any button in the Quick Access Toolbar again and choose the Show Quick Access Toolbar Below the Ribbon option.

Another Method

You also can type the underlined letter of a command to choose it or press [Enter] to choose a selected command.

Your screen should be similar to Figure 5

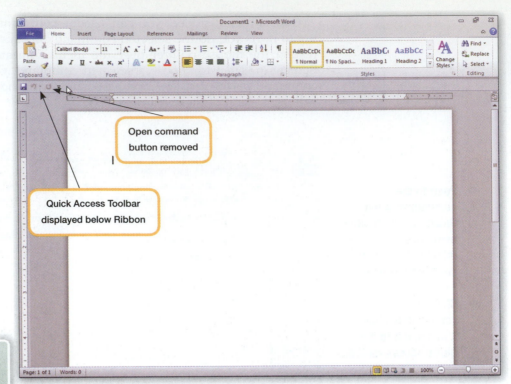

Figure 5

The Quick Access Toolbar is now displayed full size below the Ribbon. This is useful if you have many buttons on the toolbar; however, it takes up document viewing space. You will return it to its compact size.

4

- Display the Quick Access Toolbar menu.

- Choose Show Above the Ribbon.

Your screen should be similar to Figure 6

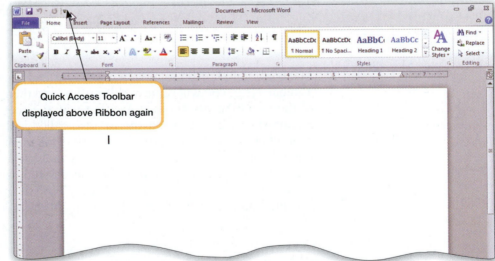

Figure 6

The Quick Access Toolbar is displayed above the Ribbon again.

Using the Ribbon

The Ribbon has three basic parts: tabs, groups, and commands (see Figure 7). **Tabs** are used to divide the Ribbon into major activity areas. Each tab is then organized into **groups** that contain related items. The related items are **commands** that consist of command buttons, a box to enter information, or a menu. Clicking on a command button performs the associated action or displays a list of additional options.

The Ribbon tabs, commands, and features vary with the different Office applications. For example, the Word Ribbon displays tabs and commands used to create a text document, whereas the Excel Ribbon displays tabs and commands used to create an electronic worksheet. Although the Ribbon commands are application specific, many are also common to all Office 2010 applications. In all applications, the Ribbon also can be customized by changing the built-in tabs or creating your own tabs and groups to personalize your workspace and provide faster access to the commands you use most.

Opening Tabs

The Word application displays the File tab and seven Ribbon tabs. The Home tab (shown in Figure 6), consisting of five groups, appears highlighted, indicating it is the open or active tab. This tab is available in all the Office 2010 applications and because it contains commands that are most frequently used when you first start an application or open a file, it is initially the open tab. In Word, the commands in the Home tab help you perform actions related to creating the text content of your document. In the other Office 2010 applications, the Home tab contains commands related to creating the associated type of document, such as a worksheet, presentation, or database. To open another tab you click on the tab name.

Additional Information

Because the Ribbon can adapt to the screen resolution and orientation, your Ribbon may look slightly different. Additionally, the Ribbon may display an Add-Ins tab if your application setup specifies that add-in applications be made available in the Add-Ins tab.

Additional Information

The File tab is not a Ribbon tab. You will learn about the File tab shortly.

1

Click on the Insert tab.

Your screen should be similar to Figure 7

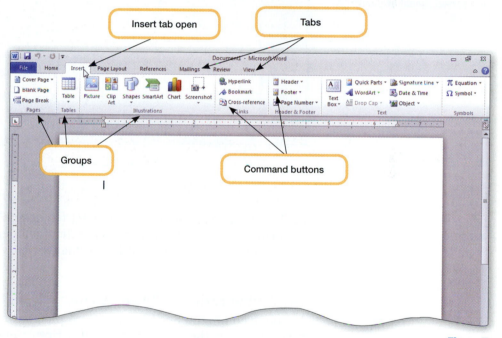

Figure 7

This Insert tab is now open and is the active tab. It contains seven groups whose commands have to do with inserting items into a document. As you use the Office applications, you will see that the Ribbon contains many of the same tabs, groups, and commands across the applications. For example, the Insert tab is available in all applications except Access. Others, such as the References tab in Word, are specific to the application. You also will see that many of the groups and commands in the common tabs, such as the Clipboard group of commands in the Home tab, contain all or many of the same commands across applications. Other groups in the common tabs contain commands that are specific to the application.

To save space, some tabs, called **contextual tabs** or **on-demand tabs**, are displayed only as needed. For example, when you are working with a picture, the Picture Tools tab appears. The contextual nature of this feature keeps the work area uncluttered when the feature is not needed and provides ready access to it when it is needed.

2

● Click on each of the other tabs, ending with the View tab, to see their groups and commands.

Additional Information

If you have a mouse with a scroll wheel, pointing to the tab area of the ribbon and using the scroll wheel will scroll the tabs.

Your screen should be similar to
Figure 8

Figure 8

Each tab relates to a type of activity; for example, the View tab commands perform activities related to viewing the document. Within each tab, similar commands are grouped together to make it easy to find the commands you want to use.

Displaying Enhanced ScreenTips

Although command buttons display graphic representations of the action they perform, often the graphic is not descriptive enough. As you have learned, pointing to a button displays the name of the button and the keyboard shortcut in a ScreenTip. To further help explain what a button does, many buttons in the Ribbon display **Enhanced ScreenTips**. For example, the Paste button in the Clipboard group of the Home tab is a two-part button. Clicking on the upper part will immediately perform an action, whereas clicking on the lower part will display additional options. You will use this feature next to see the Enhanced ScreenTips.

1

● Click on the Home tab to open it.

● Point to the upper part of the 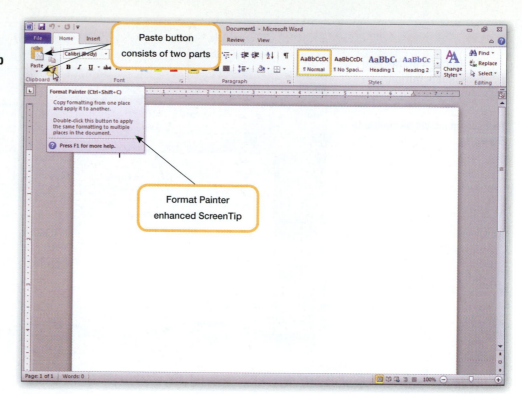 Paste button in the Clipboard group.

● Point to the lower part of the Paste button in the Clipboard group.

● Point to Format Painter in the Clipboard group.

Your screen should be similar to
Figure 9

Figure 9

Additional Information

Not all commands have keyboard shortcuts.

Additional Information

You will learn about using Help shortly.

Because the Paste button is divided into two parts, both parts display separate Enhanced ScreenTips containing the button name; the keyboard shortcut key combination, Ctrl + V; and a brief description of what action will be performed when you click on that part of the button. Pointing to Format Painter displays an Enhanced ScreenTip that provides more detailed information about the command. Enhanced ScreenTips may even display information such as procedures or illustrations. You can find out what the feature does without having to look it up using Office Help, a built-in reference source. If a feature has a Help article, you can automatically access it by pressing F1 while the Enhanced ScreenTip is displayed.

Using Command Buttons

Clicking on most command buttons immediately performs the associated action. Many command buttons, however, include an arrow as part of the button that affects how the button works. If a button includes an arrow that is separated from the graphic with a line when you point to the button (as in Bullets), clicking the button performs the associated default action and clicking the arrow displays a menu of options. If a button displays an arrow that is not separated from the graphic with a line when you point to it (as in Line Spacing), clicking the button immediately displays a menu of options. To see an example of a drop-down menu, you will open the Bullets menu.

1

Click  in the Bullets button.

Your screen should be similar to Figure 10

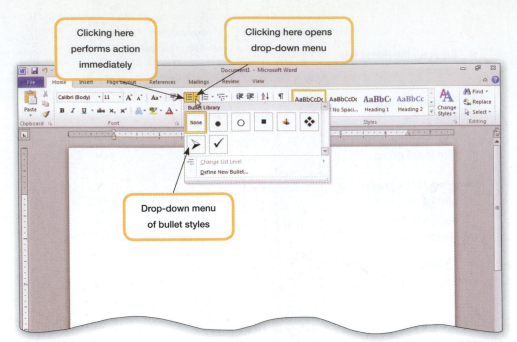

Clicking here performs action immediately

Clicking here opens drop-down menu

Drop-down menu of bullet styles

Figure 10

A drop-down menu of different bullet styles is displayed. The drop-down menu will disappear when you make a selection or click on any other area of the window.

2

Click outside the Bullet menu to clear it.

Click 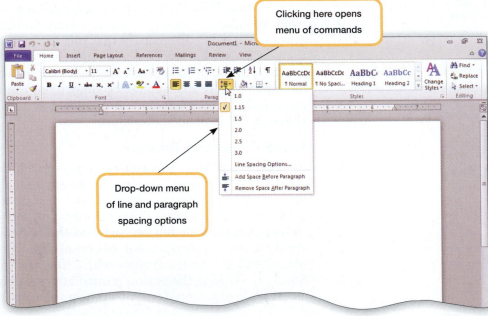 Line and Paragraph Spacing.

Your screen should be similar to Figure 11

Clicking here opens menu of commands

Drop-down menu of line and paragraph spacing options

Figure 11

Another Method

You also can open tabs and choose Ribbon commands using the access key shortcuts. Press [Alt] or [F10] to display the access key letters in KeyTips over each available feature. Then type the letter for the feature you want to use.

The menu of options opened automatically when you clicked Line and Paragraph Spacing.

WWW.MHHE.COM/OLEARY

Using the Dialog Box Launcher

Because there is not enough space, only the most used commands are displayed in the Ribbon. If more commands are available, a ⬚ button, called the **dialog box launcher**, is displayed in the lower-right corner of the group. Clicking ⬚ opens a dialog box or task pane of additional options.

1

● Click outside the Line and Paragraph Spacing menu to clear it.

● Point to the ⬚ of the Paragraph group to see the ScreenTip.

● Click ⬚ of the Paragraph group.

Your screen should be similar to
Figure 12

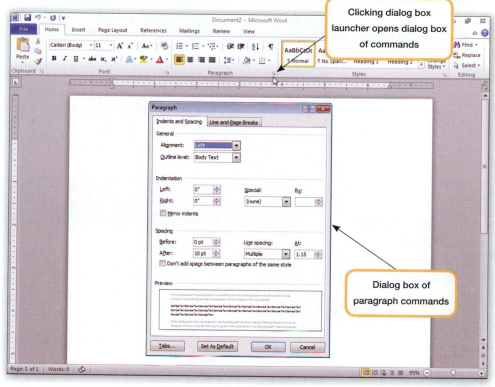

Figure 12

The Paragraph dialog box appears. It provides access to the more advanced paragraph settings options. Selecting options from the dialog box and clicking **OK** will close the dialog box and apply the options as specified. To cancel the dialog box, you can click **Cancel** or ❌ Close in the dialog box title bar.

2

● Click ❌ to close the dialog box.

● Click ⬚ in the Clipboard group.

Your screen should be similar to
Figure 13

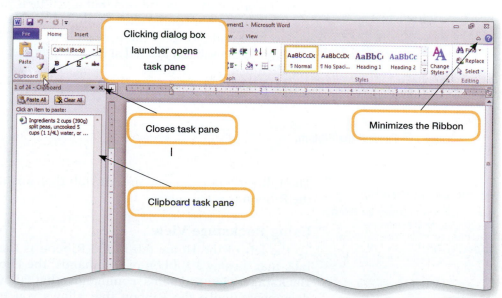

Figure 13

A task pane is open that contains features associated with the Clipboard. Unlike a dialog box, a task pane is a separate window that can be sized and moved. Generally, task panes are attached or docked to one edge of the application window. Also, task panes remain open until you close them. This allows you to make multiple selections from the task pane while continuing to work on other areas of your document.

● Click ☒ Close in the upper-right corner of the task pane to close it.

Minimize and Expand the Ribbon

Sometimes you may not want to see the entire Ribbon so that more space is available in the document area. You can minimize the Ribbon by double-clicking the active tab.

● **Double-click the Home tab.**

Your screen should be similar to Figure 14

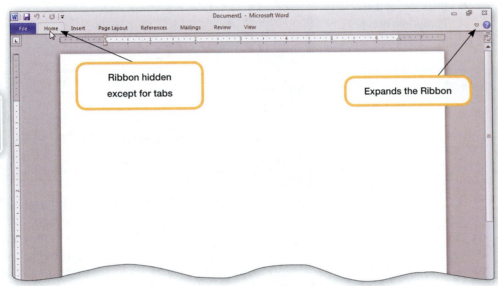

Ribbon hidden except for tabs

Expands the Ribbon

Figure 14

Now, the only part of the Ribbon that is visible is the tab area. Then, to expand the Ribbon, simply double click on the tab you want to make active. Another way to hide and redisplay the Ribbon is to click ☒ Minimize the Ribbon or ☒ Expand the Ribbon located at the far right end of the Ribbon tabs. You will unhide it using this feature.

● Click ☒ Expand the Ribbon.

The full Ribbon reappears and the tab that was active when you minimized the Ribbon is active again.

Using Backstage View

To the left of the Home tab in the Ribbon is the File tab. Unlike the other tabs that display a Ribbon of commands, the File tab opens Backstage view. **Backstage view** contains commands that allow you to work *with* your document, unlike the Ribbon that allows you to work *in* your document.

Backstage view contains commands that apply to the entire document. For example, you will find commands to open, save, print, and manage your files and set your program options. This tab is common to all the Office 2010 applications, although the menu options may vary slightly.

1

Click the File tab to open Backstage view.

Your screen should be similar to
Figure 15

Command buttons

Tabs

Command buttons

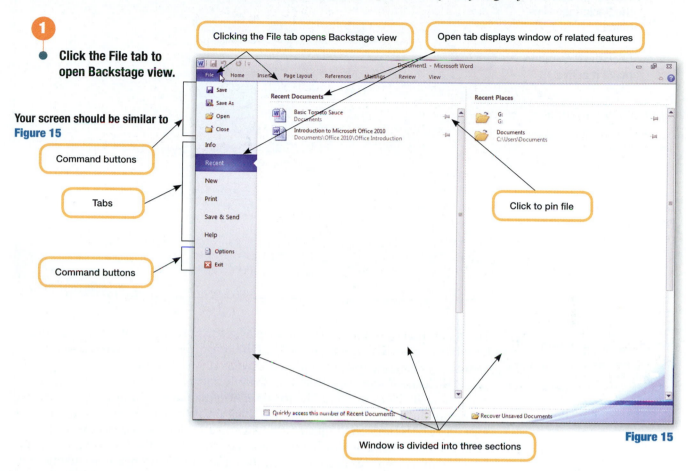

Clicking the File tab opens Backstage view

Open tab displays window of related features

Click to pin file

Window is divided into three sections

Figure 15

The document window is hidden and the Backstage view window is open. The Backstage view window completely covers the document window and is divided into sections or panes. In all Office 2010 applications, the first (left) section always displays command buttons and tabs. You can select a tab or a button by pointing to it. As you do, the selected tab or button appears highlighted. Then to choose a selected tab or button, you click on it. Choosing a command button either opens a dialog box or immediately performs the associated action. Clicking a tab opens the tab and displays the related commands and features.

When you first open Backstage view and you have not yet opened a document or started to create a new document, the Recent tab is open. It displays a list of links to recently opened Word files in the second section, making it easy to quickly locate and resume using a file. The third section displays a list of folder locations that have been recently visited. In Excel, PowerPoint, and Access, the recently opened file list displays files for the associated application. The list of files and folders changes as you work to reflect only the most recent files and folder locations. The most recently used files and folder locations appear at the top of the list.

Next, you will try out some of these features by selecting and opening different tabs and command buttons.

2

● **Point to all the tabs and commands in the Backstage view menu.**

● **Click the New tab to make it active.**

Your screen should be similar to Figure 16

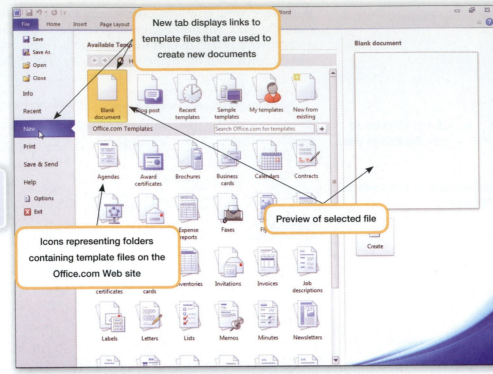

Figure 16

The second section of the New tab displays icons representing links to available templates on your computer or on the Office.com Web site. A **template** is a professionally designed document that is used as the basis for a new document. The Blank document icon is selected by default and is used to create a new Word document file from scratch. The third section displays a preview of the selected file. Icons in the Office.com area are links to different categories of template files that are contained in folders. Clicking on a folder icon opens the folder and displays file icons. Double-clicking on a file icon opens the file in Word. Again, the available templates are specific to the Office application you are using.

3

● **Click the Info tab.**

Your screen should be similar to Figure 17

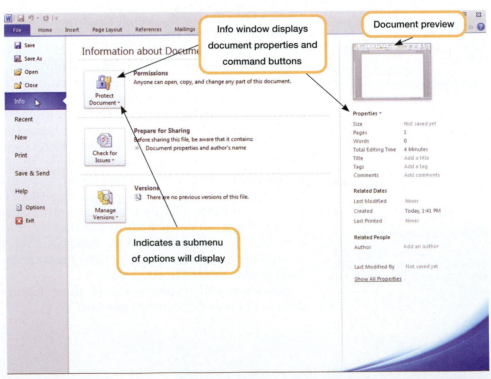

Figure 17

The Info tab displays information about your current document. The three buttons in the second section are used to define permissions, check for issues related to distribution, and manage document versions for the current document. A description of these buttons and the current document settings is shown to the right of the button. Notice that the buttons display a [▼]. This indicates that a menu of commands will be displayed when you click the button. The third section displays a preview picture of the current document and a list of the settings, called **properties**, associated with the document. The current properties displayed in the Info window show the initial or **default** properties associated with a new blank document.

Additional Information

You will learn more about document properties shortly.

4

● **Click** 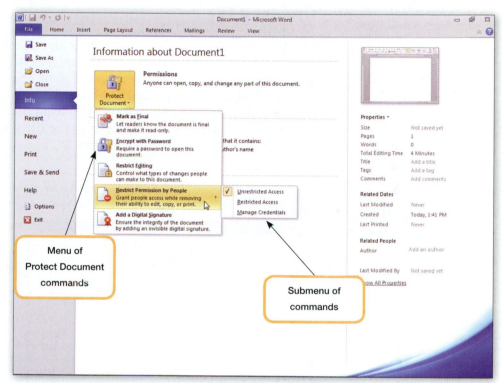 **to open the menu.**

● **Point to Restrict Permission by People.**

Your screen should be similar to Figure 18

Figure 18

The Protect Document drop-down menu displays five commands. The highlighted command displays a submenu of additional commands. Next, you will clear the Protect Document menu and close Backstage view.

5

● **Click**  **again to clear the submenu.**

● **Click the Home tab to close Backstage view and open the Home tab again.**

Another Method

You also can press [Esc], click on the File tab or any other Ribbon tab, or click on the document preview in the Info screen to close the Backstage view window.

COMMON APPLICATION FEATURES

So far you have learned about using the Office 2010 user interface features. Next, you will learn about application features that are used to work in and modify documents and are the same or similar in all Office 2010 applications. These include how to open, close, and save files; navigate, scroll, and zoom a document; enter, select, edit, and format text; and document, preview, and print a file. To do this, you will open a Word document file and make a few changes to it. Then you will save and print the revised document. Once you have gained an understanding of the basic concepts of the common features using Word, you will be able to easily apply them in the other Office applications.

Opening a File

In all Office 2010 applications, you either need to create a new file using the blank document file or open an existing file. Opening a file retrieves a file that is stored on your computer hard drive or an external storage device and places it in RAM (random access memory) of your computer so it can be read and modified. There are two main methods that can be used to open an existing file. One is to select the file to be opened from the list of recently opened documents. If you have not recently opened the file you want to use, then you use the Open command in Backstage view.

- Click the File tab to open Backstage view.

- Click [Open].

Your screen should be similar to
Figure 19

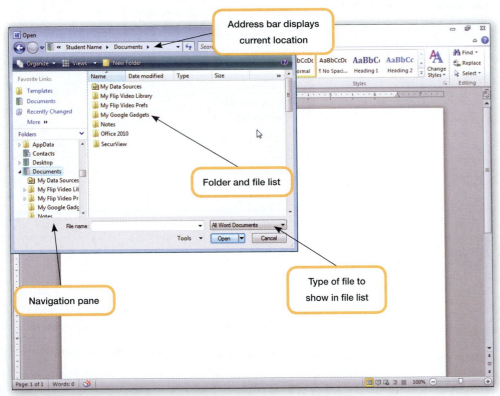

Figure 19

Additional Information

The Open dialog box is common to all programs using the Windows operating system. Your dialog box may look slightly different depending on the version of Windows on your computer.

The Open dialog box is displayed in which you specify the location where the file you want to open is stored and the file name. The location consists of identifying the hard drive of your computer or an external storage device or a remote computer followed by folders and subfolders within that location. The Address bar displays the default folder as the location to open the file. The file list displays folder names as well as the names of any Word documents in the current location. Only Word documents are listed because All Word Documents is the specified file type in the File Type list box. In Excel and Power-Point, only files of that application's file type would be displayed.

First you need to change the location to where your data files for completing these labs are stored. The file location may be on a different drive, in an external storage device, or in a folder or subfolder. There are several methods that can be used to locate files. One is to use the Address bar to specify another location by either typing the complete folder name or path or by opening the drop-down list of previously accessed locations and clicking a new location. Another is to use the Favorite Links list in the Navigation pane, which provides shortcut links to specific folders on your computer. A third is to use the Folders list in the navigation pane to navigate through the hierarchical structure of drives and folders on your computer. Clicking a link or folder from the list displays files at that location in the file list. Then, from the file list, you can continue to select subfolders until the file you want to open is located.

Change to the location where your student data files for this lab are located.

Your screen should be similar to **Figure 20**

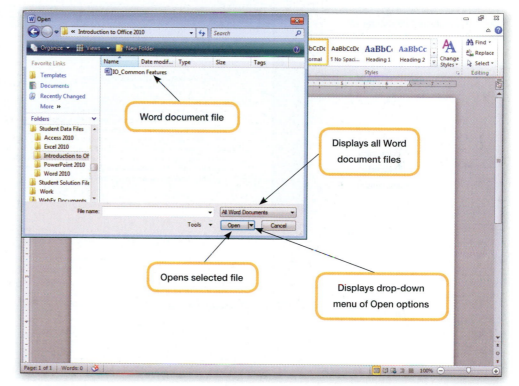

Figure 20

Now the file list displays the names of all Word files at that location. Next, you open the file by selecting it and clicking the ▭ Open ▾ button. In addition, in the Office applications you can specify how you want to open a file by choosing from the ▭ Open ▾ drop-down menu options described in the following table.

Open Options	Description
Open	Opens with all formatting and editing features enabled. This is the default setting.
Open Read-only	Opens file so it can be read or copied only, not modified in any way.
Open as Copy	Automatically creates a copy of the file and opens the copy with complete editing capabilities.
Open in Browser	Opens HTML type files in a Web browser.
Open with Transform	Opens certain types of documents and lets you change it into another type of document.
Open in Protected View	Opens files from potentially unsafe locations with editing functions disabled.
Open and Repair	Opens file and attempts to repair any damage.

You will open the file IO_Common Features. Clicking the [Open ▾] button opens the file using the default Open option so you can read and edit the file.

3

- **Select** IO_Common Features.

- **Click** [Open ▾].

Your screen should be similar to
Figure 21

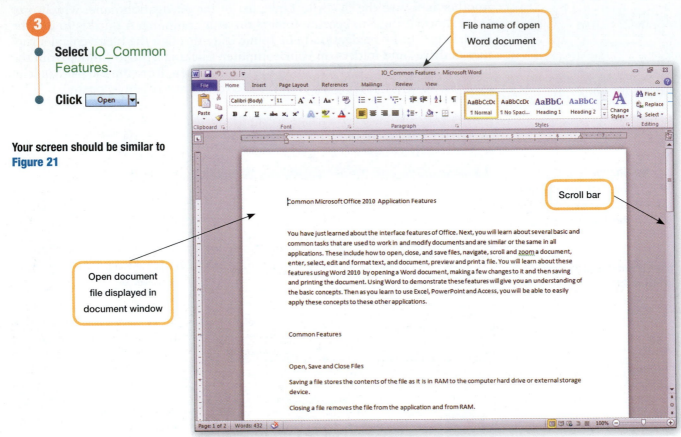

File name of open Word document

Scroll bar

Open document file displayed in document window

Figure 21

A Word document file describing the common Microsoft Office application features is displayed in the document window.

Scrolling the Document Window

As documents increase in size, they cannot be easily viewed in their entirety in the document window and much time can be spent moving to different locations in the document. All Office 2010 applications include features that make it easy to move around and view the information in a large document. The basic method is to scroll through a document using the scroll bar or keyboard. Both methods are useful, depending on what you are doing. For example, if you are entering text using the keyboard, using the keyboard method may be more efficient than using the mouse.

Additional Information

If you have a mouse with a scroll wheel, you can use it to scroll a document vertically.

The table below explains the basic mouse and keyboard techniques that can be used to vertically scroll a document in the Office 2010 applications. There are many other methods for navigating through documents that are unique to an application. They will be discussed in the specific application text.

Mouse or Key Action	Effect in:			
	Word	**Excel**	**PowerPoint**	**Access**
Click ▼ Or ↓	Moves down line by line.	Moves down row by row	Moves down slide by slide	Moves down record by record
Click ▲ Or ↑	Moves up line by line.	Moves up row by row	Moves up slide by slide	Moves up record by record
Click above/below scroll box Or Page Up / Page Down	Moves up/down window by window	Moves up/down window by window	Displays previous/next slide	Moves up/down window by window
Drag ▤ Scroll Box	Moves up/down line by line	Moves up/down row by row	Moves up/down slide by slide	Moves up/down record by record
Ctrl + Home	Moves to beginning of document	Moves to first cell in worksheet or beginning of cell entry	Moves to first slide in presentation or beginning of entry in placeholder	Moves to first record in table or beginning of field entry
Ctrl + End	Moves to end of document	Moves to last-used cell in worksheet or end of cell entry	Moves to last slide in presentation or to end of placeholder entry	Moves to last record in table or end of field entry

Additional Information

You also can scroll the document window horizontally using the horizontal scroll bar or the → and ← keys.

You will use the vertical scroll bar to view the text at the bottom of the Word document. When you use the scroll bar to scroll, the actual location in the document where you can work does not change, only the area you are viewing changes. For example, in Word, the cursor does not move and in Excel the cell you can work in does not change. To move the cursor or make another cell active, you must click in a location in the window. However, when you scroll using the keyboard, the actual location as identified by the position of the cursor in the document also changes. For example, in Word the cursor attempts to maintain its position in a line as you scroll up and down through the document. In Excel the cell you can work in changes as you move through a worksheet using the keyboard.

1

- Click ▾ in the vertical scroll bar 10 times.

- Click at the beginning of the word Scroll in the Common Features section to move the cursor.

- Press ↓ 10 times to scroll the window and move the cursor down 10 lines.

Your screen should be similar to
Figure 22

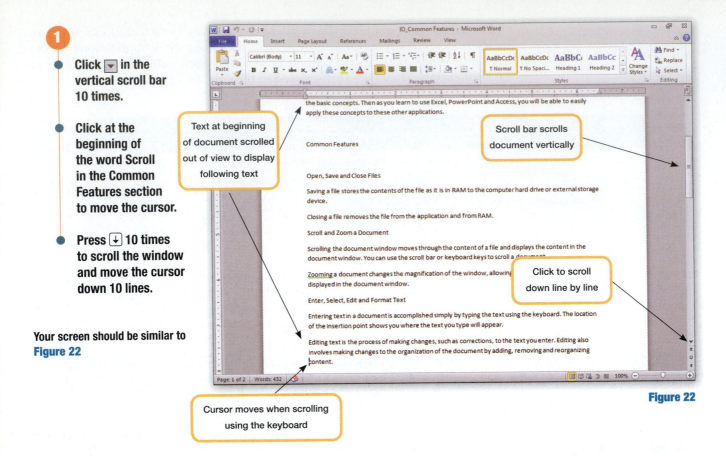

Text at beginning of document scrolled out of view to display following text

Scroll bar scrolls document vertically

Click to scroll down line by line

Cursor moves when scrolling using the keyboard

Figure 22

Having Trouble?

If your screen scrolls differently, this is a function of the type of monitor you are using.

The text at the beginning of the document has scrolled line by line off the top of the document window, and the following text is now displayed. In a large document, scrolling line by line can take a while. You will now try out several additional mouse and keyboard scrolling features that move by larger increments through the document.

2

- Click below the scroll box in the scroll bar.

- Press Ctrl + End to move to the end of the last line of the document.

- Drag the scroll box to the top of the scroll bar.

Your screen should be similar to
Figure 23

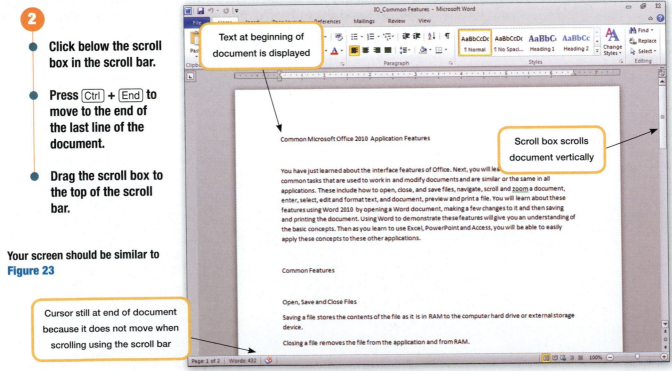

Text at beginning of document is displayed

Scroll box scrolls document vertically

Cursor still at end of document because it does not move when scrolling using the scroll bar

Figure 23

WWW.MHHE.COM/OLEARY

The document window displays the beginning of the document; however, the cursor is still at the end of the document. Using these features makes scrolling a large document much more efficient.

Using the Zoom Feature

Another way to see more or less of a document is to use the zoom feature. Although this feature is available in all Office 2010 applications, Excel and PowerPoint have fewer options than Word. In Access, the zoom feature is available only when specific features are used, such as viewing reports.

The Zoom Slider in the status bar is used to change the magnification. To use the Zoom Slider, click and drag the slider control. Dragging to the right zooms in on the document and increases the magnification whereas dragging to the left zooms out on the document and decreases the magnification. You also can change the zoom percentage by increments of 10 by clicking the ⊕ or ⊖ on each end of the slider control. In Word, the default display, 100 percent, shows the characters the same size they will be when printed. You can increase the onscreen character size up to five times the normal display (500 percent) or reduce the character size to 10 percent.

You will first "zoom out" on the document to get an overview of the file, and then you will "zoom in" to get a close-up look. When a document is zoomed, you can work in it as usual.

Additional Information

The degree of magnification varies with the different applications.

1

- **Click ⊖ in the Zoom Slider five times to decrease the zoom percentage to 50%.**

- **Press** Ctrl + Home **to move the cursor to the beginning of the document.**

- **Drag the Zoom Slider all the way to the right to increase the zoom to 500%.**

Your screen should be similar to
Figure 24

Another Method

You can also hold down Ctrl while using the scroll wheel on your mouse to zoom a document.

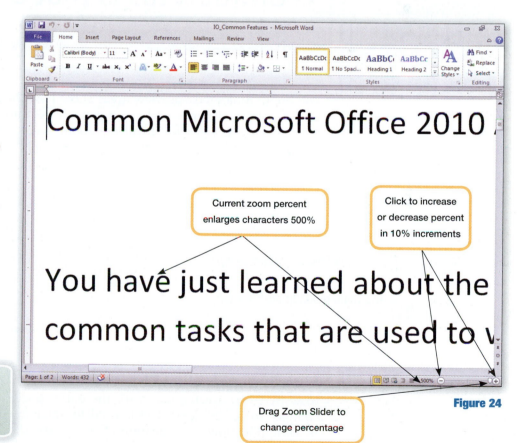

Current zoom percent enlarges characters 500%

Click to increase or decrease percent in 10% increments

Drag Zoom Slider to change percentage

Figure 24

Another Method

You can also click on the zoom percentage in the status bar to open the Zoom dialog box.

Another way to change the magnification is to use the [Zoom] button in the View tab. This method opens the Zoom dialog box containing several preset zoom options, or an option that lets you set a precise percentage using the Percent scroll box. You will use this feature next to zoom the document. This method is available in Word only.

2

- Open the View tab.

- Click 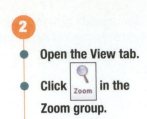 in the Zoom group.

- Click Whole Page and note that the percent value in the Percent text box and the preview area reflect the new percentage setting.

- Click the ▲ up scroll button in the Percent scroll box to increase the zoom percentage to 57.

Another Method

You could also type a value in the Percent text box to specify an exact percentage.

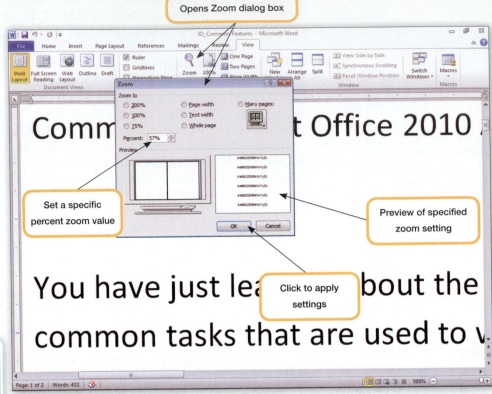

Figure 25

Your screen should be similar to Figure 25

The Zoom dialog box preview areas show how the document will appear on your screen at the specified zoom percent. Not until you complete the command by clicking [OK] will the zoom percent in the document actually change. You will complete the command to apply the 57% zoom setting. Then, you will use the 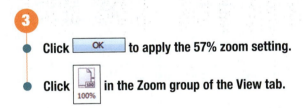 button in the Zoom group to quickly return to the default zoom setting.

3

- Click [OK] to apply the 57% zoom setting.

- Click [100%] in the Zoom group of the View tab.

The document is again at 100% magnification.

Entering and Editing Text

Now that you are familiar with the entire document, you will make a few changes to it. The keyboard is used to enter information into a document. In all applications, the location of the cursor shows you where the text will appear as you type. After text is entered into a document, you need to know how to move around within the text to edit or make changes to the text. Again, the process is similar for all Office applications.

Currently, in this Word document, the cursor is positioned at the top of the document. You will type your name at this location. As you type, the cursor moves to the right and the characters will appear to the left of the cursor. Then you will press [Enter] to end the line following your name and press [Enter] again at the beginning of a line to insert a blank line.

Additional Information

The effect of pressing [Enter] varies in the different Office applications. For example, in Excel, it completes the entry and moves to another cell. You will learn about these differences in the individual application labs.

1

- Type your first and last name.

- Press (Enter) two times.

Your screen should be similar to **Figure 26**

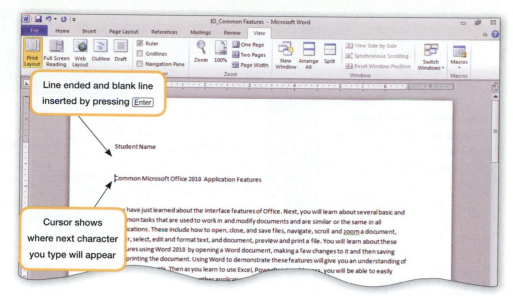

Line ended and blank line inserted by pressing (Enter)

Student Name

Common Microsoft Office 2010 Application Features

Cursor shows where next character you type will appear

Figure 26

As you typed your name, to make space for the text on the line, the existing text moved to the right. Then, when you pressed (Enter) the first time, all the text following your name moved down one line. A blank line was inserted after pressing (Enter) the second time.

Next, you want to add a word to the first line of the first paragraph. To do this, you first need to move the cursor to the location where you want to make the change. The keyboard or mouse can be used to move through the text in the document window. Depending on what you are doing, one method may be more efficient than another. For example, if your hands are already on the keyboard as you are entering text, it may be quicker to use the keyboard rather than take your hands off to use the mouse.

You use the mouse to move the cursor to a specific location in a document simply by clicking on the location. When you can use the mouse to move the cursor, the mouse pointer is shaped as an ⌶ I-beam. You use the arrow keys located on the numeric keypad or the directional keypad to move the cursor in a document. The keyboard directional keys are described in the following table.

Key	Word/PowerPoint	Excel	Access
→	Right one character	Right one cell	Right one field
←	Left one character	Left one cell	Left one field
↑	Up one line	Up one cell	Up one record
↓	Down one line	Down one cell	Down one record
Ctrl + →	Right one word	Last cell in row	One word to right in a field entry
Ctrl + ←	Left one word	First cell in row	One word to left in a field entry
Home	Beginning of line	First cell in row	First field of record
End	End of line		Last field of record

In the first line of the first paragraph, you want to add the word "common" before the word "interface" and the year "2010" after the word "Office." You will move to the correct locations using both the keyboard and the mouse and then enter the new text.

2

- Click at the beginning of the word You in the first paragraph.

- Press ⟶ four times to move to the beginning of the second word.

- Press Ctrl + ⟶ five times to move to the beginning of the seventh word.

Additional Information

Holding down a directional key or key combination moves quickly in the direction indicated, saving multiple presses of the key.

- Type **basic** and press Spacebar.

Having Trouble?

Do not be concerned if you make a typing error; you will learn how to correct them next.

- Position the I-beam between the e in Office and the period at the end of the first sentence and click.

- Press Spacebar and type **2010**

Your screen should be similar to **Figure 27**

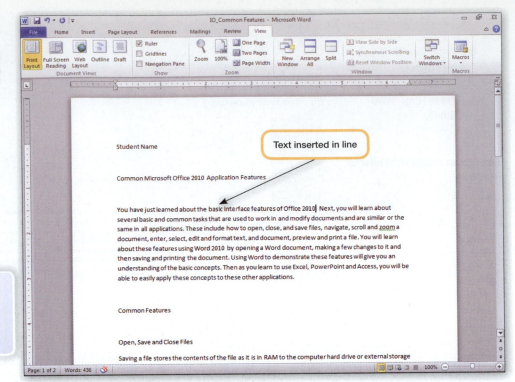

Text inserted in line

Student Name

Common Microsoft Office 2010 Application Features

You have just learned about the basic interface features of Office 2010. Next, you will learn about several basic and common tasks that are used to work in and modify documents and are similar or the same in all applications. These include how to open, close, and save files, navigate, scroll and zoom a document, enter, select, edit and format text, and document, preview and print a file. You will learn about these features using Word 2010 by opening a Word document, making a few changes to it and then saving and printing the document. Using Word to demonstrate these features will give you an understanding of the basic concepts. Then as you learn to use Excel, PowerPoint and Access, you will be able to easily apply these concepts to these other applications.

Common Features

Open, Save and Close Files

Saving a file stores the contents of the file as it is in RAM to the computer hard drive or external storage

Figure 27

Next, you want to edit the text you just entered by changing the word "basic" to "common." Removing typing entries to change or correct them is one of the basic editing tasks. Corrections may be made in many ways. Two of the most basic editing keys that are common to the Office applications are the Backspace and Delete keys. The Backspace key removes a character or space to the left of the cursor. It is particularly useful when you are moving from right to left (backward) along a line of text. The Delete key removes the character or space to the right of the cursor and is most useful when moving from left to right along a line.

You will use these features as you make the correction.

3

- Move the cursor between the s and i in "basic" (in the first sentence).

- Press `Del` to remove the two characters to the right of the insertion point.

- Press `Backspace` three times to remove the three characters to the left of the cursor.

- Type **common**

- Correct any other typing errors you may have made using `Backspace` or `Delete`.

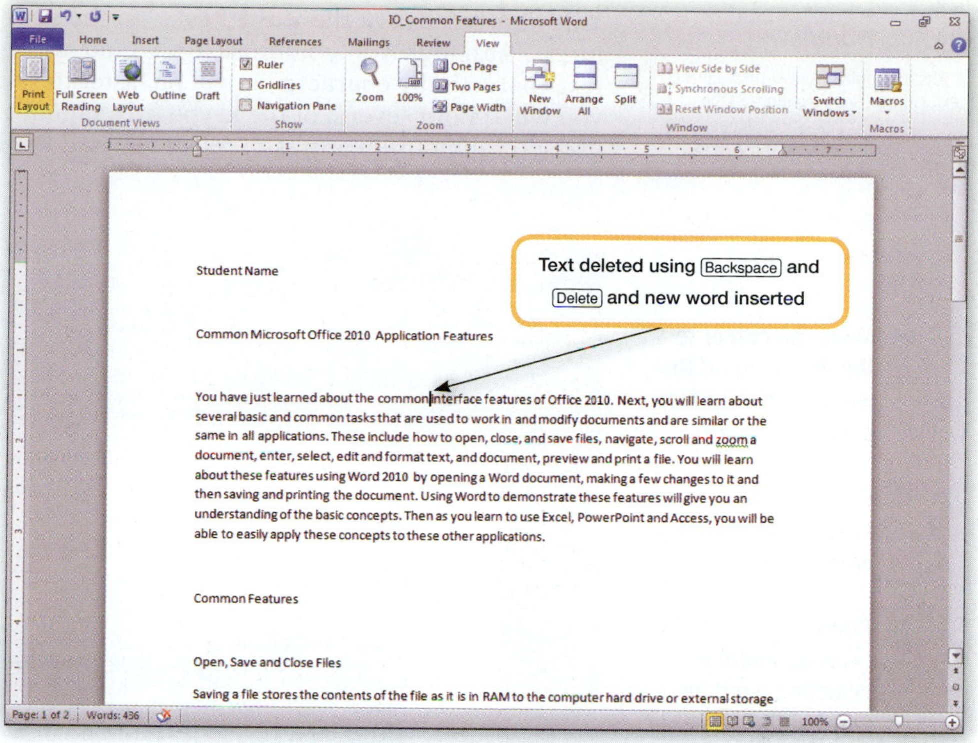

Your screen should be similar to Figure 28

Text deleted using `Backspace` and `Delete` and new word inserted

Figure 28

The word "basic" was deleted from the sentence and the word "common" was entered in its place.

Selecting Text

Additional Information

The capability to select text is common to all Office 2010 applications. However, many of the features that are designed for use in Word are not available in the other applications. Some are available only when certain modes of operation are in effect or when certain features are being used.

While editing and formatting a document, you will need to select text. Selecting highlights text and identifies the text that will be affected by your next action. To select text using the mouse, first move the cursor to the beginning or end of the text to be selected, and then drag to highlight the text you want selected. You can select as little as a single letter or as much as the entire document. You also can select text using keyboard features. The following table summarizes common mouse and keyboard techniques used to select text in Word.

To Select	Mouse	Keyboard
Next/previous space or character	Drag across space or character.	`Shift` + → / `Shift` + ←
Next/previous word	Double-click in the word.	`Ctrl` + `Shift` + → / `Ctrl` + `Shift` + ←
Sentence	Press `Ctrl` and click within the sentence.	
Line	Click to the left of a line when the mouse pointer is ⟋.	
Multiple lines	Drag up or down to the left of a line when the mouse pointer is ⟋.	
Text going backward to beginning of paragraph	Drag left and up to the beginning of the paragraph when the mouse pointer is ⟋.	`Ctrl` + `Shift` + ↑
Text going forward to end of paragraph	Drag right and down to the end of the paragraph when the mouse pointer is ⟋.	`Ctrl` + `Shift` + ↓
Paragraph	Triple-click on the paragraph or double-click to the left of the paragraph when the mouse pointer is ⟋.	
Multiple paragraphs	Drag to the left of the paragraphs when the mouse pointer is ⟋.	
Document	Triple-click or press `Ctrl` and click to the left of the text when the mouse pointer is ⟋.	`Ctrl` + A

You want to change the word "tasks" in the next sentence to "application features". Although you could use ⌈Delete⌉ and ⌈Backspace⌉ to remove the unneeded text character by character, it will be faster to select and delete the word. First you will try out several of the keyboard techniques to select text. Then you will use several mouse features to select text and finally you will edit the sentence.

1

- Move the cursor to the beginning of the word "basic" in the second sentence.

- Press ⌈Shift⌉ + ⌈→⌉ five times to select the word basic.

- Press ⌈Shift⌉ + ⌈Ctrl⌉ + ⌈→⌉ to extend the selection word by word until the entire line is selected.

- Press ⌈Shift⌉ + ⌈Ctrl⌉ + ⌈↓⌉ to extend the selection to the end of the paragraph.

Your screen should be similar to **Figure 29**

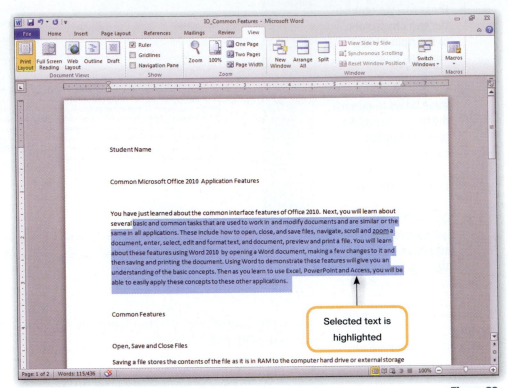

Figure 29

The text from the cursor to the end of the paragraph is selected. Next, you will clear this selection and then use the mouse to select text.

2

● Click anywhere in the paragraph to clear the selection.

● Click at the beginning of the word "basic" and drag to the right to select the text to the end of the line.

● Click in the left margin to the left of the fourth line of the paragraph when the mouse pointer is ⤢ to select the entire line.

● Double-click in the margin to the left of the paragraph when the mouse pointer is ⤢ to select the paragraph.

Your screen should be similar to Figure 30

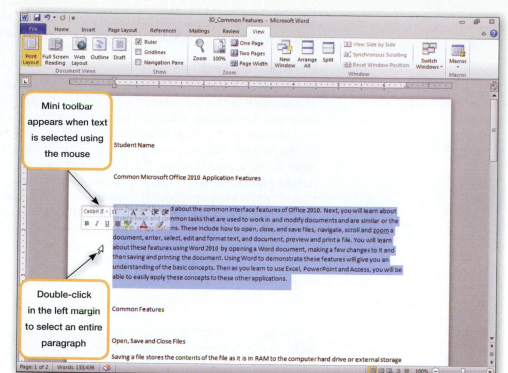

Figure 30

Additional Information

When positioned in the left margin, the mouse pointer shape changes to ⤢, indicating it is ready to select text.

When you select text using the mouse, the **Mini toolbar** appears automatically in Word, Excel, and PowerPoint. You will learn about using this feature in the next section.

Text that is selected can be modified using many different features. In this case, you want to replace the word "tasks" in the second sentence with "application features".

3

● Double-click on the word "tasks" in the second sentence.

● Type **application features**

Your screen should be similar to Figure 31

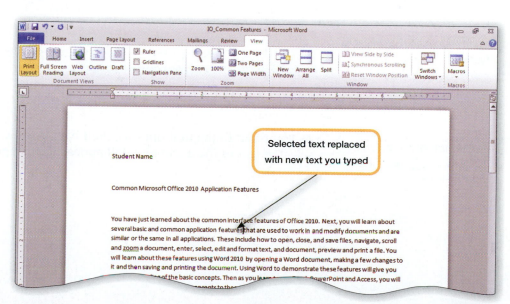

Figure 31

As soon as you began typing, the selected text was automatically deleted. The new text was inserted in the line just like any other text.

Formatting Text

An important aspect of all documents you create using Office 2010 is the appearance of the document. To improve the appearance you can apply many different formatting effects. The most common formatting features are font and character effects. A **font**, also commonly referred to as a **typeface**, is a set of characters with a specific design. The designs have names such as Times New Roman and Courier. Each font has one or more sizes. **Font size** is the height and width of the character and is commonly measured in points, abbreviated "pt." One point equals about 1/72 inch. **Character effects** are enhancements such as bold, italic, and color that are applied to selected text. Using font and character effects as design elements can add interest to your document and give readers visual cues to help them find information quickly.

First you want to change the font and increase the font size of the title of this document.

1

- **Click in the left margin next to the title line when the mouse pointer is** ⬧ **to select it.**

- **Open the Home tab.**

- **Open the** Calibri (Body) ▾ **Font drop-down menu in the Font group.**

- **Point to the Arial Black font option in the menu.**

Your screen should be similar to Figure 32

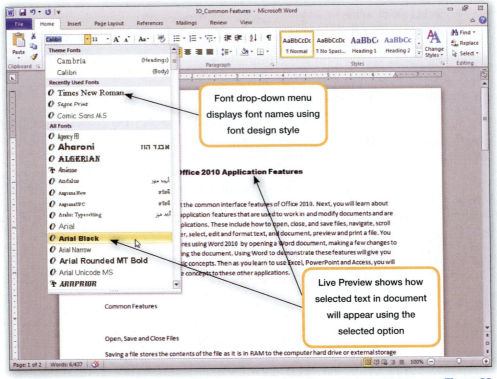

Figure 32

As you point to the font options, the **Live Preview** feature shows you how the selected text in the document will appear if this option is chosen.

Point to several different fonts in the menu to see the Live Preview.

Scroll the menu and click Segoe Print to choose it.

Your screen should be similar to Figure 33

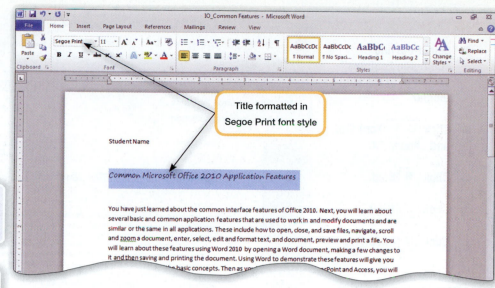

Title formatted in Segoe Print font style

Figure 33

The title appears in the selected font and the name of the font used in the selection is displayed in the Segoe Print ▾ Font button. Next you want to increase the font size. The current (default) font size of 11 is displayed in the 11 ▾ Font Size button. You will increase the font size to 16 points.

Open the 11 ▾ Font Size drop-down menu in the Font group of the Home tab.

Point to several different font sizes to see the Live Preview.

Click 16 to choose it.

Your screen should be similar to Figure 34

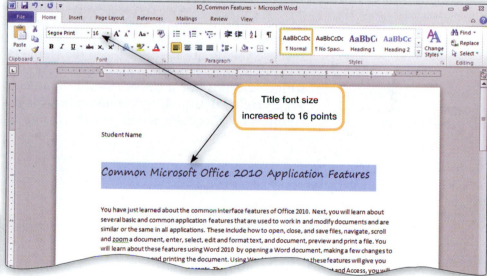

Title font size increased to 16 points

Figure 34

Now the title stands out much more from the other text in the document. Next you will use the Mini toolbar to add formatting to other areas of the document. As you saw earlier, the Mini toolbar appears automatically when you select text. Initially the Mini toolbar appears dimmed (semi-transparent) so that it does not interfere with what you are doing, but it changes to solid when you point at it. It displays command buttons for often-used commands from the Font and Paragraph groups that are used to format a document.

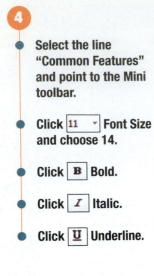

4 ● Select the line "Common Features" and point to the Mini toolbar.

● Click [11 ▾] Font Size and choose 14.

● Click **B** Bold.

● Click *I* Italic.

● Click U Underline.

Your screen should be similar to Figure 35

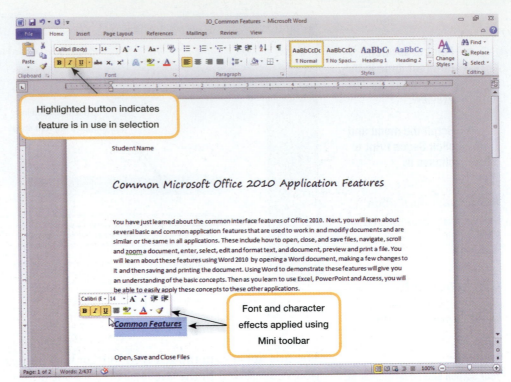

Highlighted button indicates feature is in use in selection

Font and character effects applied using Mini toolbar

Figure 35

The increase in font size as well as the text effects makes this topic head much more prominent. Notice the command button for each selected effect is highlighted, indicating the feature is in use in the selection.

Using the Mini toolbar is particularly useful when the Home tab is closed because you do not need to reopen the Home tab to access the commands. It remains available until you clear the selection or press [Esc]. If you do nothing with a selection for a while, the Mini toolbar will disappear. To redisplay it simply right-click on the selection again. This will also open the context menu.

You will remove the underline effect from the selection next.

5

- **Right-click on the selection to redisplay the Mini toolbar.**

- **Click U Underline on the Mini toolbar.**

Your screen should be similar to
Figure 36

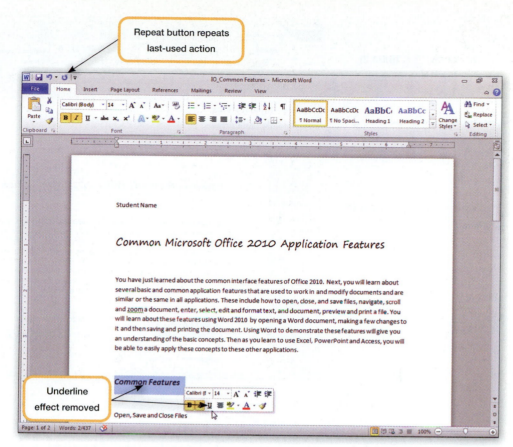

Figure 36

The context menu and Mini toolbar appeared when you right-clicked the selection. The context menu displayed a variety of commands that are quicker to access than locating the command on the Ribbon. The commands that appear on this menu change depending on what you are doing at the time. The context menu disappeared after you made a selection from the Mini toolbar. Both the Mini toolbar and context menus are designed to make it more efficient to execute commands.

Also notice that the ↻ Redo button in the Quick Access Toolbar has changed to a ↺ Repeat button. This feature allows you to quickly repeat the last-used command at another location in the document.

Undoing and Redoing Editing Changes

Instead of reselecting the **U** Underline command to remove the underline effect, you could have used ↺ ▾ Undo to reverse your last action or command. You will use this feature to restore the underline (your last action).

1

● Click 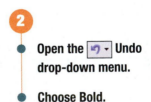 Undo in the Quick Access Toolbar.

Another Method

The keyboard shortcut is Ctrl + Z.

Your screen should be similar to
Figure 37

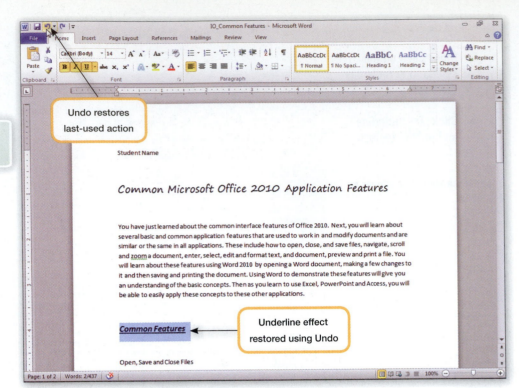

Undo restores
last-used action

Student Name

Common Microsoft Office 2010 Application Features

You have just learned about the common interface features of Office 2010. Next, you will learn about several basic and common application features that are used to work in and modify documents and are similar or the same in all applications. These include how to open, close, and save files, navigate, scroll and zoom a document, enter, select, edit and format text, and document, preview and print a file. You will learn about these features using Word 2010 by opening a Word document, making a few changes to it and then saving and printing the document. Using Word to demonstrate these features will give you an understanding of the basic concepts. Then as you learn to use Excel, PowerPoint and Access, you will be able to easily apply these concepts to these other applications.

Common Features

Underline effect
restored using Undo

Open, Save and Close Files

Figure 37

Undo reversed the last action and the underline formatting effect was restored. Notice that the Undo button includes a drop-down menu button. Clicking this button displays a menu of the most recent actions that can be reversed, with the most-recent action at the top of the menu. When you select an action from the drop-down menu, you also undo all actions above it in the menu.

2

● Open the 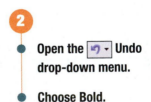 Undo drop-down menu.

● Choose Bold.

Your screen should be similar to
Figure 38

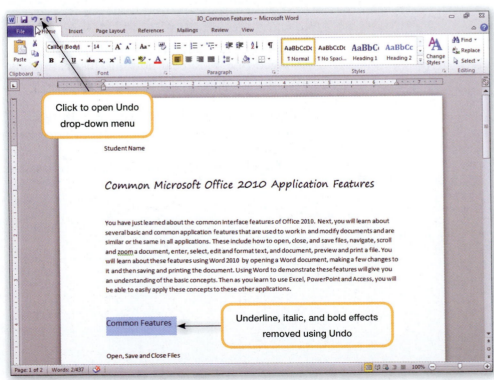

Click to open Undo
drop-down menu

Student Name

Common Microsoft Office 2010 Application Features

You have just learned about the common interface features of Office 2010. Next, you will learn about several basic and common application features that are used to work in and modify documents and are similar or the same in all applications. These include how to open, close, and save files, navigate, scroll and zoom a document, enter, select, edit and format text, and document, preview and print a file. You will learn about these features using Word 2010 by opening a Word document, making a few changes to it and then saving and printing the document. Using Word to demonstrate these features will give you an understanding of the basic concepts. Then as you learn to use Excel, PowerPoint and Access, you will be able to easily apply these concepts to these other applications.

Common Features

Underline, italic, and bold effects
removed using Undo

Open, Save and Close Files

Figure 38

The underline, italic, and bold effects were all removed. Immediately after you undo an action, the ⟲ Repeat button changes to the ⟳ Redo button and is available so you can restore the action you just undid. You will restore the last-removed format, bold.

● Click ⟳ Redo.

Copying and Moving Selections

Common to all Office applications is the capability to copy and move selections to new locations in a document or between documents, saving you time by not having to recreate the same information. A selection that is moved is cut from its original location, called the **source**, and inserted at a new location, called the **destination**. A selection that is copied leaves the original in the source and inserts a duplicate at the destination.

When a selection is cut or copied, the selection is stored in the system **Clipboard**, a temporary Windows storage area in memory. It is also stored in the **Office Clipboard**. The system Clipboard holds only the last cut or copied item, whereas the Office Clipboard can store up to 24 items that have been cut or copied. This feature allows you to insert multiple items from various Office documents and paste all or part of the collection of items into another document.

First, you will copy the text "Office 2010" to two other locations in the first paragraph.

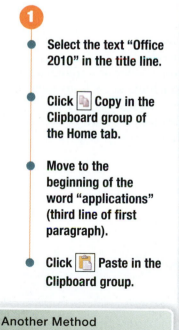

● Select the text "Office 2010" in the title line.

● Click 🗐 Copy in the Clipboard group of the Home tab.

● Move to the beginning of the word "applications" (third line of first paragraph).

● Click 📋 Paste in the Clipboard group.

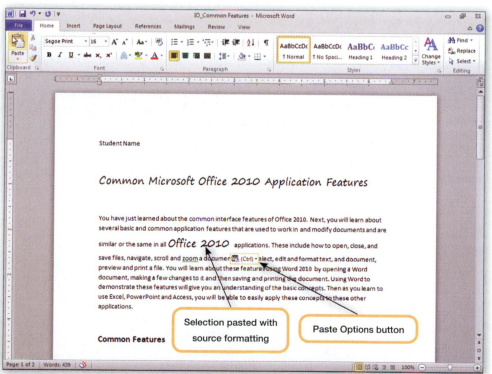

Figure 39

Your screen should be similar to Figure 39

The copied selection is inserted at the location you specified with the same formatting as it has in the title. The 📋 (Ctrl) ▾ Paste Options button appears automatically whenever a selection is pasted. It is used to control the format of the pasted item.

2

● Click the 📋 (Ctrl) ▾ Paste Options button.

Your screen should be similar to Figure 40

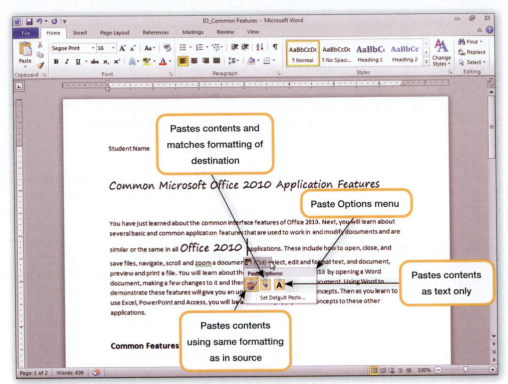

Figure 40

The Paste Options are used to specify whether to insert the item with the same formatting that it had in the source, to change it to the formatting of the surrounding destination text, or to insert text only (from a selection that is a combination of text and graphics). The default as you have seen is to keep the formatting from the source. You want to change it to the formatting of the surrounding text. As you point to a Paste Options button, a **Paste Preview** will show how that option will affect the selection. Then you will copy it again to a second location.

Additional Information

The Paste Options vary with the different applications. For example, Excel has 14 different Paste Options. The Paste Options feature is not available in Access and Paste Preview is not available in Excel.

3

- Click  Merge Formatting.

- Select "other" in the last line of the first paragraph.

- Right-click on the selection and point to each of the Paste Options in the context menu to see the Paste Preview.

- Click  Merge Formatting.

Your screen should be similar to **Figure 41**

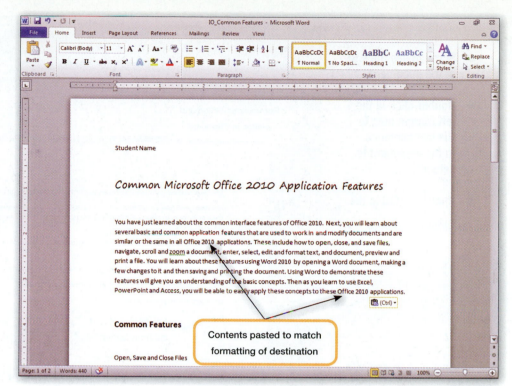

Figure 41

The selected text was deleted and replaced with the contents of the system Clipboard. The system Clipboard contents remain in the Clipboard until another item is copied or cut, allowing you to paste the same item multiple times.

Now you will learn how to move a selection by rearranging several lines of text in the description of common features. You want to move the last sentence in the document, beginning with "Opening a file", to the top of the list. The Cut and Paste commands in the Clipboard group of the Home tab are used to move selections.

4

● Scroll to see the end of the document.

● Double-click in the left margin next to the last sentence in the document to select it.

● Click ✄ Cut in the Clipboard group.

Another Method

The Cut keyboard shortcut is Ctrl + X. You also can choose Cut from the context menu.

Your screen should be similar to Figure 42

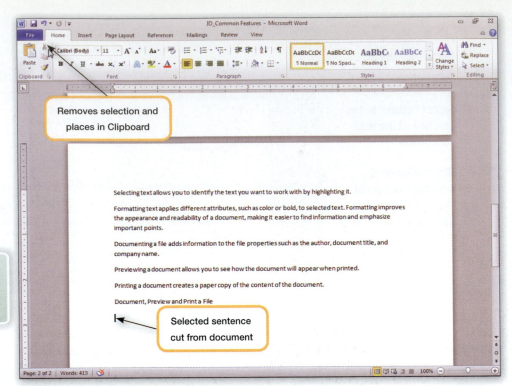

Removes selection and places in Clipboard

Selected sentence cut from document

Figure 42

The selected paragraph is removed from the source and copied to the Clipboard. Next, you need to move the cursor to the location where the text will be inserted and paste the text into the document from the Clipboard.

5

● Move to the beginning of the word "Saving" at the top of the Common Features list.

● Press Ctrl + V.

Your screen should be similar to Figure 43

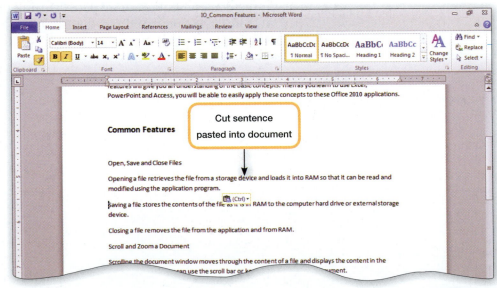

Cut sentence pasted into document

Figure 43

The cut sentence is reentered into the document at the cursor location. That was much quicker than retyping the whole sentence! Because the source has the same formatting as the text at the destination, the default setting to keep the source formatting is appropriate.

WWW.MHHE.COM/OLEARY

Office 2010

Using Drag and Drop

Another way to move or copy selections is to use the drag-and-drop editing feature. This feature is most useful for copying or moving short distances in a document. To use drag and drop to move a selection, point to the selection and drag it to the location where you want the selection inserted. The mouse pointer appears as as you drag, and a temporary insertion point shows you where the text will be placed when you release the mouse button.

Additional Information

You also can use drag and drop to copy a selection by holding down [Ctrl] while dragging. The mouse pointer shape is .

1

- **Select the last line of text in the document.**

- **Drag the selection to the beginning of the word "Documenting" (four lines up).**

Additional Information

You also can move or copy a selection by holding down the right mouse button while dragging. When you release the mouse button, a context menu appears with the available move and copy options.

Your screen should be similar to Figure 44

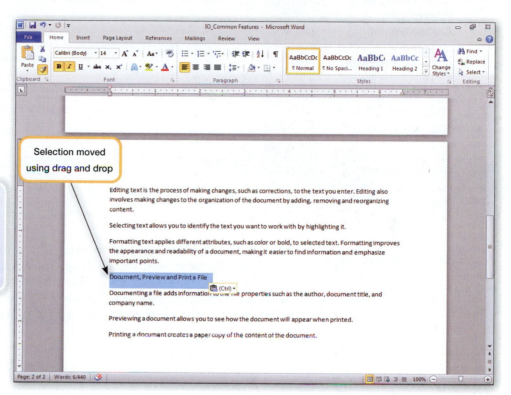

Figure 44

The selection moved to the new location. However, the selection is not copied and stored in the Clipboard and cannot be pasted to multiple locations in the document.

Copying Formats

Many times, you will find you want to copy the formats associated with a selection, but not the text. It is easy to do this using the Format Painter tool.

1

- Apply bold and italic effects and increase the font size to 14 of the currently selected text.

- Click 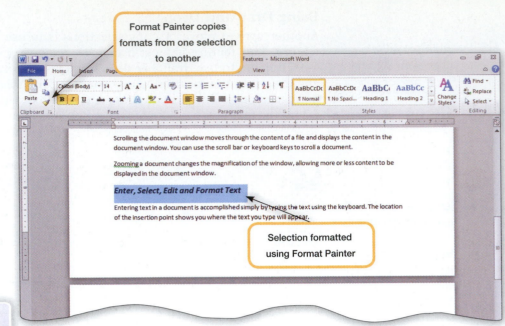 Format Painter in the Clipboard group.

- Scroll the document up and select the topic line of text "Enter, Select, Edit and Format text".

Additional Information

The mouse pointer appears as when this feature is on.

Figure 45

Format Painter copies formats from one selection to another

Selection formatted using Format Painter

Your screen should be similar to Figure 45

The text you selected is formatted using the same formats. This feature is especially helpful when you want to copy multiple formats at one time. Next, you want to format the other topic heads in the Common Features list using the same formats. To do this, you can make the Format Painter "sticky" so that it can be used to copy the format multiple times in succession.

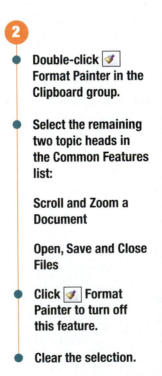

2

- Double-click Format Painter in the Clipboard group.

- Select the remaining two topic heads in the Common Features list:

- Scroll and Zoom a Document

- Open, Save and Close Files

- Click Format Painter to turn off this feature.

- Clear the selection.

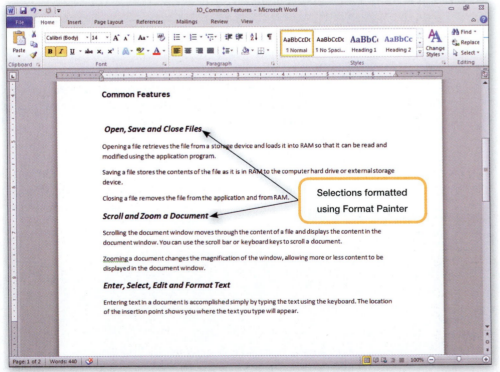

Common Features

Open, Save and Close Files

Opening a file retrieves the file from a storage device and loads it into RAM so that it can be read and modified using the application program.

Saving a file stores the contents of the file as it is in RAM to the computer hard drive or external storage device.

Closing a file removes the file from the application and from RAM.

Scroll and Zoom a Document

Scrolling the document window moves through the content of a file and displays the content in the document window. You can use the scroll bar or keyboard keys to scroll a document.

Zooming a document changes the magnification of the window, allowing more or less content to be displayed in the document window.

Enter, Select, Edit and Format Text

Entering text in a document is accomplished simply by typing the text using the keyboard. The location of the insertion point shows you where the text you type will appear.

Selections formatted using Format Painter

Figure 46

Your screen should be similar to Figure 46

Specifying Document Properties

In addition to the content of the document that you create, all Office 2010 applications automatically include details about the document that describe or identify it called **metadata** or document **properties**. Document properties include details such as title, author name, subject, and keywords that identify the document's topic or contents (described below). Some of these properties are automatically generated. These include statistics such as the number of words in the file and general information such as the date the document was created and last modified. Others such as author name and tags or keywords are properties that you can specify. A **tag** or **keyword** is a descriptive word that is associated with the file and can be used to locate a file using a search.

By specifying relevant information as document properties, you can easily organize, identify, and search for your documents later.

Property	Action
Title	Enter the document title. This title can be longer and more descriptive than the file name.
Tags	Enter words that you associate with the presentation to make it easier to find using search tools.
Comments	Enter comments that you want others to see about the content of the document.
Categories	Enter the name of a higher-level category under which you can group similar types of presentations.
Author	Enter the name of the presentation's author. By default this is the name entered when the application was installed.

You will look at the document properties that are automatically included and add documentation to identify you as the author, and specify a document title and keywords to describe the document.

1

● Open the File tab.

● Click the "Show all properties" link at the bottom of the Properties panel in the Info window to display all properties.

Your screen should be similar to
Figure 47

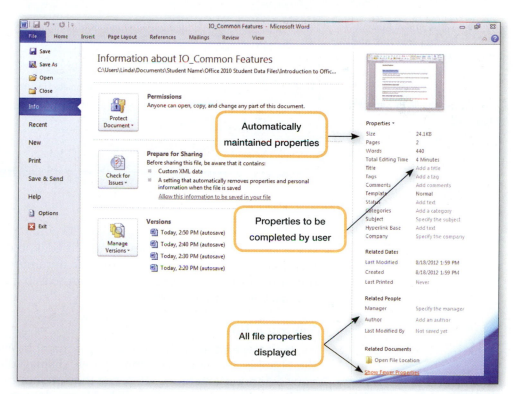

Figure 47

The Properties panel in the right section of the Info tab is divided into four groups and displays the properties associated with the document. Properties such as the document size, number of words, and number of pages are automatically maintained. Others such as the title and tag properties are blank waiting for you to specify your own information.

You will add a title, a tag, and your name as the author name.

2

● Click in the Title text box and type **Common Office Features**

● In the same manner, enter **common**, **features**, **interface** as the tags.

● Click in the Add an Author text box and enter your name.

Your screen should be similar to Figure 48

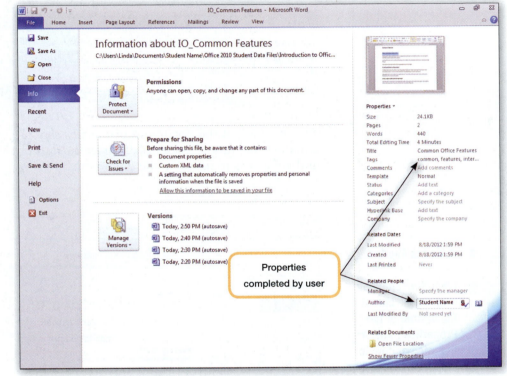

Properties completed by user

Figure 48

Once the document properties are specified, you can use them to identify and locate documents. You also can use the automatically updated properties for the same purpose. For example, you can search for all files created by a specified user or on a certain date.

Saving a File

As you enter and edit text to create a document in Word, Excel, and PowerPoint, the changes you make are immediately displayed onscreen and are stored in your computer's memory. However, they are not permanently stored until you save your work to a file on a disk. After a document has been saved as a file, it can be closed and opened again at a later time to be edited further. Unlike Word, Excel, and PowerPoint, where you start work on a new document and then save your changes, Access requires that you name the new database file first and create a table for your data. Then, it saves your changes to the data automatically as you work. This allows multiple users to have access to the most up-to-date data at all times.

As a backup against the accidental loss of work from power failure or other mishap, Word, Excel, and PowerPoint include an AutoRecover feature. When this feature is on, as you work you may see a pulsing disk icon briefly appear in the status bar. This icon indicates that the program is saving your work to a temporary recovery file. The time interval between automatic saving can be set to any period you specify; the default is every 10 minutes. After a problem has occurred, when you restart the program, the recovery file is automatically opened containing all changes you made up to the last time it was saved by AutoRecover. You then need to save the recovery file. If you do not save it, it is deleted when closed. AutoRecover is a great feature for recovering lost work but should not be used in place of regularly saving your work.

You will save the work you have done so far on the document. You use the Save or Save As commands to save files. The 🖫 **Save** command on the File tab or the 🖫 Save button on the Quick Access Toolbar will save the active file using the same file name by replacing the contents of the existing disk file with the document as it appears on your screen. The 🔣 **Save As** command on the File tab is used to save a file using a new file name, to a new location, or as a different file type. This leaves the original file unchanged. When you create a new document, you can use either of the Save commands to save your work to a file on the disk. It is especially important to save a new document very soon after you create it because the AutoRecover feature does not work until a file name has been specified.

You will save this file using a new file name to your solution file location.

1

Click  in the left section of Backstage view.

Your screen should be similar to **Figure 49**

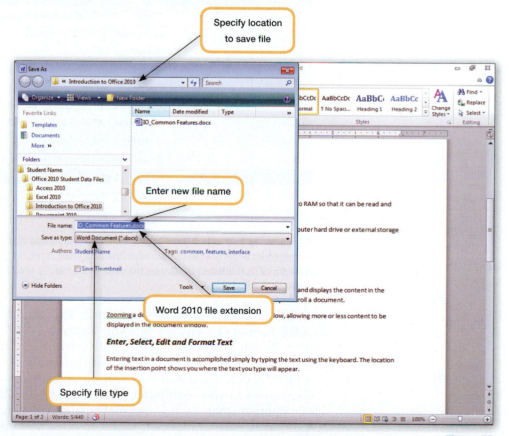

Figure 49

The Save As dialog box is used to specify the location where you will save the file and the file name. The Address bar displays the folder location from which the file was opened and the File name text box displays the name of the open file. The file name is highlighted, ready for you to enter a new file name. The Save as type box displays "Word Document.docx" as the default format in which the file will be saved. Word 2010 documents are identified by the file extension .docx. The file type you select determines the file extension that will be automatically added to the file name when the file is saved. The file types and extensions for the four Office 2010 applications are described in the following table.

Extensions	File Type
Word 2010	
.docx	Word 2007-2010 document without macros or code
.dotx	Word 2007-2010 template without macros or code
.docm	Word 2007-2010 document that could contain macros or code
.xps	Word 2007-2010 shared document (see Note)
.doc	Word 95–2003 document
Excel 2010	
.xlsx	Excel 2007-2010 default workbook without macros or code
.xlsm	Excel 2007-2010 default workbook that could contain macros
.xltx	Excel 2007-2010 template without macros
.xltm	Excel 2007-2010 template that could contain macros
.xps	Excel 2007-2010 shared workbook (see Note)
.xls	Excel 97–2003 workbook
PowerPoint	
.pptx	PowerPoint 2007-2010 default presentation format
.pptm	PowerPoint 2007-2010 presentation with macros
.potx	PowerPoint 2007-2010 template without macros
.potm	PowerPoint 2007-2010 template that may contain macros
.ppam	PowerPoint 2007-2010 add-in that contains macros
.ppsx	PowerPoint 2007-2010 slide show without macros
.ppsm	PowerPoint 2007-2010 slide show that may contain macros
.thmx	PowerPoint 2007-2010 theme
.ppt	PowerPoint 2003 or earlier presentation
Access	
.accdb	Access 2007-2010 database
.mdb	Access 2003 or earlier database

NOTE XPS file format is a fixed-layout electronic file format that preserves document formatting and ensures that when the file is viewed online or printed, it retains exactly the format that you intended. It also makes it difficult to change the data in the file. To save as an XPS file format, you must have installed the free add-in.

Office 2007 and 2010 save Word, Excel, and PowerPoint files using the XML format (Extensible Markup Language) and a four-letter file extension. This format makes your documents safer by separating files that contain macros (small programs in a document that automate tasks) to make it easier for a virus checker to identify and block unwanted code or macros that could be dangerous to your computer. It also makes file sizes smaller by compressing the content upon saving and makes files less susceptible to damage. In addition, XML format makes it easier to open documents created with an Office application using another application.

Previous versions of Word, Excel, and PowerPoint did not use XML and had a three-letter file extension. If you plan to share a file with someone using an Office 2003 or earlier version, you can save the document using the three-letter file type; however, some features may be lost. Otherwise, if you save it as a four-letter file type, the recipient may not be able to view all features. There also may be loss of features for users of Office 2007 (even though it has an XML file type) because the older version does not support several of the new features in Office 2010. Office 2010 includes a feature that checks for compatibility with previous versions and advises you what features in the document may be lost if opened by an Office 2007 user or if the document is saved in the 2003 format.

If you have an Office Access 2007 (.accdb) database that you want to save in an earlier Access file format (.mdb), you can do so as long as your .accdb database does not contain any multivalued lookup fields, offline data, or attachments. This is because older versions of Access do not support these new features. If you try to convert an .accdb database containing any of these elements to an .mdb file format, Access displays an error message.

First you may need to change the location to the location where the file will be saved. The same procedures you used to specify a location to open a file are used to specify the location to save a file. Then, you will change the file name to Common Features using the default Word document type (.docx).

2

- If necessary, select the location where you save your solution files.

- If necessary, triple-click or drag in the File Name text box to highlight the existing file name.

- Type **Common Features**

- Click [Save].

Your screen should be similar to **Figure 50**

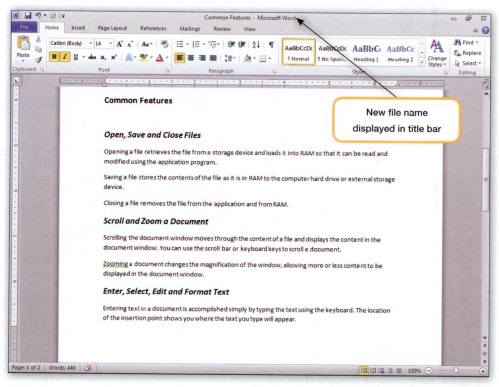

Figure 50

The document is saved as Common Features.docx at the location you selected, and the new file name is displayed in the Word application window title bar.

Printing a Document

Once a document appears how you want, you may want to print a hard copy for your own reference or to give to others. All Office 2010 applications include the capability to print and have similar options. You will print this document next.

1

Open the File tab and choose Print.

Another Method

The keyboard shortcut for the Print command is Ctrl + P.

Your screen should be similar to Figure 51

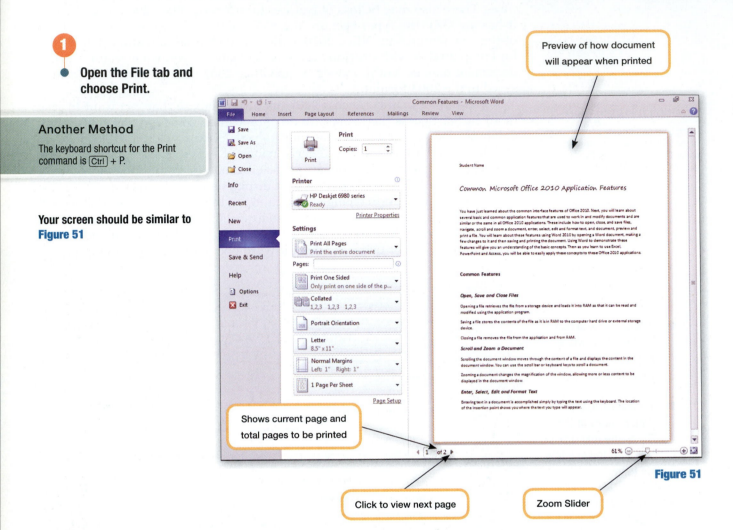

Preview of how document will appear when printed

Shows current page and total pages to be printed

Click to view next page

Zoom Slider

Figure 51

Having Trouble?

If necessary, use the Zoom Slider to change the preview zoom to 60%.

The right section of the Print window displays a preview of the current page of your document. To save time and unnecessary printing and paper waste, it is always a good idea to preview each page of your document before printing. Notice below the preview, the page scroll box shows the page number of the page you are currently viewing and the total number of pages. The scroll buttons on either side are used to scroll to the next and previous pages. Additionally, a Zoom Slider is available to adjust the size of the preview.

2

● Click ▶ to view the second page of the document.

● Increase the zoom to 70%.

Your screen should be similar to **Figure 52**

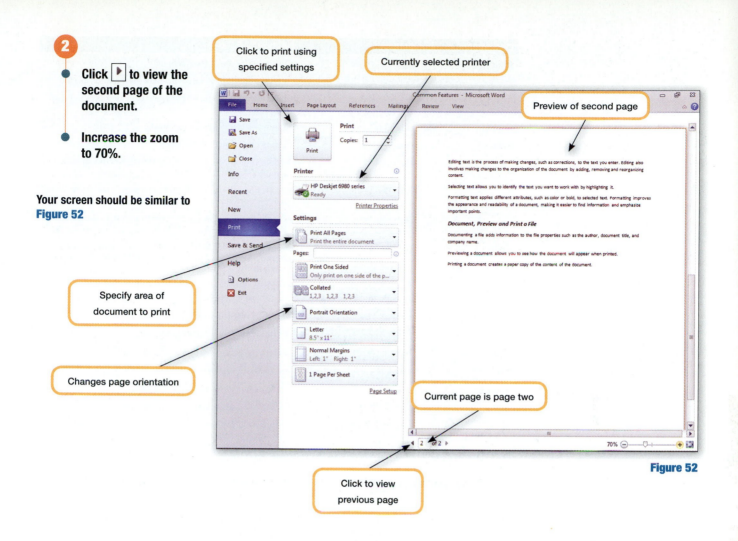

Click to print using specified settings

Currently selected printer

Preview of second page

Specify area of document to print

Changes page orientation

Current page is page two

Click to view previous page

Figure 52

If you see any changes you want to make to the document, you would need to close the File tab and make the changes. If the document looks good, you are ready to print.

The second section of the Print window is divided into three areas: Print, Printer, and Settings. In the Print section you specify the number of copies you want printed. The default is to print one copy. The Printer section is used to specify the printer you will use and the printer properties such as paper size and print quality. The name of the default printer on your computer appears in the list box. The Settings area is used to specify what part of the document you want to print, whether to print on one or both sides of the paper or to collate (sort) the printed output, the page orientation, paper size, margins, and sheet settings. The Word print setting options are explained in the following table. The Print settings will vary slightly with the different Office applications. For example, in Excel, the options to specify what to print are to print the entire worksheet, entire workbook, or a selection. The differences will be demonstrated in the individual labs.

Option	Setting	Action
Print what	All	Prints entire document (default)
	Current page	Prints selected page or page where the cursor is located.
	Pages	Prints pages you specify by typing page numbers in Pages text box
	Selection	Prints selected text only (default)
Sides	One	Prints on one side of the paper.
	Both (short)	Prints on both sides by flipping the page vertically using a duplex printer
	Both (long)	Prints on both sides by flipping the page horizontally using a duplex printer
	Manually both	Reload the paper when prompted to print on the other side
Collate	Collated	Prints all of specified document before printing second or multiple copies; for example, pages 1,2 then 1,2 again (default)
	Uncollated	Prints multiple copies of each specified page sequentially (for example, pages 1,1 then 2,2)
Orientation	Portrait	Prints across the width of the paper (default)
	Landscape	Prints across the length of the paper
Paper	Size	Select the paper size (8.5 × 11 is default)
	Envelope	Select an envelope size
Margins	Normal	One-inch margins all around (default)
	Narrow, Wide	Select alternative margin settings
Sheet	One Page Per Sheet	Prints each page of the document on a separate sheet (default)
	Multiple pages per sheet	Specify number of pages to print on a sheet

NOTE Please consult your instructor for printing procedures that may differ from the following directions.

You will specify several different print settings to see the effect on the preview, then you will print using the default print settings.

3

- If you need to change the selected printer to another printer, open the Printer drop-down menu and choose the appropriate printer (your instructor will tell you which printer to select).

- Click

  Print All Pages
  Print the entire document

  and choose Print Current Page from the drop-down menu.

- Click

  Portrait Orientation

  and choose Landscape Orientation from the drop-down menu.

Your screen should be similar to Figure 53

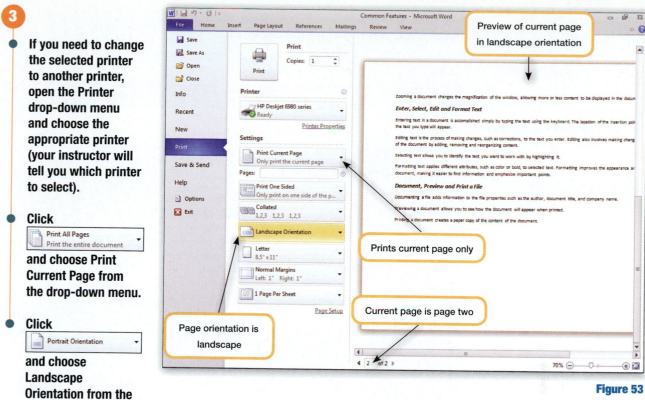

Figure 53

The preview window displays the current page in landscape orientation and the page indicator shows that page two of two will print. You will return these settings to their defaults and then print the document.

4

- Click Print Current Page / Only print the current page and choose Print All Pages from the drop-down menu.

- Click Landscape Orientation and choose Portrait Orientation from the drop-down menu.

- Click Print .

Your printer should be printing the document.

Closing a File

Finally, you want to close the document.

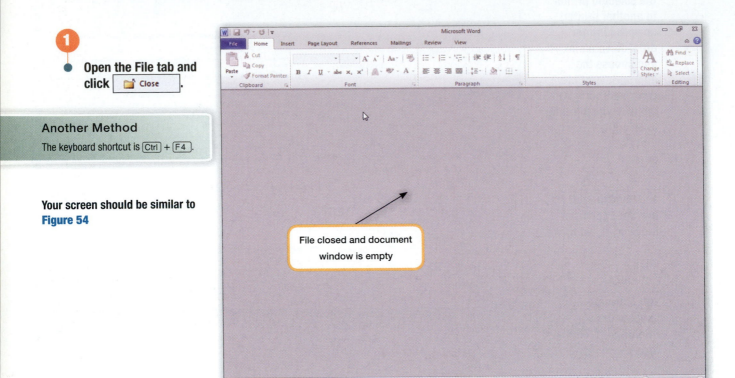

File closed and document window is empty

Now the Word window displays an empty document window. Because you did not make any changes to the document since saving it, the document window closed immediately. If you had made additional changes, the program would ask whether you wanted to save the file before closing it. This prevents the accidental closing of a file that has not been saved first.

USING OFFICE HELP

Notice the ⊘ in the upper-right corner of the Ribbon. This button is used to access the Microsoft Help system. The Help button is always visible even when the Ribbon is hidden. Because you are using the Microsoft Word 2010 application, Word Help will be accessed.

1

- Click Microsoft Word Help.

- If a Table of Contents pane is not displayed along the left side of the Help window, click Show Table of Contents in the Help window toolbar to open it.

Your screen should be similar to Figure 55

Additional Information

Click Hide Table of Contents in the Help window toolbar to hide the Table of Contents pane when it is open.

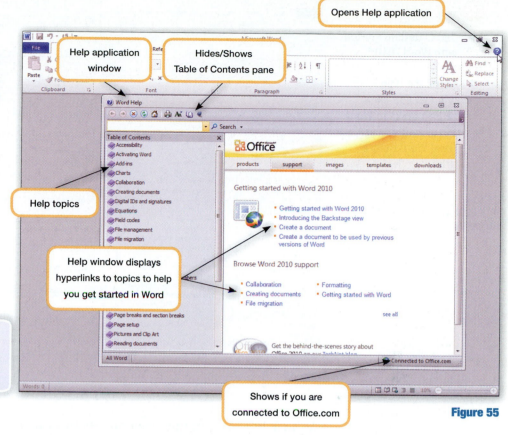

Figure 55

Additional Information

Because Help is an online feature, the information is frequently updated. Your screens may display slightly different information than those shown in the figures in this lab.

The Word Help feature is a separate application and is opened and displayed in a separate window. The Help window on your screen will probably be a different size and arrangement than in Figure 56. A list of help topics is displayed in the Table of Contents pane along the left side of the window and the Help window on the right side displays several topics to help you get started using Word. If you are connected to the Internet, the Microsoft Office Online Web site, Office.com, is accessed and help information from this site is displayed in the window. If you are not connected, the offline help information that is provided with the application and stored on your computer is located and displayed. Generally, the listing of topics is similar but fewer in number.

Additional Information

Depending on the size of your Help window, you may need to scroll the window to see all the Help information provided.

Selecting Help Topics

There are several ways you can get help. The first is to select a topic from the listing displayed in the Help window. Each topic is a **hyperlink** or connection to the information located on the Office.com Web site or in Help on your computer. When you point to a hyperlink, it appears underlined and the mouse pointer appears as . Clicking the hyperlink accesses and displays the information associated with the hyperlink.

Having Trouble?

In addition to being connected to the Internet, the Help feature to show content from the Internet must be selected. If necessary, click at the bottom of the Help window and choose Show content from Office.com.

1

● Click "Getting started with Word 2010."

● Scroll the Help window and click "Basic tasks in Word 2010" in the Never Used Word Before area.

Your screen should be similar to
Figure 56

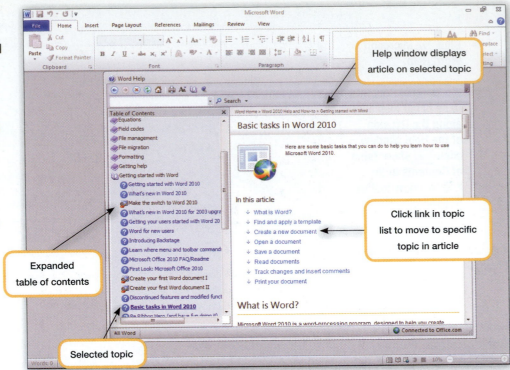

Figure 56

An article containing information about basic features of Word 2010 is displayed and the table of contents has expanded and current topic is underlined to show your location in Help. A topic list appears at the top of the article. You can either scroll the article to read it, or you can jump to a specific location in the article by clicking on a topic link.

2

● Click "Create a new document."

Your screen should be similar to
Figure 57

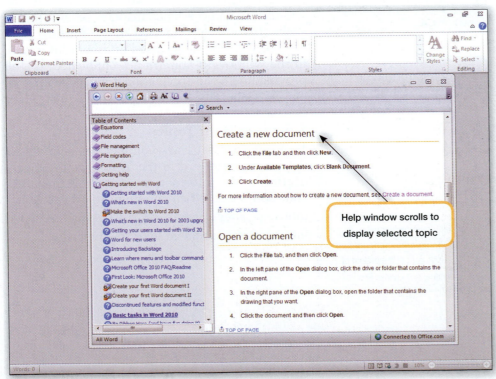

Figure 57

The information on the selected topic is displayed in the window. Notice, as you made selections in the Help window, that the Table of Contents pane shows your current location in Help.

Using the Help Table of Contents

Choosing a topic from the Table of Contents is another method of locating Help information. Using this method allows you to browse the entire list of Help topics to locate topics of interest to you. In this case, the Getting Started with Word topic has expanded to show the subtopics and the topic you are currently viewing is underlined, indicating it is selected. Notice the 📖 Open Book and 📗 Closed Book icons in the Table of Contents. The 📖 Open Book icon identifies those chapters that are open. Clicking on an item preceded with a 📗 Closed Book icon opens a chapter, which expands to display additional chapters or topics. Clicking on an item preceded with 📄 displays the specific Help information.

Additional Information

Pointing to a topic that is not fully displayed in the Table of Contents displays a ScreenTip of the entire topic heading.

1

● Click "Word for new users" in the Table of Contents list.

● Click "A tour of the Word user interface" in the Help window.

Your screen should be similar to **Figure 58**

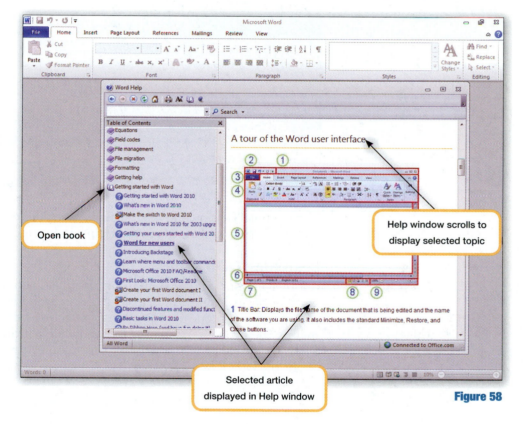

Open book

Help window scrolls to display selected topic

Selected article displayed in Help window

Figure 58

Now information about the user interface features of Word 2010 is displayed in the Help window. To move through previously viewed Help topics, you can use the ◀ Back and ▶ Forward buttons in the Help toolbar. You can quickly redisplay the opening Help window using 🏠 Home on the Help toolbar.

2

- Click ◀ Back to display the previous topic.

- Click ⌂ Home in the Help window toolbar.

- Click "Getting started with Word" in the Table of Contents pane to close this topic.

Your screen should be similar to Figure 59

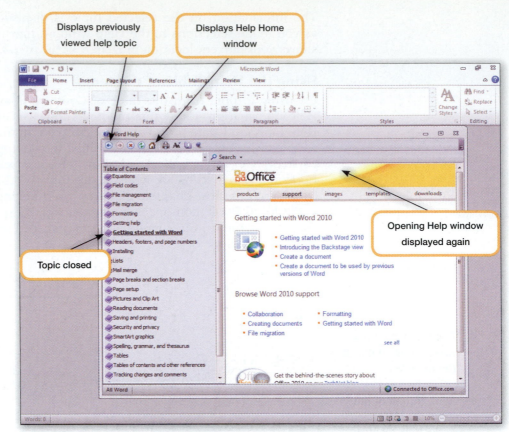

Figure 59

The opening Help window is displayed, the Table of Contents topic is closed, and the ▶ Forward button in the Help window toolbar is now available for use.

Searching Help Topics

Another method to find Help information is to conduct a search by entering a word or phrase you want help on in the Search text box. When searching, you can specify the scope of the search by selecting from the 🔍 Search ▾ drop-down menu. The broadest scope for a search, All Word under Content from Office .com, is preselected. You will use this feature to search for Help information about the Office user interface.

1

● **Click in the Search text box to display the cursor and type user interface**

Additional Information

The search is not case sensitive.

● **Click** 🔍 Search ▾ **.**

● **Scroll the Help window to see the search results.**

Additional Information

You also could press Enter to start the search.

Your screen should be similar to Figure 60

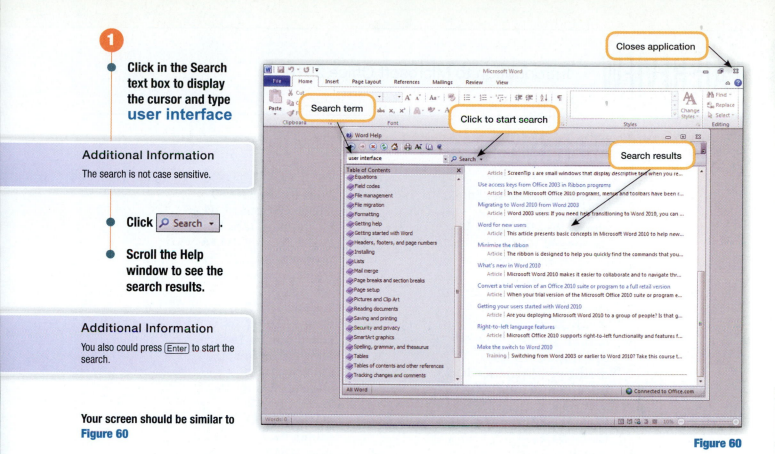

Figure 60

The Help window displays links to articles that contain both the words "user" and "interface." The results are shown in order of relevance, with the most likely matches at the top of the list.

EXITING AN OFFICE 2010 APPLICATION

Now you are ready to close the Help window and exit the Word program. The 🗙 Close button located on the right end of the window title bar can be used to exit most application windows. Alternatively, you can use the 🗙 Exit command on the File tab. If you attempt to close an application without first saving your document, a warning appears asking if you want to save your work. If you do not save your work and you exit the application, any changes you made since last saving it are lost.

1

● Click 🗙 Close in the Help window title bar to close the Help window.

● Click 🗙 Close in the Word window title bar to exit Word.

Another Method

The keyboard shortcut for the Exit command is Alt + F4.

The program window is closed and the Windows desktop is visible again.

KEY TERMS

Backstage view IO.24
buttons IO.15
character effects IO.40
Clipboard IO.45
commands IO.18
context menu IO.17
contextual tabs IO.20
cursor IO.15
database IO.7
default IO.27
destination IO.45
dialog box launcher IO.23
document window IO.15
edit IO.3
Enhanced ScreenTip IO.20
fields IO.7
font IO.40
font size IO.40
format IO.3
groups IO.18
hyperlink IO.61
insertion point IO.15
keyboard shortcut IO.16
keyword IO.51
Live Preview IO.40
metadata IO.51

Mini toolbar IO.39
Office Clipboard IO.45
on-demand tabs IO.20
Paste Preview IO.46
properties IO.27, 51
Quick Access Toolbar IO.15
records IO.7
Ribbon IO.15
ScreenTip IO.16
scroll bar IO.15
shortcut menu IO.17
slide IO.10
slide shows IO.10
source IO.45
status bar IO.15
tables IO.7
tabs IO.18
tag IO.51
task pane IO.23
template IO.26
tooltip IO.16
typeface IO.40
user interface IO.14
View buttons IO.15
worksheet IO.5
Zoom Slider IO.15

COMMAND SUMMARY

Command/Button	Shortcut	Action
Quick Access Toolbar		
⤺ ▾ Undo	Ctrl + Y	Restores last change
↻ Redo	Ctrl + Y	Restores last Undo action
↻ Repeat	Ctrl + Y	Repeats last action
❓ Microsoft Word Help	F1	Opens Microsoft Help

COMMAND SUMMARY (CONTINUED)

Command/Button	Shortcut	Action
File tab		
🔲 Save	Ctrl + S or 🔲	Saves document using same file name
🔲 Save As	F12	Saves document using a new file name, type, and/or location
🔲 Open	Ctrl + O	Opens existing file
🔲 Close	Ctrl + F4 or ⊠	Closes document
Info		Displays document properties
Print/ 🖨 Print	Ctrl + P	Prints document using specified settings
⊠ Exit	Alt + F4 or ⊠	Exits Office program
View tab		
Zoom group		
🔍 Zoom		Changes magnification of document
Home tab		
Clipboard group		
📋 Paste	Ctrl + V	Inserts copy of Clipboard at location of cursor
✂ Cut	Ctrl + X	Removes selection and copies to Clipboard
📋 Copy	Ctrl + C	Copies selection to Clipboard
🖌 Format Painter		Duplicates formats of selection to other locations
Font group		
Calibri (Body) ▾ Font	Ctrl + Shift + F	Changes typeface
11 ▾ Font Size	Ctrl + Shift + P	Changes font size
B Bold	Ctrl + B	Adds/removes bold effect
I Italic	Ctrl + I	Adds/removes italic effect
U̲ Underline	Ctrl + U	Adds/removes underline effect

STEP-BY-STEP

EXPLORING EXCEL 2010

1. In this exercise you will explore the Excel 2010 application and use many of the same features you learned about while using Word 2010 in this lab.

    a. Use the Start menu or a shortcut icon on your desktop to start Office Excel 2010.

    b. What shape is the mouse pointer when positioned in the document window area? _____

    c. Excel has _____ tabs. Which tabs are not the same as in Word? _____

    d. Open the Formulas tab. How many groups are in the Formulas tab? _____

    e. Which tab contains the group to work with charts? _____

    f. From the Home tab, click the Number group dialog box launcher. What is the name of the dialog box that opens? _____ How many number categories are there? _____ Close the dialog box.

    g. Display ScreenTips for the following buttons located in the Alignment group of the Home tab and identify what action they perform.

        ▤ _____

        ▤ _____

        ▤ _____

    h. Open the Excel Help window. From the Help window choose "Getting started with Excel 2010" and then choose "Basic tasks in Excel 2010." Read this article and answer the following question: What is Excel used for? _____

    i. In the Table of Contents, open the "Worksheets" topic and then "Entering Data." Read the topic "Enter data manually in worksheet cells" and answer the following:

    • What is the definition of worksheet? Hint: Click on the grayed term "worksheet" to view a definition.

    _____

    • What four types of data can be entered in a worksheet? _____, _____, _____, _____

    j. Read the topic "Quick Start: Edit and enter data in a worksheet." If you have an Internet connection, click the Watch the video link and view the video. Close your browser window.

    k. Enter the term "formula" in the Search text box. Look at several articles and answer the following question: All formula entries begin with what symbol? _____

    l. Close the Help window. Exit Excel.

EXPLORING POWERPOINT 2010

2. In this exercise you will explore the PowerPoint 2010 application and use many of the same features you learned about while using Word 2010 in this lab.

a. Use the Start menu or a shortcut icon on your desktop to start Office PowerPoint 2010.

b. PowerPoint has _____ tabs. Which tabs are not the same as in Word?
_____

c. Open the Animations tab. How many groups are in this tab? _____

d. Which tab contains the group to work with themes? _____

e. Click on the text "Click to add title." Type your name. Select this text and change the font size to 60; add italic and bold. Cut this text. Click in the box containing "Click to add subtitle" and paste the cut selection. Use the Paste Options to keep the source formatting.

f. Click on the text "Click to add title" and type the name of your school. Select the text and apply a font of your choice.

g. Open the PowerPoint Help window. From the Help window, choose "Getting Started with PowerPoint 2010" and then choose "Basic tasks in PowerPoint 2010." Read the information in this article and answer the following questions:

- In the "What is PowerPoint?" topic, what is the primary use of PowerPoint?_____.

- In the "Save a presentation" topic, what is the default file format for a presentation? _____

- What is the first tip in the "Tips for creating an effective presentation" topic?
_____

h. Enter the term "placeholder" in the Search text box. Look at several articles and write the definition of this term. Hint: Click on a word in an article that appears in light gray to view a definition.
_____

i. In the Table of Contents, open the "Delivering your presentation" topic. Choose "Create and print notes pages" and answer the following questions:

- What are notes pages?
_____

- What is the Green Idea?
_____

j. Close the Help window. Exit PowerPoint and do not save the changes you made to the presentation.

LAB EXERCISES

EXPLORING ACCESS 2010

3. As noted in this Introduction to Microsoft Office 2010, when you start Access 2010 you need to either open an existing database file or create and name a new database. Therefore, in this exercise, you simply explore the Access 2010 Help information without opening or creating a database file.

   a. Use the Start menu or a shortcut icon on your desktop to start Office Access 2010.

   b. Open the Help tab in Backstage view and choose Microsoft Office Help.

   c. From the Help window, choose "Basic tasks in Access 2010." Read the information in this article and answer the following questions:

   - In the "What is Access?" topic, what are the two locations where you can keep your data? _____ and _____.

   - In the "Create a Database from Scratch" topic, what are the two choices? _____ or _____.

   d. In the Table of Contents pane, open the "Access basics" topic. Choose "Database basics" and answer the following questions:

   - In the "What is a database?" topic, define "database." _____

   - In "The parts of an Access database" topic, what are the six main parts? _____, _____, _____, _____, _____, _____.

   - In "The parts of an Access database" topic, how is data in a table stored? _____ and _____.

   - In "The parts of an Access database" topic, each row in a table is referred to as a _____.

   e. Enter the term "field" in the Search text box. Look at several articles and write the definition of this term. Hint: Click on a word in an article that appears in light gray to view a definition. _____

   f. Close the Help window. Exit Access.

ON YOUR OWN

EXPLORING WORD HELP

1. In addition to the Help information you used in this lab, Office 2010 Help also includes many interactive tutorials. Selecting a Help topic that starts a tutorial will open the browser program on your computer. Both audio and written instructions are provided. You will use one of these tutorials to learn more about using Word 2010.

   Start Word 2010. Open Help and choose "Getting started with Word" from the Help window. Click on the training topic "Create your first Word document I." Follow the directions in your browser to run the tutorial. When you are done, close the browser window, close Help, and exit Word 2010.

Objectives

After completing this lab, you will know how to:

1 Plan, create, and modify a database.

2 Create and save a table structure.

3 Define field names, data types, field properties, and primary key fields.

4 Enter and edit data.

5 Add attachments.

6 Change views.

7 Adjust column widths.

8 Use the Best Fit feature.

9 Create a second table.

10 Navigate among records.

11 Add, copy, and move fields.

12 Add and delete records.

13 Document a database.

14 Preview and print a table.

15 Change page orientation.

16 Close and open a table and database.

Lifestyle Fitness Club

You have recently accepted a job as a human resources administrator with Lifestyle Fitness Club. Like many fitness centers, Lifestyle Fitness Club includes exercise equipment, free weights, aerobics classes, tanning and massage facilities, a swimming pool, a steam room and sauna, and child-care facilities. In addition, it promotes a healthy lifestyle by including educational seminars on good nutrition and proper exercise. It also has a small snack bar that serves healthy drinks, sandwiches, and snacks.

The Lifestyle Fitness Clubs are a franchised chain of clubs that are individually owned. You work at a club owned by Felicity and Ryan Albright, who also own two others in California. Accounting and employment functions for all three clubs are handled centrally at the Landis location.

You are responsible for maintaining the employment records for all employees, as well as records for traditional employment activities such as hiring and benefits. Currently the club employment records are maintained on paper forms and are stored in file cabinets organized alphabetically by last name. Although the information is well organized, it still takes time to manually look through the folders to locate the information you need and to compile reports from this data.

The club has recently purchased new computers, and the owners want to update the employee record-keeping system to an electronic database management system. The software tool you will use to create the database is the database application Microsoft Access 2010. In this lab, you will learn about entering, editing, previewing, and printing information in the database you create for the club.

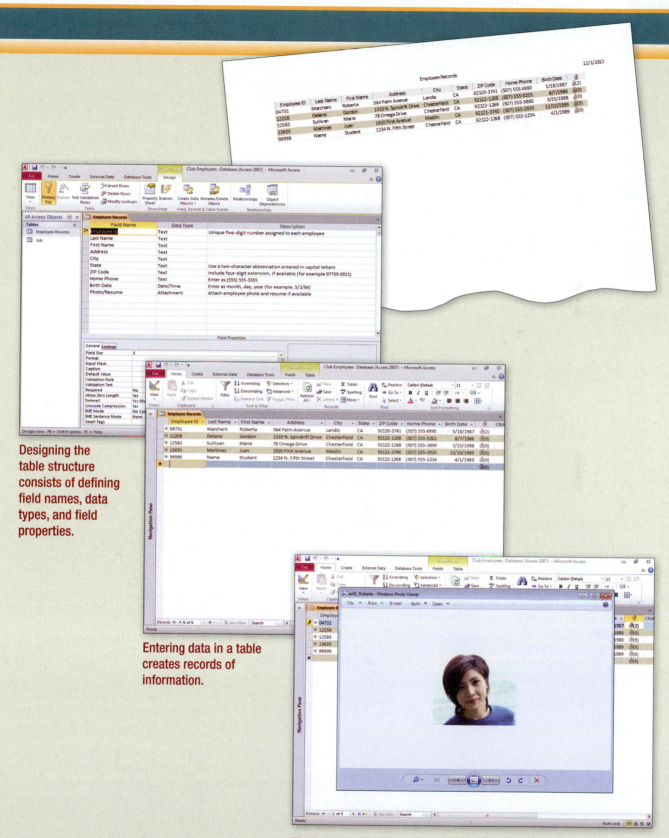

Designing the table structure consists of defining field names, data types, and field properties.

Entering data in a table creates records of information.

Fields can contain attachments such as pictures or files.

Concept Preview

The following concepts will be introduced in this lab:

1 **Database** A database is an organized collection of related information.

2 **Object** An Access database is made up of several types of objects, such as a table or report, consisting of many elements. An object can be created, selected, and manipulated as a unit.

3 **Data Type** The data type defines the type of data the field will contain. Access uses the data type to ensure that the right kind of data is entered in a field.

4 **Field Property** A field property is a characteristic that helps define the appearance and behavior of a field.

5 **Primary Key** A primary key is a field that uniquely identifies each record.

6 **Relationship** A relationship establishes the association between common fields in two tables.

7 **Subdatasheet** A subdatasheet is a data table nested within a main data table; it contains information that is related or joined to the main table.

Designing a New Database

The Lifestyle Fitness Club recently purchased the 2010 Microsoft Office System software suite. You are very excited about learning to use the Access 2010 database management system to store and maintain the club's records.

Concept Database

A **database** is an organized collection of related information. Typically, the information in a database is stored in a **table** consisting of vertical columns and horizontal rows. Each row contains a **record**, which is all the information about one person, thing, or place. Each column is a **field**, which is the smallest unit of information about a record. Access databases can contain multiple tables that can be linked to produce combined output from all tables. This type of database is called a **relational database**. Read more about relational databases in the Introduction to Microsoft Office 2010.

The Lifestyle Fitness Club plans to use Access to maintain several different types of databases. The database you will create will contain information about each club employee. Other plans for using Access include keeping track of members and inventory. To keep the different types of information separate, the club plans to create a database for each group.

Good database design follows two basic principles: Do not include duplicate information (also called redundant data) in tables and enter accurate and complete information. Redundant data wastes space, wastes the time that is required to enter the same information multiple times, and consequently increases the possibility of errors and inconsistencies between tables. The information that is stored in a database may be used to make business decisions and if the information is inaccurate, any decisions that are based on the information will be misinformed.

To attain these principles, the database design process is very important and consists of the following steps: plan, design, develop, implement, and refine and review. You will find that you will generally follow these steps in order as you create your database. However, you will probably retrace steps as the final database is developed.

Step	Description
Plan	The first step in the development of a database is to define the purpose of the database in writing. This includes establishing the scope of the database, determining its feasibility, and deciding how you expect to use it and who will use it.
Design	Using the information gathered during the planning step, you can create an implementation plan and document the functional requirements. This includes finding and organizing the information required for the database and deciding how this information should be divided into subject groups. You also need to think about the types of questions you might want the database to answer and determine the types of output you need such as reports and mailings.
Develop	Using the design you created, you are ready to create tables to hold the necessary data. Create separate tables for each of the major subjects to make it easier to locate and modify information. Define fields for each item that you want to store in each table. Determine how tables are related to one another, and include fields to clarify the relationships as needed. Try not to duplicate information in the different tables.
Implement	After setting up the tables, populate the tables by entering sample data to complete each record. Then work with the data to make sure it is providing the information you need.
Refine and Review	Refine the design by adding or removing fields and tables and continue to test the data and design. Apply the data normalization rules to see if the tables are structured correctly. Periodically review the database to ensure that the initial objectives have been met and to identify required enhancements.

As you develop the employee database for the Lifestyle Fitness Club, you will learn more about the details of the design steps and how to use Access 2010 to create a well-designed and accurate database.

PLANNING THE CLUB DATABASE

Your first step is to plan the design of your database tables: the number of tables, the data they will contain, and the relationship between the tables. You need to decide what information each table in the employee database should contain and how it should be structured or laid out.

You can obtain this information by analyzing the current record-keeping procedures used in the company. You need to understand the existing procedures so that your database tables will reflect the information that is maintained by different departments. You should be aware of the forms that serve as the basis for the data entered into the department records and of the information that is taken from the records to produce periodic reports. You also need to determine whether there is information that the department heads would like to be able to obtain from the database that may be too difficult to generate with current procedures.

After looking over the existing record-keeping procedures and the reports that are created from the information, you decide to create several separate tables of data in the database file. Each table should only contain information about the subject of the table. Additionally, try not to duplicate information in different tables. If this occurs, create a separate table for this information. Creating several smaller tables of related data rather than one large table makes it easier to use the tables and faster to process data. This is because you can join several tables together as needed.

The main table will include the employee's basic information, such as employee number, name, birth date, and address. Another will contain the employee's job title and work location only. A third will contain data on pay rate and hours worked each week. To clarify the organization of the database, you sketched the structure for the employee database as shown below.

Club Records Database

Employee Records Table

Emp #	Last Name	First Name	Street	City	State	Zipcode	Phone	Birth Date
7721	Brown	Linda	——	——	——	——	——	——
7823	Duggan	Michael	——	——	——	——	——	——

link on common field

link on common field

Clubs Table

Emp #	Location	Position
7721	Iona	Greeter
7823	Fort Myers	Server

Pay Table

Emp #	Pay	Hours
7721	8.25	30
7823	7.50	20

Creating and Naming the Database File

Now that you have decided what information you want to include in the tables, you are ready to create a new database for the employee information using the Microsoft Access 2010 database management program.

1 Start the Access 2010 application.

Having Trouble?

See the Introduction to Microsoft Office 2010 for information about starting an Office application and for a discussion of features that are common to all Office 2010 applications.

Your screen should be similar to Figure 1.1

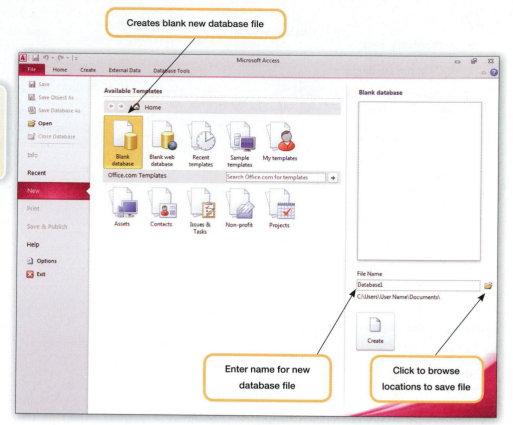

Creates blank new database file

Enter name for new database file

Click to browse locations to save file

Figure 1.1

Additional Information

Backstage view can be accessed anytime by opening the File tab.

When Microsoft Access first opens, the New tab of Backstage view is open and ready for you to create a new database. Several methods can be used to create a new database. One method is to use one of the many templates that are provided by Microsoft as the basis for your new database. A database template generally includes the data structure, tables, queries, forms, and reports for the selected type of database. Another method is to start with a blank database that contains the basic database objects and then add your own content. Although using a template is sometimes the fastest way to create a database, it often requires a lot of work to adapt the template to suit the needs of the existing data. A third option is to copy or import data from another source into an Access database file. Finally, you can use a custom template that you created and saved as the basis for your new database.

You decide to create the club database from a blank database file. The Blank Database template includes the basic structure for a database file, but it does not include a data structure that is specific to a type of database.

Additional Information

Depending on your Windows settings, your screens may not display file extensions.

Additionally, when creating a new database, you need to enter a file name and specify the location on your computer where you want it saved. The File Name box displays Database1, the default database file name. After you specify the file name you want to use and the location to which it should be saved, Access will display the file extension .accdb after the file name. This identifies the file as an Access 2010 database.

Having Trouble?

For information on how to save a file, refer to the Saving a File section in the Introduction to Microsoft Office 2010 lab.

2

- If necessary, click 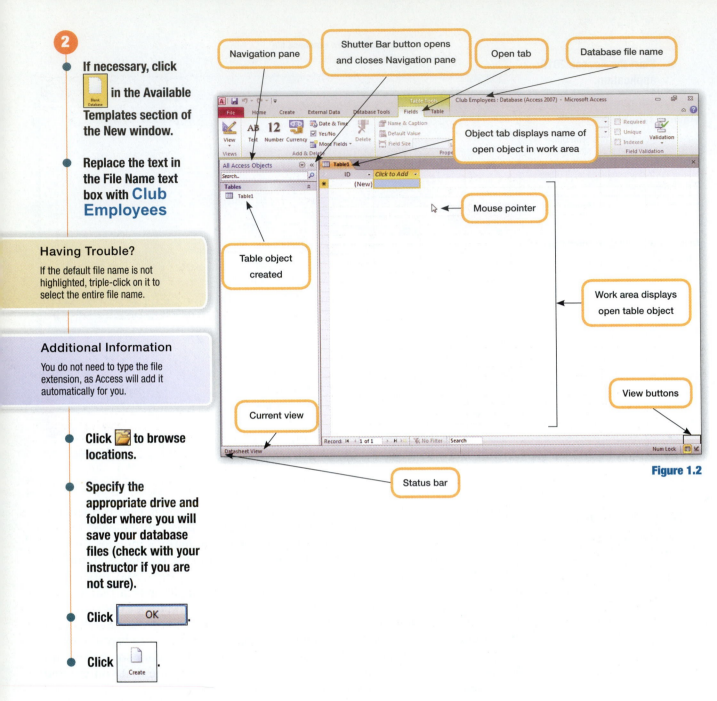 in the Available Templates section of the New window.

- Replace the text in the File Name text box with **Club Employees**

Having Trouble?

If the default file name is not highlighted, triple-click on it to select the entire file name.

Additional Information

You do not need to type the file extension, as Access will add it automatically for you.

- Click 📂 to browse locations.

- Specify the appropriate drive and folder where you will save your database files (check with your instructor if you are not sure).

- Click **OK**.

- Click **Create**.

Your screen should be similar to Figure 1.2

Navigation pane

Shutter Bar button opens and closes Navigation pane

Open tab

Database file name

Object tab displays name of open object in work area

Mouse pointer

Table object created

Work area displays open table object

View buttons

Current view

Status bar

Figure 1.2

Having Trouble?

If your screen looks slightly different, this is because Access remembers settings that were on when the program was last used.

The blank database file is opened in the Access application window. The name of the database, Club Employees, followed by the application name appears in the window title bar.

EXPLORING THE ACCESS WINDOW

Additional Information

Read "Common Interface Features" in the Introduction to Microsoft Office 2010 lab for more information about the File tab, Ribbon, galleries, and other features that are common to all Office 2010 applications.

Located below the title bar is the Access 2010 Ribbon, which contain the commands and features you will use to create and modify database objects. The Access Ribbon always has four main tabs available: Home, Create, External Data, and Database Tools. Additional contextual tabs will appear as you perform different tasks and open various windows. In this case, the Table Tools Fields and Table contextual tabs are available to help you create a new table. The Table Tools Fields tab is currently open and contains command buttons that are used to perform basic database functions specifically relating to the fields within the table.

The mouse pointer appears as on your screen. The mouse pointer changes shape depending upon the task you are performing or where the pointer is located in the window.

The large area below the Ribbon is the work area where different Access components are displayed as you are using the program. When a new database file is created, it includes one empty table named Table1. A table is the main structure in a database that holds the data. It is one of several different database components or objects that can be included within the database file.

Concept 2 Object

An Access database is made up of several types of objects, such as a table or report, consisting of many elements. An **object** is a database component that can be created, selected, and manipulated as a unit. The basic database objects are described below.

Object	Use
Table	Store data.
Query	Find and display selected data.
Form	View, add, and update data in tables.
Report	Analyze and print data in a specific layout.

The table object is the basic unit of a database and must be created first, before any other types of objects are created. Access displays each different type of object in its own window. You can open multiple objects from the same database file in the work area; however, you cannot open more than one database file at a time in a single instance of Access. To open a second database file, you need to start another instance of Access and open the database file in it.

The work area displays a tab containing the table name for the open table. It is used to switch between open objects in the work area. There is currently just one tab because only one object is open.

Additional Information

You will learn more about tables and the different database views shortly.

Just below the work area, the status bar provides information about the task you are working on and about the current Access operation. Currently, the left end of the status bar displays Datasheet view and the right end displays two buttons that are used to change the view. In addition, the status bar displays messages such as instructions to help you use the program more efficiently.

USING THE NAVIGATION PANE

The **Navigation pane** along the left edge of the work area displays all the objects in the database and is used to open and manage the objects. Because your database only contains one object, Table1, that is the only object listed in the pane. When there are many different objects, the pane organizes the objects into categories and groups within each category. It is used to quickly access the different objects.

The Navigation pane is always displayed, but it can be collapsed to a bar to provide more space in the work area. The Shutter Bar close button « , located in the upper-right corner of the pane, is used to show or hide the pane.

Additional Information

The items in the Navigation pane can be organized differently by using the menu at the top of the pane.

1

● Click « to close the Navigation pane.

Your screen should be similar to Figure 1.3

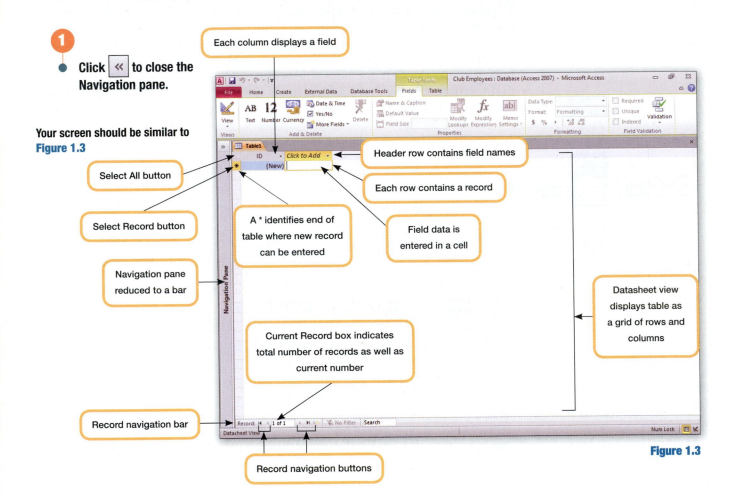

Each column displays a field

Header row contains field names

Each row contains a record

Select All button

Select Record button

A * identifies end of table where new record can be entered

Field data is entered in a cell

Navigation pane reduced to a bar

Datasheet view displays table as a grid of rows and columns

Current Record box indicates total number of records as well as current number

Record navigation bar

Record navigation buttons

Figure 1.3

Another Method

You also can press F11 to open/close the Navigation pane.

The Navigation pane is reduced to a bar along the left side of the window, and the work area expands to fill the space. The pane can be easily displayed again by clicking » . You will learn more about using the Navigation pane throughout the labs.

Creating a Table

In anticipation of your entering information in the table, Access displays the blank table in Datasheet view, one of several different window formats, called **views**, that are used to display and work with the objects in a database. Each view includes its own Ribbon tab that contains commands that are designed to work with the object in that view. The available views change according to the type of object you are using. For example, when working with reports the available views are report view, print preview, layout view, and design view; yet when working with datasheets the viewing options are design view and datasheet view. The basic views are described in the following table.

View	Purpose
Datasheet view	Provides a row-and-column view of the data in tables or query results.
Form view	Displays the records in a form.
Report view	Displays the table data in a report layout.
Design view	Used to create a table, form, query, or report. Displays the underlying design structure, not the data.
Layout view	Displays the object's data while in the process of designing the object.
Print Preview	Displays a form, report, table, or query as it will appear when printed.

Additional Information

Entering information in Datasheet view is very similar to working in a Microsoft Excel worksheet.

Datasheet view is a visual representation of the data that is contained in a database table. It consists of a grid of rows and columns that is used to display each field of a table in a column and each record in a row. The field names are displayed in the **header row** at the top of the datasheet.

Below the header row is a blank row. The intersection of the row and column creates a **cell** where you will enter the data for the record. The square to the left of each row is the **Select Record** button and is used to select an entire record. The record containing the insertion point is the **current record** and is identified by the color in the Select Record button. The * in the Select Record button signifies the end of the table or where a new record can be entered.

The bottom of the work area displays a Current Record box and record navigation buttons. The **Current Record box** shows the number of the current record as well as the total number of records in the table. Because the table does not yet contain records, the indicator displays "Record: 1 of 1" in anticipation of your first entry. On both sides of the record number are the **record navigation buttons**, which are used to move through records with a mouse. In addition, two buttons that are used to filter and search for data in a table are displayed. You will learn about using all these features throughout the text.

DEFINING TABLE FIELDS

Now you are ready to begin defining the fields for the table. You have already decided that the main table in this database will include the employee's basic information such as employee number, name, birth date, and address. Next, you need to determine what information you want to appear in each column (field) about the subject recorded in the table. For example, you know you want to include the employee's name. However, should the entire name be in a single column or should it appear as two separate columns: first name and last name? Because you may want to sort or search for information based on the employee's name, it is better to store the information in separate columns. Similarly, because the address actually consists of four separate parts— address, city, state, and zip code—it makes sense to store them in separate columns as well.

Generally, when deciding how to store information about a subject in a table, break down the information into its smallest logical parts. If you combine more than one kind of information in a field, it is difficult to retrieve individual facts later.

After looking at the information currently maintained in the personnel folder for each employee, you have decided to include the following fields in the table: Employee #, Hire Date, Last Name, First Name, Address, City, State, Zip Code, Home Phone, Birth Date, and Photo. The data for the first employee record you will enter is shown below.

Field Name	Data
Employee #	04731
Hire Date	August 19, 2005
Last Name	Marchant
First Name	Roberta
Address	564 Palm Avenue
City	Landis
State	CA
Zip Code	92120–3741
Home Phone	(507) 555–4990
Birth Date	May 18, 1987
Photo/Resume	Roberta.jpg

ENTERING FIELD DATA

Notice that the first field in the table, ID, is already defined. The ID field is always included in a table when it is first created. It automatically assigns a number to each record as it is added to a table and is useful for maintaining record order. The second column header displays *Click to Add* and is used to add a new field in the table.

In Datasheet view, you can enter data for a record and create a new field at the same time. The first field of data you will enter is the employee number, which is assigned to each employee when hired. Each new employee is given the next consecutive number, so that no two employees can have the same number. Each number is a maximum of five digits.

When you enter data in a record, it should be entered accurately and consistently. The data you enter in a field should be typed exactly as you want it to appear. This is important because any printouts of the data will display the information exactly as entered. It is also important to enter data in a consistent form. For example, if you decide to abbreviate the word "Avenue" as "Ave." in the Address field, then it should be abbreviated the same way in every record where it appears. Also be careful not to enter a blank space before or after a field entry. This can cause problems when using the table to locate information.

Having Trouble?

For more information on moving through, entering, and editing text, refer to the section Entering and Editing Text in the Introduction to Microsoft Office 2010.

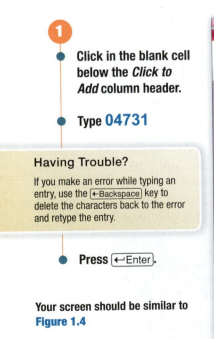

1

● Click in the blank cell below the *Click to Add* column header.

● Type **04731**

Having Trouble?

If you make an error while typing an entry, use the ← Backspace key to delete the characters back to the error and retype the entry.

● Press ← Enter .

Your screen should be similar to Figure 1.4

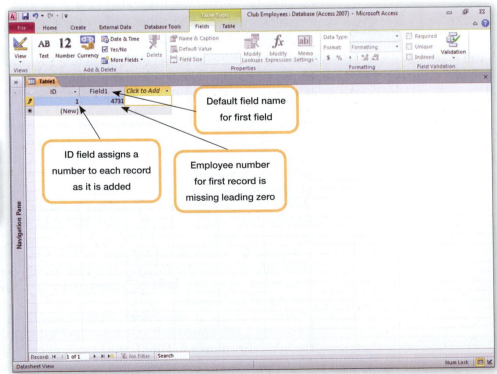

Figure 1.4

The employee number for the first record is entered in the table and Access is ready for you to enter the data for the next field. However, notice the leading zero is no longer displayed in the employee number you just typed. You will learn the reason for this and how to correct it shortly.

The new field has been assigned the default field name of Field1. Also notice that the ID field displays the number 1 for the first record entered in the table.

CHANGING FIELD NAMES

Before entering more data, you want to replace the default field name with a more descriptive field name. A **field name** is used to identify the data stored in the field. A field name should describe the contents of the data to be entered in the field. It can be up to 64 characters long and can consist of letters, numbers, spaces, and special characters, except a period, an exclamation point, an accent grave (`), or brackets ([]). You also cannot start a field name with a space. It is best to use short field names to make the tables easier to manage.

1

● Double-click on the Field1 column header.

● Type **Employee #** (be sure to include a space before the #).

Another Method

You also can choose Rename Column from the column header's shortcut menu.

Additional Information

The field name can be typed in uppercase or lowercase letters. It will be displayed in your database table exactly as you enter it.

Your screen should be similar to Figure 1.5

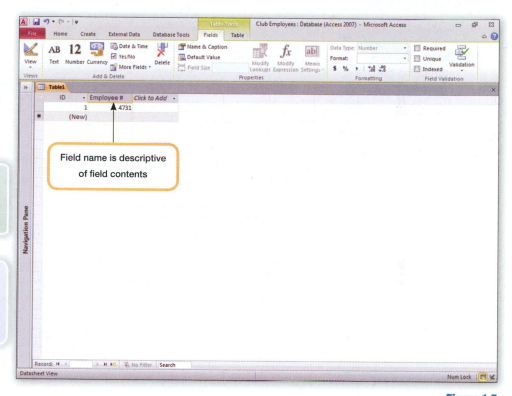

Field name is descriptive of field contents

Figure 1.5

The highlighted text is deleted and replaced by the new field name you typed. You realize that "Employee ID" is the more common term used on company forms, so you decide to use this as the field name instead. As you enter text, you are bound to make typing errors that need to be corrected. You also may want to edit or update information. In this case, you want to edit the field name you are currently working on. The insertion point is already in the correct position and you just need to delete the character to the left of it.

2

- Press ←Backspace to delete the # symbol.

- Type **ID**

- Press ←Enter.

- Press Esc to close the Data Type shortcut menu that appears for the next field.

Additional Information

You will learn about the Data Type shortcut menu shortly.

- Click in the cell containing the Employee ID number.

Your screen should be similar to
Figure 1.6

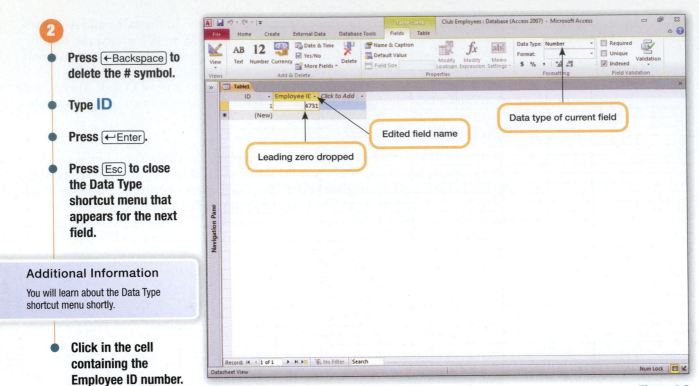

Figure 1.6

The field name has been completed, and it is now easy to know what the data in that column represents.

DEFINING FIELD DATA TYPE

As you noticed, the leading zero of the Employee ID number has been dropped. This is because Access automatically detects and assigns a data type to each field based upon the data that is entered. In this case, the field entry consisted of numbers only, and Access assigned the field a Number data type. This data type drops any leading zeros.

Concept ③ Data Type

The **data type** defines the type of data the field will contain. Access uses the data type to ensure that the right kind of data is entered in a field. It is important to choose the right data type for a field before you start entering data in the table. You can change a data type after the field contains data, but if the data types are not compatible, such as a text entry in a field whose data type accepts numbers only, you may lose data. The data types are described in the following table.

Data Type	Purpose
Text	Use in fields that contain alphanumeric data (words, combinations of words and numbers, and numbers that are not used in calculations). Text field entries can be up to 255 characters in length. Names and phone numbers are examples of Text field entries. Text is the default data type.
Memo	Use in fields where you want to store more than 255 characters of alphanumeric data. A Memo field holds up to 1 GB of characters or 2 GB of storage, of which 65,535 characters can be displayed. Text in this field can be formatted.
Number	Use in fields that contain numeric data only and that will be used to perform calculations on the values in the field. Number of units ordered is an example of a Number field entry. Leading zeros are dropped. Do not use in fields involving money or that require a high degree of accuracy because Number fields round to the next highest value. Fields that contain numbers only but will not be used in calculations are usually assigned a Text data type.
Date/Time	Use in fields that will contain dates and times. Access allows dates from AD January 1, 100, to December 31, 9999. Access correctly handles leap years and checks all dates for validity. Even though dates and times are formatted to appear as a date or time, they are stored as **serial values** so that they can be used in calculations. The date serial values are consecutively assigned beginning with 1, which corresponds to the date January 1, 1900, and ending with 2958465, which is December 31, 9999.
Currency	Use in number fields that are monetary values or that you do not want rounded. Numbers are formatted to display decimal places and a currency symbol.
AutoNumber	Use when you need a unique, sequential number that is automatically incremented by one whenever a new record is added to a table. After a number is assigned to a record, it can never be used again, even if the record is deleted.
Yes/No	Use when the field contents can only be a Yes/No, True/False, or On/Off value. Yes values are stored as a 1 and No values as 0 so that they can be used in expressions.
OLE Object	Use in fields to store an object from another Microsoft Windows program, such as a document or graph. Stores up to 1 GB. The object is converted to a bitmap image and displayed in the table field, form, or report. An OLE server program must be on the computer that runs the database in order to render the object. Generally, use the Attachment field type rather than OLE Object field type because the objects are stored more efficiently and doing so does not require the OLE server.
Hyperlink	Use when you want the field to store a link to an object, document, Web page, or other destination.
Attachment	Use to add multiple files of different types to a field. For example, you could add a photograph and set of resumes for each employee. Unlike OLE Object fields, the files are not converted to bitmap images and additional software is not needed to view the object, thereby saving space. Attachments also can be opened and edited from within Access in their parent programs. Size limit is 256 MB per individual file, with a total size limit of 2 GB.
Calculated	Use this data type to create a calculated field in a table. For example, you could calculate the units on hand by the cost to determine the inventory value. You can then easily display or use the results of the calculation throughout your database. Whenever a record is edited, Access automatically updates the Calculated fields, thereby constantly maintaining the correct value in the field. Note that a Calculated field cannot refer to fields in other tables or queries.

Additional Information

If Access does not have enough information to determine the data type, it sets the data type to Text.

Notice in Figure 1.6 that the Data Type box in the Formatting group shows the current data type for the field is Number. Access accurately specified this data type because the Employee ID field contains numbers. However, unless the numbers are used in calculations, the field should be assigned the Text data type. This designation allows other characters, such as the parentheses or hyphens in a telephone number, to be included in the entry. Also, by specifying the type as Text, leading zeros will be preserved.

You need to override the data type decision and change the data type for this field to Text.

1

• Open the

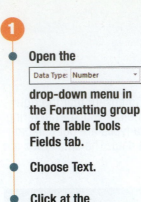

Data Type: Number

drop-down menu in the Formatting group of the Table Tools Fields tab.

• Choose Text.

• Click at the beginning of the Employee ID entry to place the insertion point and type **0**

• Press **End** to move to the end of the entry.

• Press **→** to move to the next column.

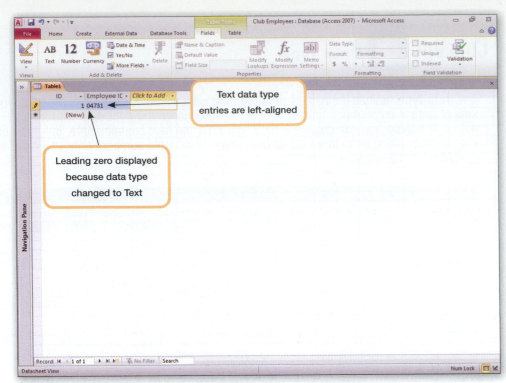

Figure 1.7

Your screen should be similar to Figure 1.7

The leading zero is now correctly displayed. Also notice that the entry is now left-aligned in the cell space whereas it was right-aligned when the data type was set to Number. Many data types also include formatting settings that control the appearance of the data in the field. In this case, the Text field format is to align the text with the left edge of the cell space. You will learn more about formatting later in the lab.

Now you are ready to enter the data for the next field, Hire Date.

2

• Type **Aug 19, 2001**

• Press **← Enter**.

• Right-click the Field1 column name and choose Rename Field from the shortcut menu.

• Type **Hire Date**

• Press **← Enter**.

• Press **Esc** to close the Data Type shortcut menu that appears for the next field.

• Click on the hire date.

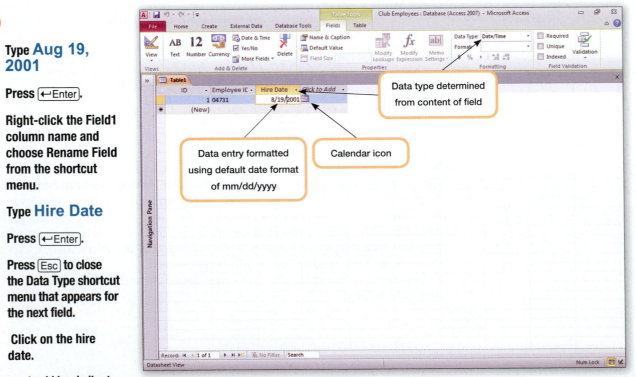

Your screen should be similar to Figure 1.8

Figure 1.8

Access correctly determined that the entry is a Date type and displays the date using the default date format of mm/dd/yyyy.

USING THE QUICK ADD FEATURE

The next few fields you need to enter include employee name and address information.

First you will add a field for the employee's last name.

Click on *Click to Add*.

Your screen should be similar to Figure 1.9

Additional Information

The ⊞ calendar icon displays the month calendar for that date when you click on it.

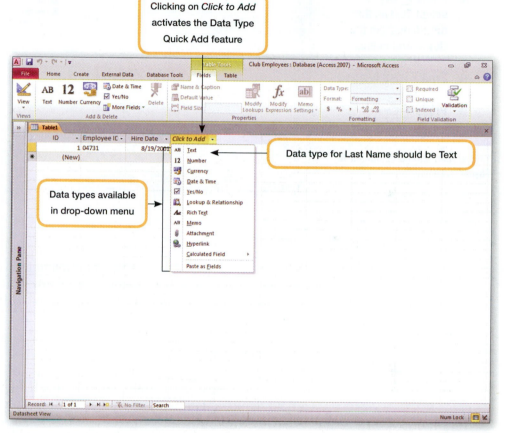

Figure 1.9

Additional Information

Rich text allows formatting such as color, bold and italics.

The Data Type Quick Add menu displays. It lists available data types as well as formatting that can be used. For example, the Rich Text option is really the Memo data type with the format property set to Rich Text.

You will choose the Text data type for this field and then define the same data type for the next field, First Name.

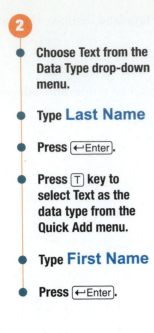

2

- Choose Text from the Data Type drop-down menu.

- Type **Last Name**

- Press ⏎Enter.

- Press T key to select Text as the data type from the Quick Add menu.

- Type **First Name**

- Press ⏎Enter.

Your screen should be similar to Figure 1.10

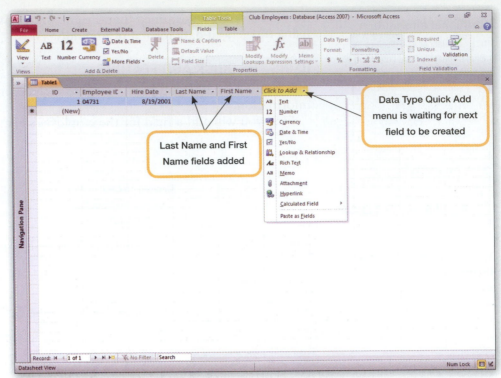

Figure 1.10

Using the Data Type Quick Add menu made it easy to quickly define the data type and specify the field name. It is again waiting for you to choose your next field type. You will add the remaining address fields using a different technique.

USING FIELD MODELS

Another way you can specify field names is to select them from a menu of predefined fields called **field models**. Each field model definition includes a field name, a data type, and other settings that control the appearance and behavior of the field.

Some field models consist of a set of several fields that are commonly used together. For example, the Address field model comes with a field for the street address, city, state, and zip code. You will use the Address field model to add the address fields next.

1

Click

More Fields ▾

in the Add & Delete group of the Table Tools Fields tab.

Scroll the menu until you see the Quick Start section.

Choose Address.

Your screen should be similar to
Figure 1.11

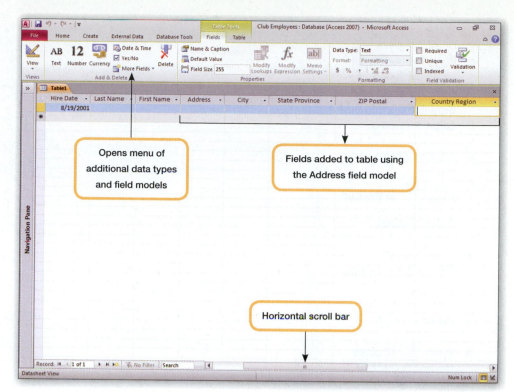

> Opens menu of additional data types and field models

> Fields added to table using the Address field model

> Horizontal scroll bar

Figure 1.11

The Address, City, State Province, ZIP Postal and Country Region field names quickly appear in the table headings. Using field models saves time and provides the basis from which you can start. Once inserted, the field name and data type can be modified like any other fields.

A horizontal scroll bar may display at the bottom of the work area. This means there are more fields in the datasheet than can be viewed in the currently visible work space.

The last remaining field to add is Home Phone. You might have noticed the Phone option in the More Fields menu of Quick Start Field Models. Because the Phone field model contains three fields (Home Phone, Fax, and Mobile), it would not be the best option to use for this table. You will add the Home Phone field using the Add & Delete group.

2

- Move the horizontal scroll bar to the right to see the next available *Click to Add* column heading.

- Click on *Click to Add*.

- Click [12 Number] in the Add & Delete group.

- Type **Home Phone** for the field name.

- Press ⏎Enter.

- Press Esc to close the last Quick Add menu.

Your screen should be similar to
Figure 1.12

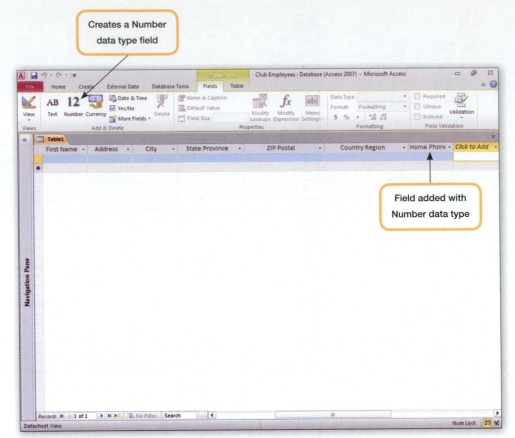

Creates a Number data type field

Field added with Number data type

Figure 1.12

DELETING A FIELD IN DATASHEET VIEW

The Country Region field that was added as part of the Address field model is not needed, so you will delete it. Deleting a field permanently removes the field column and all the data in the field from the table.

1

- Click in the Country Region field.

- Click  in the Add & Delete group.

- Click **Yes** in response to the message to confirm that you want to permanently delete the field.

Your screen should be similar to **Figure 1.13**

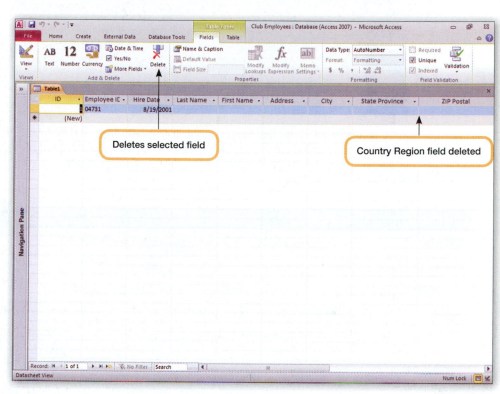

Deletes selected field

Country Region field deleted

Figure 1.13

The field is permanently removed from the table.

Modifying Field Properties

In addition to data type, there are many other field properties associated with a field.

Concept 4 Field Property

A **field property** is a characteristic that helps define the appearance and behavior of a field. Each field has a set of field properties associated with it, and each data type has a different set of field properties. Setting field properties enhances the way your table works. Some of the more commonly used properties and their functions are described in the following table.

Field Property	Description
Field Size	Sets the maximum number of characters that can be entered in the field.
Format	Specifies the way data displays in a table and prints.
Input Mask	Simplifies data entry by controlling the data that is required in a field and the way the data is to be displayed.
Caption	Specifies a field label other than the field name that is used in queries, forms, and reports.
Default Value	Automatically fills in a certain value for this field in new records as you add to the table. You can override a default value by typing a new value into the field.
Validation Rule	Limits data entered in a field to values that meet certain requirements.
Validation Text	Specifies the message to be displayed when the associated Validation Rule is not satisfied.
Required	Specifies whether a value must be entered in a field.
Allow Zero Length	Specifies whether an entry containing no characters is valid. This property is used to indicate that you know no value exists for a field. A zero-length string is entered as "" with no space between the quotation marks.
Indexed	Sets a field as an index field (a field that controls the order of records). This speeds up searches on fields that are searched frequently.

To view and change the field properties, you use Design view.

SWITCHING VIEWS

You can easily switch between views using the button in the Table Tools Fields tab. The graphic in the button changes to indicate the view that will be displayed when selected. Currently the button displays the graphic for Design view. If the view you want to change to is displayed in the button, you can simply click on the upper part of the button to change to that view. Otherwise, you can click on the lower part of the button to open the button's drop-down menu and select the view you want to use. Before you can change views, you will be asked to save the table.

WWW.MHHE.COM/OLEARY

Click ⟩⟩ to open the Navigation pane.

Click 🖉 Design View in the Views group.

1

Click ⟩⟩ to open the Navigation pane.

Click 🖉 Design View in the Views group.

Another Method

You also can click [View ▾] to open the View drop-down menu and choose Design View or click 🖉 Design View in the status bar. Alternatively, you can right-click the object tab and choose Design View.

Your screen should be similar to Figure 1.14

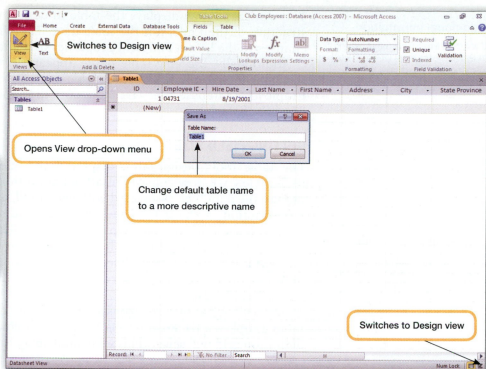

Figure 1.14

Additional Information

You also could click 📇 Save in the Records group of the Home tab, or use the keyboard shortcut ⇧Shift + ↵Enter, or click 💾 Save in the Quick Access Toolbar to save changes to the table at any time.

When you first create a new table and switch views, you are asked to save the table by replacing the default table name, Table1, with a more descriptive name. A table name follows the same set of standard naming conventions or rules that you use when naming fields. It is acceptable to use the same name for both a table and the database, although each table in a database must have a unique name. You will save the table using the table name Employee Records.

2

Type **Employee Records**

Click [OK].

Your screen should be similar to Figure 1.15

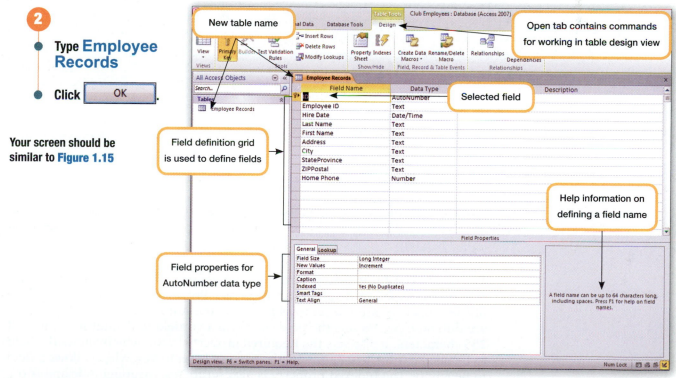

Figure 1.15

Modifying Field Properties **AC1.23**

The work area now displays the table in design view. This view displays the structure of the table, not the table data. Therefore, it is only used to make changes to the layout and field properties of the table.

Additionally, the new table name appears in the Navigation pane and in the Table tab. You have created a table named Employee Records in the Club Employees database file. The table structure and data are saved within the database file.

SETTING FIELD SIZE

The Table Tools Design tab is displayed and open. The upper section of the design view window consists of a field definition grid that displays the field names, the data type associated with each field, and an area in which to enter a description of the field. The lower section displays the properties associated with each field and a Help box that provides information about the current task. The first field in the field definition grid, ID, is the selected field or **current field** and will be affected by any changes you make. It has a data type of AutoNumber. The properties associated with the current field are displayed in the Field Properties section.

You will look at the properties associated with the first field you added to the table, Employee ID. Positioning the insertion point in any column of the field definition grid will select that field and display the associated field properties.

1 **Click on the Employee ID field name.**

Your screen should be similar to Figure 1.16

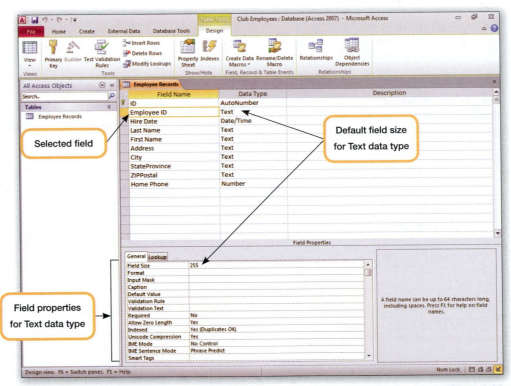

Figure 1.16

The data type of this field is Text, and the default properties associated with a Text data type are displayed in the Field Properties area. Although some of the properties are the same as those for the AutoNumber data type, most are different. Access sets the field size for a Text field to default maximum of 255 characters. It also sets the Required property to No, which allows the field to be blank. The Allow Zero Length property is set to Yes, which allows a field to be empty. The Indexed property is also set to Yes, meaning indexing is on, and duplicate entries are allowed in the field, as, for example, the same name could be entered in the Name field of multiple records. All these settings seem appropriate, except for the field size, which is much too large.

Although Access uses only the amount of storage space necessary for the text you actually store in a Text field, setting the field size to the smallest possible size can decrease the processing time required by the program. Additionally, if the field data to be entered is a specific size, setting the field size to that number restricts the entry to the maximum number.

Because the employee number will never be more than five digits long, you will change the field size from the default of 255 to 5.

2

● **Click the Field Size property text box.**

Another Method

You also can press [F6] to switch between the upper and lower areas of the Design window.

● **Click the words Field Size in the row header to automatically select its contents of 255.**

Another Method

You can select text (highlight by dragging or double-clicking) and then press the [Delete] key to erase the selection.

● **Type 5 to replace the default entry.**

Additional Information

You can cancel changes you are making in the current field at any time before you move on to the next field. Just press [Esc] and the original entry is restored.

Your screen should be similar to Figure 1.17

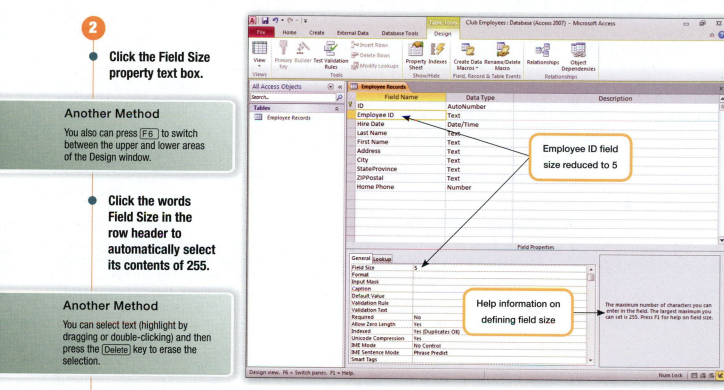

Figure 1.17

The maximum number of characters that can be entered in this field is now restricted to 5. Notice the Help box displays a brief description of the selected property.

Likewise, you will adjust the field sizes of several other fields.

3

- Change the field sizes to those shown for the fields in the following table.

Field	Size
Last Name	25
First Name	25
Address	50
City	25
StateProvince	2
ZIPPostal	10

Your screen should be similar to
Figure 1.18

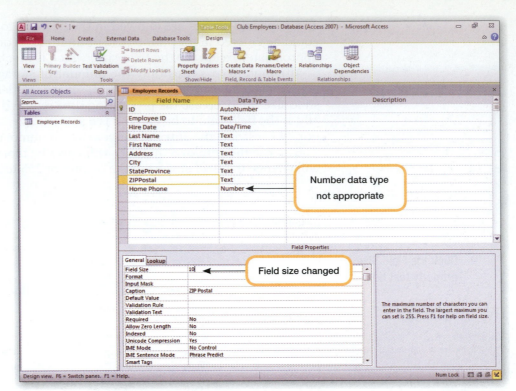

Figure 1.18

CHANGING DATA TYPE

As you look at the field definitions, it is important to make sure the correct data type has been assigned to the field. You can see that the ZIPPostal field has been correctly assigned a data type of Text because it will not be used in calculations and you may use a dash to separate the digits. For the same reasons, you realize the Home Phone field should have a Text data type instead of Number. You will correct the data type for the Home Phone field.

1

- Click in the Data Type column for the Home Phone field.

- Click  to open the drop-down menu and choose Text.

- Change the field size for Home Phone to **15**

Your screen should be similar to
Figure 1.19

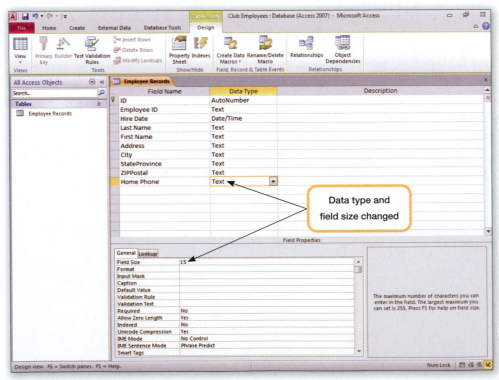

Figure 1.19

WWW.MHHE.COM/OLEARY

EDITING FIELD NAMES

As you continue to look over the fields, you decide to change the field names for the StateProvince and ZIPPostal fields that were assigned when you selected the Address field model.

● Click on the StateProvince field.

Your screen should be similar to Figure 1.20

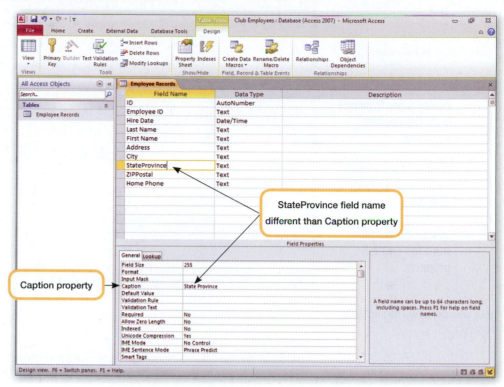

Figure 1.20

Notice that the StateProvince field name appears spelled with no space between the words, while the Caption property displays the State Province with a space. A **caption** is the text that displays in the column heading while in Datasheet view. It is used when you want the label to be different from the actual field name. If there is no text in the Caption field property, the field name will appear as the column heading in Datasheet view. You will change the field name to State and remove the caption for this field. Likewise, you will change the ZIPPostal field name to ZIP Code and clear the caption.

2

- Change the StateProvince field name to **State**

Having Trouble?

Double-click on the field name to select it.

- **Delete State Province from the Caption property.**

- **Change the ZIPPostal field name to ZIP Code**

- **Delete Zip Postal from the Caption property.**

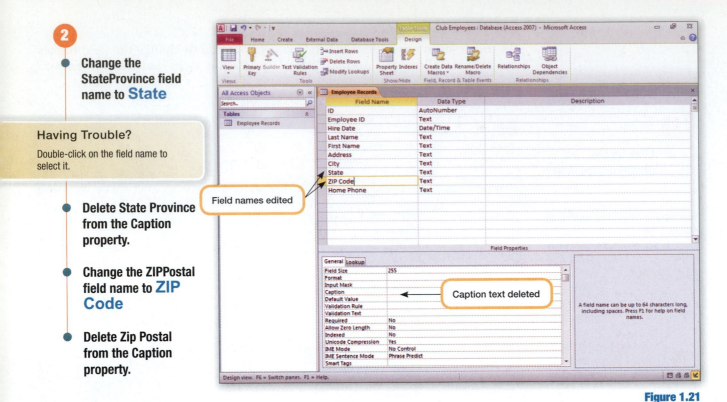

Field names edited

Caption text deleted

Figure 1.21

Your screen should be similar to **Figure 1.21**

The field names have been corrected and captions removed. The field names will automatically be used as the default text for the column headings.

DEFINING A FIELD AS A PRIMARY KEY

The next change you want to make is to define the Employee ID field as a primary key field.

Concept ⑤ Primary Key

A **primary key** is a field that uniquely identifies each record and is used to associate data from multiple tables. To qualify as a primary key field, the data in the field must be unique for each record. For example, a Social Security Number field could be selected as the primary key because the data in that field is unique for each employee. Other examples of primary key fields are part numbers or catalog numbers. (One example of a field that should not be used as the primary key is a name field because more than one person can have the same last or first name.) A second requirement is that the field can never be empty or null. A third is that the data in the field never, or rarely, changes.

A primary key prevents duplicate records from being entered in the table and is used to control the order in which records display in the table. This makes it faster for databases to locate records in the table and to process other operations.

Most tables have at least one field that is selected as the primary key. Some tables may use two or more fields that, together, provide the primary key of a table. When a primary key uses more than one field, it is called a **composite key**.

Notice the  icon that is displayed to the left of the ID field. This indicates that this field is a primary key field. You want to define the Employee ID field so that duplicate employee ID numbers will not be allowed.

1

- **Click on the Employee ID field name.**

- **Click** [Primary Key] **in the Tools group.**

Your screen should be similar to Figure 1.22

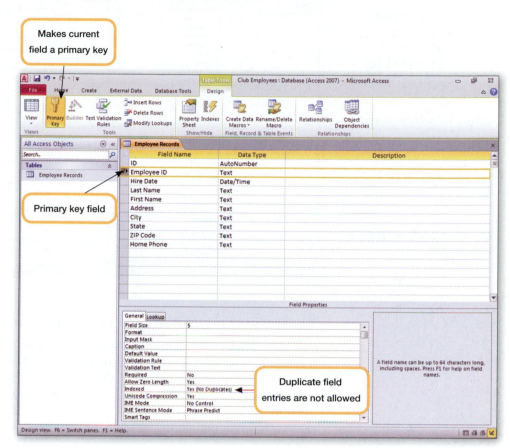

Figure 1.22

Notice the Indexed property setting for this field has changed to Yes (No Duplicates) because the field is defined as the primary key field. This setting prohibits duplicate values in a field. Also, the primary key status has been removed from the default ID field.

ENTERING FIELD DESCRIPTIONS

To continue defining the Employee ID field, you will enter a brief description of the field. Although it is optional, a field description makes the table easier to understand and update because the description is displayed in the status bar when you enter data into the table.

1

- Click the **Description text box** for the **Employee ID field.**

- Type **Unique five-digit number assigned to each employee**

Additional Information

The Description box scrolls horizontally as necessary to accommodate the length of the text entry. The maximum length is 255 characters.

Your screen should be similar to **Figure 1.23**

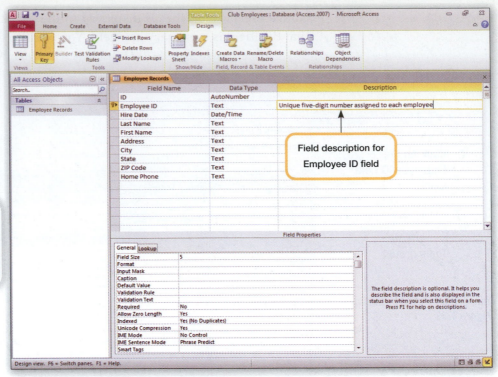

Field description for Employee ID field

Figure 1.23

You also want to add field descriptions to several other fields. As you do, the Property Update Options button will appear when you complete the entry by moving outside the Description text box. Clicking on this button opens a menu whose option will update the description in the status bar everywhere the field is used. Because this database only contains one table, there is no need to update the description anyplace else. The button will disappear automatically when you continue working.

2

- **Add descriptions to the fields as shown in Figure 1.24.**

Your screen should be similar to **Figure 1.24**

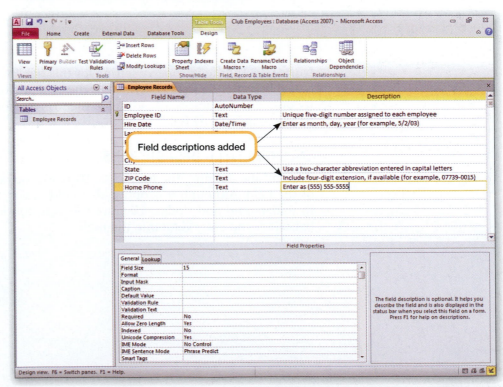

Field descriptions added

Figure 1.24

DELETING A FIELD IN DESIGN VIEW

Because the ID field essentially duplicates the purpose of the Employee ID field, you will delete the ID field. Just like deleting a field in Datasheet view, deleting a field in Design view permanently removes the field column and all the data in the field from the table.

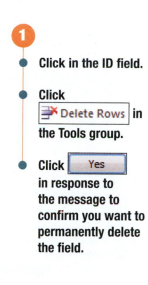

- Click in the ID field.

- Click
  Delete Rows in
  the Tools group.

- Click **Yes**
  in response to
  the message to
  confirm you want to
  permanently delete
  the field.

**Your screen should be similar to
Figure 1.25**

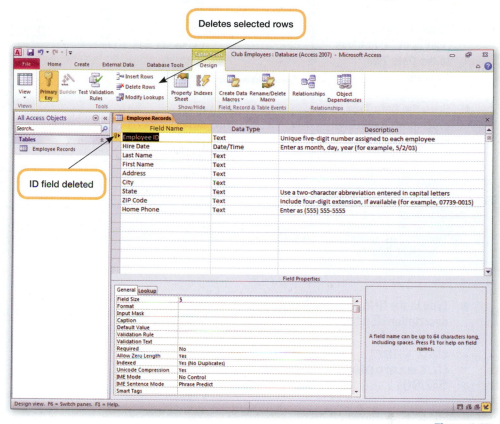

Figure 1.25

The field is permanently removed from the table.

CREATING A FIELD IN DESIGN VIEW

You still need to add two fields to the table: one for the employee's date of birth and the other to display the employee's photo. You will add the new fields and define their properties in Design view.

1

- Click in the blank Field Name row below the Home Phone field name.

- Type **Birth Date**

- Press ⏎Enter, Tab ⇄, or → to move to the Data Type column.

- Open the Data Type drop-down menu and choose Date/Time.

- Type in the field description: **Enter as month, day, year (for example, 5/2/90)**

Your screen should be similar to Figure 1.26

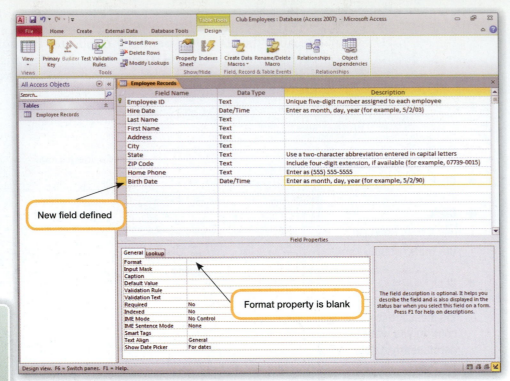

Figure 1.26

The default field properties for the selected data type are displayed. Because the format line is blank, you decide to check the format to make sure that the date will display as you want.

2

- Click in the Format property box.

- Click ⏷ to open the drop-down menu of format options.

Your screen should be similar to Figure 1.27

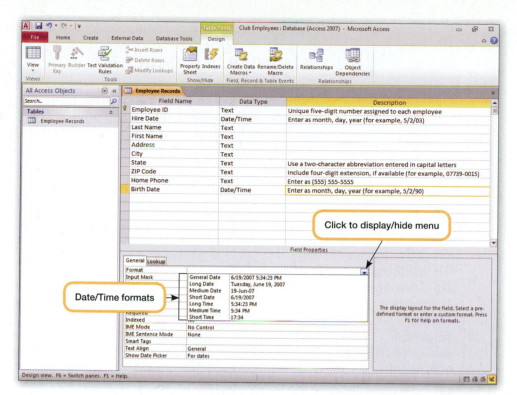

Figure 1.27

The names of the seven predefined layouts for the Date/Time field type are displayed in the list. An example of each layout appears to the right of the name. Although not displayed in the Format property box, the General Date format is the default format. It displays dates using the Short Date format. If a time value is entered, it also will display the time in the Long Time format. You will choose this format so that the setting will be displayed in the Format property box.

3

- Choose General Date.

Your screen should be similar to Figure 1.28

Additional Information

Access automatically assumes the first two digits of a year entry. If you enter a year that is between /30 and /99, Access reads this as a 20th century date (1930 to 1999). A year entry between /00 and /29 is assumed to be a 21st century date (2000 to 2029).

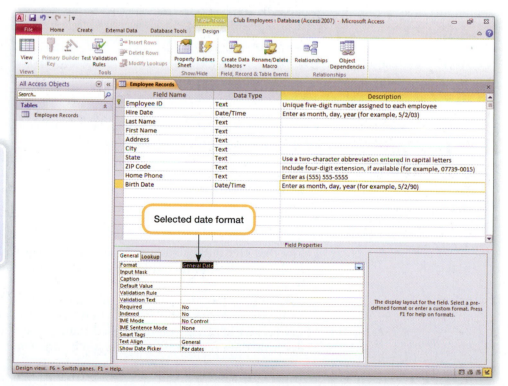

Figure 1.28

Modifying Field Properties   **AC1.33**

The Date/Time property setting is now displayed in the Format text box.

CREATING AN ATTACHMENT FIELD

The last field you will enter will display a photo and resume if available for each employee. The data type for this type of input is Attachment. Once a field has been assigned, this data type cannot be changed. You can, however, delete the field and then redefine it if you think you made an error.

1

- In the next blank field name row, enter the field name **Photo/Resume** with a data type of Attachment.

- Include the description **Attach employee photo and resume if available**

Your screen should be similar to Figure 1.29

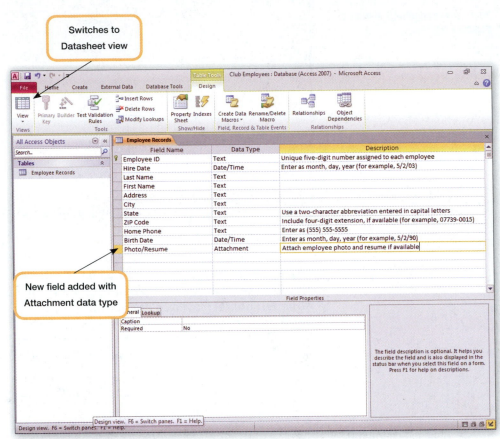

Figure 1.29

Specifying the Attachment data type allows you to store multiple files of different file types in a single field.

Entering and Editing Records

Now that the table structure is complete, you want to continue entering the employee data into the table. To do this, you need to switch back to Datasheet view.

Because you have made many changes to the table design, you will be asked to save the changes before you switch views. You also will be advised that data may be lost because you decreased field sizes in several fields. Since there is very little data in the table, this is not a concern.

1

- Click 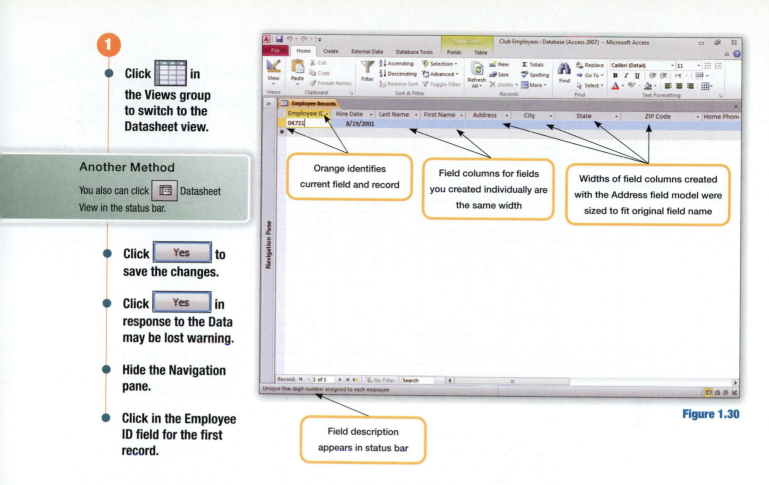 in the Views group to switch to the Datasheet view.

Another Method

You also can click 🔳 Datasheet View in the status bar.

- Click [Yes] to save the changes.

- Click [Yes] in response to the Data may be lost warning.

- Hide the Navigation pane.

- Click in the Employee ID field for the first record.

Your screen should be similar to Figure 1.30

Figure 1.30

Additional Information

You will learn how to change the column width shortly.

Because you deleted the ID field, it is no longer displayed and the new fields you defined are ready for you to enter the remaining data for the first record. The first field, Employee ID, of the first record is outlined in orange, indicating that the program is ready to accept data in this field. The field name and Select Record button also are highlighted in orange to identify the current field and current record. The status bar displays the description you entered for the field.

Notice also in this view that the column widths for the fields you created individually are all the same, even though you set different field sizes in the Table Design window. This is because the Table Datasheet view has its own default column width setting. The column widths of the fields that were created using the Address field model were sized to fit the original field name for each column.

VERIFYING DATA ACCURACY AND VALIDITY

To see how field properties help ensure data accuracy, you will reenter the employee number for the first record and try to enter a number that is larger than the field size of five that you defined in Table Design view.

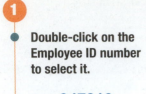

1

● Double-click on the Employee ID number to select it.

● Type **047310**

Your screen should be similar to **Figure 1.31**

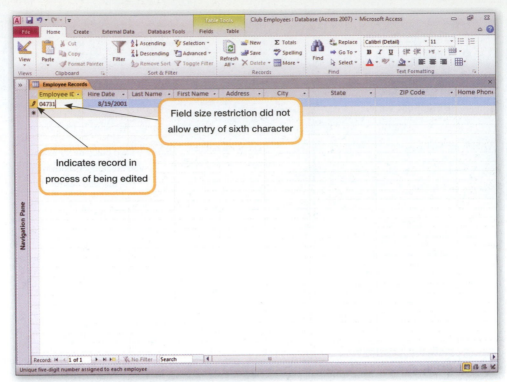

Field size restriction did not allow entry of sixth character

Indicates record in process of being edited

Figure 1.31

The program accepted only the first five digits and would not let you type a sixth. The field size restriction helps control the accuracy of data by not allowing an entry larger than has been specified. Notice also that the current record symbol has changed to 🖉. The pencil symbol means the record is in the process of being entered or edited and has not yet been saved.

Next, you will intentionally enter an invalid date to see what happens.

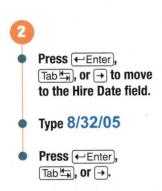

2

● Press ⏎Enter, Tab⇥, or → to move to the Hire Date field.

● Type **8/32/05**

● Press ⏎Enter, Tab⇥, or →.

Your screen should be similar to **Figure 1.32**

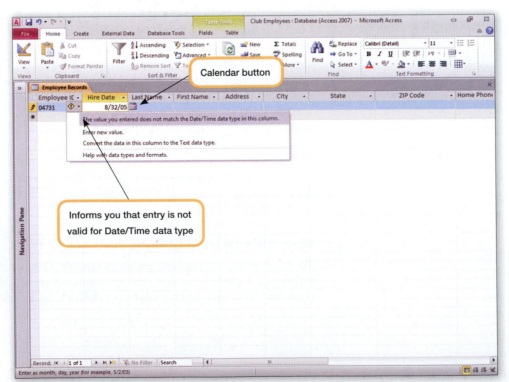

Calendar button

The value you entered does not match the Date/Time data type in this column.

Enter new value.

Convert the data in this column to the Text data type.

Help with data types and formats.

Informs you that entry is not valid for Date/Time data type

Figure 1.32

WWW.MHHE.COM/OLEARY

An informational message box is displayed advising you that the entry is not valid. In this case, the date entered (8/32/05) could not be correct because a month cannot have 32 days. Access automatically performs some basic checks on the data as it is entered based upon the field type specified in the table design. This is another way that Access helps you control data entry to ensure the accuracy of the data.

You will need to edit the date entry to correct it.

Additional Information

The calendar button appears automatically whenever a Date data type field is active. Clicking it displays a calendar for the current month from which you can quickly find and choose a date.

3

● Select Enter new value from the message box.

● Double-click on 32 to select it.

● Type **19**

● Press `Tab ⇥`.

Your screen should be similar to Figure 1.33

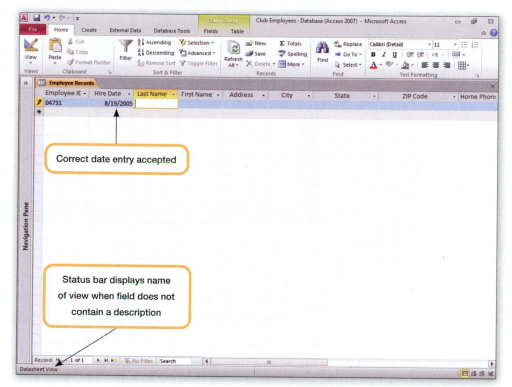

Figure 1.33

The corrected date is accepted, and the insertion point moves to the Last Name field. The year in the date changed to four digits, which reflects the date format you specified in the field's property.

Because you did not enter a description for the Last Name field, the status bar displays "Datasheet View," the name of the current view, instead of a field description.

USING AUTOCORRECT

Now you are ready to continue entering the data for the first record. As you are typing, you may make errors and they may be corrected automatically for you. This is because the AutoCorrect feature automatically corrects obvious errors such as capitalizing names of days, the first letter of sentences, and other common typing errors and misspellings such as words starting with two initial capital letters. The AutoCorrect Options button  will appear next to any text that was corrected. You have the option of undoing the correction or leaving it as is. Most of the time, the typing error is not corrected, and you will need to fix it manually.

To see how this works, you will enter the last name incorrectly by typing the first two letters using capital letters.

1

● Type **MArchant**

● Press [Tab ⇆].

Your screen should be similar to
Figure 1.34

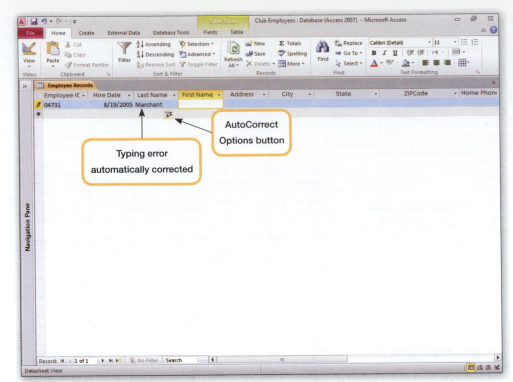

Figure 1.34

The name was automatically corrected, and the AutoCorrect Options button
📝 appears. You will leave the correction as is and continue to enter data for
this record.

2

● Enter the data
shown in the table
on the next page
for the remaining
fields, typing the
information exactly
as it appears.

Additional Information

The fields will scroll in the window as
you move to the right in the record.

Your screen should be similar to
Figure 1.35

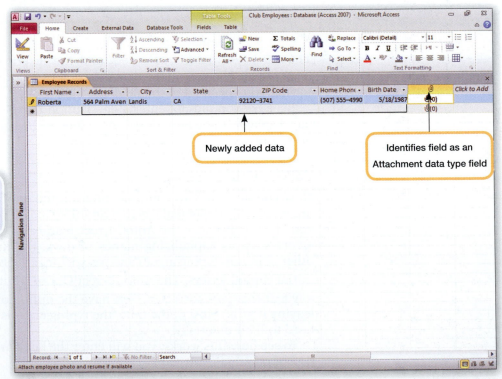

Figure 1.35

Field Name	Data
First Name	Roberta
Address	564 Palm Avenue
City	Landis
State	CA
ZIP Code	92120–3741
Home Phone	(507) 555–4990
Birth Date	May 18, 1987 (press ⇥Tab to complete the entry)

All the information for the first record is now complete, except for the last field for the employee photo and resume.

ATTACHING FILES TO RECORDS

Notice that the field name in the header for this field is not Photo/Resume, as you defined in Design view. This is because Access does not use the field name for Attachment data types. Instead it displays a paper clip icon in the field header to show that the field has an Attachment data type. However, you can specify a caption for this field that will display as the field name. Before making this change, you want to add the data for this field.

You plan to attach the employee photo and a copy of the employee's resume if it is available. A photo is one of several different types of graphic objects that can be added to a database table. A **graphic** is a nontext element or object. A graphic can be a simple **drawing object** consisting of shapes such as lines and boxes that can be created using a drawing program such as Paint, or it can be a picture. A **picture** is an illustration such as a scanned photograph. A resume is a text document that is typically created using a word processor application.

Because you have not organized all the employees' badge photographs yet, you will only insert the photo for Roberta Marchant to demonstrate this feature to the club owners. You also will attach a sample resume that was created using Word 2010.

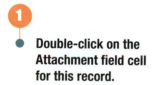

1 ● Double-click on the Attachment field cell for this record.

Another Method

You also can choose Manage Attachments from the field's shortcut menu.

Your screen should be similar to Figure 1.36

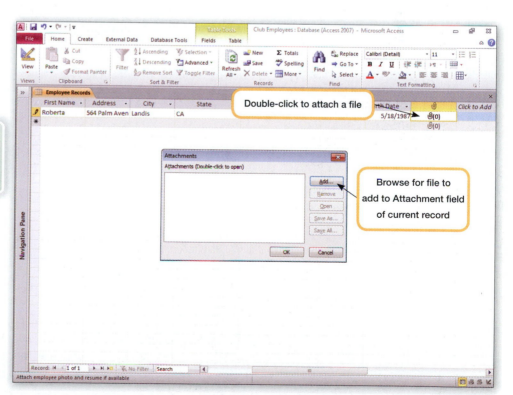

Figure 1.36

Entering and Editing Records **AC1.39**

The Attachments dialog box is used to manage the items that are in an attachment field. Because there are currently no attachments associated with this field, it is empty. You will select the photo and resume files you want to add to the field.

2

● Click **Add...** .

● If necessary, specify the location of your data files in the Choose File dialog box.

● Select ac01_ Roberta and ac01_ Resume from the file list box.

Having Trouble?

Hold down Ctrl while clicking on the file names to select multiple files.

● Click **Open** in the Choose File dialog box.

Your screen should be similar to Figure 1.37

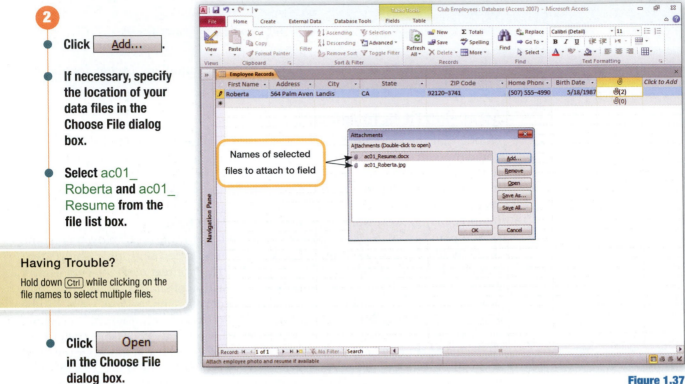

Figure 1.37

The Attachments dialog box is displayed again and now displays the names of the selected files.

Additional Information

To remove a file from the Attachment field, select the file name from the list and click **Remove** .

3

• Click **OK** in the Attachments dialog box.

Your screen should be similar to Figure 1.38

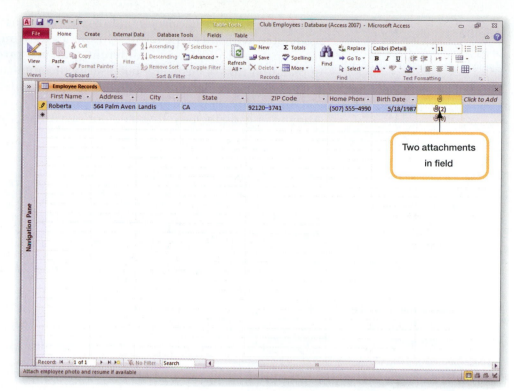

Two attachments in field

Figure 1.38

The selected files are inserted as attachments and identified with the number 2 in the cell. The number indicates how many attachments have been added to the field. You will now display the photograph from the Attachment field to check that it has been inserted properly.

4

• Double-click the cell containing the attachments for Roberta.

• Select the ac01_ Roberta file from the Attachments dialog box.

• Click **Open**.

Another Method

You also can double-click the file to both select and open it.

Your screen should be similar to Figure 1.39

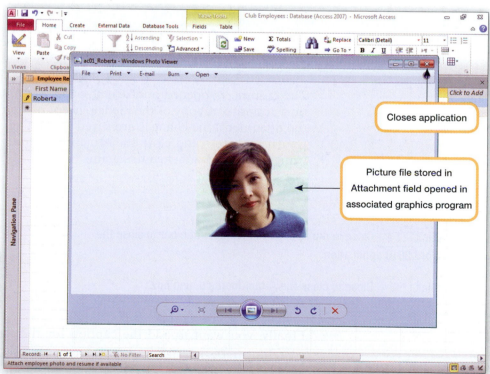

Closes application

Picture file stored in Attachment field opened in associated graphics program

Figure 1.39

Entering and Editing Records   **AC1.41**

The picture object is opened and displayed in the graphics program that is associated with this type of file—in this case, Windows Photo Viewer. Yours may open and display in a different graphics program such as Paint. The application that opens is not necessarily the application in which the file was created. If the application in which it opens includes features that can be used to edit the file, you will be prompted to save any changes before closing the Attachments dialog box. If you do not save them, the changes will be lost.

5

- Click ✕ Close in the graphics application window title bar to close the application.

- Select and open the ac01_Resume attachment.

- If necessary, maximize the Word application window.

Your screen should be similar to Figure 1.40

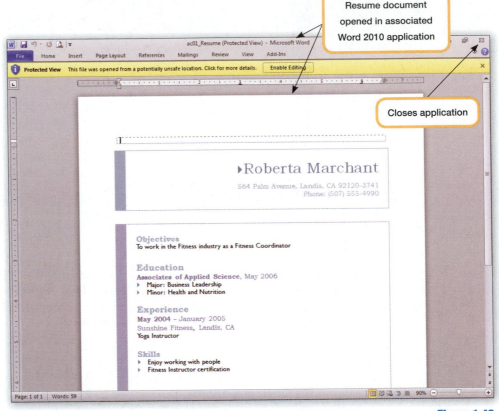

Resume document opened in associated Word 2010 application

Closes application

Figure 1.40

The resume is opened and displayed in the associated Word 2010 application program. A copy of the file is placed in a temporary folder. If you change the document, the changes are saved to the temporary copy. Then, when you return to Access and close the Attachments dialog box, you are asked if you want to save the attached file again.

6

- Click ✕ Close in the application window title bar to close the Word 2010 application.

- Click ✕ Close to close the Attachments dialog box.

Finally, you want to add the caption for the Attachment field. Rather than switching to Design view to make this change, you can use the 📝 Name & Caption button in the Properties group of the Table Tools Fields tab.

7

- Click  in the Properties group of the Table Tools Fields tab.

- In the Caption text box of the Enter Field Properties dialog box, type **Photo/Resume**

- Click **OK**.

Your screen should be similar to Figure 1.41

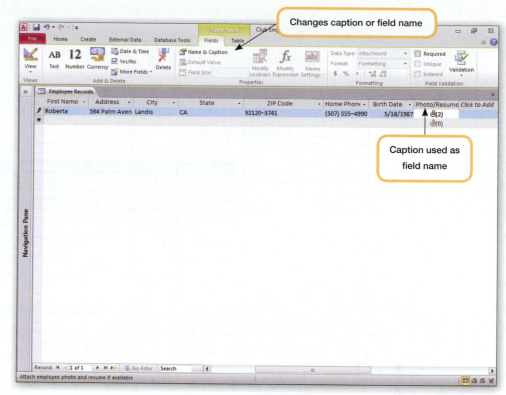

Changes caption or field name

Caption used as field name

Figure 1.41

The field column now displays the caption associated with the field. This clarifies the field contents and makes it much easier for others to understand.

8

- Press **←Enter** to move to the beginning of the next record.

Your screen should be similar to Figure 1.42

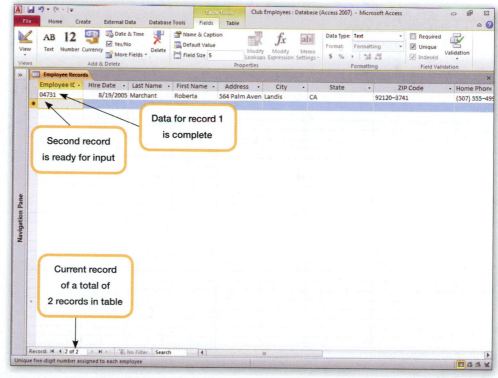

Data for record 1 is complete

Second record is ready for input

Current record of a total of 2 records in table

Figure 1.42

The information for the first record is now complete. The cursor moves to the first field in the next row and waits for input of the employee number for the next record. As soon as the cursor moves to another record, the data is saved to the table file and the number of the new record appears in the status bar. The second record was automatically assigned the record number 2.

MOVING BETWEEN FIELDS

Next, you will check the first record for accuracy. To quickly move from one field to another in a record, you can first select (highlight) the entire field contents and then you can use the keyboard keys shown in the following table to move quickly between field columns.

Key	Movement
→ or Tab↹	Next field
← or ⇧Shift + Tab↹	Previous field
↑	Current field in previous record
↓	Current field in next record
Home	First field in record
End	Last field in record

You will select the Employee ID field for the first record and then move to the Address field to check its contents.

1

- **Point to the left end of the Employee ID field for the first record. When the mouse pointer appears as ⊹, click the mouse button.**

- **Press → four times.**

Your screen should be similar to Figure 1.43

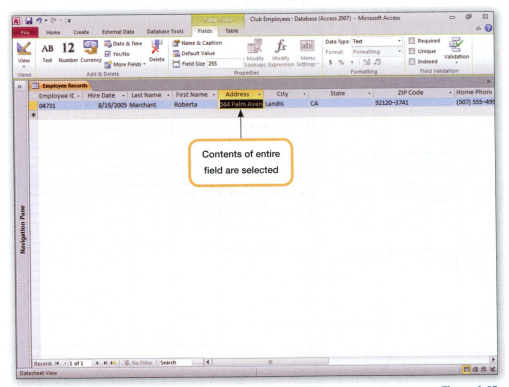

Contents of entire field are selected

Figure 1.43

Additional Information

If you press Delete or ←Backspace while the entire field is selected, the entire field contents will be deleted.

Because the entire field contents are selected, you need to be careful that you do not type a character, as that will delete the selection and replace it with the new text. To switch back to editing, you need to display the cursor in the field and then edit the entry.

2 Click the Address field with the mouse pointer shaped as an I-beam.

Your screen should be similar to **Figure 1.44**

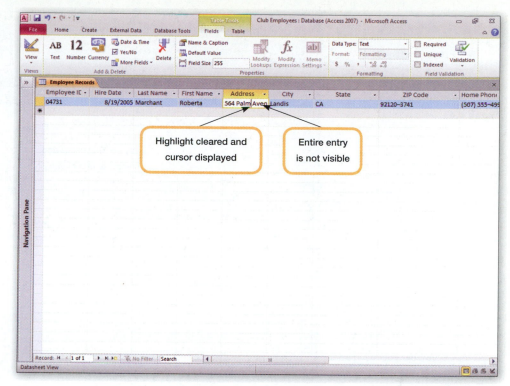

Highlight cleared and cursor displayed

Entire entry is not visible

Figure 1.44

Additional Information

You can press [F2] to switch between editing an entry (the cursor is displayed) and navigating (the field is selected) through the datasheet.

The highlight is cleared and the cursor is visible in the field. Now, using the directional keys moves the cursor within the field and you can edit the field contents if necessary.

ZOOMING A FIELD

The beginning of the field looks fine, but because the column width is too narrow, you cannot see the entire entry. You will move the cursor to the end of the address so you can check the rest of the entry.

Entering and Editing Records **AC1.45**

1 Press End.

Your screen should be similar to
Figure 1.45

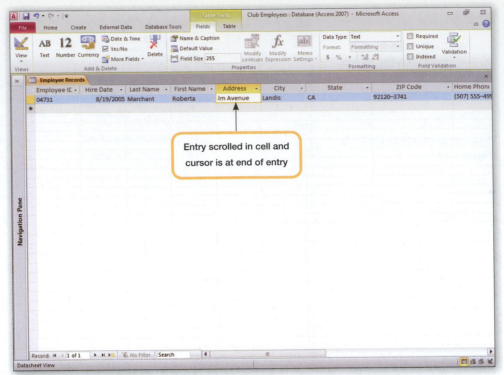

> Entry scrolled in cell and
> cursor is at end of entry

Figure 1.45

The text scrolled in the field, and the cursor is positioned at the end of the entry. However, now you cannot see the beginning of the entry, which makes it difficult to edit. Another way to view the field's contents is to expand the field.

2 Press ⇧Shift + F2.

Your screen should be similar to
Figure 1.46

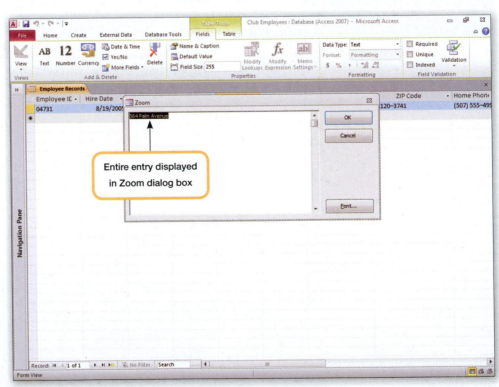

> Entire entry displayed
> in Zoom dialog box

Figure 1.46

The entry is fully displayed in the Zoom dialog box. You can edit in the dialog box just as you can in the field.

WWW.MHHE.COM/OLEARY

Access 2010

- **If the entry contains an error, correct it.**

- **Click** OK **to close the Zoom dialog box.**

- **Press** Tab **to move to the next field.**

- **Continue to check the first record for accuracy and edit as needed.**

- **Enter the data for the second record as shown in the table to the right (you will leave the Attachment field empty).**

- **Check the second record for accuracy and edit it if necessary.**

- **Move to the first field of the blank record row.**

Your screen should be similar to Figure 1.47

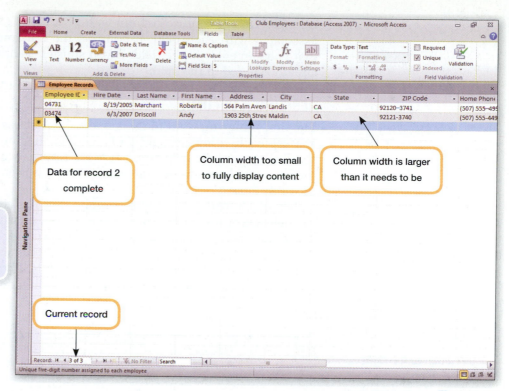

Data for record 2 complete

Column width too small to fully display content

Column width is larger than it needs to be

Current record

Figure 1.47

Field Name	Data
Employee ID	03474
Hire Date	June 3, 2007
Last Name	Driscoll
First Name	Andy
Address	1903 25th Street
City	Maldin
State	CA
ZIP Code	92121-3740
Home Phone	(507) 555-4494
Birth Date	October 10, 1986

The record indicator in the status bar tells you that record 3 is the current record of a total of three records.

Changing Column Width

As you have noticed, some of the fields (such as the Address field) do not display the entire entry, while other fields (such as the State field) are much larger than the field's column heading or contents. This is because the default width of a column in the datasheet is not the same size as the field sizes you specified in Design view. **Column width** refers to the size of a field column in a datasheet. The column width does not affect the amount of data you can enter into a field, but it does affect the data that you can see.

You can adjust the column width to change the appearance of the datasheet. Usually you should adjust the column width so that the column is slightly larger than the column heading or longest field contents, whichever is longer. Do not confuse column width with field size. Field size is a property associated with each field; it controls the maximum number of characters that you can enter in the field. If you shorten the field size, you can lose data already entered in the field.

RESIZING A COLUMN

The first thing you want to do is make the Address column wider so that you can see each complete field entry without having to move to the field and scroll or expand the field box. There are several ways that you can manipulate the rows and columns of a datasheet so that it is easier to view and work with the table data.

To quickly resize a column, simply drag the right column border line in the field selector in either direction to increase or decrease the column width. The mouse pointer shape is ↔ when you can drag to size the column. As you drag, a column line appears to show you the new column border. When you release the mouse button, the column width will be set. First you will increase the width of the Address field so that the entire address will be visible.

1

- Point to the right column border line for the Address field.

- When the mouse pointer shape is ↔, click and drag to the right until you think the column width will be wide enough to display the field contents.

- Adjust the column width again if it is too wide or not wide enough.

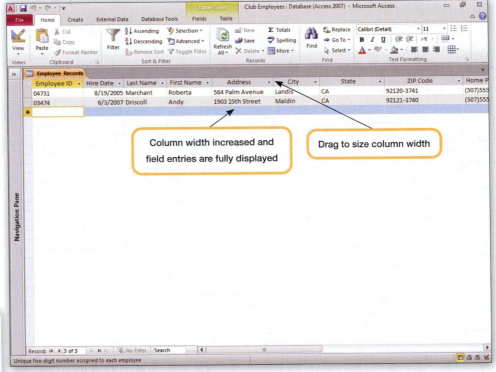

Figure 1.48

Another Method

You also can adjust the column width to a specific number of characters using More ▾ in the Records group of the Home tab and choosing Field Width. This command is also on the shortcut menu when an entire column is selected.

Your screen should be similar to Figure 1.48

USING BEST FIT

Rather than change the widths of all the other columns individually, you can select all columns and change their widths at the same time using the **Best Fit** feature. To select multiple columns, point to the column heading in the header row of the first or last column you want to select. Then, when the mouse pointer changes to ↓, click, and without releasing the mouse button, drag in either direction across the column headings. You also can quickly select the entire table by clicking the ◢ Select All button to the left of the first field name.

1

● Drag across the first four field columns ↓ to select them.

● Click the ◢ Select All button to select the entire table.

Your screen should be similar to Figure 1.49

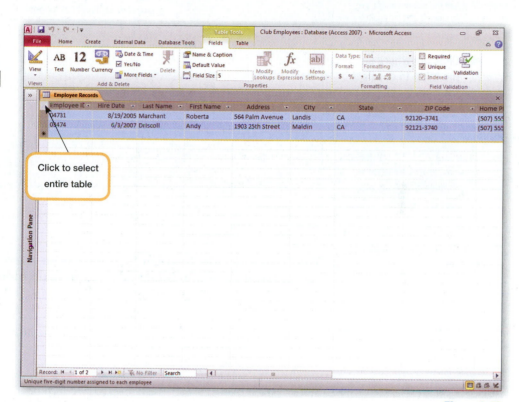

Click to select entire table

Figure 1.49

All the table columns are highlighted. Now, if you were to drag the column border of any selected column, all the selected columns would change to the same size. However, you want the column widths to be adjusted appropriately to fit the data in each column. To do this, you can double-click the column border to activate the Best Fit feature. The Best Fit feature automatically adjusts the column widths of all selected columns to accommodate the longest entry or column heading in each of the selected columns.

2

- Double-click any column border line (in the field name row) when the mouse pointer shape is ⟷.

Having Trouble?

If the *Click to Add* menu opens while trying to adjust the column width, just press Esc to close it and try again.

- Click anywhere on the table to deselect the datasheet.

Another Method

You also can use ▦ More ▾ in the Records group of the Home tab and choose Field Width/Best Fit.

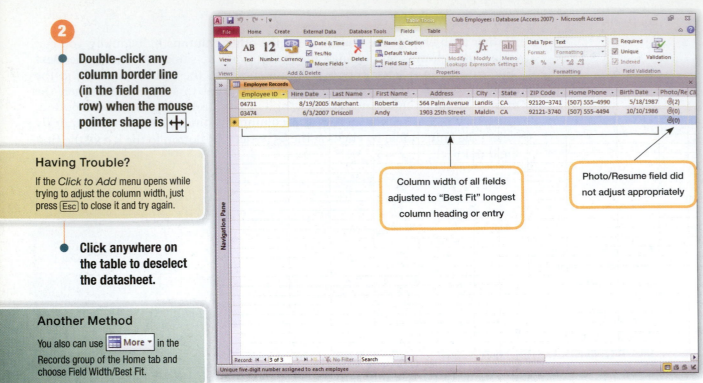

Column width of all fields adjusted to "Best Fit" longest column heading or entry

Photo/Resume field did not adjust appropriately

Figure 1.50

Your screen should be similar to Figure 1.50

The column widths for each field have been sized to accommodate the longest entry or column heading. Also, as you add more records to the table that contain longer field entries, you will need to use Best Fit again to readjust the column widths.

3

- Check each of the records again and edit any entries that are incorrect.

- Add the data shown in the following table as record 3.

- Press ⏎Enter twice to skip the Photo/Resume field and complete the record.

Your screen should be similar to Figure 1.51

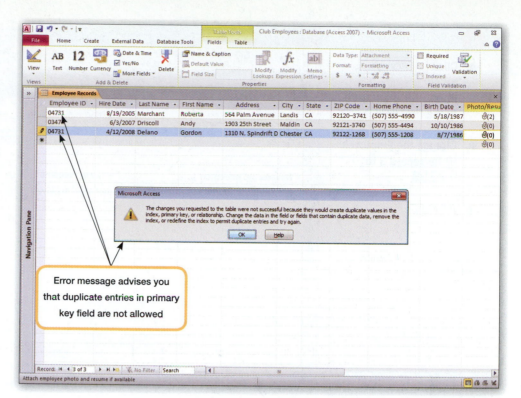

Error message advises you that duplicate entries in primary key field are not allowed

Figure 1.51

Field Name	Data
Employee ID	04731
Hire Date	April 12, 2008
Last Name	Delano
First Name	Gordon
Address	1310 N. Spindrift Drive
City	Chesterfield
State	CA
ZIP Code	92122-1268
Phone	(507) 555-1208
Birth Date	August 7, 1986

As soon as you complete the record, an error message dialog box appears indicating that Access has located a duplicate value in a primary key field. The key field is Employee ID. You realize you were looking at the employee number from Roberta Marchant's record when you entered the employee number for this record. You need to clear the message and enter the correct number.

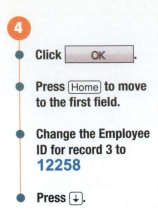

● Click [OK].

● Press [Home] to move to the first field.

● Change the Employee ID for record 3 to **12258**

● Press [↓].

Your screen should be similar to
Figure 1.52

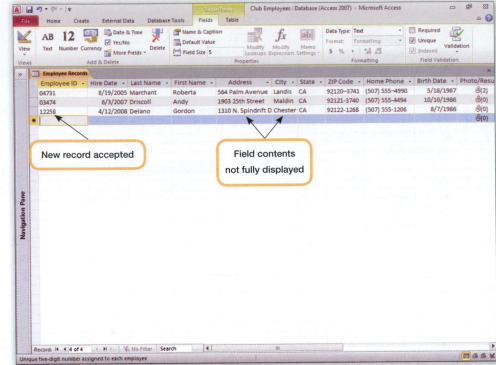

New record accepted

Field contents
not fully displayed

Figure 1.52

The record is accepted with the new employee number. However, you notice that the address and city for this record are not fully displayed in the fields.

● Best Fit the Address and City fields.

Your screen should be similar to
Figure 1.53

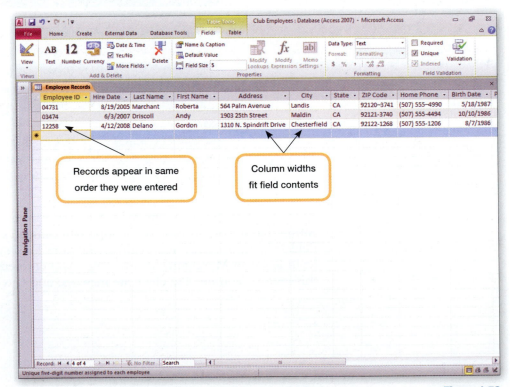

Records appear in same
order they were entered

Column widths
fit field contents

Figure 1.53

When you add new records in a datasheet, the records are displayed in the order in which you enter them. However, they are stored inside the database file in order by the primary key field.

You will add three more records to the table. If data for some fields, such as the City, State, or ZIP Code, is the same from record to record, you can save yourself some typing by copying the data from one of the other records. Just select the field contents and click [Copy] in the Clipboard group on the Home ribbon. Then move to the field where you want the copy to appear and click [Paste] in the Clipboard group.

6

● Enter the data for the two records shown in the following table.

● Enter a final record using your first and last name. Enter **99999** as your employee ID and the current date as your date hired. Use **Chesterfield, CA 92122-1268** for the city, state, and zip code. The information you enter in all other fields can be fictitious.

Field	Record 4	Record 5
Employee ID	13635	12583
Hire Date	January 2, 2011	April 20, 2011
Last Name	Martinez	Sullivan
First Name	Juan	Marie
Address	1920 First Avenue	78 Omega Drive
City	Maldin	Chesterfield
State	CA	CA
ZIP Code	92121-3740	92122-1268
Phone	(507) 555-2935	(507) 555-3890
Birth Date	December 10, 1989	March 15, 1988

● Check each of the records and correct any entry errors.

Your screen should be similar to **Figure 1.54**

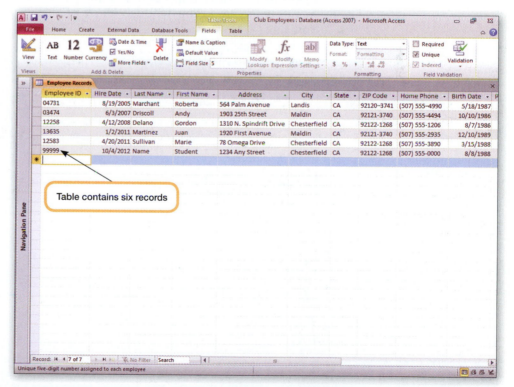

Table contains six records

Figure 1.54

There are now a total of six records in the table.

Navigating among Records

You have found that with the addition of records, it takes longer to move around in the datasheet. Typical database tables are very large and consequently can be cumbersome to navigate. Learning how to move around in a large table will save time and help you get the job done faster.

MOVING USING THE KEYBOARD

In a large table, there are many methods you can use to quickly navigate through records in Datasheet view. You can always use the mouse to move from one field or record to another. However, if the information is not visible in the window, you must scroll the window using the scroll bar first. The following table presents several keyboard methods that will help you move around in the datasheet.

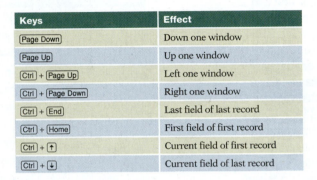

Keys	Effect
Page Down	Down one window
Page Up	Up one window
Ctrl + Page Up	Left one window
Ctrl + Page Down	Right one window
Ctrl + End	Last field of last record
Ctrl + Home	First field of first record
Ctrl + ↑	Current field of first record
Ctrl + ↓	Current field of last record

Currently, records 1 through 6 of the Employee Records table are displayed in the work area. You will use many of these methods to move around the datasheet.

1

Select the Employee ID field of the first record.

Press Page Down.

Your screen should be similar to
Figure 1.55

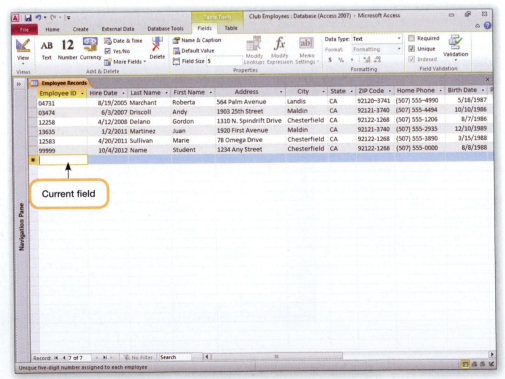

If you were working on a very large table, the next page of records would display, with the first record in the window being the current record. Because this table is small, pressing Page Down moved the cursor to the last position in the window, the row to add a new record. To see an example of moving in a wide table, you will expand the Navigation pane. Because there are numerous fields of various widths, not all of the fields are able to display in the window at the same time. Rather than scrolling the window horizontally to see the additional fields, you can quickly move to the right one window at a time.

2

● **Expand the Navigation pane.**

● **Click on First Name field for the second record.**

● **Press Ctrl + Page Down.**

Your screen should be similar to Figure 1.56

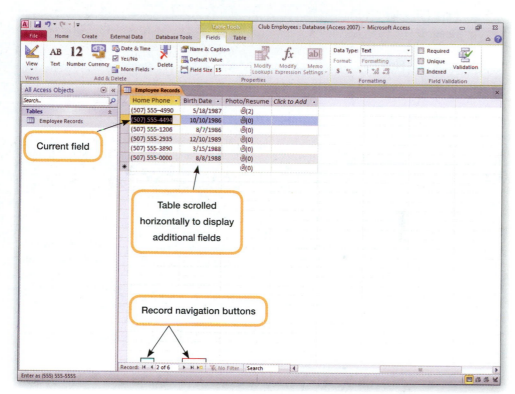

Figure 1.56

The table scrolled horizontally one window to the right, and the last three field columns in the table are now visible. The current field is the first field of this screen, but on the second record's row.

MOVING USING THE RECORD NAVIGATION BUTTONS

The record navigation buttons in the status bar also provide navigation short-cuts. These buttons are described in the following table.

Another Method

You also can use ⇒ Go To ▾ in the Find group of the Home tab to access the record navigation buttons.

Button	Effect
I◀	First record, same field
◀	Previous record, same field
▶	Next record, same field
▶I	Last record, same field
▶*	New (blank) record

You will use the record navigation buttons to move to the same field that is currently selected in the last record, and then back to the same field of the first record. Then you will move to the first field of the first record.

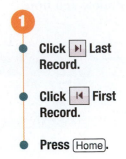

- Click ▶| Last Record.

- Click |◀ First Record.

- Press Home.

Your screen should be similar to Figure 1.57

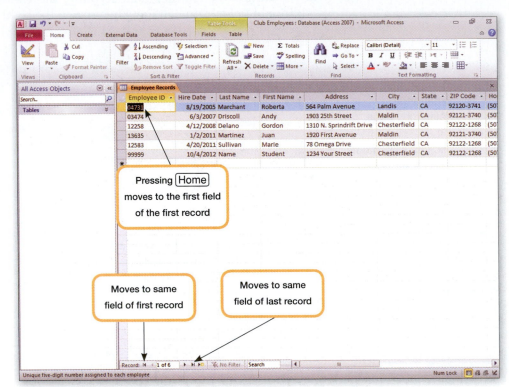

Figure 1.57

The first field of the first record is selected.

MOVING TO A SPECIFIC RECORD

You have moved the location of the cursor to the first record by using the record navigation buttons. You can also quickly move to a specific record by simply typing the record number into the Current Record box in the record navigation bar. This method is especially helpful when navigating around a large table when you know the record number you are looking for. Now you will practice moving to a specific record number.

1

- Click in the Current Record box.

- Press ⌫Backspace or Delete to delete the number 1.

- Type in 5 and press ⏎Enter.

Your screen should be similar to Figure 1.58

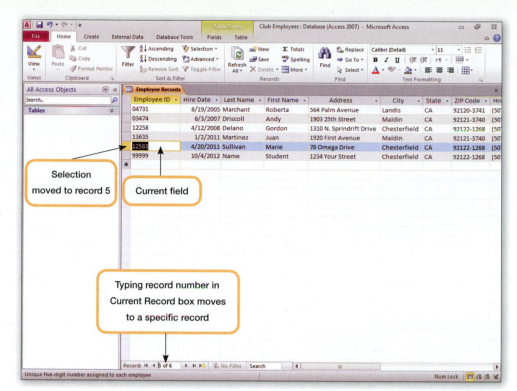

Figure 1.58

The specified record is now selected.

Deleting Records

Additional Information

You can select multiple noncontiguous records by holding down Ctrl while clicking the Select Record button of each record. To select contiguous records, click and drag along the Select Record buttons.

While you are entering the employee records, you find a memo from one of your managers stating that Andy Driscoll is no longer working at the club and asking you to remove his record from the employee files.

You can remove records from a table by selecting the entire record and pressing the Delete key. After pressing Delete, you will be asked to confirm that you really want to delete the selected record. This is because this action cannot be reversed.

1

- **Point to the Select Record button for record 2 (Andy Driscoll), and click when the mouse shape is ➡.**

Another Method

You also can move to the record and choose Select from the ⟨ Select ▾⟩ drop-down list in the Find group of the Home tab.

- **Press** Delete.

Another Method

You also can use ✂ Cut in the Clipboard group to delete a selected record.

Your screen should be similar to Figure 1.59

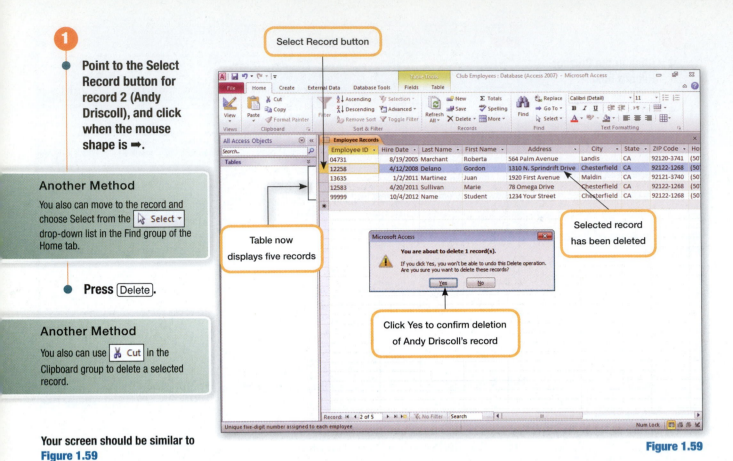

Select Record button

Table now displays five records

Selected record has been deleted

Click Yes to confirm deletion of Andy Driscoll's record

Figure 1.59

Although Andy Driscoll's record has been removed from the table, it will not be permanently deleted from the database until you confirm the deletion. If you change your mind, you can click ⟨ No ⟩ to restore the record.

2

- **Click**  **to confirm that you want to delete the record.**

The record has been permanently deleted and the table now consists of five employee records.

Another Method

You also can choose Delete Record from the ✕ Delete drop-down list in the Records group of the Home tab. The current record is both selected and deleted at the same time.

Creating a Table in Design View

Following your plan for the employee database, you will add another table to the existing database file. This table will hold information about the employee's work location and job title.

There are several ways to create a new table in an existing database. You can insert a blank table and define the fields in Datasheet view as you already have done, or you can create a table based on a table model. You also can import from or link to data from another source, such as another database, an Excel worksheet, or a SharePoint list. Finally, you can create a new table starting in Design view. You will use this last method to define the two fields in the table, Location and Job Title.

Additional Information

A SharePoint list is a list of data that is stored on a SharePoint server and is available to others in an organization.

1

- Open the Create tab and click 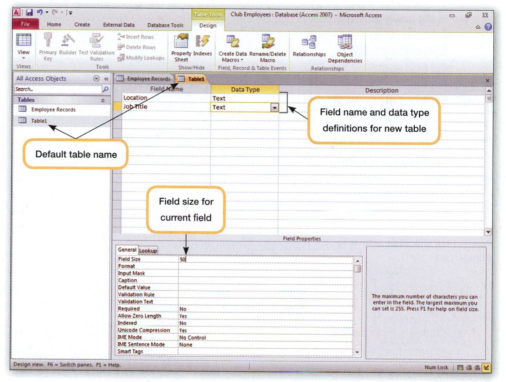 in the Tables group.

- Define the fields using the settings shown in the following table.

Your screen should be similar to Figure 1.60

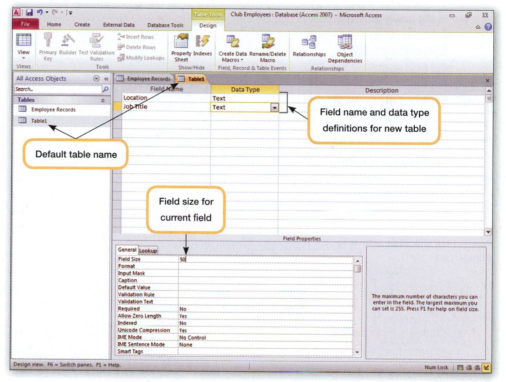

Figure 1.60

The new table has a default table name of Table1.

Field Name	Data Type	Field Size
Location	Text	20
Job Title	Text	50

INSERTING A FIELD

As you look at the table you realize you need a field to identify which employee the information belongs to. You want this field to be the first field in the table. To do this, you will insert the new field above the Location field.

1

- Make Location the current field.

- Click 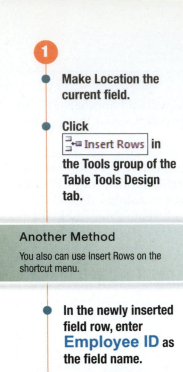Insert Rows in the Tools group of the Table Tools Design tab.

Another Method

You also can use Insert Rows on the shortcut menu.

- In the newly inserted field row, enter **Employee ID** as the field name.

- Specify a data type of Text and a field size of **5**

- Set the Employee ID field as the primary key for this table.

Your screen should be similar to **Figure 1.61**

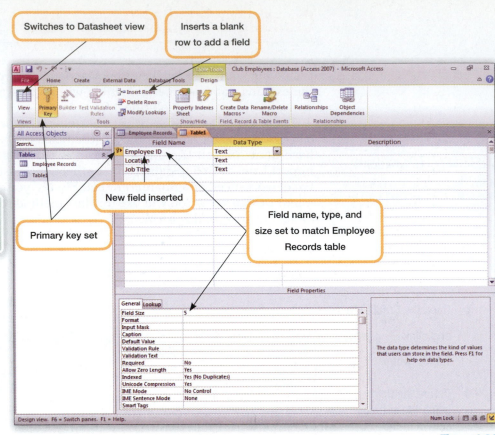

Switches to Datasheet view

Inserts a blank row to add a field

New field inserted

Field name, type, and size set to match Employee Records table

Primary key set

Figure 1.61

The Employee ID field is now inserted above the Location field in Design view. The Text data type and field size of 5 will match the existing property settings from the Employee Records table. Now you will switch to Datasheet view and save the table.

2

- Click 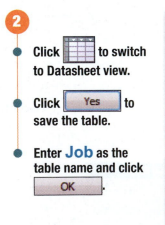 to switch to Datasheet view.

- Click Yes to save the table.

- Enter **Job** as the table name and click OK.

Your screen should be similar to **Figure 1.62**

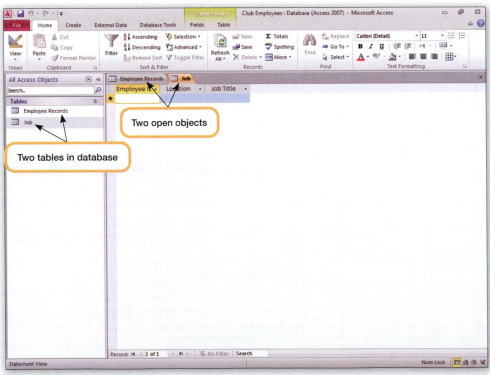

Two open objects

Two tables in database

Figure 1.62

As you consider the contents of the two tables, you realize that the Hire Date information should be in the Job table because the subject matter is related to the employee's job, not to his or her personal information.

3

- Click in the **Job Title field.**

- Click 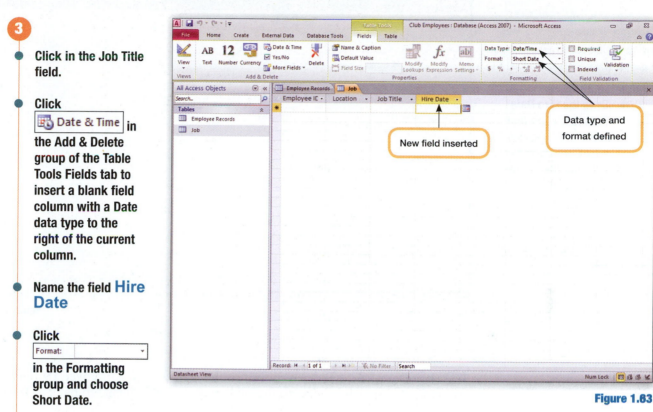 **Date & Time** in the **Add & Delete group of the Table Tools Fields tab to insert a blank field column with a Date data type to the right of the current column.**

- **Name the field Hire Date**

- Click **Format:** [▼] in the **Formatting group and choose Short Date.**

- **Click in the Hire Date field to confirm your settings.**

Your screen should be similar to **Figure 1.63**

Data type and format defined

New field inserted

Figure 1.63

The new field has been inserted and defined.

MOVING A FIELD

The Hire Date field was inserted as the last field in the Job table. While in Datasheet view, you decide to move the Hire Date field next to the Employee ID field. To move a field column, select the column and then drag the selected column to the new location. As you drag, a heavy black bar shows where the column will be placed when you stop dragging.

1

● Select the Hire Date
column.

Having Trouble?

Point to the field column name and click
when the mouse pointer appears as ↓.

● Drag the Hire Date
field to the left and
release the mouse
when the black bar
is to the right of the
Employee ID field
column.

Your screen should be similar to
Figure 1.64

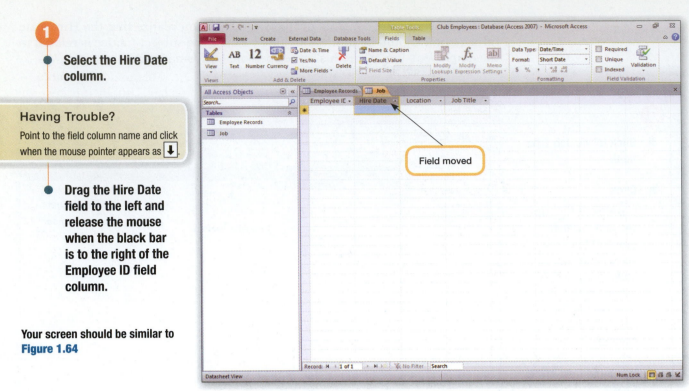

Field moved

Figure 1.64

The Hire Date field has been moved to the right of the Employee ID field. To
compare the Datasheet view to the Design view, you will switch back to Design
view.

2

● Click  to switch
back to Design view.

Your screen should be similar to
Figure 1.65

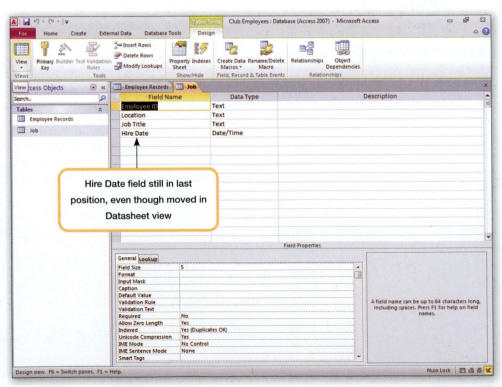

Hire Date field still in last
position, even though moved in
Datasheet view

Figure 1.65

Notice the Hire Date field is still last in the list of field names in Design view, even though you moved it to the second position in Datasheet view. The order in which the fields display can differ between the two views. This enables you to aesthetically display the order of the fields in the table and yet be able to arrange them in a specific structural order in Design view. Usually it is best for the field order to be the same in both views. You want to move the Hire Date below the Employee ID to match the placement in the datasheet. Moving a field in Design view is similar to doing so in Datasheet view, except that a row rather than a column is selected.

3

- Position the mouse in the gray row selector button next to Hire Date.

- Click when the mouse symbol changes to ➡ to select the Hire Date field row.

- While pointing to the row selector for the Hire Date row, drag up until the black move indicator line is below the Employee ID field.

- Release the mouse to place the Hire Date field row in its new position in Design view.

Your screen should be similar to Figure 1.66

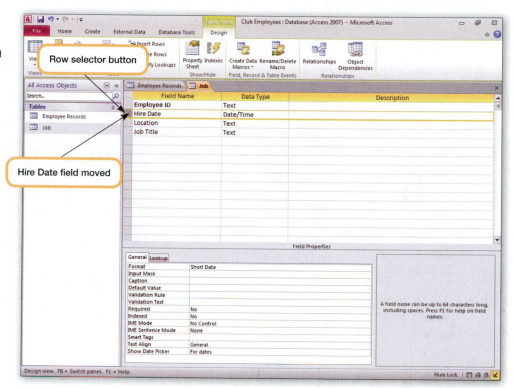

Figure 1.66

The field order in Design view now matches the order in which the fields are displayed in the datasheet.

4

- Click 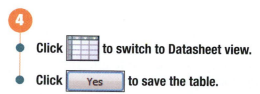 to switch to Datasheet view.

- Click Yes to save the table.

The Job table is now ready for you to input the data.

COPYING FIELD CONTENT

Having Trouble?

To review how to copy and paste, refer to the Copying and Moving Selections section in the Introduction to Microsoft Office 2010 lab.

Another Method

You can also press Ctrl + F6 to cycle between open table windows.

To save yourself time and prevent possible errors in typing, you will copy the data from the Employee ID and Hire Date fields in the Employee Records table into the new fields in the Job table. To switch between open tables, simply click on the table's tab. It then becomes the active table, or the table you can work in.

- Click on the Employee Records tab to make the table active.

- Select the Employee ID column.

- Click 📋 Copy in the Clipboard group of the Home tab.

- Click on the Job tab to make the table active.

- Select the Employee ID column.

- Click 📋 Paste in the Clipboard group of the Home tab.

- Click Yes to confirm the paste operation.

- Repeat these steps to copy the hire date information from the Employee Records table into the Job table.

Your screen should be similar to Figure 1.67

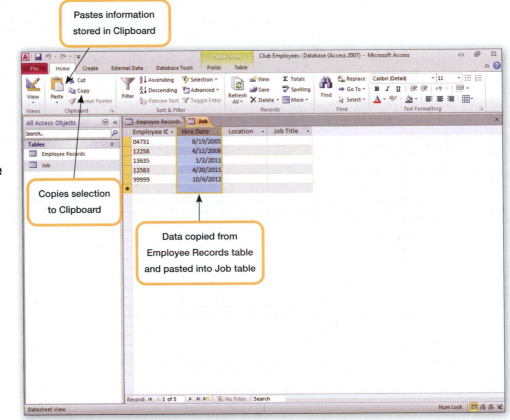

Figure 1.67

The table now includes information on the employee ID and hire date for the same records as in the Employee Records table. Now, all you need to do is delete the Hire Date field in the Employee Records table and then enter the rest of the data for the employees' job locations and titles.

2

- Make the Employee Records table active.

- Press Delete and click [Yes] to remove the still-selected Hire Date field from the Employee Records table.

- Add the information shown below to the appropriate records in the Job table.

- Best Fit the columns.

Your screen should be similar to Figure 1.68

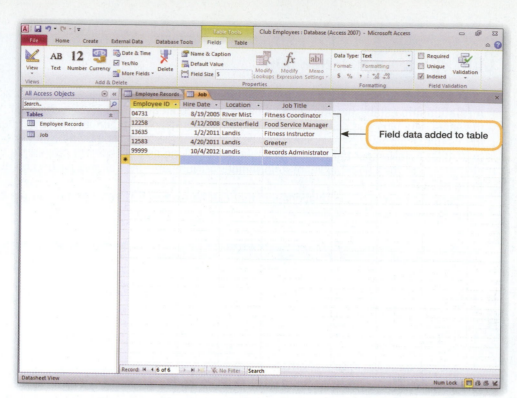

Field data added to table

Figure 1.68

Employee ID	Location	Job Title
04731	River Mist	Fitness Coordinator
12258	Chesterfield	Food Service Manager
12583	Landis	Greeter
13635	Landis	Fitness Instructor
99999	Landis	Records Administrator

Now the Employee Records table only contains the employee's personal information, and the Job table contains information about the employee's job.

Creating Relationships

Now that the database contains two tables, a relationship needs to be created between the tables to link the data together.

Concept ⑥ Relationship

A **relationship** establishes the association between common fields in two tables. The related fields must be of the same data type and contain the same kind of information but can have different field names. The exception to this rule occurs when the primary key field in one of the tables is the AutoNumber type, which can be related to another AutoNumber field or to a Number field, as long as the field size property is the same for both. This is also the case when both fields are AutoNumber or Number—they always have to be the same field size in order to be related.

There are three types of relationships that can be established between tables: one-to-one, one-to-many, and many-to-many.

Relationship Type	Description
One-to-one 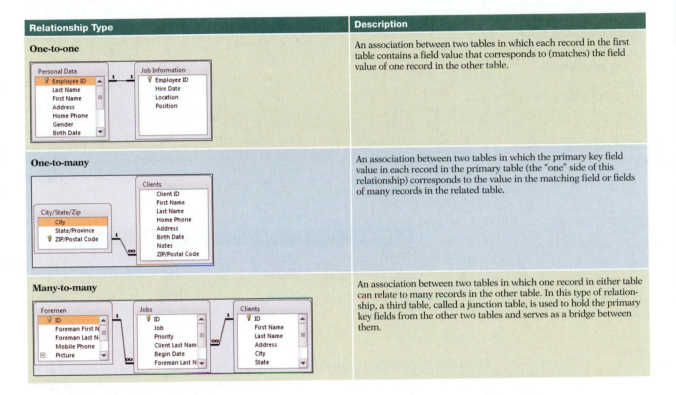	An association between two tables in which each record in the first table contains a field value that corresponds to (matches) the field value of one record in the other table.
One-to-many	An association between two tables in which the primary key field value in each record in the primary table (the "one" side of this relationship) corresponds to the value in the matching field or fields of many records in the related table.
Many-to-many	An association between two tables in which one record in either table can relate to many records in the other table. In this type of relationship, a third table, called a junction table, is used to hold the primary key fields from the other two tables and serves as a bridge between them.

Once relationships are established, rules can be enforced, called the rules of **referential integrity**, to ensure that relationships between tables are valid and that related data is not accidentally changed or deleted. The rules ensure that a record in a primary table cannot be deleted if matching records exist in a related table, and a primary key value cannot be changed in the primary table if that record has related records.

The Employee ID field is the field that the two tables have in common in this database and on which you will establish a relationship to link the tables together. To be able to create or edit relationships, you must close all open objects.

CLOSING TABLES

You close a table by closing its window and saving any layout changes you have made. Because you changed the column widths of the table, you will be prompted to save the layout changes before the table is closed. If you do not save the table, your column width settings will be lost.

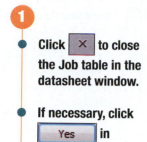

● Click ☒ to close the Job table in the datasheet window.

● If necessary, click Yes in response to the prompt to save the table.

● In a similar manner, close the Employee Records table.

Your screen should be similar to Figure 1.69

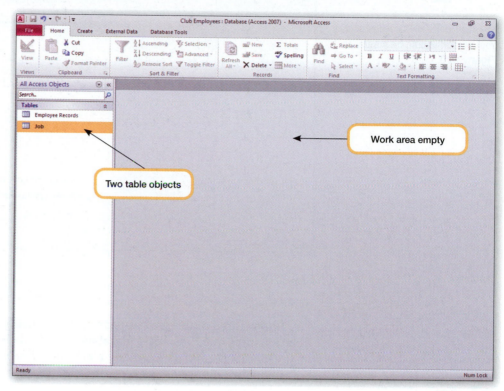

Figure 1.69

Both tables are closed and the work area is empty. The Navigation pane continues to display the names of the two table objects.

VIEWING RELATIONSHIPS

The Relationships window is used to create and edit relationships. It displays a field list for each table in the database and identifies how the tables are associated with relationship lines. However, the first time you open the Relationships window for a database, you need to select the tables to display in the window and then establish the relationship between the tables.

1

Click  in the
Relationships group
of the Database Tools
tab.

Your screen should be similar to
Figure 1.70

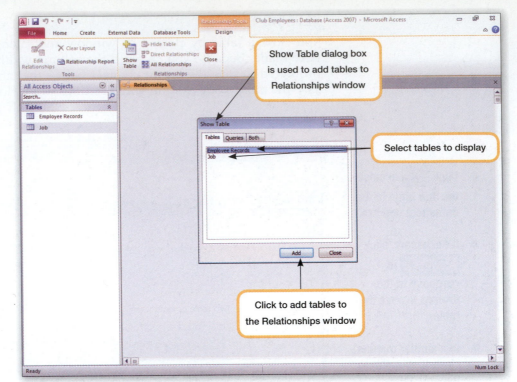

Figure 1.70

The Show Table dialog box appears automatically the first time you open the
Relationships window for a database. It displays the names of both tables
in the database and is used to select the tables you want displayed in the
Relationships window.

2

Click [Add]
to add the selected
table, Employee
Records, to the
Relationships
window.

Click Job in the
Tables list to select
the table and then
click [Add].

Click [Close].

Your screen should be similar to
Figure 1.71

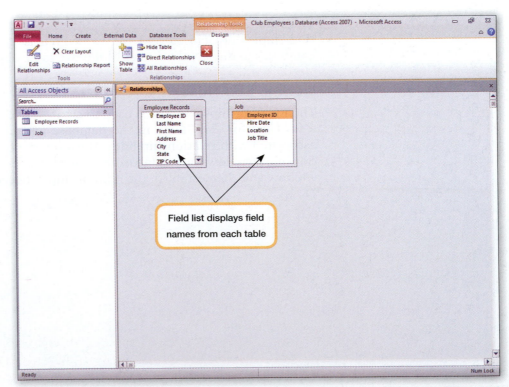

Figure 1.71

As you selected each table, a field list box displaying the field names from the table was added to the Relationships window. Next, you need to establish the relationship between the tables.

DEFINING RELATIONSHIPS

When creating relationships between the tables, study them first to determine what field the two tables have in common, and then determine which table is the main table. The common field in the lesser table, called a **foreign key** field, will be used to refer back to the primary key field of the main table. The field names of these two fields do not have to match, although their data types must be the same. As we have established, the Employee ID field is the common field between the two tables in this database. The Employee Records table is the main table, as it contains the main information about the employee. The Employee ID field in the Job table is the foreign key field.

Now you must connect the Employee Records' Employee ID field to its related field in the Job table. To create the relationship, you drag the field from the field list of one table to the common field in the field list of the other table.

As you point to the foreign key field, the mouse pointer will appear as ▨, indicating a relationship is being established.

1

● Click on the Employee ID field in the Employee Records table and drag to the same field in the Job table.

Your screen should be similar to Figure 1.72

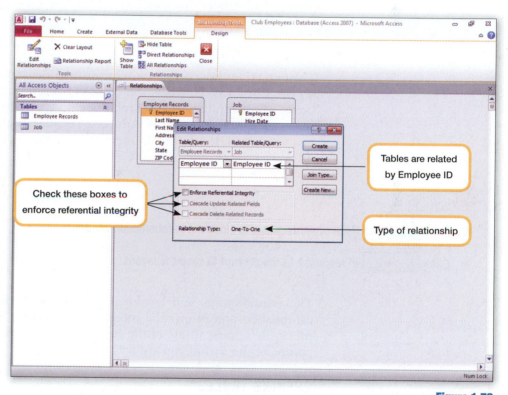

Figure 1.72

The Edit Relationships dialog box appears and shows how the tables will be related. You also want to enforce referential integrity between the tables. Selecting this option will make the Cascade Update and Cascade Delete options available. Again, you will select these options to ensure that if you change a primary key or delete a record, all fields that reference the primary key of that record are likewise updated or deleted in both tables. This prevents inconsistent and **orphaned records** (records that do not have a matching primary key record in the associated table). In addition, you can see that Access has correctly defined the type of relationship as one-to-one.

2

- Choose **Enforce Referential Integrity.**

- Choose both **Cascade** options.

- Click [**Create**].

- Click on the Job field list title bar to clear the selection from the relationship line.

Your screen should be similar to **Figure 1.73**

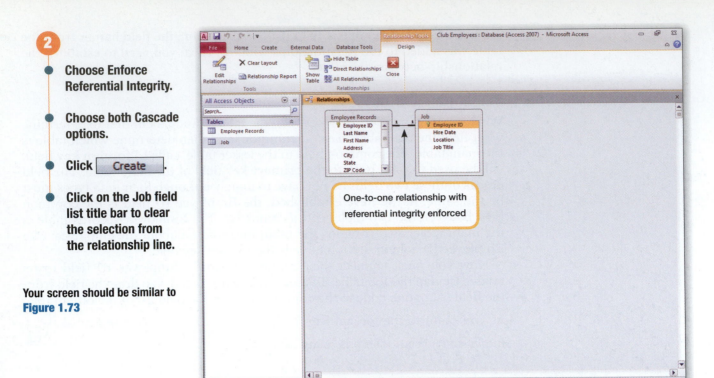

One-to-one relationship with referential integrity enforced

Figure 1.73

The two tables now display a relationship line that shows the tables are related on the Employee ID field. You can tell from the number 1 above each end of the relationship line that the relationship type is one-to-one. You can also tell that referential integrity is enforced because the relationship line is thicker near each end. If referential integrity were not enforced, the line would not be thicker at the ends.

3

- Click 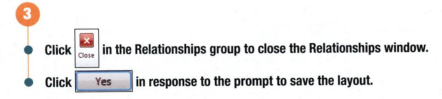 in the Relationships group to close the Relationships window.

- Click [**Yes**] in response to the prompt to save the layout.

The relationships and layout are saved. Now that a relationship has been established and referential integrity enforced, a warning message will automatically appear if one of the rules is broken, and you will not be allowed to complete the action you are trying to do.

OPENING TABLES

Now that you have established relationships between the tables, you will open the Employee Records table to see how the change has affected it. To open a table object, double-click on the name in the Navigation pane.

1

● Double-click
Employee Records in
the Navigation pane.

Another Method

You also can drag the object from the
Navigation pane to the work area to
open it, or right-click the object name in
the Navigation pane and choose Open.

Your screen should be similar to
Figure 1.74

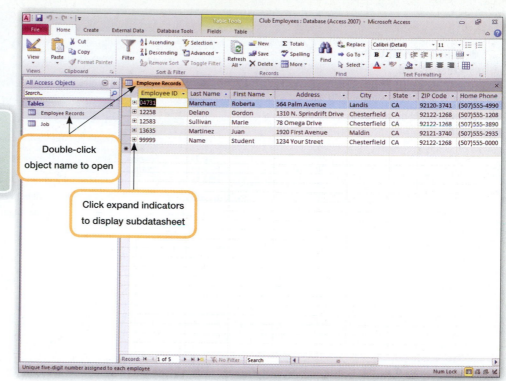

**Double-click
object name to open**

**Click expand indicators
to display subdatasheet**

Figure 1.74

The Employee Records table is open in the work area. Notice the records are
no longer in the same order they were entered, but are now in ascending order
by the primary key, Employee ID. There are also expand indicators ⊞ at the
beginning of each row. This indicates there is a subdatasheet linked to the
records in this table.

Concept ⑦ Subdatasheet

A **subdatasheet** is a data table nested within a main data table that contains information that is related or
joined to the main table. A subdatasheet allows you to easily view and edit related data. Subdatasheets are created automatically whenever relationships are established between tables.

In this case, the subdatasheet is the Job table. Clicking ⊞ will expand the table
to show the information in the subdatasheet table, Job.

2

● Click ⊞ next to the first record.

Your screen should be similar to Figure 1.75

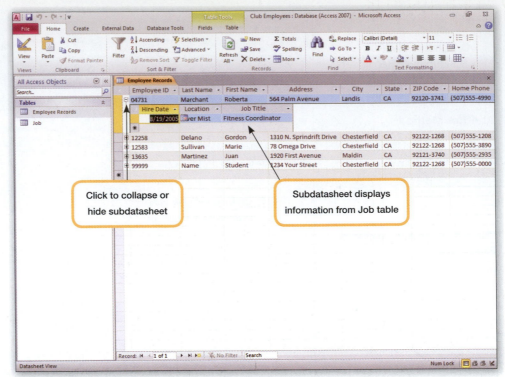

Figure 1.75

<table>
<tr><td colspan="2">**Additional Information**</td></tr>
<tr><td colspan="2">You will learn more about relationships and subdatasheets in later labs.</td></tr>
</table>

A subdatasheet appears and displays the location and job title information contained in the Job table for Roberta Marchant. Similarly, the Job table will display a subdatasheet to the Employee Records table.

Then, to hide or collapse the subdatasheet again, you click the collapse indicator ⊟.

3

● Click ⊟ next to the first record.

● Close the table.

You have created a database file that contains two tables and follows the two basic principles of database design: Do not include redundant information in tables, and enter accurate and complete information. Although you may think the employee number is redundant data, it is the only way the information in the two tables can be associated. The database attains the goals of **normalization**, a design technique that identifies and eliminates redundancy by applying a set of rules to your tables to confirm that they are structured properly.

Closing and Opening a Database

You are ready to show the manager your database to get approval on the setup of the data. But first you want to make sure you know how to close and open the file.

It is always a good idea to close all open objects in the work area before closing the database. Since you have already closed the tables, the work area is empty and there are no open objects. Next, you will close the database, but not the Access program.

CLOSING A DATABASE

When closing a database file, unlike other types of files, you do not need to save first, as each time changes are made to the data they are automatically saved as part of the process. Changes to an object's design, however, need to be saved for the changes to be permanent.

①

Open the File tab and click

Close Database

.

Your screen should be similar to Figure 1.76

Recently used files may also be listed here

Open the Recent tab to access list of recently used database files

Figure 1.76

Additional Information

To review file types, refer to the Saving a File section in the Introduction to Microsoft Office 2010 lab.

The New tab in Backstage view is displayed again so you can create another new database or open an existing one. If you plan to share an Access 2007 or 2010 .accdb file with someone using Access 2003 or earlier, before closing the database open the Save & Publish tab in Backstage view, choose the Save Database As option and save it as the .mdb file type. Be aware some features may be lost when saving to an older version of Access.

OPENING A DATABASE

Additional Information

See the section Opening a File in the Introduction to Microsoft Office 2010 to review the basics on how to open a file.

Just as there are several methods to create a new database, there are several methods you can use to open an existing database. The first is to click ⮞ Open , which displays the Open dialog box through which you browse to specify the location and name of the file you want to open. Another is to open the Recent tab and select from a list of recently used database files. A third is to select from the list of recently used database files above the Info tab if the feature to display recent databases in this location is selected.

You also can open database files that were created in previous versions of Access that used the .mdb file extension. These older file types must be converted to the Access 2010 file format if you want to take advantage of the new features in Access 2010.

You will open the Recent Databases window list to see the list of recently opened database files and use this method to open the database.

- Click the Recent tab to open the Recent Databases window.

Your screen should be similar to Figure 1.77

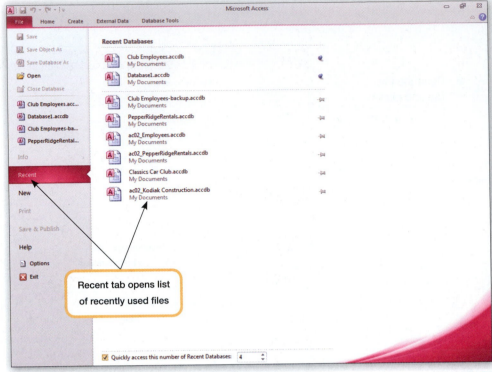

Recent tab opens list of recently used files

Figure 1.77

Additional Information

Items can be removed from the Recent list by right-clicking the file name and choosing Remove from list.

The Recent Databases window by default displays up to 17 names of recently used database files on the computer you are using. The file names listed, however, are not always accurate as files may have been moved or deleted since they were last accessed.

2

• **Choose** Club Employees **from the Recent Databases list.**

• **If necessary, click**

Enable Content

in the Security Warning message bar below the Ribbon to fully utilize the database.

Having Trouble?

Depending upon the security settings on your system, a Security Warning may be displayed below the Ribbon.

• **Double-click on the Employee Records table.**

Another Method

You also can drag the object from the Navigation pane to the work area to open it.

Your screen should be similar to Figure 1.78

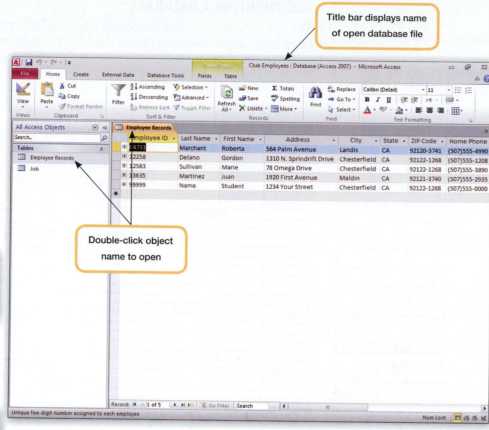

Figure 1.78

The database file and table are open again and appear just as they were when you closed them.

Setting Database and Object Properties

Now, you want to look at the file properties or settings that are associated with the database file. Some of these properties are automatically generated. These include statistics such as the date the file was created and last modified. Others such as a description of the file are properties you can add.

DOCUMENTING A DATABASE

Having Trouble?

See Specifying Document Properties in the Introduction to Microsoft Office 2010 for more information about this feature.

The information you can associate with the file includes a title, subject, author, keywords, and comments about the file. You will look at the file properties and add documentation to identify you as the author and a title for the database.

1

- Open the File tab and, if necessary, choose Info.

- Click on the View and edit database properties link, located below the database preview.

- Open each tab in the Properties dialog box and look at the recorded information.

- Open the Summary tab.

- Enter the following information in the Summary tab.

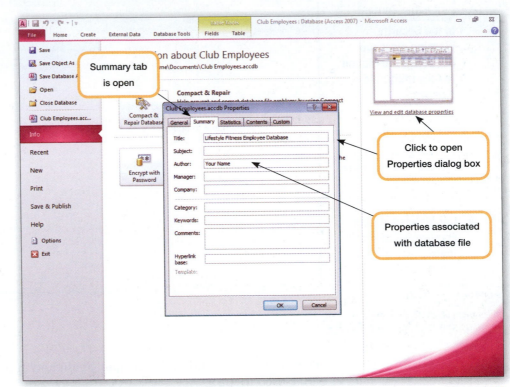

Figure 1.79

Title	**Lifestyle Fitness Employee Database**
Author	**Your Name**

Having Trouble?

The Title and Author text boxes may be blank or may already show information. Clear the existing contents first if necessary.

You also want to create a custom property to identify the completion date.

Your screen should be similar to Figure 1.79

2

- Open the Custom tab.

- Choose Date completed from the Name list.

- Choose Date as the Type.

- Enter the current date in the Value text box.

- Click  .

Your screen should be similar to Figure 1.80

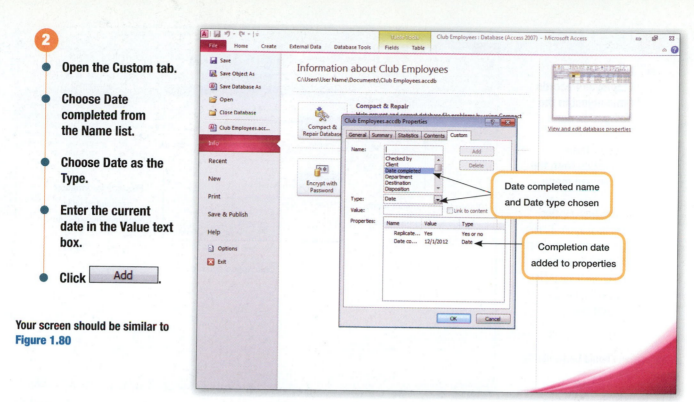

Figure 1.80

You are now finished entering information in the Database properties.

3

- Click OK .

- Click the Home tab to close Backstage view.

DOCUMENTING A TABLE OBJECT

You have completed adding the properties to the file. You also can add limited documentation to each object in a database. You will add documentation to the Employee Records table object.

1

- **Right-click the Employee Records table object in the Navigation pane.**

- **Choose Table Properties from the drop-down menu.**

- **In the Description text box, type This table is under construction and currently contains 5 records.**

Your screen should be similar to Figure 1.81

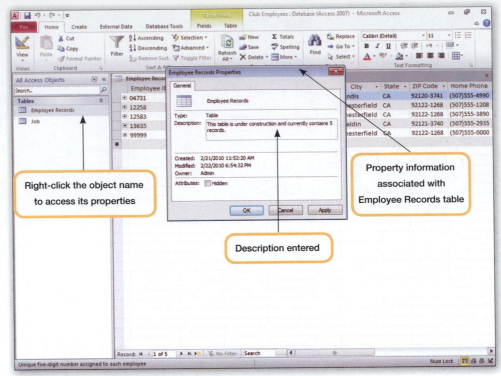

Figure 1.81

You have added property information to both the database file and the Employee Records table.

2

- **Click** OK **to close the Properties dialog box.**

Previewing and Printing a Table

Now that you have completed designing and entering some sample data in the two tables, you want to print a copy of the tables to get your manager's approval before you begin entering more employee records. Before printing the tables, you will preview them onscreen to see how they will look when printed.

PREVIEWING THE TABLE

Previewing a table displays each page in a reduced size so you can see the layout. Then, if necessary, you can make changes to the layout before printing to save time and avoid wasting paper.

1

- Open the Job table.

- Open the File tab.

- Open the Print tab and choose Print Preview.

- Hide the Navigation pane.

Your screen should be similar to
Figure 1.82

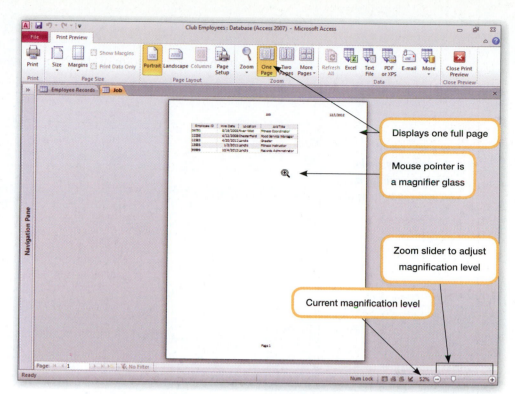

Figure 1.82

Additional Information

The current magnification level is displayed in the status bar.

The Print Preview window displays how the table will appear when printed. The Print Preview contextual tab is open and includes commands that are used to modify the print settings.

2

- Click on the table.

Additional Information

The location where you click will determine the area that is displayed initially.

Your screen should be similar to
Figure 1.83

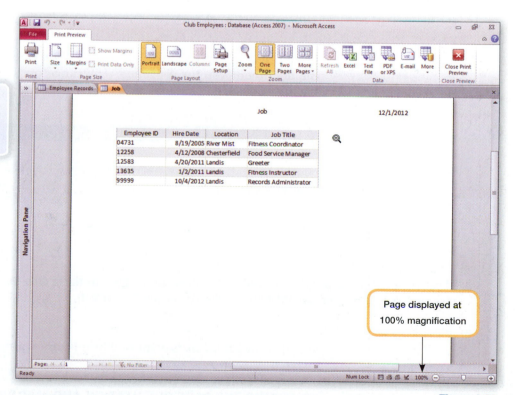

Figure 1.83

The table appears in 100 percent magnification. This is the size it will appear when printed.

PRINTING A TABLE

The  button in the Print group of the Print Preview tab is used to define the printer settings and print the document.

1

● If necessary, make sure your printer is on and ready to print.

● Click  .

Another Method

The keyboard shortcut is Ctrl + P.

Having Trouble?

Please consult your instructor for printing procedures that may differ from the directions given here.

Your screen should be similar to Figure 1.84

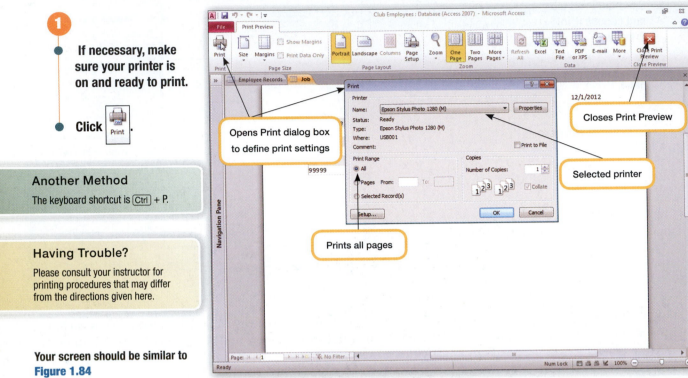

Figure 1.84

The Print Range area of the Print dialog box is used to specify the amount of the document you want printed. The range options are described in the following table.

Option	Action
All	Prints the entire document.
Pages	Prints pages you specify by typing page numbers in the text box.
Selected Records	Prints selected records only.

You will print the entire document.

2

● If you need to change the selected printer to another printer, open the Name drop-down list box and select the appropriate printer (your instructor will tell you which printer to select).

● Click OK .

A status message box is displayed briefly, informing you that the table is being printed.

CHANGING THE PAGE ORIENTATION AND MARGINS

Next, you will preview and print the Employee Records table.

1

- Click [Close Print Preview] in the **Close Preview** group.

- Make the **Employee Records** table active.

- Open the **File** tab.

- Open the **Print** tab and then choose **Print Preview.**

- Click on the table to zoom the preview.

Your screen should look similar to **Figure 1.85**

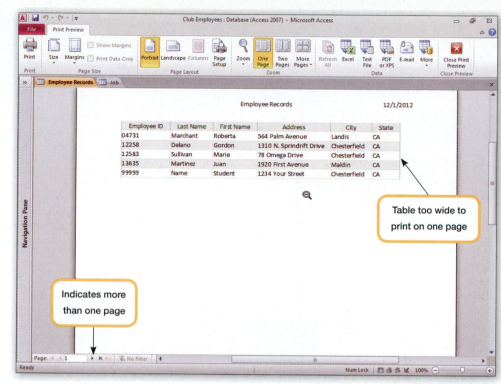

Table too wide to print on one page

Indicates more than one page

Figure 1.85

Notice that because the table is too wide to fit across the width of a page, only the first six fields are displayed on the page. Tables with multiple columns are typically too wide to fit on an 8½- by 11-inch piece of paper. You would like to see both pages displayed onscreen.

2

- Click [Two Pages] in the **Zoom** group.

Your screen should be similar to **Figure 1.86**

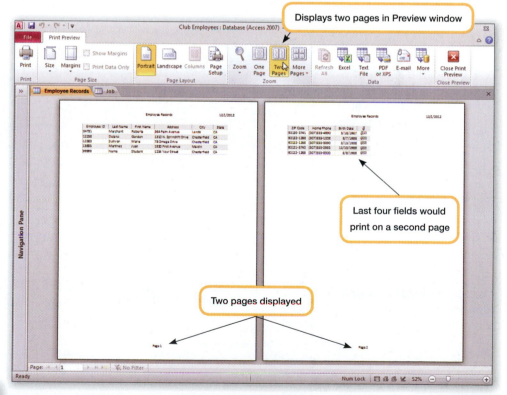

Displays two pages in Preview window

Last four fields would print on a second page

Two pages displayed

Figure 1.86

Having Trouble?

Refer to the section Printing a Document in the Introduction to Microsoft Office 2010 lab to review page orientation.

Rather than print the table on two pages, you decide to see whether changing the page orientation from portrait to landscape will allow you to print the table on one page.

3

● Click 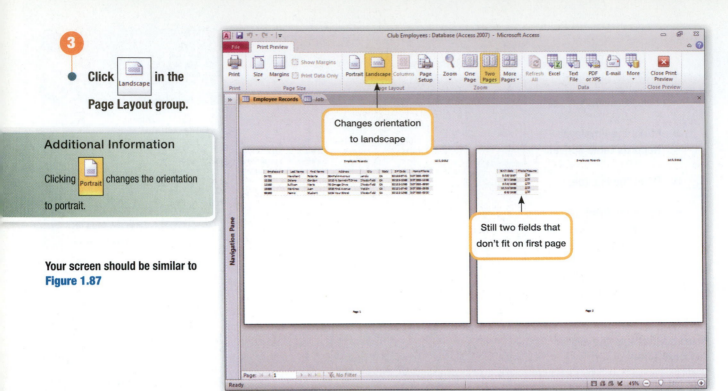 **Landscape** in the

Page Layout group.

Your screen should be similar to
Figure 1.87

Changes orientation
to landscape

Still two fields that
don't fit on first page

Figure 1.87

Although this helps, there are still two fields that do not fit on the page. To
fix this, you will try reducing the size of the page margins. The **margin** is the
blank space around the edge of a page. You will decrease the right and left
margin settings to 0.25 inch to see if this allows all fields to fit on one page.

4

● Click **Margins** in the

**Page Size group of
the Print Preview tab.**

● **Choose Normal.**

● Click **One Page**.

● **Increase the
magnification to 90%.**

Your screen should be similar to
Figure 1.88

Adjust page margins

	Employee Records								12/1/2012
Employee ID	Last Name	First Name	Address	City	State	ZIP Code	Home Phone	Birth Date	Photo/Resume
04731	Marchant	Roberta	564 Palm Avenue	Landis	CA	92120-3741	(507)555-4990	5/18/1987	(2)
12258	Delano	Gordon	1310 N. Sprindrift Drive	Chesterfield	CA	92122-1268	(507)555-1208	8/7/1986	(0)
12583	Sullivan	Marie	78 Omega Drive	Chesterfield	CA	92122-1268	(507)555-3890	3/15/1988	(0)
13635	Martinez	Juan	1920 First Avenue	Maldin	CA	92121-3740	(507)555-2935	12/10/1989	(0)
99999	Name	Student	1234 Your Street	Chesterfield	CA	92122-1268	(507)555-0000	8/8/1988	(0)

Normal margins have .25" left and
right and .75" top and bottom

All fields fit on one page

Grayed-out arrow
indicates there are no more
pages after page 1

Magnification at 90%

Figure 1.88

You can now see that all the fields will print on one page.

- Print the table.

- Close the Print Preview window.

Exiting Access

You will continue to build and use the database of employee records in the next lab. Until then, you can exit Access.

Click ⊠ Close in the Access window title bar.

> **Another Method**
>
> You also can open the File tab and choose ✕ Exit.

Notice that this time you were not prompted to save the tables because you did not made any layout changes to them since opening them. If you had made layout changes, you would be prompted to save the tables before exiting Access.

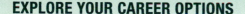

FOCUS ON CAREERS

EXPLORE YOUR CAREER OPTIONS

Admitting Nurse

Can you imagine trying to organize the information of hundreds of patients in a busy emergency room? This is the job of an admitting nurse, who must be able to enter, edit, and format data; add and delete records; and so on. This information is used by all departments of the hospital, from the doctors, to the pharmacy, and to the billing department. Without a proper understanding of database software, a hospital cannot run efficiently. The average salary of an admitting nurse is in the $40,000 to $50,000 range. The demand for nurses is expected to remain high.

Database (AC1.4)

A database is an organized collection of related information.

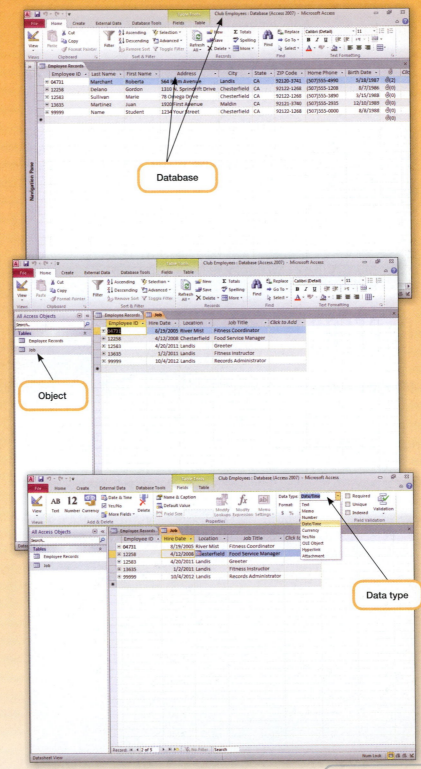

Database

Object (AC1.9)

An Access database is made up of several types of objects, such as a table or report, consisting of many elements. An object can be created, selected, and manipulated as a unit.

Object

Data Type (AC1.15)

The data type defines the type of data the field will contain. Access uses the data type to ensure that the right kind of data is entered in a field.

Data type

Field Property (AC1.22)

A field property is a characteristic that helps define a field. A set of field properties is associated with each field.

Primary Key (AC1.28)

A primary key is a field that uniquely identifies each record.

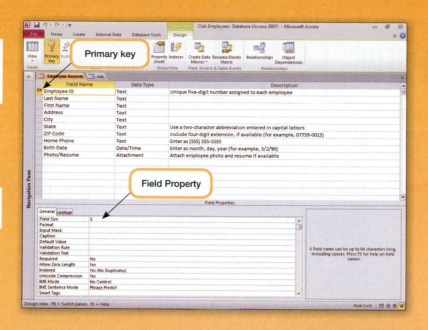

Relationship (AC1.66)

A relationship establishes the association between common fields in two tables.

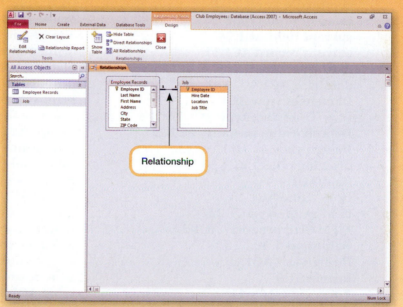

Subdatasheet (AC1.71)

A subdatasheet is a data table nested within a main data table; it contains information that is related or joined to the main table.

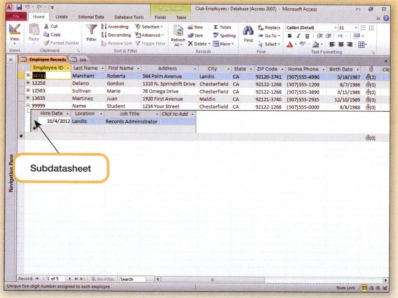

KEY TERMS

Allow Zero Length property AC1.22
Attachment data type AC1.15
AutoNumber data type AC1.15
Best Fit feature AC1.49
Calculated data type AC1.15
caption AC1.27
Caption property AC1.22
cell AC1.11
column width AC1.47
composite key AC1.28
Currency data type AC1.15
current field AC1.24
current record AC1.11
data type AC1.15
database AC1.4
Datasheet view AC1.11
Date/Time data type AC1.15
Default Value property AC1.22
Design view AC1.11
drawing object AC1.39
field AC1.4
field name AC1.13
field property AC1.22
Field Size property AC1.22
field model AC1.18
foreign key AC1.69
form AC1.9
Form view AC1.11
Format property AC1.22
graphic AC1.39
header row AC1.11
Hyperlink data type AC1.15
Indexed property AC1.22
Input Mask property AC1.22

Layout view AC1.11
margin AC1.82
Memo data type AC1.15
navigation buttons AC1.11
Navigation pane AC1.10
normal form AC1.72
normalization AC1.72
Number data type AC1.15
object AC1.9
OLE Object data type AC1.15
one-to-many AC1.66
one-to-one AC1.66
orphaned records AC1.69
picture AC1.39
primary key AC1.28
Print Preview AC1.11
query AC1.9
record AC1.4
referential integrity AC1.66
relational database AC1.4
relationship AC1.66
report AC1.9
Report view AC1.11
Required property AC1.22
Select Record button AC1.11
serial value AC1.15
subdatasheet AC1.71
table AC1.4, 9
Text data type AC1.15
Validation Rule property AC1.22
Validation Text property AC1.22
view AC1.10
Yes/No data type AC1.15

COMMAND SUMMARY

Command	Shortcut	Action
File Tab		
New		Opens a new blank database
Open	Ctrl + O	Opens an existing database
Save	Ctrl + S	Saves database object
Recent		Displays a list of recently used database files
Print/Print	Ctrl + P	Specifies print settings and prints current database object
Print/Print Preview		Displays file as it will appear when printed
Close Database		Closes open window
✕ Exit		Closes Access
Home Tab		
Views group		
Design View		Displays object in Design view
Datasheet View		Displays object in Datasheet view
Clipboard group		
✂ Cut	Ctrl + X	Removes selected item and copies it to the Clipboard
Copy	Ctrl + C	Duplicates selected item and copies to the Clipboard
Paste	Ctrl + V	Inserts copy of item from Clipboard
Records group		
✕ Delete	Delete	Deletes current record
More ▾ /Field Width		Adjusts width of selected column
Find group		
Select ▾ /Select		Selects current record

LAB REVIEW

COMMAND SUMMARY (CONTINUED)

Command	Shortcut	Action
Table Tools Field Tab		
Views group		
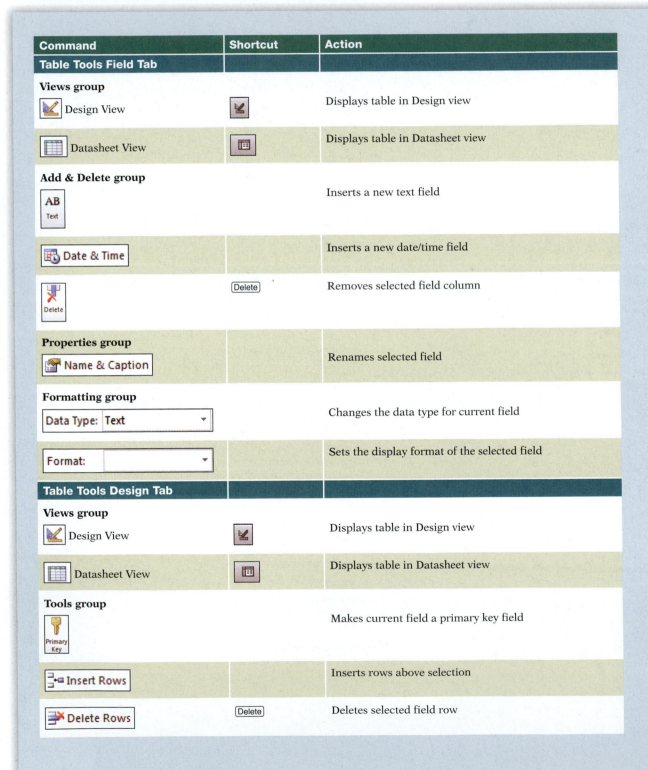 Design View		Displays table in Design view
Datasheet View		Displays table in Datasheet view
Add & Delete group		
AB Text		Inserts a new text field
Date & Time		Inserts a new date/time field
Delete	Delete	Removes selected field column
Properties group		
Name & Caption		Renames selected field
Formatting group		
Data Type: Text		Changes the data type for current field
Format:		Sets the display format of the selected field
Table Tools Design Tab		
Views group		
Design View		Displays table in Design view
Datasheet View		Displays table in Datasheet view
Tools group		
Primary Key		Makes current field a primary key field
Insert Rows		Inserts rows above selection
Delete Rows	Delete	Deletes selected field row

COMMAND SUMMARY (CONTINUED)

Command	Shortcut	Action
Database Tools Tab		
Relationships		Opens relationships window
Print Preview Tab		
Print group		
Print	Ctrl + P	Prints displayed object
Page Layout group		
Portrait		Changes print orientation to portrait
Landscape		Changes print orientation to landscape
Zoom group		
One Page		Displays one entire page in Print Preview
Two Pages		Displays two entire pages in Print Preview
Close Preview group		
Close Print Preview		Closes Print Preview window

LAB EXERCISES

SCREEN IDENTIFICATION

1. On the following Access screen, several items are identified by letters. Enter the correct term for each item in the spaces provided.

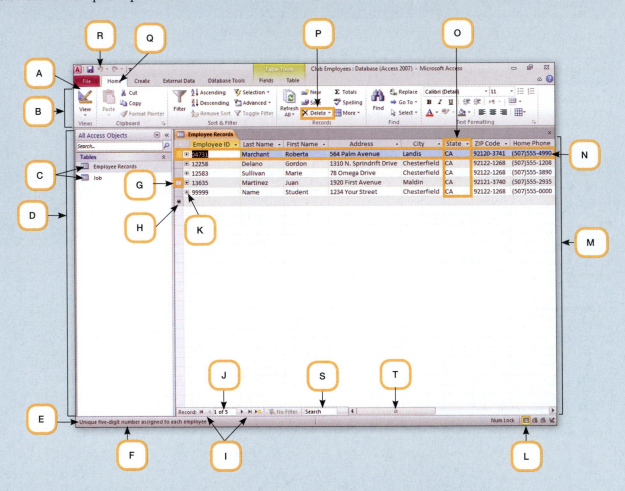

Possible answers for the screen identification are:

Cell	Quick Access Toolbar	**A.** _____	**K.** _____
Current Record box	Record	**B.** _____	**L.** _____
Datasheet View button	Record navigation buttons	**C.** _____	**M.** _____
Delete record	Ribbon	**D.** _____	**N.** _____
Design view	Scroll bar	**E.** _____	**O.** _____
Field	Search	**F.** _____	**P.** _____
Field description	Select Record button	**G.** _____	**Q.** _____
Navigation pane	Status bar	**H.** _____	**R.** _____
New Record/End of table marker	Subdatasheet indicator	**I.** _____	**S.** _____
	Tab	**J.** _____	**T.** _____
Object	Work area		
Open object tab			
Primary key indicator			

MATCHING

Match the numbered item with the correct lettered description.

1. Datasheet view   ____ a. contains multiple tables linked by a common field
2. Attachment   ____ b. used to define the table structure
3. Design view   ____ c. used to open and manage database objects
4. field size   ____ d. a data type that stores multiple files of different file types in a single field
5. data type   ____ e. field that uniquely identifies each record
6. object   ____ f. displays table in row and column format
7. record   ____ g. defines the type of data the field will contain
8. relational database   ____ h. controls the maximum number of characters that can be entered in a field
9. primary key   ____ i. collection of related fields
10. Navigation pane   ____ j. a unit of a database

TRUE/FALSE

Circle the correct answer to the following statements.

1. A foreign key is a field in one table that refers to the primary key field in another table and indicates how the tables are related.	True	False
2. Tables and queries are two types of database objects.	True	False
3. Caption text can be different from the field's name.	True	False
4. A table is a required object in a database.	True	False
5. Changing the column width in the datasheet changes the field size.	True	False
6. A field description is a required part of the field definition.	True	False
7. Interactive databases define relationships between tables by having common data in the tables.	True	False
8. A field contains information about one person, thing, or place.	True	False
9. The data type defines the information that can be entered in a field.	True	False
10. You can format the text in a Memo field.	True	False

LAB EXERCISES

FILL-IN

Complete the following statements by filling in the blanks with the correct terms.

1. The _____ data type can be used to store a graphic file in a field.
2. A(n) _____ is used to create a preformatted field or a set of several fields commonly used together.
3. An Access database is made up of several types of _____.
4. A(n) _____ is a data table nested in another data table that contains data that is related or joined to the table where it resides.
5. The field property that limits a Text data type to a certain size is called a(n) _____.
6. Using _____ orientation prints across the length of the paper.
7. The _____ data type restricts data to digits only.
8. A field name is used to identify the _____ stored in a field.
9. The _____ field property specifies how data displays in a table.
10. You use the _____ located at the left of the work area to select the type of object you want to work with.

MULTIPLE CHOICE

Circle the letter of the correct response.

1. _____ view is only used to modify the table structure.
   a. Design
   b. Report
   c. Datasheet
   d. Query
2. The basic database objects are _____.
   a. panes, tables, queries, and reports
   b. tables, queries, forms, and reports
   c. forms, reports, data, and files
   d. portraits, keys, tables, and views
3. Graphics can be inserted into a field that has a(n) _____ data type.
   a. Graphic
   b. Text
   c. Attachment
   d. Memo
4. Another way to create fields is to select from a list of predefined fields called _____.
   a. value fields
   b. data types
   c. field models
   d. attachment fields

5. A _____ is a field in one table that refers to the primary key field in another table and indicates how the tables are related.
   a. foreign key
   b. common key
   c. related key
   d. data key

6. _____ affects the amount of data that you can enter into a field.
   a. Column width
   b. Field size
   c. Format
   d. Description size

7. You may lose data if your data and _____ are incompatible.
   a. field name
   b. data type
   c. default value
   d. field size

8. A _____ is often used as the primary key.
   a. phone number
   b. catalog number
   c. last name
   d. first name

9. _____ is a design technique that identifies and eliminates redundancy by applying a set of rules to your tables.
   a. Database development
   b. Normalization
   c. Validation
   d. Orientation

10. The last step of database development is to _____.
    a. design
    b. develop
    c. review
    d. plan

LAB EXERCISES | Hands-On Exercises

STEP-BY-STEP

OAK RIDGE SCHOOL PARENT CONTACT DATABASE ★

1. Oak Ridge Elementary School has decided to set up a database with the contact information for all students. As a parent, you have volunteered to do the initial database creation and teach the secretary at the school to maintain it. The database table you create will have the following information: student's last name, student's first name, guardian's name, home address, and home phone number. When you have finished, a printout of your completed database table should look similar to the one shown here.

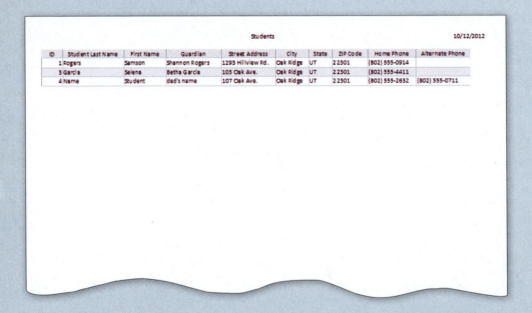

a. Create a blank database named Oak Ridge School. Create a table in Datasheet view using the following field information. When creating the address fields, use the Address field model to create the Address, City, State, and ZIP Code fields. Switch to Design view and save the table as Students. Make the ID field the primary key field. Delete the Country Region field generated from the Address field model and then modify the field names and properties to match those shown below.

Field Name	Data Type	Description	Field Size/Format
ID	AutoNumber		Long Integer
Student Last Name	Text	Student's legal last name	25
First Name	Text	Include student's nickname in parentheses	25
Guardian	Text	First and last names of primary guardian	55
Street Address	Text		75
City	Text		20
State	Text	Two-letter abbreviation	2
ZIP Code	Text		5
Home Phone	Text		15

b. In Datasheet view, enter the following records into the table, using Copy and Paste for fields that have the same data (such as the city):

	Record 1	Record 2	Record 3
Student Last Name	Rogers	Wilson	Garcia
First Name	Samson	Avette	Selena
Guardian	Shannon Rogers	Rita Wilson-Montoya	Betha Garcia
Street Address	1293 Hillview Rd.	102 4th Street	103 Oak Ave.
City	Oak Ridge	Oak Ridge	Oak Ridge
State	UT	UT	UT
ZIP Code	22301	22301	22301
Home Phone	(802) 555-0914	(802) 555-3375	(802) 555-4411

c. Adjust the column widths appropriately.

d. Delete record 2. Add another record with the following data:

[Your last name]

[Your first name]

[Your parent's name]

107 Oak Ave.

Oak Ridge

UT

22301

(802) 555-2632

e. Add a new field after the Home Phone field with the following definitions:

Field Name: Alternate Phone

Data Type: Text

Field Size: 15

f. Change the ZIP Code field size to 10

g. Enter the Alternate Phone number of (802) 555-0711 and the ZIP Code of 22301-4459 for the record with ID number 4

h. Best Fit all columns.

i. In the database properties, add your name as the author and Oak Ridge School as the title. Add the description Exercise 1 in Access Lab 1 to the table properties.

i. View the table in Print Preview; change the page orientation to landscape and margins to Normal.

j. Print, save, and close the table.

LAB EXERCISES

PEPPER RIDGE RENTALS DATABASE ★ ★

2. You manage a real estate rental business and decide to implement a database to track the rental properties. A database will be useful to look up any information about the rental, including its location, how many bedrooms and bathrooms, square footage, and date available. This will help you find rentals within the desired home size and price range of your clients. When you are finished, your printed database table should be similar to the one shown here.

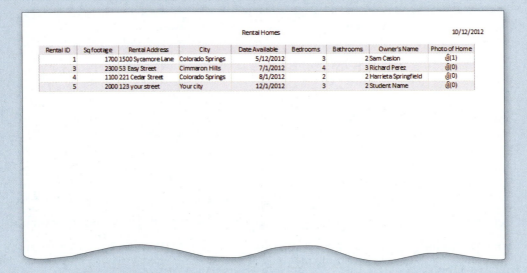

a. Create a blank database named PepperRidgeRentals

b. Add the following fields to the new table:

> **Rental Address**
>
> **City**
>
> **Date Available**
>
> **Bedrooms**
>
> **Bathrooms**
>
> **Sq Footage**
>
> **Owner's Name**

c. Switch to Design view. Save the table as **Rental Homes**

d. Change the ID field name to **Rental ID**

e. Add an Attachment field and name it **Photo of Home**. Use this name for the Caption property as well.

f. Change the field size of the Address and Owner's Name fields to **40**

g. Change the field size of the City field to **20**

h. Set the Date Available data type to Date, Short format.

i. The data type for Bedrooms, Bathrooms, and Sq Footage should be Number.

j. Return to Datasheet view. Add the following records to the table:

Address	1500 Sycamore Lane	8900 Sparrows Nest	53 Easy Street	221 Cedar Street
City	Colorado Springs	Cascade	Cimarron Hills	Colorado Springs
Date Available	5/12/2012	6/1/2012	7/1/2012	8/1/2012
Bedrooms	3	2	4	2
Bathrooms	2	1	3	2
Sq Footage	1700	840	2300	1100
Owner's Name	Sam Caslon	Betty Rose	Richard Perez	Harrieta Springfield

k. Insert the image file ac01_1500SycamoreHouse in the Attachment field of the first record.

l. Adjust the column widths using the Best Fit feature.

m. Delete the record for the address 8900 Sparrows Nest. Add a new record with fictional information, your name in the Owner's Name field, and the current date in the Date Available field.

n. In the database properties, add **your name** as the author and **Pepper Ridge Rentals** as the title. Add the description **Exercise 2 in Access Lab 1** to the table properties.

o. Preview and print the table in landscape orientation with normal margins.

p. Save and close the table. Exit Access.

LAB EXERCISES

CAR CLUB MEMBERS DATABASE ★ ★

3. You are a member of the local car club. Even though the club was founded only last year, the membership has grown considerably. Because of your computer skills, you have been asked to create a database with the membership number, membership date, first name, last name, address, city, state, zip, phone number, car year, and car model. This will help the club president contact members about events, the treasurer to mail out dues notices, and the events coordinator to mail out newsletters. Your printed database tables and relationships should be similar to those shown here.

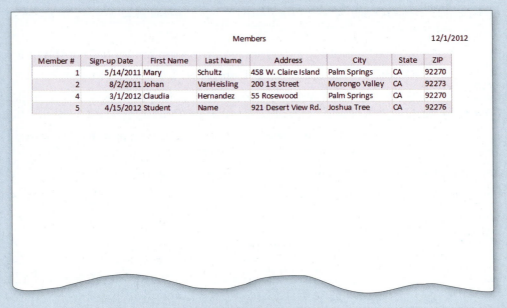

Members   12/1/2012

Member #	Sign-up Date	First Name	Last Name	Address	City	State	ZIP
1	5/14/2011	Mary	Schultz	458 W. Claire Island	Palm Springs	CA	92270
2	8/2/2011	Johan	VanHeisling	200 1st Street	Morongo Valley	CA	92273
4	3/1/2012	Claudia	Hernandez	55 Rosewood	Palm Springs	CA	92270
5	4/15/2012	Student	Name	921 Desert View Rd.	Joshua Tree	CA	92276

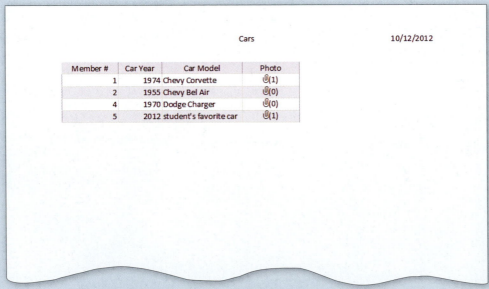

Cars   10/12/2012

Member #	Car Year	Car Model	Photo
1	1974	Chevy Corvette	(1)
2	1955	Chevy Bel Air	(0)
4	1970	Dodge Charger	(0)
5	2012	student's favorite car	(1)

a. Create a blank database named Classics Car Club

b. Add the following fields to the new table:

Sign-up Date

Member Name

Address (use the Address field model)

c. Switch to Design view. Save the table as **Members**

d. Edit the field properties using the following information:

Field Name	Data Type	Description	Field Size/Format
Change ID to **Member #**	AutoNumber		
Sign-up Date	Date/Time	**Date member joined club**	Short Date
Change Member Name to **First Name**	Text	**Member's first name**	**25**
Address		**Mailing address**	**50**
Change State Province to **State**		**Two-letter state abbreviation**	**2**
Change ZIP Postal to **ZIP**		**ZIP code, ex: 99999 or 99999-1234**	**10**

e. Insert a row above the Address field and add the following field there:

Field Name	Data Type	Description	Field Size
Last Name	Text	**Member's last name**	**25**

f. Delete the Country Region field that was created as part of the Address field model.

g. Switch to Datasheet view and enter the following records into the table:

	Record 1	Record 2	Record 3	Record 4
Membership date	**5/14/2011**	**8/2/2011**	**12/20/2011**	**3/1/2012**
First Name	**Mary**	**Johan**	**Frank**	**Claudia**
Last Name	**Schultz**	**Van Heisling**	**Bonaire**	**Hernandez**
Address	**458 W. Claire Island**	**200 1st Street**	**890 Lakeside Dr.**	**55 Rosewood Circle**
City	**Palm Springs**	**Morongo Valley**	**Indio**	**Palm Springs**
State	**CA**	**CA**	**CA**	**CA**
ZIP	**92270**	**92273**	**92275**	**92270**

h. Best Fit all column widths.

i. Create a second table named **Cars** with the following fields:

Field Name	Data Type	Description	Field Size
Car Year	Number	**Car's year of manufacture**	
Car Model	Text	**Car's make and model (e.g., Ford Mustang)**	**50**
Vehicle Photo	Attachment	**Photo of car in Classics Car show**	

j. Change the Caption property for the Vehicle Photo to read **Photo**

Since you need a way to link the two tables together, you will obtain the member information from the Members table and paste it into the Cars table.

k. Switch to Datasheet view. Make the Members table active. Copy the Member # column.

l. Make the Cars table active. Right-click the Car Year field name and choose Insert field from the shortcut menu. Click Paste to complete the copy process, bringing the Member # field and information into the Cars table.

m. Enter the following records into the Cars table:

Member #	1	2	3	4
Car Year	1974	1955	1930	1970
Car Model	Chevy Corvette	Chevy Bel Air	Studebaker	Dodge Charger
Photo	ac01_1974Corvette			

n. Best Fit all column widths.

o. Close the tables. Establish the relationship between the Members table and the Cars table (hint: one member can have many cars). Enforce referential integrity and check the Cascade delete and update options. Close and save the relationship.

p. Open the Members table. Delete record 3. Add a new record with the following data:

Membership Date:	4/15/2012
First Name:	Your first name
Last Name:	Your last name
Address:	921 Desert View Rd
City:	Joshua Tree
State:	CA
Zip:	92276

q. Open the Cars table and add your car information as a new record. (Your Member # should be 5.)

Car Year:	your favorite car year or use 1961
Car Model:	your favorite car model or use Ferrari
Photo:	attach photo of your car or use ac01_1961Ferrari

r. Check the tables in Print Preview. Print in portrait orientation with normal margins. Save and close both tables. Exit Access.

DOWNTOWN INTERNET CAFÉ INVENTORY DATABASE ★ ★ ★

4. The Downtown Internet Café, which you helped get off the ground, is an overwhelming success. The clientele is growing every day, as is the demand for the beverages the café serves. Up until now, the information about the vendors has been kept in an alphabetical card file. This has become quite unwieldy, however, and Evan, the owner, would like a more sophisticated tracking system. He would like you to create a database containing each supply item and the contact information for the vendor that sells that item. When you are finished, your database tables should be similar to those shown here.

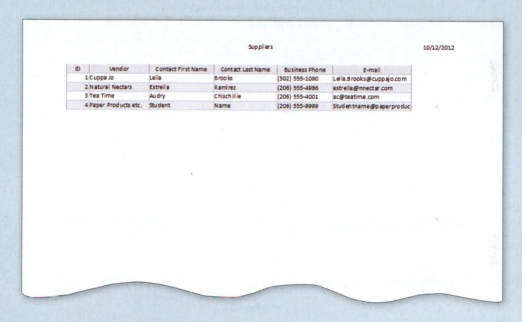

Suppliers — 10/12/2012

ID	Vendor	Contact First Name	Contact Last Name	Business Phone	E-mail
1	Cuppa Jo	Leila	Brooks	(502) 555-1090	Leila.Brooks@cuppajo.com
2	Natural Nectars	Estrella	Ramirez	(206) 555-4986	estrella@nnectar.com
3	Tea Time	Audry	Chischillie	(206) 555-4001	ac@teatime.com
4	Paper Products etc.	Student	Name	(206) 555-9999	Studentname@paperproduc

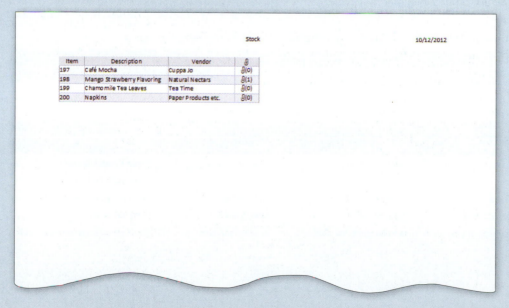

Stock — 10/12/2012

Item	Description	Vendor	
197	Café Mocha	Cuppa Jo	𝕌(0)
198	Mango Strawberry Flavoring	Natural Nectars	𝕌(1)
199	Chamomile Tea Leaves	Tea Time	𝕌(0)
200	Napkins	Paper Products etc.	𝕌(0)

LAB EXERCISES

a. Create a blank database named Cafe Inventory

b. Design a table with the field names **Item** and **Description**

c. Switch to Design view. Save the table as **Stock**

d. Delete the ID field. Make Item the primary key field.

e. Add the following information to the field properties:

Field Name	Data Type	Description	Field Size
Item	Text	Unique three-digit product number	3
Description	Text	Name of product	50

f. Create a second table using the following field names:

Company

First Name

Last Name

Business Phone

E-mail Address

g. Switch to Design view. Save the table as **Suppliers**

h. Edit the field properties as shown here:

Field Name	Data Type	Description	Field Size
Change Company to **Vendor**	Text	Company name of supplier	50
Change First Name to **Contact First Name**	Text		50
Change Last Name to **Contact Last Name**	Text		50
Business Phone	Text	Include the area code in parentheses: (800) 555-5555	15
Change E-mail Address to **E-mail**	Text	E-mail address of contact person	50

i. Enter the following records into the Stock and Suppliers tables:

Stock table		
Record 1	Record 2	Record 3
197	198	199
Café Mocha	Mango Strawberry Flavoring	Chamomile Tea Leaves

Suppliers table			
Record 1	Record 2	Record 3	Record 4
Cuppa Jo	Natural Nectars	Tea Time	Paper Products etc.
Leila	Estrella	Audry	Enter your first name
Brooks	Ramirez	Chischillie	Enter your last name
(502) 555-1090	(206) 555-4986	(206) 555-4001	(206) 555-9999
lbrooks@cuppajo.com	estrella@nnectar.com	ac@teatime.com	Yourname@paperproducts.com

j. Add the existing field, Vendor, from the Suppliers table as the last field in the Stock table.

k. In the Stock table, select Cuppa Jo as the vendor for the first record, Natural Nectars for the second record, and Tea Time for the third record.

l. In the Suppliers table, edit the record for ID 1 by changing the e-mail address to **Leila.Brooks@ cuppajo.com**

m. Add a new attachment data type field to the Stock table. Assign the new field the name and caption of **Picture**. For item number 198 insert the file ac01_Flavoring

n. Add the following new item to the Stock file.

Item:	**200**
Description:	**Napkins**
Vendor:	**Paper Products etc**

o. Adjust the column widths in both tables using Best Fit.

p. Make sure there is a relationship line connecting the Suppliers table ID field to the Stock table Vendor field. Edit the relationship line to enforce referential integrity, and the cascade update and delete options.

q. Preview the Suppliers table. Change to landscape orientation. Change the margins to wide and print the table.

r. Preview the Stock table. Change to landscape orientation. Change the margins to wide and print the table.

s. Close the database. Exit Access.

LAB EXERCISES

KODIAK CONSTRUCTION DATABASE ★ ★ ★

5. You have just been hired by Kodiak Paint and Construction to create and maintain a database containing information about their clients and jobs. The company has grown rapidly, and they need ready access to information about jobs spread across the city. When you are finished, your tables should be similar to those shown here.

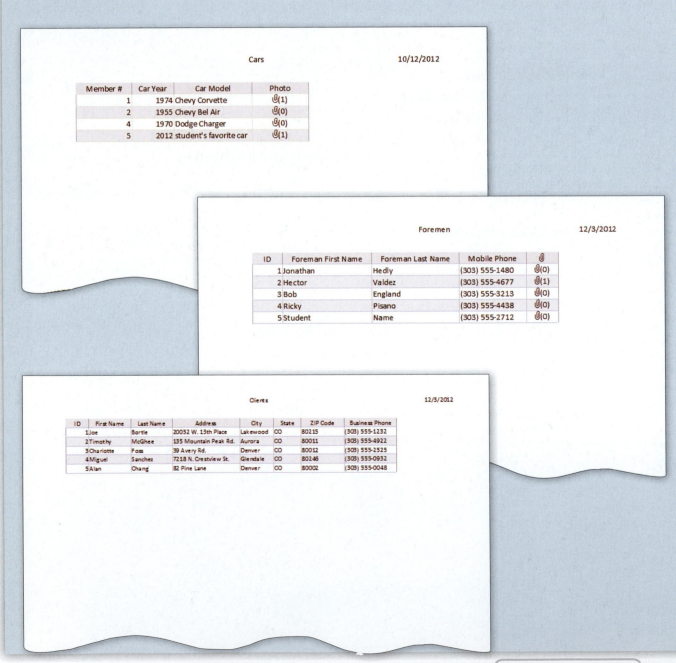

		Cars		10/12/2012
Member #	Car Year	Car Model	Photo	
1	1974	Chevy Corvette	(1)	
2	1955	Chevy Bel Air	(0)	
4	1970	Dodge Charger	(0)	
5	2012	student's favorite car	(1)	

		Foremen		12/3/2012
ID	Foreman First Name	Foreman Last Name	Mobile Phone	
1	Jonathan	Hedly	(303) 555-1480	(0)
2	Hector	Valdez	(303) 555-4677	(1)
3	Bob	England	(303) 555-3213	(0)
4	Ricky	Pisano	(303) 555-4438	(0)
5	Student	Name	(303) 555-2712	(0)

			Clients				12/3/2012
ID	First Name	Last Name	Address	City	State	ZIP Code	Business Phone
1	Joe	Bortle	20032 W. 13th Place	Lakewood	CO	80215	(303) 555-1232
2	Timothy	McGhee	135 Mountain Peak Rd.	Aurora	CO	80011	(303) 555-4922
3	Charlotte	Foss	39 Avery Rd.	Denver	CO	80012	(303) 555-2525
4	Miguel	Sanchez	7218 N. Crestview St.	Glendale	CO	80246	(303) 555-0932
5	Alan	Chang	82 Pine Lane	Denver	CO	80002	(303) 555-0048

a. Create a blank database named Kodiak Construction. Design a table using the following field names:

Project Name

Begin Date

End Date

b. Add the following additional fields to the table.

Field Name	Type
Job Description	Memo
Job Location	Text
Job Estimate	Currency

c. Save the table as Jobs. Switch to Design view.

d. Change the Project Name field name to Job. Delete the End Date field. Add field descriptions and make the changes to the field properties shown in the following table:

Field Name	Data Type	Description	Field Size	Format
ID	Text	Unique three-digit job ID	3	
Job		Project Name	75	
Begin Date				Short date
Job Description		Brief description of project		
Job Location	Text	Enter city only	25	

e. Enter the following records into the table:

Record 1	Record 2	Record 3	Record 4	Record 5
034	062	010	053	112
Summit Lakes	Sandalwood Villa	Ridgeline Condos	R Bar C Ranch	Williams Retreat
4/13/2008	9/15/2008	2/18/2008	7/18/2008	12/13/2008
Remodel golf club	Remodel restaurant	New construction of 75 condo units	Private home guest addition	New construction
Denver	Aurora	Aurora	Glendale	Golden
1,200,000	750,000	2,500,000	125,000	925,000

f. Adjust the column widths using Best Fit.

g. Delete the record for the Summit Lakes job.

LAB EXERCISES

h. Create a second table for the client information using the following field names: (Use the
Address field model to create the address fields.)

First Name

Last Name

Address

City

State Province

ZIP Postal Code

Business Phone

i. Save the table as **Clients**

j. Add field descriptions and make the changes to the field properties shown in the following table:

Field Name	Data Type	Description	Field Size
First Name	Text	First name of client	25
Last Name	Text	Last name of client	25
Address		Mailing address	50
City	Text		50
Change State Province to **State**		Use two-character abbreviation	2
Change ZIP Postal Code to **ZIP Code**		Enter 10 digit code, if available	10
Business Phone	Text	Enter phone as (###) ###-####	14

k. Add the following client information:

	Record 1	Record 2	Record 3	Record 4	Record 5
First Name	Joe	Timothy	Charlotte	Miguel	Alan
Last Name	Bortle	McGhee	Foss	Sanchez	Chang
Address	20032 W. 13th Place	135 Mountain Peak Rd.	39 Avery Rd.	7218 N. Crestview St.	82 Pine Lane
City	Lakewood	Aurora	Denver	Glendale	Denver
State	CO	CO	CO	CO	CO
ZIP Code	80215	80011	80012	80246	80002
Business Phone	(303) 555-1232	(303) 555-4922	(303) 555-2525	(303) 555-0932	(303) 555-0048

l. Create a third table for the foreman information with the following fields:

Field Name	Data Type	Description	Field Size
Foreman First Name	Text		25
Foreman Last Name	Text		25
Mobile Phone	Text	Enter phone as (###) ###-####	14
Picture	Attachment	Photo of foreman	

m. Save the table as **Foremen**

n. Enter the following information for the five foremen.

Jonathan Hedly	Hector Valdez	Bob England	Ricky Pisano	Your Name
(303) 555-1480	(303) 555-4677	(303) 555-3213	(303) 555-4438	(303) 555-2712

o. Add the file ac01_Valdez to the Attachment field for Hector Valdez.

p. Create a new field in the Jobs table that matches the Foreman Last Name from the Foreman table. Place the field after the Begin Date field. Use the field name **Foreman Last Name**

q. Enter the following foremen for each job:

Job	Foreman
010	Pisano
053	England
062	Your Name
112	Valdez

r. Create a field that matches the Last Name from the Client table after the Job field in the Jobs table. Rename the field **Client Last Name**

s. Enter the following clients for each job:

Job	Client
010	Foss
053	Sanchez
062	McGhee
112	Bortle

t. Establish relationships between tables: create a relationship between the Client Last Name field of the Client table and the Client Last Name field of the Jobs table; create another relationship between the Foreman Last Name field of the Foremen table and the Foreman Last Name field of the Jobs table.

u. Best Fit all fields in all tables.

v. Preview and print the Jobs table in landscape orientation with normal margins. Print the Foremen table in portrait orientation with wide margins. Print the Client table in landscape orientation with wide margins.

w. Save and close all tables and exit Access.

LAB EXERCISES

ON YOUR OWN

MUSIC COLLECTION DATABASE ★

1. You have just purchased a 200-disc CD carousel, and now you would like to organize and catalog your CDs. You realize that without an updatable list, it will be difficult to maintain an accurate list of what is in the changer. To get the most out of your new purchase, you decide a database is in order. Create a new database called Music Collection and a table called CD Catalogue. The table you create should include Artist's Name, Album Title, Genre, and Position Number fields. Make the Position Number field the primary key (because you may have multiple CDs by a given artist). Enter at least 15 records. Include an entry that has your name as the artist. Preview and print the table when you are finished.

VALLEY VIEW NEWSLETTER ADVERTISING DATABASE ★

2. Your homeowner's association distributes a monthly newsletter, *Valley View News*, to keep residents up to date with neighborhood news. In the past year, there has been rapid growth in building, including more houses and small office complexes. There are also plans to build an elementary school, fire station, and shopping center in the community. Consequently, the newsletter is now the size of a small newspaper, and the homeowners' dues are not covering the expense of publishing it.

   The editorial staff has already begun selling ad space in the newsletter to local businesses, and, based on your background in database management, they have asked you to set up a database to keep track of the advertiser contact information. You agree to design such a database, called Valley View News, and tell them you will have something to show them at the next meeting. Your finished database should include each advertiser's billing number, business name and address, and contact name and phone number in a table named Advertisers. Enter 10 records and include a record that has your name as the contact name. Preview and print the table when you are finished.

PATIENT DATABASE ★

3. You are the manager of a newly opened dental office. As one of your first projects, you need to create a patient database. Create a database called Dental Patients and a table named Patient Information. The database table you set up should contain patient identification numbers, last and first names, addresses, and phone numbers. Also include a field named "Referred by" and another field named "Patient since." Use appropriate field sizes and make the ID number field the primary key. Enter at least 10 records, adjusting the column widths as necessary. Include a record that contains your name as the patient. Preview and print the table.

OLD WATCH DATABASE USING THE WEB ★ ★

4. You have a small online business, Timeless Treasures, that locates and sells vintage wrist and pocket watches. Your business and inventory have grown large enough now that you have decided to use a database to track your inventory. Create a simple database named Timeless Treasures with a table named **Watches** that contains identification numbers, manufacturer (Waltham, Hamilton, Melrose), category (pocket watch, wrist watch), description, price, and quantity on hand. Size the fields appropriately and assign a primary key to one of them. Enter at least 10 records in the table. To obtain data about watches to include in your table, do a Web search on "old watches." Use the information you locate to complete the data for the records in your table. Adjust column widths as necessary. Include your name as the manufacturer in one of the records. Preview and print the table.

EXPENSE TRACKING DATABASE ★ ★ ★

5. You work in the accounting department at a start-up company called AMP Enterprises. One of your duties is to reimburse employees for small, company-related expenses, which up until now has been a simple task of having the employees fill out a form that they submit to you for payment. You then cut checks for them that are charged to the general expense fund of the company. However, the company has grown tremendously in the last year, adding employees and departments at a rapid rate, and the executive team has decided that it is time to start managing the income and expenses on a much more detailed level. To this end, you need to create a database that includes the employee ID, employee name, submission date, expense type, and expense amount for each expense report that is turned in. Name the database AMP Enterprises. Create two tables, one for the employee information named **Employee Info** and the other for employee expenses named **Employee Expenses**. Include the Employee ID, First Name, and Last Name fields in the Employee Info table. Include the Employee ID, Submission Date, Expense Type, and Expense Amount fields in the Employee Expenses table. Use the Currency data type for the Expense Amount field, and appropriate data types for all other fields. Size the fields appropriately. Delete the ID field from the Employee Info table and make the Employee ID field the primary key. Enter at least 15 records. Adjust the column widths as necessary. Delete one of the records you just entered, and then edit one of the remaining records so it contains your name as the employee. Enter 10 records in the Employee Expenses table (one should be an expense record for the record containing your name). Preview and print both tables.

Modifying and Filtering a Table and Creating a Form Lab 2

Objectives

After completing this lab, you will know how to:

1. Change field format properties.

2. Set default field values.

3. Define validation rules.

4. Hide and redisplay fields.

5. Create a lookup field.

6. Search, find, and replace data.

7. Sort records.

8. Format a datasheet.

9. Filter a table.

10. Create and use a form.

11. Modify the layout of a form.

12. Add a record using a form.

13. Organize the Navigation Pane

14. Preview, print, close, and save a form.

15. Identify object dependencies.

Lifestyle Fitness Club

Lifestyle Fitness Club owners, Ryan and Felicity, are very pleased with your plans for the organization of the database and with your progress in creating the first table of basic employee data. As you have seen, creating a database takes planning and a great deal of time to set up the structure and enter the data. As you have continued to add more employee records to the table, you have noticed several errors. You also realize that you forgot to include a field for the employee's gender. Even with the best of planning and care, errors occur and the information may change. You will see how easy it is to modify the database structure

and to customize field properties to provide more control over the data that is entered in a field.

Even more impressive, as you will see in this lab, is the program's ability to locate information in the database. This is where all the hard work of entering data pays off. With a click of a button, you can find data that might otherwise take hours to locate. The result saves time and improves the accuracy of the output.

You also will see how you can make the data you are looking at onscreen more pleasing and easier to read by creating and using a form.

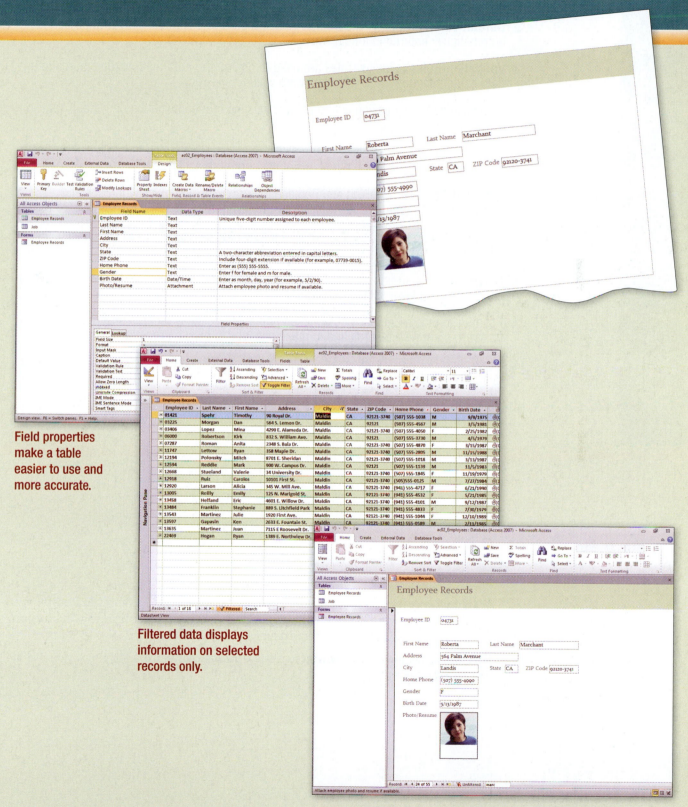

Field properties make a table easier to use and more accurate.

Filtered data displays information on selected records only.

Forms can be used to display information in an easy-to-read manner and make data entry easier.

The following concepts will be introduced in this lab:

1 Format Property The Format property is used to specify the way that numbers, dates, times, and text in a field are displayed and printed.

2 Default Value Property The Default Value property is used to specify a value that is automatically entered in a field when a new record is created.

3 Validation Rule Validation rules are used to control the data that can be entered in a field by defining the input values that are valid or allowed.

4 Expression An expression is a formula consisting of a combination of symbols that will produce a single value.

5 Lookup Field A lookup field provides a list of values from which the user can choose to make entering data into that field simpler and more accurate.

6 Find and Replace The Find and Replace feature helps you quickly find specific information and automatically replace it with new information.

7 Sorting Sorting rearranges the order of the records in a table based on the value in each field.

8 Filter A filter is a restriction placed on records in the open datasheet or form to quickly isolate and display a subset of records.

9 Form A form is a database object used primarily to display records onscreen to make it easier to enter new records and to make changes to existing records.

10 Controls Controls are objects that display information, perform actions, or enhance the design of a form or report.

11 Theme A theme is a predefined set of formatting choices that can be applied to an entire document in one simple step.

Customizing Fields

You have continued to add more records to the Lifestyle Fitness Club employee database. You want to open the expanded database to continue working on and refining the Employee Records table.

NOTE Before you begin, you may want to create a backup copy of the ac02_Employees file by copying and renaming it.

1

- Start Microsoft Access 2010.

- Open the database file ac02_Employees.

- If necessary, click

  Enable Content

  in the Security Warning bar below the Ribbon.

- Open the Employee Records table.

Your screen should be similar to **Figure 2.1**

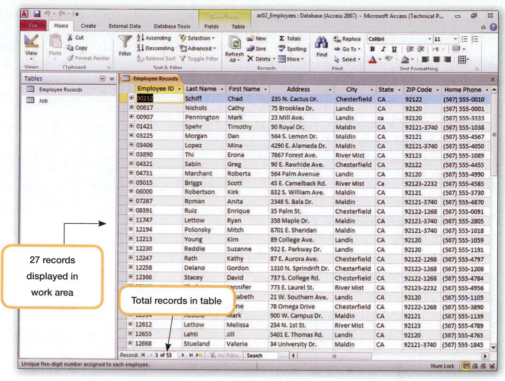

Figure 2.1

Having Trouble?

Your screen may display more or fewer records, depending upon your monitor settings.

As you can see from the record number indicator, the updated table now contains 53 records, but only the first 27 records are displayed. To see the rest of the records, you will move about the table using the keyboard and the record navigation buttons.

2

- Press Page Down to look at the next page of records.

- Press Ctrl + End to move to the last field of the last record.

Your screen should be similar to **Figure 2.2**

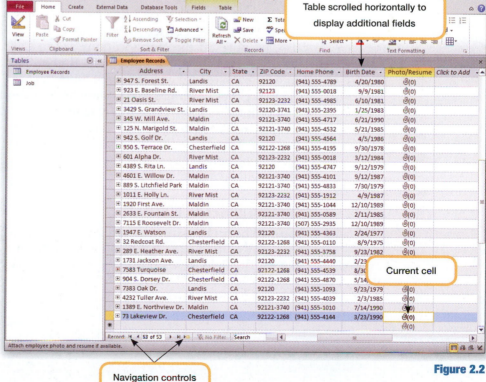

Figure 2.2

First the table moved down one full window to display records 27 through 53. Then the table scrolled horizontally one window to the right, and now the last fields in the table are visible. The last field in the last record is currently active.

3

● Click the ⏮ **First record navigation** button to move to the first record.

● Press Home to move to the first field of the first record.

Your screen should be similar to Figure 2.3

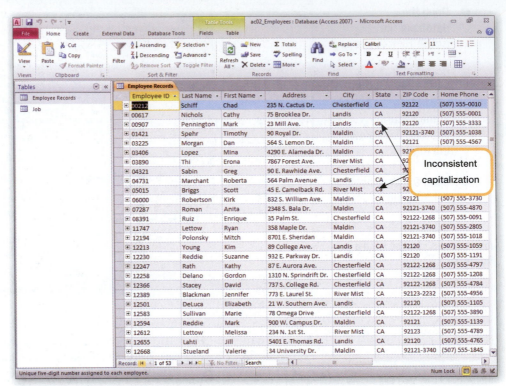

Figure 2.3

As you look through the records, you notice that record 3 has a lowercase entry in the State field and that record 10 has a mixed-case entry. You want all the State field entries to be consistently entered in all uppercase letters. Also, because all the club locations are in California, it is unlikely that any club employees live in another state. Rather than repeatedly entering the same state for each record, you want the State field to automatically display CA. You will make these changes to the State field by modifying its properties.

Additionally, you realize that you forgot to include a field for each employee's gender. While developing a table, you can modify and refine how the table operates. You can easily add and delete fields and add restrictions on the data that can be entered in a field as well as define the way that the data entered in a field will be displayed.

SETTING DISPLAY FORMATS

You will begin by fixing the display of the entries in the State field. Instead of manually editing each field, you will fix the entries by defining a display format for the field to customize the way the entry is displayed.

Concept 1 Format Property

The **Format property** is used to specify the way that numbers, dates, times, and text in a field are displayed and printed. Format properties do not change the way Access stores data, only the way the data is displayed. To change the format of a field, you can select from predefined formats or create a custom format by entering different symbols in the Format text box. For example, four common format symbols used in Text and Memo data types are shown in the following table.

Symbol	Meaning	Example
@	Requires a text character or space	@@@-@@-@@@@ would display 123456789 as 123-45-6789. Nine characters or spaces are required.
>	Forces all characters to uppercase	> would display SMITH whether you entered SMITH, smith, or Smith.
<	Forces all characters to lowercase	< would display smith whether you entered SMITH, smith, or Smith.
&	Allows an optional text character	@@-@@& would display 12345 as 12-345 and 1234 as 1-234. Four out of five characters are required, and a fifth is optional.

You want to change the format of the State field to display the entries in all uppercase characters.

1

- Click 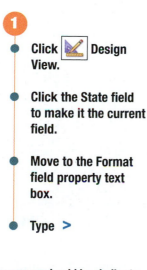 Design View.

- Click the State field to make it the current field.

- Move to the Format field property text box.

- Type **>**

Your screen should be similar to
Figure 2.4

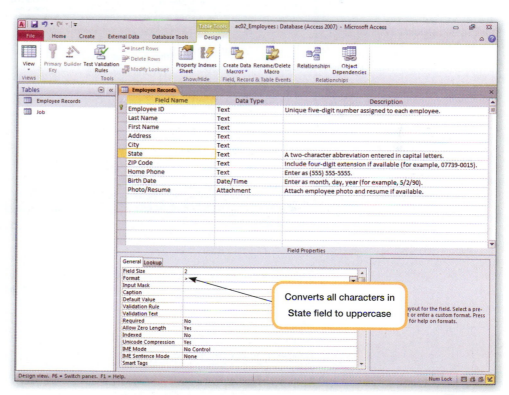

Converts all characters in State field to uppercase

Figure 2.4

SETTING DEFAULT VALUES

Next, you want to change the State field for new records to automatically display CA. To do this, you specify a Default Value property.

Concept 2 Default Value Property

The **Default Value property** is used to specify a value that is automatically entered in a field when a new record is created. This property is commonly used when most of the entries in a field will be the same for the entire table. That default value is then displayed automatically in the field. When users add a record to the table, they can either accept this value or enter another value. This saves time while entering data.

You will set the State field's default value to display CA.

- Click in the Default Value property text box.

- Type **CA**

- Press ↵Enter.

Your screen should be similar to
Figure 2.5

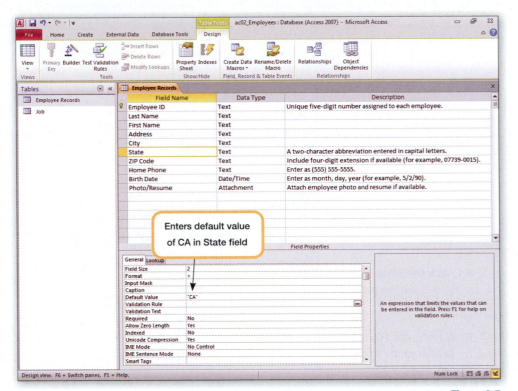

Figure 2.5

The default value is automatically enclosed in quotation marks to identify the entry as a group of characters called a **character string**. To see the effect on the table of setting a default value, you will return to Datasheet view and look at a new blank record.

First, you want to see the effect of the modifications to the State field's properties on the table.

2

● Click 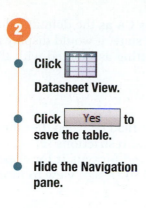 Datasheet View.

● Click [Yes] to save the table.

● Hide the Navigation pane.

Your screen should be similar to **Figure 2.6**

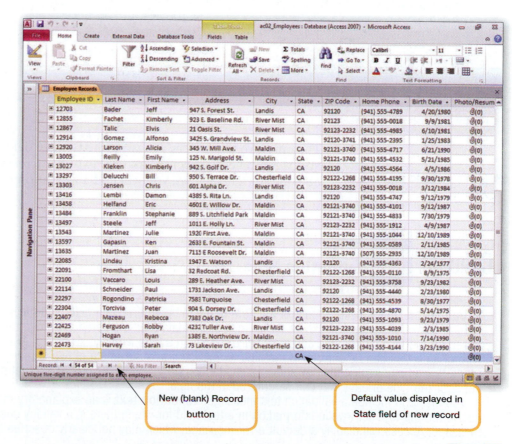

Figure 2.6

You can see that records 3 (Mark Pennington) and 10 (Scott Briggs) now correctly display the state in capital letters. Setting the format for the field will prevent this type of error from occurring again.

3

● Click ▶ New (blank) Record on the navigation bar to move to a new record.

Your screen should be similar to **Figure 2.7**

Figure 2.7

The new blank record at the end of the table displays CA as the default value for the State field. If you did need to enter a different state, it would display in all capital letters because of the Format property setting associated with the field.

DEFINING VALIDATION RULES

After looking at the fields, you decide to add a Gender field between the Home Phone and Birth Date fields. The field will need to have restrictions set so that it only accepts a single character, either "f" or "m", and formats it for uppercase. To create this customized field, you will switch to Design view to insert and define the new field.

1

- Switch to Design view.

- Make the Birth Date field current.

- Click ⊐⋅◼ Insert Rows in the Tools group of the Design tab to insert a blank field definition row.

- Enter the new field definitions from the table shown here:

Field Name	Gender
Data Type	Text
Description	Enter f for female and m for male.
Field Size	1
Format	>

Your screen should be similar to Figure 2.8

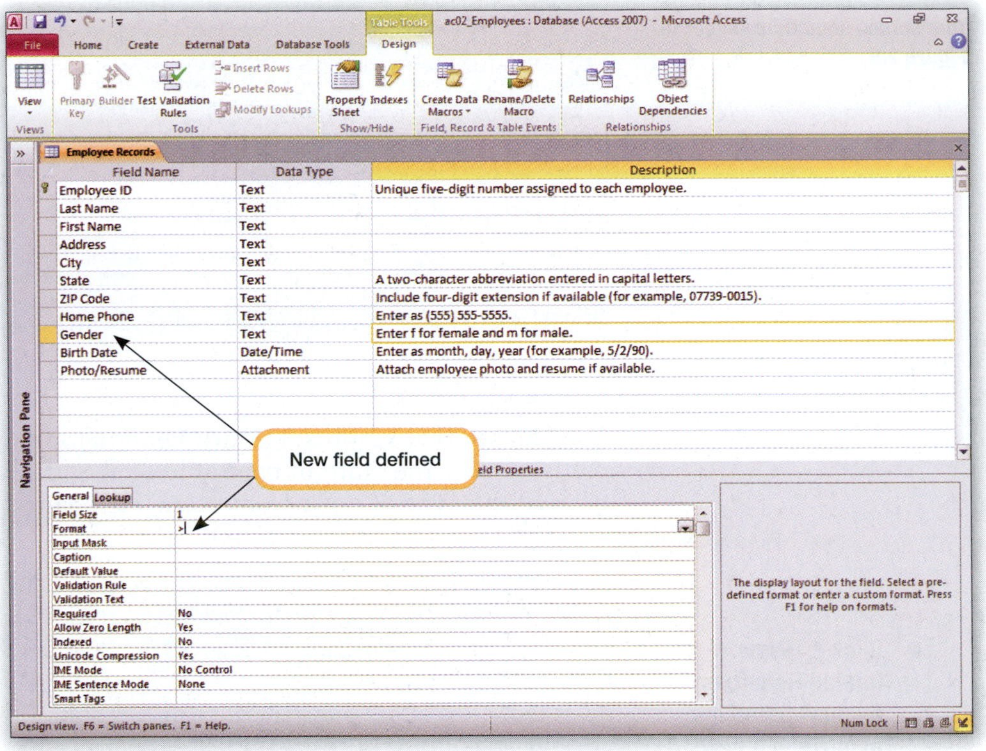

Figure 2.8

The only two characters you want the Gender field to accept are F for female and M for male. To specify that these two characters are the only entries acceptable in the Gender field, you will add a validation rule to the field's properties.

Concept **3** Validation Rule

A **validation rule** is used to control the data that can be entered in a field by defining the input values that are valid or allowed. Certain checks on the validity of the data that is entered in a field are performed automatically based on the field's data type and size. For example, in a field whose data type is Number and size is five, the type of data that can be entered in the field is restricted to a maximum of five numeric entries. You can further refine these basic restrictions by adding a validation rule to the field's properties that defines specific restrictions for the type of data that can be entered in the field.

You also can include a validation text message. **Validation text** is an explanatory message that appears if a user attempts to enter invalid information in a text field for which there is a validity check. If you do not specify a message, Access will display a default error message, which may not clearly describe the reason for the error.

You will create a validation rule for the Gender field to restrict the data entry to the two valid characters. A validation rule is specified by entering an expression in the **Validation Rule property** that limits the values that can be entered in the field.

Concept 4 Expression

An **expression** is a formula consisting of a combination of symbols that will produce a single value. You create an expression by combining identifiers, operators, constants, and functions to produce the desired results. An **identifier** is an element that refers to the value of a field, a graphical object, or a property. In the expression [Sales Amount] + [Sales Tax], [Sales Amount] and [Sales Tax] are identifiers that refer to the values in the Sales Amount and Sales Tax fields. Identifiers are separated by dots or exclamation points. Each part of an identifier is surrounded by square brackets.

An **operator** is a symbol or word that indicates that an operation is to be performed. Common mathematical operators are + for addition, - for subtraction, * for multiplication, and / for division. A **comparison operator** is a symbol that allows you to make comparisons between two items. The following table describes the comparison operators:

Operator	Meaning
=	Equal to
< >	Not equal to
<	Less than
>	Greater than
<=	Less than or equal to
>=	Greater than or equal to

In addition, the OR and AND operators allow you to enter additional criteria in the same field or different fields.

Constants are numbers, dates, or character strings. Character strings such as "F", "M", or "Workout Gear" are enclosed in quotation marks. Dates are enclosed in pound signs (#), as in #1/1/99#. **Functions** are built-in formulas that perform certain types of calculations automatically. Functions begin with the function name, such as SUM, and are followed by the function **argument**, which specifies the data the function should use. Arguments are enclosed in parentheses.

The following table shows some examples of possible expressions.

Expression	Result
[Sales Amount] + [Sales Tax]	Sums values in two fields.
"F" OR "M"	Restricts entry to the letters F or M only.
>= #1/1/99# AND <= #12/31/99#	Restricts entries to dates greater than or equal to 1/1/99 and less than or equal to 12/31/99.
"Workout Gear"	Allows the entry Workout Gear only.
SUM([Pay])	Totals the values in the Pay field.

You will learn much more about entering expressions in later labs.

You will enter the expression to restrict the data entry in the Gender field to the letters "f" or "m." As you do, a drop-down list of available functions that begin with the character you are typing, in this case f or m, will be displayed. The context-sensitive menu appears anytime you can enter an expression and suggests identifiers and functions that could be used. This is the **IntelliSense** feature, which is designed to help you quickly type expressions and ensure their accuracy. You can continue typing to narrow the list of functions or identifiers, or you can select an item from the list and press ⏎Enter or Tab⇥, to have the highlighted suggestion entered for you. By continuing to type or by pressing an arrow key to move on, you can continue entering the expression and ignore the IntelliSense suggestions. You will also enter text in the **Validation Text property** to display a message to the user if data is entered incorrectly.

1

- **Move to the Validation Rule field property text box.**

- **Type f or m**

Additional Information

The AND and OR operators can be entered using uppercase or lowercase characters.

- **Press Esc to clear the drop-down list of functions, and then press Enter to complete the entry.**

- **For the validation text, type The only valid entry is f or m.**

Your screen should be similar to Figure 2.9

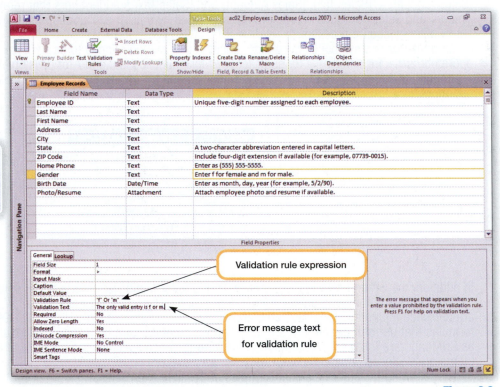

Figure 2.9

The expression you entered for the validation rule states that the only acceptable data values for this field must be equal to an F or an M. Notice that when you finished typing the validation rule, Access automatically added quotation marks around the two character strings and changed the "o" in "or" to uppercase. Because the Format property has been set to convert all entries to uppercase, a lowercase entry of f or m is as acceptable as the capitalized letters F or M.

Next, you will switch back to Datasheet view to test the validation rule by entering data for the Gender field. In addition to a message box asking whether you want to save the design changes, another message box will appear to advise you that the data integrity rules have been changed. When you restructure a table, you often make changes that could result in a loss of data. Changes such as shortening field sizes, creating validation rules, or changing field types can cause existing data to become invalid. Because the field is new, it has no data values to verify, and a validation check is unnecessary at this time.

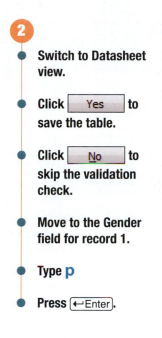

2

- **Switch to Datasheet view.**
- **Click [Yes] to save the table.**
- **Click [No] to skip the validation check.**
- **Move to the Gender field for record 1.**
- **Type p**
- **Press [↵Enter].**

Your screen should be similar to **Figure 2.10**

Figure 2.10

The new field was added to the table between the Home Phone and Birth Date fields. Because the letter p is not a valid entry, Access displays the error message you entered as the validation text for the field. You will clear the error message and correct the entry.

3

- Click [OK].

- Press [←Backspace].

- Type **m**

- Press [↓].

Your screen should be similar to Figure 2.11

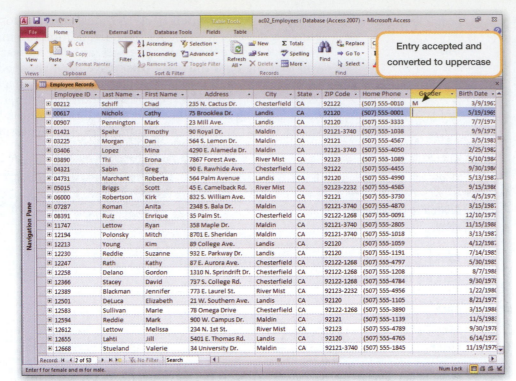

Figure 2.11

The entry for the first record is accepted and displayed as an uppercase M.

Hiding and Redisplaying Fields

To enter the gender data for the rest of the fields, you will use the First Name field as a guide. Unfortunately, the First Name and Gender fields are currently on opposite sides of the screen and will require you to look back and forth across each record. You can eliminate this problem by hiding the fields you do not need to see, and then redisplaying them when you have finished entering the gender data.

HIDING FIELDS

A quick way to view two fields side by side (in this case, the First Name and Gender fields) is to hide the fields that are in between (the Address through Home Phone fields).

1

● **Select the Address field through the Home Phone field.**

Additional Information

Drag along the column headings when the mouse pointer is to select the fields.

● **Right-click on the selection.**

● **Choose Hide Fields from the shortcut menu.**

Another Method

You also can click 🟦 More ▾ in the Records group of the Home tab and choose Hide Fields.

Your screen should be similar to Figure 2.12

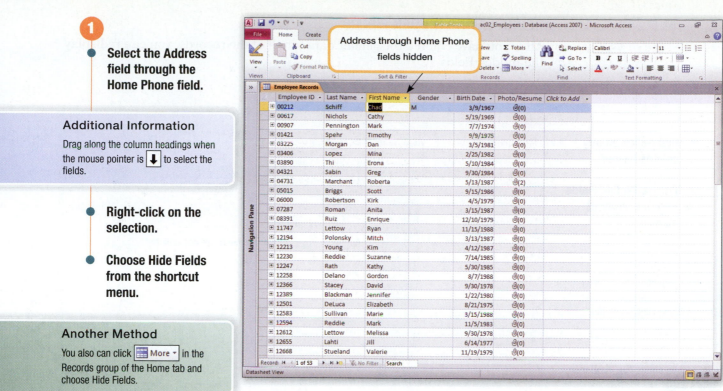

Figure 2.12

Now that the First Name and Gender columns are next to each other, you can refer to the first name in each record to enter the correct gender data.

2

● **Enter the Gender field values for the remaining records by looking at the First Name field to determine whether the employee is male or female.**

● **Reduce the size of the Gender column using the Best Fit command.**

Having Trouble?

Remember, to Best Fit data in a column, you double-click its right border.

Your screen should be similar to Figure 2.13

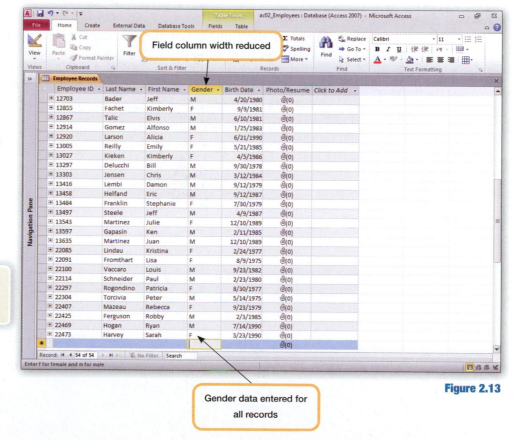

Gender data entered for all records

Figure 2.13

REDISPLAYING HIDDEN FIELDS

After you have entered the gender data for all of the records, you can redisplay the hidden fields.

- **Right-click on any column header.**

- **Choose Unhide Fields from the shortcut menu.**

Another Method

You also can click [More ▾] in the Records group of the Home tab and choose Unhide Columns.

Your screen should be similar to Figure 2.14

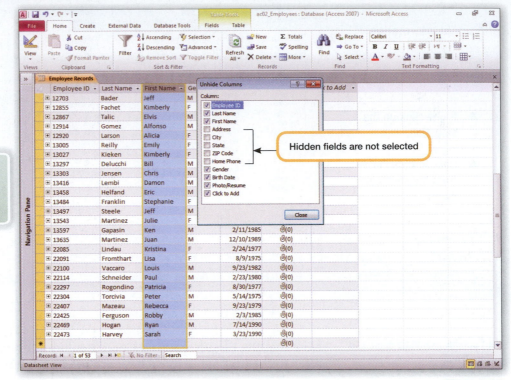

Figure 2.14

You use the Unhide Columns dialog box to select the currently hidden columns you want to redisplay. A checkmark in the box next to a column name indicates that the column is currently displayed; column names with no checkmarks indicate that they are currently hidden. You want to unhide all hidden columns in your table.

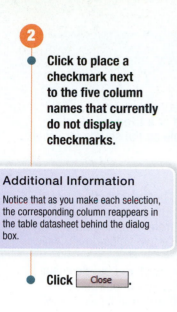

2 Click to place a checkmark next to the five column names that currently do not display checkmarks.

Additional Information

Notice that as you make each selection, the corresponding column reappears in the table datasheet behind the dialog box.

● Click Close .

Your screen should be similar to Figure 2.15

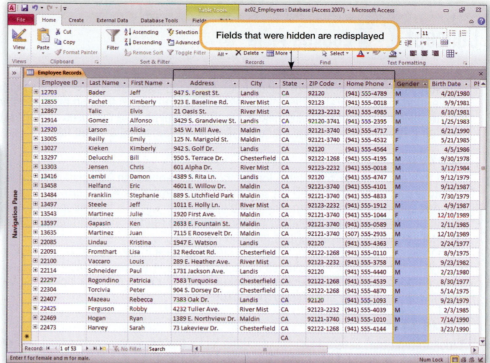

Figure 2.15

All of the fields are displayed again.

Creating a Lookup Field

Next you decide to change the Location field in the Job table to a lookup field that will make entering the location information easier, faster, and less prone to errors.

Concept 5 Lookup Field

A **lookup field** provides a list of values from which the user can choose to make entering data into that field simpler and more accurate. The lookup field can get the values from an existing table or a fixed set of values that are defined when the lookup field is created. A lookup field that uses another table as the source for values is called a **lookup list**, and one that uses fixed values is called a **value list**.

Lookup List

When the lookup field uses a table for the values it displays, an association is created between the two tables. Picking a value from the lookup list sets the foreign key value in the current record to the primary key value of the corresponding record in the related table. A foreign key is a field in one table that refers to the primary key field in another table and indicates how the tables are related. The field names of these two fields do not have to match, although their data types must be the same.

The related table displays but does not store the data in the record. The foreign key is stored but does not display. For this reason, any updates made to the data in the related table will be reflected in both the list and records in the table containing the lookup field. You must define a lookup list field from the table that will contain the foreign key and display the lookup list.

Value List

A lookup field that uses a fixed list of values looks the same as a lookup field that uses a table, except the fixed set of values is entered when the lookup field is created. A value list should be used only for values that will not change very often and do not need to be stored in a table. For example, a list for a Salutation field containing the abbreviations Mr., Mrs., or Ms. would be a good candidate for a value list. Choosing a value from a value list will store that value in the record—it does not create an association to a related table. For this reason, if you change any of the original values in the value list later, they will not be reflected in records added before this change was made.

There are three club locations: Landis, Chesterfield, and River Mist. You want the club locations to be displayed in a drop-down list so that anyone entering a new employee record can simply choose from this list to enter the club location.

USING THE LOOKUP WIZARD

The **Lookup Wizard** is used to create a lookup field that will allow you to select from a list of values. A **wizard** is a feature that guides you step by step through the process to perform a task. You will use the Lookup Wizard to change the existing Location field to a lookup field that uses fixed values.

1

- **Close the Employee Records table, saving any changes.**

- **Display the Navigation pane and open the Job table.**

- **Hide the Navigation pane and switch to Design view.**

- **Make the Location field active.**

- **Open the Data Type drop-down menu and choose Lookup Wizard.**

Your screen should be similar to Figure 2.16

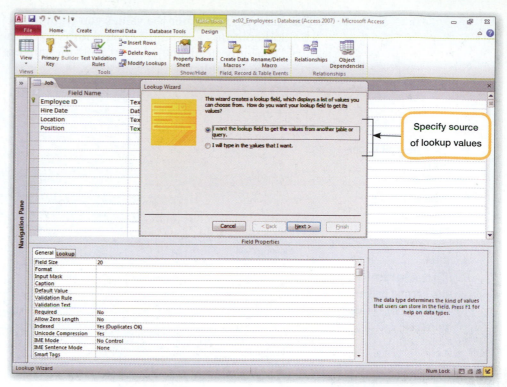

Specify source of lookup values

Figure 2.16

Additional Information

In Datasheet view, you can use in the Add & Delete group of the Table Tools Fields tab and choose More Fields ▾ to create a new field column and start the Lookup Wizard.

In the first Lookup Wizard dialog box, you specify the source for the values for the lookup field. You will enter your own values, the club locations, for this field.

2

- **Choose "I will type in the values that I want."**

- **Click Next >.**

Your screen should be similar to Figure 2.17

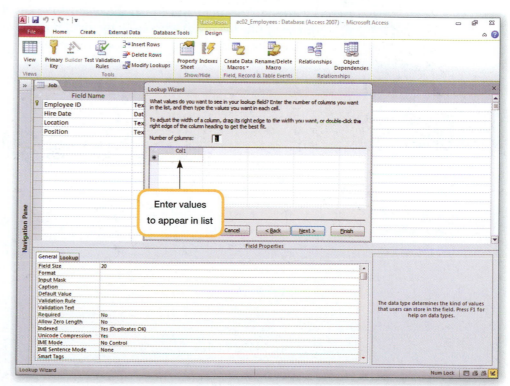

Enter values to appear in list

Figure 2.17

Creating a Lookup Field

The next step is to enter the values you want listed in the lookup field. You also can add columns and adjust their widths to fit the values you enter, if necessary. You only need one column, and the current width is sufficient for the values you will enter.

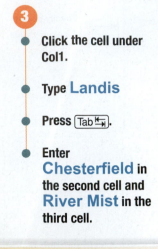

3

- Click the cell under **Col1.**

- Type **Landis**

- Press [Tab ⇆].

- Enter **Chesterfield** in the second cell and **River Mist** in the third cell.

Having Trouble?

You can correct these entries the same way you do when entering data into any other field.

Your screen should be similar to
Figure 2.18

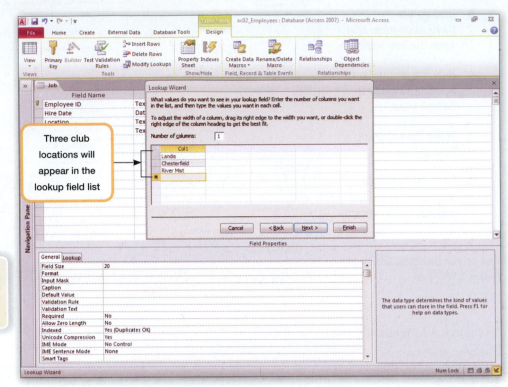

Figure 2.18

After entering the field values, you will move to the next step to enter a label for the lookup field and finish the wizard. You will leave the field name label as Location. Then you will check the field property settings established for this field to see whether any changes are necessary.

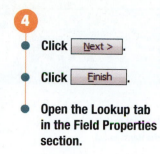

4

- Click **Next >**.

- Click **Finish**.

- Open the **Lookup** tab in the Field Properties section.

Your screen should be similar to **Figure 2.19**

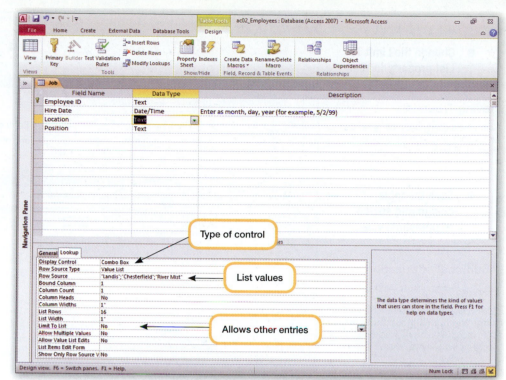

Type of control

List values

Allows other entries

Figure 2.19

Before you clicked on the Lookup tab, you may have noticed that the property settings for the Location field looked like nothing had changed; the data type is still Text. By clicking the Lookup tab, you can see the values you typed in the Lookup Wizard listed in the Row Source property box. The Row Source Type is a Value List and will display in a Combo Box (drop-down list) control when in Datasheet view, as well as on any forms where this field is used. The other properties are set to the defaults for lookup fields. The only change you want to make is to restrict the data entry in that field to values in the lookup list. Then you will test that the Location field is performing correctly by entering a location that is not in the list.

5 Change the Limit To List property to Yes.

Having Trouble?

Select the property and click at the end of the box to open the drop-down menu of options.

● Save the table design and switch to Datasheet view.

Additional Information

The Save button in the Quick

Access Toolbar will save the table design changes. If you do not save the table design before switching views, Access will prompt you to save it.

● Click in the Location field of the first record.

● Select and replace the current entry by typing **Maldin** and pressing ↵Enter.

Your screen should be similar to **Figure 2.20**

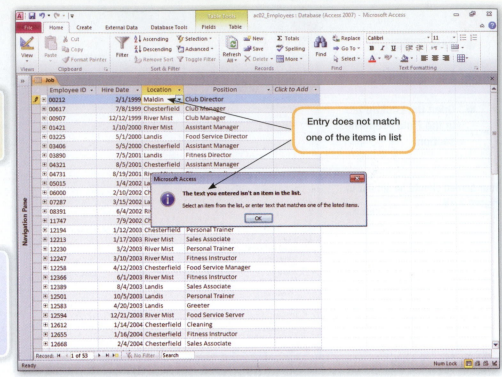

Figure 2.20

A warning box advises you that the entry is not one of the listed items because you restricted the field entries in the Location field to the lookup values you specified.

6

● Click [OK].

● Choose Landis from the list of locations.

● Press [←Enter].

Your screen should be similar to **Figure 2.21**

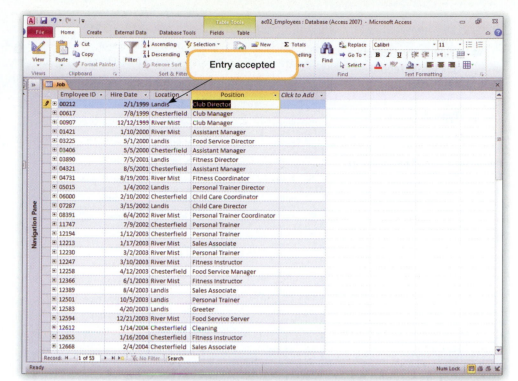

Figure 2.21

The Location lookup field is working correctly. Using a lookup field makes entering repetitive information faster and more accurate.

Searching for, Finding, and Replacing Data

Over the past few days, you have received several change request forms to update the employee records and a request to know how many fitness instructors there are in the company. Rather than having to scroll through all the records to locate the ones that need to be modified, you can use various methods to search for, find, and/or replace the data.

SEARCHING FOR DATA

While working in the Job table, you decide to find out how many fitness instructors are employed in the company first. One way to do this is to use the Search box to locate this information. The Search box is a useful tool to find any character(s) anywhere in the database. For example, it could be used to quickly locate a particular Employee ID number in order to update an address change. When you type in the Search box, Access will simultaneously highlight any possible fields that match. The more characters you type in the Search box, the more accurate the search response will be. Additionally, this feature is not case sensitive.

You want to search for "Fitness Instructor".

1

● Click in the Search box in the record navigation bar.

● Type in **fi**

Your screen should be similar to Figure 2.22

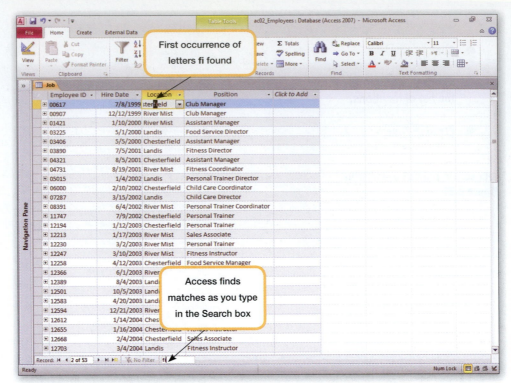

Figure 2.22

Notice that Access highlighted the "fi" in Chester**fi**eld. You will continue to type the word "Fitness" in the Search box, and notice that as you enter more text, the search is refined to more closely locate what you are looking for.

2

● Continue to type the word **fitness** in the Search box (Fitness Director is located)

● Press Spacebar and type **in** to locate the first record containing the text Fitness Instructor.

● Press ←Enter to move to the next record containing the search text.

Your screen should be similar to Figure 2.23

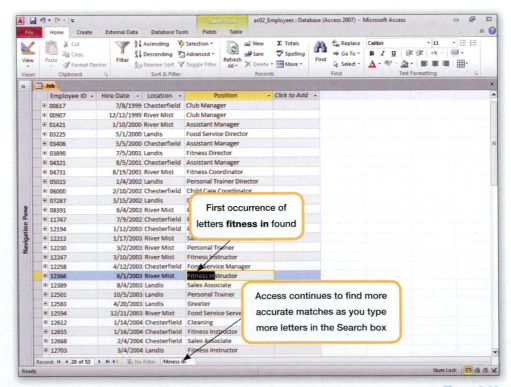

Figure 2.23

The next record in the search that matches the characters "fitness in" is selected. Because it is now locating the information you want to find, you do not need to complete the word "instructor". Notice that each time the enter key is pressed, the selection moves to the next record until it reaches the last matching set of characters.

3

Continue pressing to locate all fitness instructor records.

When the last field matching the search text is selected, it will remain highlighted and Access will go no further; no message will appear telling you there are no more matches. If you were counting, there were seven fitness instructors. Although this method worked to find out the number of fitness instructors, you will learn later in this lab about another, more effective way to gather this information.

FINDING DATA

Now you will work on making the changes to update the employee records from the change requests forms you have received. Rather than use the Search box to locate the records to change, you will use the Find and Replace feature.

Concept 6 Find and Replace

The **Find and Replace** feature helps you quickly find specific information and automatically replace it with new information. The Find command will locate all specified values in a field, and the Replace command will both find a value and automatically replace it with another. For example, in a table containing supplier and item prices, you may need to increase the price of all items supplied by one manufacturer. To quickly locate these items, you would use the Find command to locate all records with the name of the manufacturer and then update the price appropriately. Alternatively, you could use the Replace command if you knew that all items priced at $11.95 were increasing to $15.99. This command would locate all values matching the original price and replace them with the new price.

Finding and replacing data is fast and accurate, but you need to be careful when replacing not to replace unintended matches.

The first change request is for Melissa Lettow, who recently married and has both a name and address change. To quickly locate the correct record, you will use the Find command. This information is in the Last Name field of the Employee Records table.

1

- Close the Job table.

- Open the Employee Records table.

- Close the Navigation Pane.

- Click in the Last Name field of record 1 in the Employee Records table.

- Click 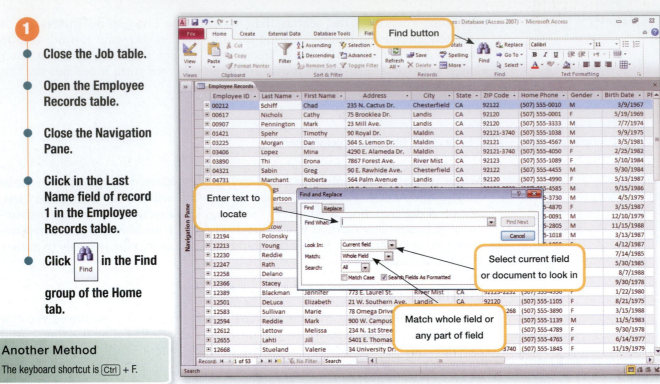 in the Find group of the Home tab.

Another Method

The keyboard shortcut is Ctrl + F.

Figure 2.24

Your screen should be similar to Figure 2.24

You use the Find and Replace dialog box to specify the information you are looking for and the way that you want Access to search the table. In the Find What text box, you specify the **criteria**, or a set of limiting conditions, records must meet by entering the text you want to locate. You can enter a specific character string or use wildcards to specify the criteria. **Wildcards** are symbols that are used to represent characters. The * symbol represents any collection of characters and the ? symbol represents any individual character. For example, ?ar will locate any three-letter text such as bar, far, and car. In contrast, *ar will locate the same text, but in addition will expand the criteria to locate any text ending with ar, such as star, popular, and modular.

Access defaults to search the entire current document, and matches any part of the field. You can change these settings and further refine your search by using the options described in the following table.

Option	Effect
Look In	Searches the current field or the entire table for the specified text.
Match	Locates matches to the whole field, any part of the field, or the start of the field.
Search	Specifies the direction in which the table will be searched: All (search all records); Down (search down from the current insertion point location in the field); or Up (search up from the current insertion point location in the field).
Match Case	Finds words that have the same pattern of uppercase letters as entered in the Find What text box. Using this option makes the search case sensitive.
Search Fields as Formatted	Finds data based on its display format.

With the cursor in the field you want to search, you will change the Look In location to search only that field. If you wanted to search on a different field, you could click on the field you want in the datasheet without closing the dialog box. You also will change it to match the whole field. The other default option to search all records is appropriately set.

Once your settings are as you want them, you will use the * wildcard to find all employees whose last names begin with "L".

2

- Change the Look In setting to Current field.

- Change the Match setting to Whole Field.

- Type **l*** in the Find What text box.

- Click [Find Next] eight times to move from one located record to the next.

Your screen should be similar to Figure 2.25

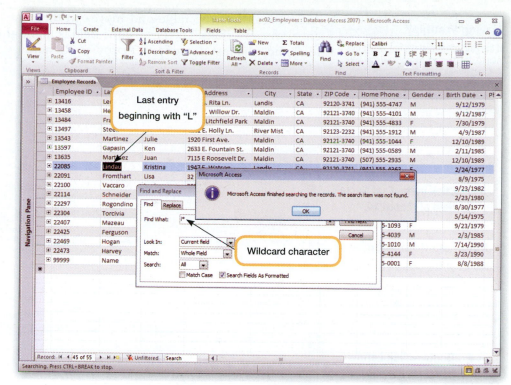

Figure 2.25

Using the wildcard located seven employees whose last names start with the letter "L". The more specific you can make your criteria, the more quickly you can locate the information you want to find. In this case, you want to find a specific last name, so you will enter the complete name in the Find What text box.

3

- Click [OK] to close the finished searching informational box.

- Select the entry in the Find What text box and type **lettow**

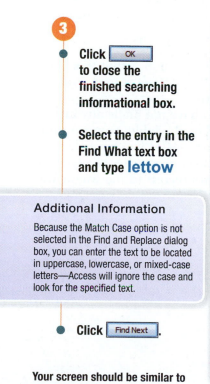

Additional Information

Because the Match Case option is not selected in the Find and Replace dialog box, you can enter the text to be located in uppercase, lowercase, or mixed-case letters—Access will ignore the case and look for the specified text.

- Click [Find Next].

Your screen should be similar to Figure 2.26

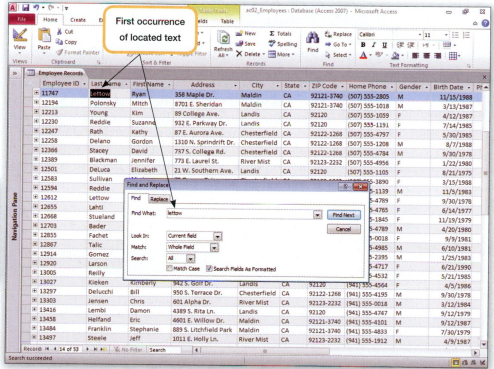

Figure 2.26

Having Trouble?

If the Find command did not locate this record, try it again. Make sure that you entered the name "lettow" (uppercase or lowercase) correctly and that Last Name is the selected field in the Look In box.

Access searches the table and moves to the first located occurrence of the entry you specified. The Last Name field is highlighted in record 14. You need to change the last name from Lettow to Richards.

- **Click in the Last Name field of record 14.**

Additional Information

You do not need to close the Find and Replace dialog box before you make a change to the table. You will be using this dialog box again to perform more searches, so leave it open for now.

- **Double-click Lettow to select the entry.**

- **Type Richards**

- **Press** ⏎Enter.

Your screen should be similar to Figure 2.27

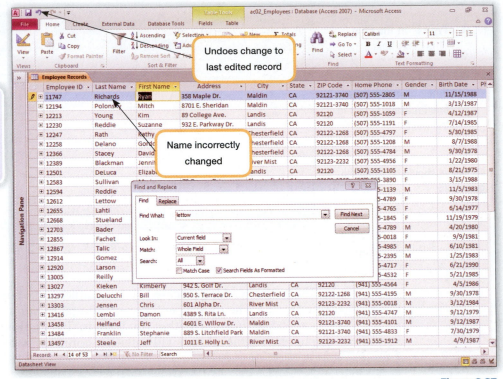

Figure 2.27

Now that the highlight is on the First Name field, you notice that this is the record for Ryan Lettow, not Melissa. You changed the wrong record. You will use the Undo command next to quickly fix this error.

Undo will cancel your last action as long as you have not made any further changes to the table. Even if you save the record or the table, you can undo changes to the last edited record by clicking ↶ Undo. After you have changed another record or moved to another window, however, the earlier change cannot be undone. You will use Undo to return Ryan's record to the way it was before you made the change.

Additional Information

Refer to the section Undoing and Redoing Editing Changes in the Introduction to Microsoft Office 2010 to review the Undo feature.

5 ● Click 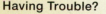 Undo.

Another Method

The keyboard shortcut is Ctrl + Z.

Your screen should be similar to Figure 2.28

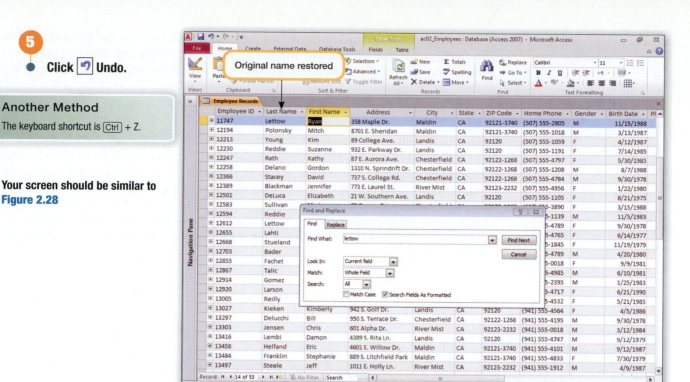

Figure 2.28

The original field value of Lettow is restored. Now you want to continue the search to locate the next record with the last name of Lettow.

6

● Move back to the Last Name field of record 14.

● Click Find Next in the Find and Replace dialog box.

● When Access locates the record for Melissa Lettow (record 25), change her last name to **Richards** and the address to **5522 W. Marin Lane**

Having Trouble?

If necessary, move the Find and Replace dialog box.

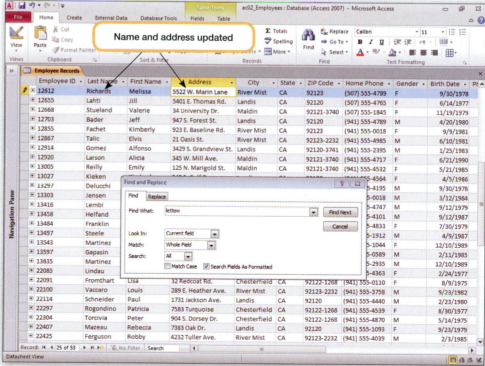

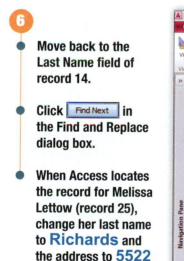

Your screen should be similar to Figure 2.29

Figure 2.29

The Find method works well when you need to locate an individual field in order to view the data and/or modify it. However, when you need to make the same change to more than one record, the Replace command is the quicker method because it both finds and replaces the data.

REPLACING DATA

You have checked with the U.S. Postal Service and learned that all ZIP Codes of 92120 have a four-digit extension of 3741. To locate all the records with this ZIP Code, you could look at the ZIP Code field for each record to find the match and then edit the field to add the extension. If the table is small, this method would be acceptable. For large tables, however, this method could be quite time-consuming and more prone to errors. A more efficient way is to search the table to find specific values in records and then replace the entry with another.

1

- Move to the ZIP Code field of record 1.

- Open the Replace tab.

Another Method

You can use ab̲ac Replace in the Find group, or the keyboard shortcut of Ctrl + H, to open the Find and Replace dialog box and display the Replace tab.

Your screen should be similar to Figure 2.30

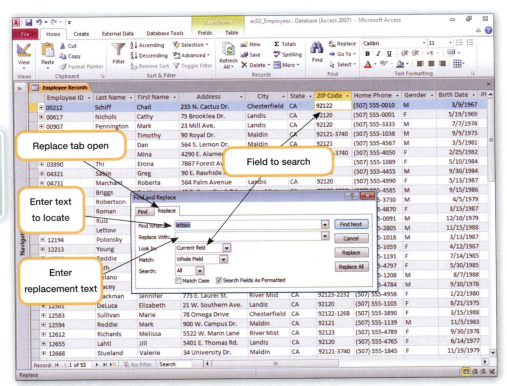

Figure 2.30

The options in the Replace tab are the same as those in the Find tab, with the addition of a Replace With text box, where you enter the replacement text exactly as you want it to appear in your table.

2

- In the Find What text box, type **92120**

- Press [Tab] to move to the Replace With text box.

- Type **92120-3741**

- Click [Find Next].

Your screen should be similar to
Figure 2.31

Having Trouble?

If necessary, move the dialog box so you can see the highlighted entry.

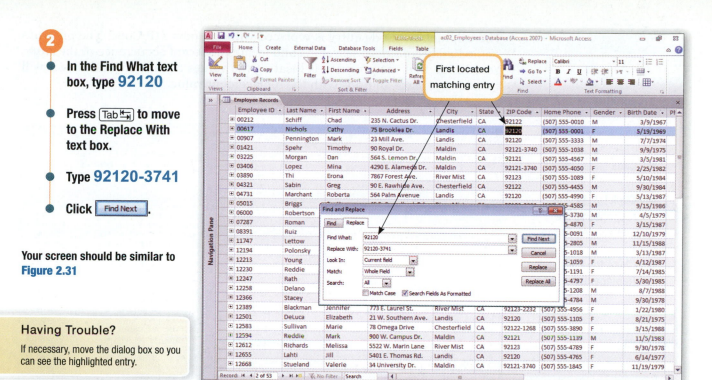

Figure 2.31

Immediately, the highlight moves to the first occurrence of text in the document that matches the Find What text and highlights it. You can now replace this text with the click of a button.

3

- Click [Replace].

Your screen should be similar to
Figure 2.32

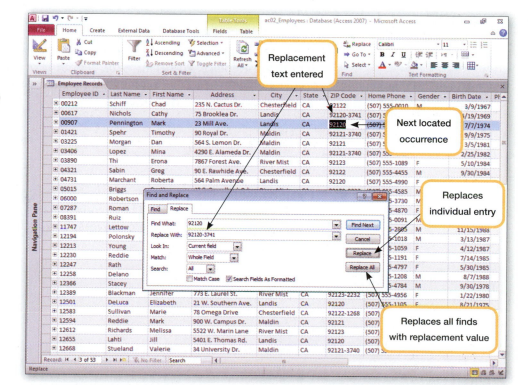

The original ZIP Code entry is replaced with the new ZIP Code. The program immediately continues searching and locates a second occurrence of the entry. You decide that the program is locating the values accurately and that it will be safe to replace all finds with the replacement value.

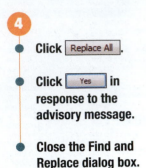

4

- Click Replace All.

- Click Yes in response to the advisory message.

- Close the Find and Replace dialog box.

Your screen should be similar to Figure 2.33

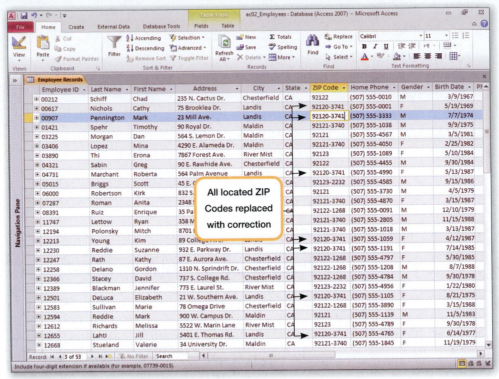

Figure 2.33

All matches are replaced with the replacement text. It is much faster to use Replace All than to confirm each match separately. However, exercise care when using Replace All because the search text you specify might be part of another field and you may accidentally replace text you want to keep.

Sorting Records

As you may recall from Lab 1, the records are ordered according to the primary key field, Employee ID. The accounting manager, however, has asked you for an alphabetical list of all employees. To do this, you will sort the records in the table.

Concept **7** Sorting

Sorting rearranges the order of the records in a table based on the value in each field. Sorting data helps you find specific information more quickly without having to browse the data. You can sort data in **ascending sort order** (A to Z or 0 to 9) or **descending sort order** (Z to A or 9 to 0).

You can sort all records in a table by a single field, such as State, or you can select adjacent columns and sort by more than one field, such as State and then City. When sorting on multiple fields, you begin by selecting the columns to sort. Access sorts records starting with the column farthest left (the outermost field) and then moves to the right across the selected columns to sort the innermost fields. For example, if you want to sort by state, and then by city, the State field must be to the left of the City field. The State field is the outermost field and the city field is the innermost field.

Access saves the new sort order with your table data and reapplies it automatically each time you open the table. To return to the primary key sort order, you must remove the temporary sort.

SORTING ON A SINGLE FIELD

You will sort the records on a single field, Last Name. To perform a sort on a single field, you move to the field on which you will base the sort and click the button that corresponds to the type of sort you want to do. In this case, you will sort the Last Name field in ascending alphabetical order.

1

- **Move to the Last Name field of any record.**

- **Click** ⬆️ Ascending **in the Sort & Filter group of the Home tab.**

Additional Information

Clicking ⬇️ Descending arranges the data in descending sort order.

Your screen should be similar to Figure 2.34

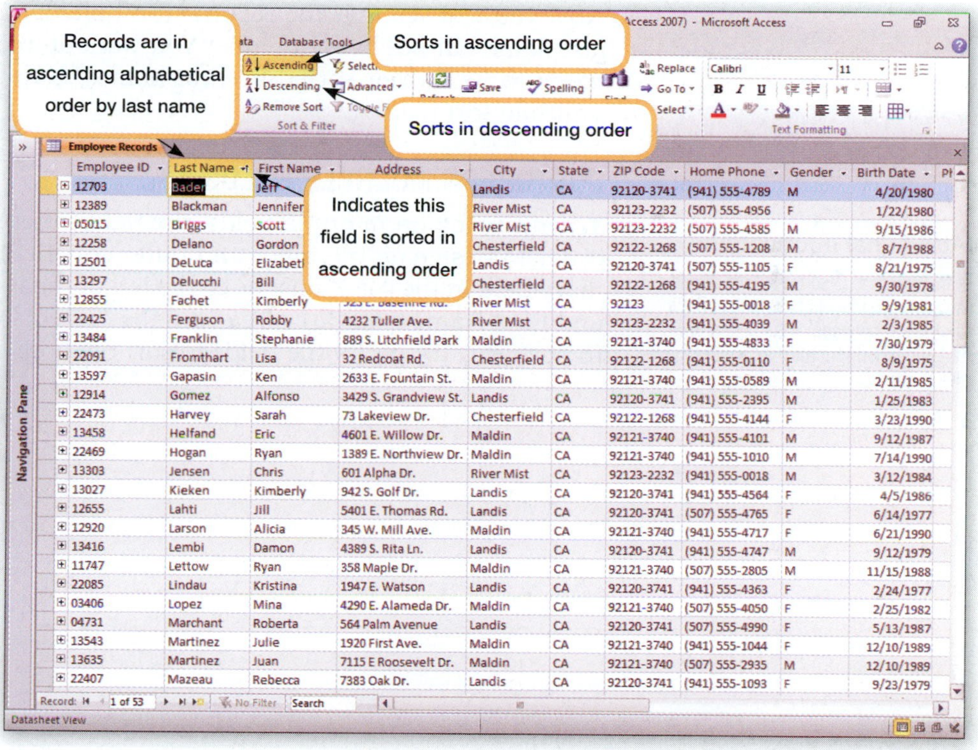

Figure 2.34

The employee records are displayed in alphabetical order by last name. The Last Name field header displays a 🔽 to show that the field is in ascending sorted order. Next, you want to check the rest of the table to see if there is anything else you need to do.

2

● Use the scroll box to scroll down to record 25.

Additional Information

As you drag the scroll box, the record location is displayed in a Screen Tip (for example, "Record 25 of 53").

Your screen should be similar to Figure 2.35

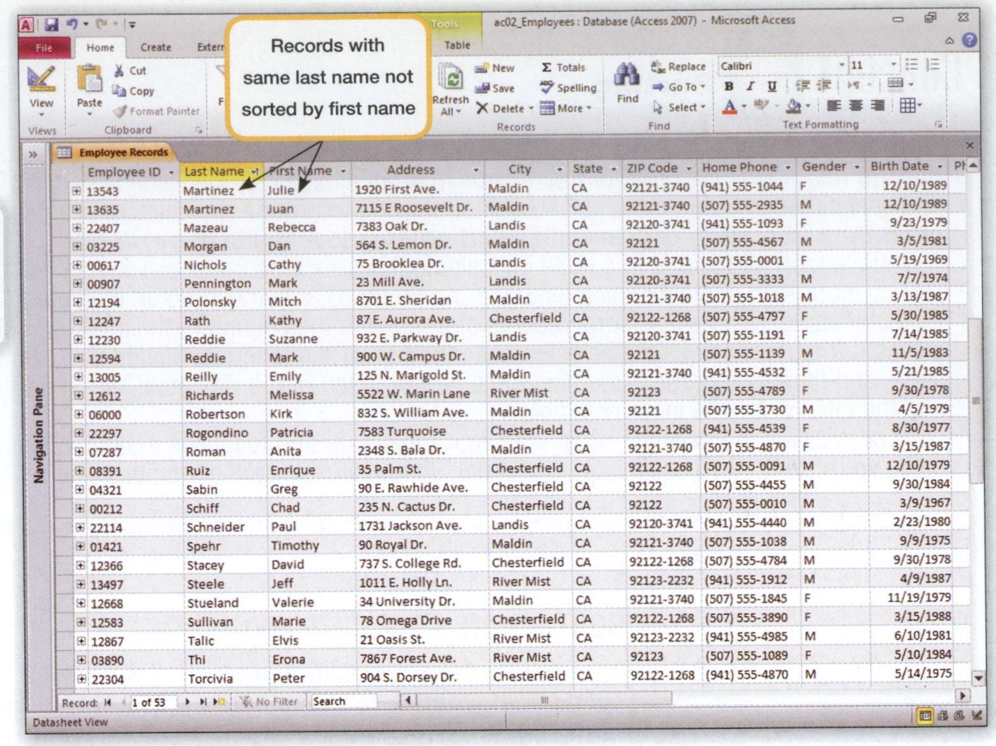

Figure 2.35

Now you can see that the records for Julie and Juan Martinez are sorted by last name but not by first name. You want all records that have the same last name to be further sorted by first name. To do this, you need to sort using multiple sort fields.

SORTING ON MULTIPLE FIELDS

Additional Information

If the columns to sort were not already adjacent, you would hide the columns that are in between. If the columns were not in the correct order, you would move the columns.

When sorting on multiple fields, the fields must be adjacent to each other in order to designate the inner and outer sort fields. The **outer sort field** (primary field in the sort) must be to the left of the inner sort field. The Last Name and First Name fields are already in the correct locations for the sort you want to perform. To specify the fields to sort on, both columns must be selected.

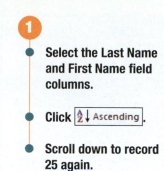

1

- Select the **Last Name** and **First Name** field columns.

- Click ⬇️ Ascending.

- Scroll down to record 25 again.

Your screen should be similar to Figure 2.36

Records with same last name also sorted by first name

Employee ID	Last Name	First Name	Address	City	State	ZIP Code	Home Phone	Gender	Birth Date	Ph
⊞ 13635	Martinez	Juan	7115 E Roosevelt Dr.	Maldin	CA	92121-3740	(507) 555-2935	M	12/10/1989	
⊞ 13543	Martinez	Julie	1920 First Ave.	Maldin	CA	92121-3740	(941) 555-1044	F	12/10/1989	
⊞ 22407	Mazeau	Rebecca	7383 Oak Dr.	Landis	CA	92120-3741	(941) 555-1093	F	9/23/1979	
⊞ 03225	Morgan	Dan	564 S. Lemon Dr.	Maldin	CA	92121	(507) 555-4567	M	3/5/1981	
⊞ 00617	Nichols	Cathy	75 Brooklea Dr.	Landis	CA	92120-3741	(507) 555-0001	F	5/19/1969	
⊞ 00907	Pennington	Mark	23 Mill Ave.	Landis	CA	92120-3741	(507) 555-3333	M	7/7/1974	
⊞ 12194	Polonsky	Mitch	8701 E. Sheridan	Maldin	CA	92121-3740	(507) 555-1018	M	3/13/1987	
⊞ 12247	Rath	Kathy	87 E. Aurora Ave.	Chesterfield	CA	92122-1268	(507) 555-4797	F	5/30/1985	
⊞ 12594	Reddie	Mark	900 W. Campus Dr.	Maldin	CA	92121	(507) 555-1139	M	11/5/1983	
⊞ 12230	Reddie	Suzanne	932 E. Parkway Dr.	Landis	CA	92120-3741	(507) 555-1191	F	7/14/1985	
⊞ 13005	Reilly	Emily	125 N. Marigold St.	Maldin	CA	92121-3740	(941) 555-4532	F	5/21/1985	
⊞ 12612	Richards	Melissa	5522 W. Marin Lane	River Mist	CA	92123	(507) 555-4789	F	9/30/1978	
⊞ 06000	Robertson	Kirk	832 S. William Ave.	Maldin	CA	92121	(507) 555-3730	M	4/5/1979	
⊞ 22297	Rogondino	Patricia	7583 Turquoise	Chesterfield	CA	92122-1268	(941) 555-4539	F	8/30/1977	
⊞ 07287	Roman	Anita	2348 S. Bala Dr.	Maldin	CA	92121-3740	(507) 555-4870	F	3/15/1987	
⊞ 08391	Ruiz	Enrique	35 Palm St.	Chesterfield	CA	92122-1268	(507) 555-0091	M	12/10/1979	
⊞ 04321	Sabin	Greg	90 E. Rawhide Ave.	Chesterfield	CA	92122	(507) 555-4455	M	9/30/1984	
⊞ 00212	Schiff	Chad	235 N. Cactus Dr.	Chesterfield	CA	92122	(507) 555-0010	M	3/9/1967	
⊞ 22114	Schneider	Paul	1731 Jackson Ave.	Landis	CA	92120-3741	(941) 555-4440	M	2/23/1980	
⊞ 01421	Spehr	Timothy	90 Royal Dr.	Maldin	CA	92121-3740	(507) 555-1038	M	9/9/1975	
⊞ 12366	Stacey	David	737 S. College Rd.	Chesterfield	CA	92122-1268	(507) 555-4784	M	9/30/1978	
⊞ 13497	Steele	Jeff	1011 E. Holly Ln.	River Mist	CA	92123-2232	(941) 555-1912	M	4/9/1987	
⊞ 12668	Stueland	Valerie	34 University Dr.	Maldin	CA	92121-3740	(507) 555-1845	F	11/19/1979	
⊞ 12583	Sullivan	Marie	78 Omega Drive	Chesterfield	CA	92122-1268	(507) 555-3890	F	3/15/1988	
⊞ 12867	Talic	Elvis	21 Oasis St.	River Mist	CA	92123-2232	(941) 555-4985	M	6/10/1981	
⊞ 03890	Thi	Erona	7867 Forest Ave.	River Mist	CA	92123	(507) 555-1089	F	5/10/1984	
⊞ 22304	Torcivia	Peter	904 S. Dorsey Dr.	Chesterfield	CA	92122-1268	(941) 555-4870	M	5/14/1975	

Record: 1 of 53   No Filter   Search

Datasheet View

Figure 2.36

The record for Juan Martinez now appears before the record for Julie. As you can see, sorting is a fast, useful tool. The sort order remains in effect until you remove the sort or replace it with a new sort order. Although Access remembers your sort order even when you exit the program, it does not actually change the table records.

You can remove the sort at any time to restore the records to the primary key sort order. You decide to return to primary key sort order and re-sort the table alphabetically for the Accounting department later, after you have finished making changes to it.

2

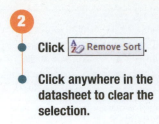

- Click **Remove Sort**.

- Click anywhere in the datasheet to clear the selection.

Your screen should be similar to Figure 2.37

Employee ID	Last Name	First Name	Address	City	State	ZIP Code	Home Phone	Gender	Birth Date
⊞ 00212	Schiff	Chad	235 N. Cactus Dr.	Chesterfield	CA	92122	(507) 555-0010	M	3/9/1967
⊞ 00617	Nichols	Cathy	75 Brooklea Dr.	Landis	CA	92120-3741	(507) 555-0001	F	5/19/1969
⊞ 00907	Pennington	Mark	23 Mill Ave.	Landis	CA	92120-3741	(507) 555-3333	M	7/7/1974
⊞ 01421	Spehr	Timothy	90 Royal Dr.	Maldin	CA	92121-3740	(507) 555-1038	M	9/9/1975
⊞ 03225	Morgan	Dan	564 S. Lemon Dr.	Maldin	CA	92121	(507) 555-4567	M	3/5/1981
⊞ 03406	Lopez	Mina	4290 E. Alameda Dr.	Maldin	CA	92121-3740	(507) 555-4050	F	2/25/1982
⊞ 03890	Thi	Erona	7867 Forest Ave.	River Mist	CA	92123	(507) 555-1089	F	5/10/1984
⊞ 04321	Sabin	Greg	90 E. Rawhide Ave.	Chesterfield	CA	92122	(507) 555-4455	M	9/30/1984
⊞ 04731	Marchant	Roberta	564 Palm Avenue	Landis	CA	92120-3741	(507) 555-4990	F	5/13/1987
⊞ 05015	Briggs	Scott	45 E. Camelback Rd.	River Mist	CA	92123-2232	(507) 555-4585	M	9/15/1986
⊞ 06000	Robertson	Kirk	832 S. William Ave.	Maldin	CA	92121	(507) 555-3730	M	4/5/1979
⊞ 07287	Roman	Anita	2348 S. Bala Dr.	Maldin	CA	92121-3740	(507) 555-4870	F	3/15/1987
⊞ 08391	Ruiz	Enrique	35 Palm St.	Chesterfield	CA	92122-1268	(507) 555-0091	M	12/10/1979
⊞ 11747	Lettow	Ryan	358 Maple Dr.	Maldin	CA	92121-3740	(507) 555-2805	M	11/15/1988
⊞ 12194	Polonsky	Mitch	8701 E. Sheridan	Maldin	CA	92121-3740	(507) 555-1018	M	3/13/1987
⊞ 12213	Young	Kim	89 College Ave.	Landis	CA	92120-3741	(507) 555-1059	F	4/12/1987
⊞ 12230	Reddie	Suzanne	932 E. Parkway Dr.	Maldin	CA	92120-3741	(507) 555-1191	F	7/14/1985
⊞ 12247	Rath	Kathy	87 E. Aurora Ave.	Chesterfield	CA	92122-1268	(507) 555-4797	F	5/30/1985
⊞ 12258	Delano	Gordon	1310 N. Sprindrift Dr.	Chesterfield	CA	92122-1268	(507) 555-1208	M	8/7/1988
⊞ 12366	Stacey	David	737 S. College Rd.	Chesterfield	CA	92122-1268	(507) 555-4784	M	9/30/1978
⊞ 12389	Blackman	Jennifer	773 E. Laurel St.	River Mist	CA	92123-2232	(507) 555-4956	F	1/22/1980
⊞ 12501	DeLuca	Elizabeth	21 W. Southern Ave.	Landis	CA	92120-3741	(507) 555-1105	F	8/21/1975
⊞ 12583	Sullivan	Marie	78 Omega Drive	Chesterfield	CA	92122-1268	(507) 555-3890	F	3/15/1988
⊞ 12594	Reddie	Mark	900 W. Campus Dr.	Maldin	CA	92121	(507) 555-1139	M	11/5/1983
⊞ 12612	Richards	Melissa	5522 W. Marin Lane	River Mist	CA	92123	(507) 555-4789	F	9/30/1978
⊞ 12655	Lahti	Jill	5401 E. Thomas Rd.	Landis	CA	92120-3741	(507) 555-4765	F	6/14/1977
⊞ 12668	Stueland	Valerie	34 University Dr.	Maldin	CA	92121-3740	(507) 555-1845	F	11/19/1979

Records sorted by primary key value

Clears sort order

Unique five-digit number assigned to each employee.

Record: 1 of 53   No Filter   Search

Figure 2.37

All the sorts are cleared, and the data in the table is now in order by the primary key field, Employee ID.

FORMATTING THE DATASHEET

Finally, you want to format or enhance the appearance of the datasheet on the screen to make it more readable or attractive by applying different effects. Datasheet formats include settings that change the appearance of the cell, gridlines, background and gridline colors, and border and line styles. In addition, you can change the text color and add text effects such as bold and italics to the datasheet. Datasheet formats affect the entire datasheet appearance and cannot be applied to separate areas of the datasheet.

CHANGING BACKGROUND AND GRIDLINE COLORS

The default datasheet format displays alternate rows in white and light gray backgrounds with a gridline color of blue. The text color is set to black. You want to see the effect of changing the color of the alternate rows and gridlines in the datasheet.

Additional Information

Refer to the section Formatting Text in the Introduction to Microsoft Office 2010 to review formatting features.

1

Click ⬜ in the Text Formatting group of the Home tab to open the Datasheet Formatting dialog box.

Your screen should be similar to Figure 2.38

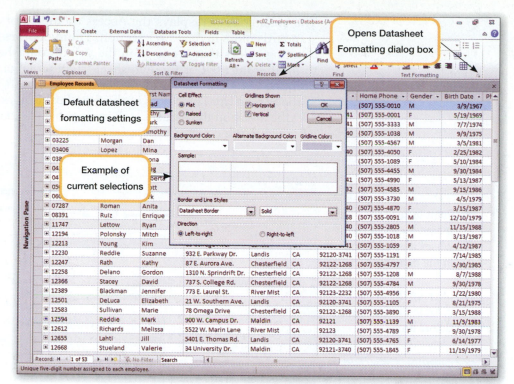

Figure 2.38

The default datasheet formatting settings are displayed in the dialog box, and the Sample area shows how the settings will appear in the datasheet. You will leave the background color white and change the color of the alternate rows.

2

Open the Alternate Background Color drop-down menu.

Your screen should be similar to Figure 2.39

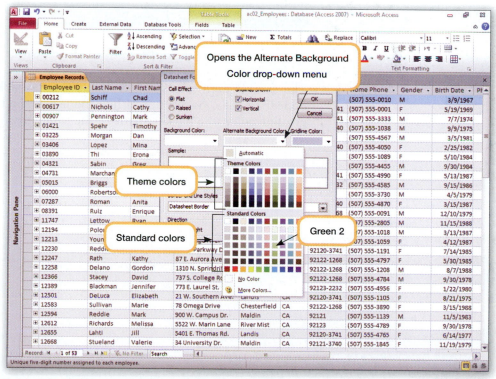

Figure 2.39

The color gallery displays the Access theme colors in the upper section and standard colors in the lower section. **Theme colors** are a combination of coordinating colors that are used in the default datasheet. Each color is assigned to a different area of the datasheet, such as label text or table background. Pointing to a theme color identifies the name of the color and where it is used in the ScreenTip. The colors in the Standard Colors gallery are not assigned to specific areas on the datasheet. Pointing to a standard color displays the name assigned to the color.

3

• Point to several theme colors to see where they are used in the datasheet.

• Click on the Green 2 color in the Standard Colors area.

Another Method

You also can use [icon] ▾ Alternate Row Color in the Text Formatting group to change the color.

Your screen should be similar to **Figure 2.40**

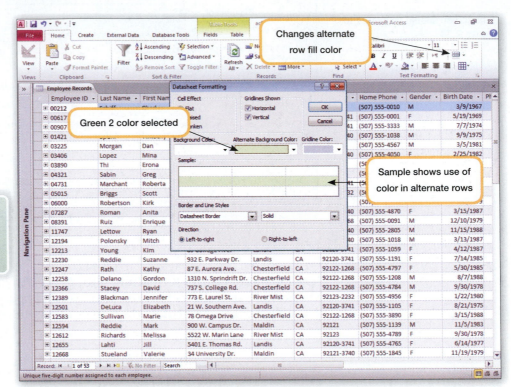

Figure 2.40

The sample area displays how the alternate background color selection will appear in the datasheet. You like the green shading and want to change the gridline color to a darker shade of the same green.

4

- Open the Gridline Color drop-down menu.

- Choose Green 5 from the Standard Colors area.

- Click [OK].

Your screen should be similar to
Figure 2.41

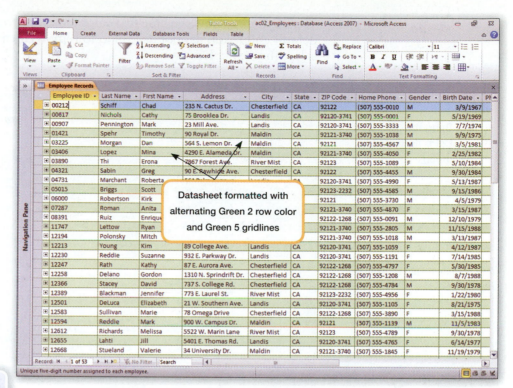

Datasheet formatted with alternating Green 2 row color and Green 5 gridlines

Figure 2.41

Additional Information

You can use Gridlines in the Text Formatting group to change the display of the gridlines.

The selected alternating row and gridline color formatting has been applied to the datasheet.

CHANGING THE TEXT COLOR

The datasheet background colors brighten the screen appearance, but you think the text is a little light, making it difficult to read. You will change the text color to a dark blue and bold.

1

- Open the [A▾] Font Color drop-down menu in the Text Formatting group.

- Select Dark Blue from the Standard Colors section of the color gallery.

- Click [B] Bold in the Text Formatting group.

Your screen should be similar to
Figure 2.42

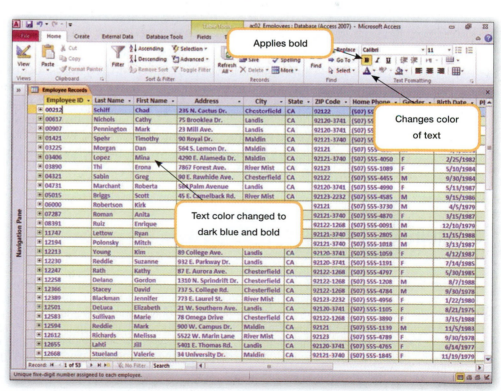

Applies bold

Changes color of text

Text color changed to dark blue and bold

Figure 2.42

Sorting Records **AC2.39**

You do not like how the blue text color looks and want to change it back to the default color. You cannot use Undo to remove formatting, so you will need to select the text color again.

2
- Open the Font Color drop-down menu.

- Choose Automatic to restore the default font color.

Your screen should be similar to Figure 2.43

Employee ID	Last Name	First Name	Address	City	State	ZIP Code	Home Phone	Gender	Birth Date
00212	Schiff	Chad	235 N. Cactus Dr.	Chesterfield	CA	92122	(507) 555-0010	M	3/9/1967
00617	Nichols	Cathy	75 Brooklea Dr.	Landis	CA	92120-3741	(507) 555-0001	F	5/19/1969
00907	Pennington	Mark	23 Mill Ave.	Landis	CA	92120-3741	(507) 555-3333	M	7/7/1974
01421	Spehr	Timothy	90 Royal Dr.	Maldin	CA	92121-3740	(507) 555-1038	M	9/9/1975
03225	Morgan	Dan	564 S. Lemon Dr.	Maldin	CA	92121	(507) 555-4567	M	3/5/1981
03406	Lopez	Mina	4290 E. Alameda Dr.	Maldin	CA	92121-3740	(507) 555-4050	F	2/25/1982
03890	Thi	Erona	7867 Forest Ave.	River Mist	CA	92123	(507) 555-1089	F	5/10/1984
04321	Sabin	Greg	90 E. Rawhide Ave.	Chesterfield	CA	92122	(507) 555-4455	M	9/30/1984
04731	Marchant	Roberta	564 Palm Avenue	Landis	CA	92120-3741	(507) 555-4990	F	5/13/1987
05015	Briggs	Scott			CA	92123-2232	(507) 555-4585	M	9/15/1986
06000	Robertson	Kirk			CA	92121	(507) 555-3730	M	4/5/1979
07287	Roman	Anita			CA	92121-3740	(507) 555-4870	F	3/15/1987
08391	Ruiz	Enrique	35 Palm St.	Chesterfield	CA	92122-1268	(507) 555-0091	M	12/10/1979
11747	Lettow	Ryan	358 Maple Dr.	Maldin	CA	92121-3740	(507) 555-2805	M	11/15/1988
12194	Polonsky	Mitch	8701 E. Sheridan	Maldin	CA	92121-3740	(507) 555-1018	M	3/13/1987
12213	Young	Kim	89 College Ave.	Landis	CA	92120-3741	(507) 555-1059	F	4/12/1987
12230	Reddie	Suzanne	932 E. Parkway Dr.	Landis	CA	92120-3741	(507) 555-1191	F	7/14/1985
12247	Rath	Kathy	87 E. Aurora Ave.	Chesterfield	CA	92122-1268	(507) 555-4797	F	5/30/1985
12258	Delano	Gordon	1310 N. Sprindrift Dr.	Chesterfield	CA	92122-1268	(507) 555-1208	M	8/7/1988
12366	Stacey	David	737 S. College Rd.	Chesterfield	CA	92122-1268	(507) 555-4784	M	9/30/1978
12389	Blackman	Jennifer	773 E. Laurel St.	River Mist	CA	92123-2232	(507) 555-4956	F	1/22/1980
12501	DeLuca	Elizabeth	21 W. Southern Ave.	Landis	CA	92120-3741	(507) 555-1105	F	8/21/1975
12583	Sullivan	Marie	78 Omega Drive	Chesterfield	CA	92122-1268	(507) 555-3890	F	3/15/1988
12594	Reddie	Mark	900 W. Campus Dr.	Maldin	CA	92121	(507) 555-1139	M	11/5/1983
12612	Richards	Melissa	5522 W. Marin Lane	River Mist	CA	92123	(507) 555-4789	F	9/30/1978
12655	Lahti	Jill	5401 E. Thomas Rd.	Landis	CA	92120-3741	(507) 555-4765	F	6/14/1977
12668	Stueland	Valerie	34 University Dr.	Maldin	CA	92121-3740	(507) 555-1845	F	11/19/1979

Text is black and bold

Record: 1 of 53 ▸ No Filter Search

Unique five-digit number assigned to each employee.

Figure 2.43

The black text color is restored. The text is still bolded and is easier to read.

Filtering a Table

Juan Martinez, an employee at the Landis location, is interested in forming a car pool. He recently approached you about finding other employees who also may want to carpool. You decide this would be a great opportunity to use the table of employee data to find this information. To find the employees, you could sort the table and then write down the needed information. This could be time-consuming, however, if you had hundreds of employees in the table. A faster way is to apply a filter to the table records to locate this information.

Concept **8** Filter

A **filter** is a restriction placed on records in the open table or form to quickly isolate and display a subset of records. A filter is created by specifying the criteria that you want records to meet in order to be displayed. A filter is ideal when you want to display the subset for only a brief time and then return immediately to the full set of records. You can print the filtered records as you would any form or table. A filter is only temporary, and all records are redisplayed when you remove the filter or close and reopen the table or form. The filter results cannot be saved. However, the last filter criteria you specify can be saved with the table, and the results can be quickly redisplayed.

USING FILTER BY SELECTION

Juan lives in Maldin and works at the Lifestyle Fitness Club located in Landis. You can locate other employees who live in Maldin quite easily by using the Filter by Selection feature. Filter by Selection displays only records containing a specific value. This method is effective when the table contains only one value that you want to use as the criterion for selecting and displaying records.

The process used to select the value determines the results that will be displayed. Placing the cursor in a field selects the entire field's contents. The filtered subset will include all records containing an exact match. Selecting part of a value in a field (by highlighting it) displays all records containing the selection. For example, in a table for a book collection, you could position the cursor anywhere in a field containing the name of the author Stephen King, choose the Filter by Selection command, and only records for books whose author matches the selected name, "Stephen King," would be displayed. Selecting just "King" would include all records for authors Stephen King, Martin Luther King, and Barbara Kingsolver.

You want to filter the table to display only those records with a City field entry of Maldin. To specify the city to locate, you select an example of the data in the table.

Additional Information

If the selected part of a value starts with the first character in the field, the subset displays all records with values that begin with the same selected characters.

1

Move to the City field of record 4.

Click Selection **in the Sort & Filter group of the Home tab.**

Your screen should be similar to Figure 2.44

Figure 2.44

The drop-down menu of commands contains the current selected value in the field. The commands that appear will vary depending on the data type of the selected value. Also, the commands will vary depending on how much of the value is selected. If the selection is a partial selection, the commands allow you to specify a filter using the beginning, middle, or end of a field value. In this case, the entire value is selected and the four commands allow you to specify whether you want the selection to equal, not equal, contain, or not contain the value.

2 Choose Equals "Maldin".

Another Method

You also can display the Filter by Selection commands using the selection's shortcut menu.

Your screen should be similar to
Figure 2.45

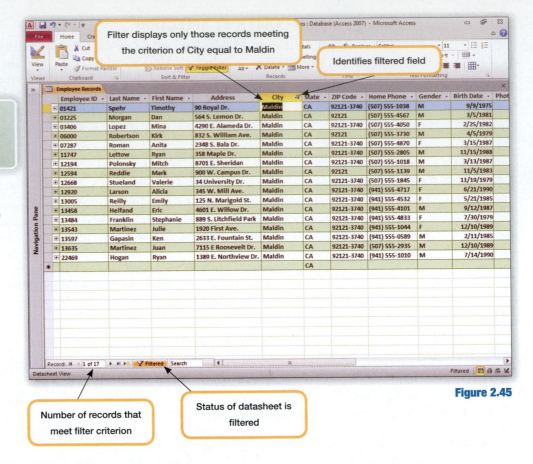

Filter displays only those records meeting the criterion of City equal to Maldin

Identifies filtered field

Employee ID	Last Name	First Name	Address	City	State	ZIP Code	Home Phone	Gender	Birth Date	Phot
01421	Spehr	Timothy	90 Royal Dr.	Maldin	CA	92121-3740	(507) 555-1038	M	9/9/1975	
03225	Morgan	Dan	564 S. Lemon Dr.	Maldin	CA	92121	(507) 555-4567	M	3/5/1981	
03406	Lopez	Mina	4290 E. Alameda Dr.	Maldin	CA	92121-3740	(507) 555-4050	F	2/25/1982	
06000	Robertson	Kirk	832 S. William Ave.	Maldin	CA	92121	(507) 555-3730	M	4/5/1979	
07287	Roman	Anita	2348 S. Bala Dr.	Maldin	CA	92121-3740	(507) 555-4870	F	3/15/1987	
11747	Lettow	Ryan	358 Maple Dr.	Maldin	CA	92121-3740	(507) 555-2805	M	11/15/1988	
12194	Polonsky	Mitch	8701 E. Sheridan	Maldin	CA	92121-3740	(507) 555-1018	M	3/13/1987	
12594	Reddie	Mark	900 W. Campus Dr.	Maldin	CA	92121	(507) 555-1139	M	11/5/1983	
12668	Stueland	Valerie	34 University Dr.	Maldin	CA	92121-3740	(507) 555-1845	F	11/19/1979	
12920	Larson	Alicia	345 W. Mill Ave.	Maldin	CA	92121-3740	(941) 555-4717	F	6/21/1990	
13005	Reilly	Emily	125 N. Marigold St.	Maldin	CA	92121-3740	(941) 555-4532	F	5/21/1985	
13458	Helfand	Eric	4601 E. Willow Dr.	Maldin	CA	92121-3740	(941) 555-4101	M	9/12/1987	
13484	Franklin	Stephanie	889 S. Litchfield Park	Maldin	CA	92121-3740	(941) 555-4833	F	7/30/1979	
13543	Martinez	Julie	1920 First Ave.	Maldin	CA	92121-3740	(941) 555-1044	F	12/10/1989	
13597	Gapasin	Ken	2633 E. Fountain St.	Maldin	CA	92121-3740	(941) 555-0589	M	2/11/1985	
13635	Martinez	Juan	7115 E Roosevelt Dr.	Maldin	CA	92121-3740	(507) 555-2935	M	12/10/1989	
22469	Hogan	Ryan	1389 E. Northview Dr.	Maldin	CA	92121-3740	(941) 555-1010	M	7/14/1990	
*					CA					

Record: 1 of 17   Filtered   Search

Datasheet View

Figure 2.45

Number of records that meet filter criterion

Status of datasheet is filtered

Additional Information

You can print a filtered datasheet just like any other table.

The table displays only those records that contain the selected city. All other records are temporarily hidden. The record navigation bar displays the **Filtered** button to show that the datasheet is filtered, and the record number indicator shows that the total number of filtered records is 17. The City field name also displays a filter icon to identify the field on which the table was filtered.

After seeing how easy it was to locate this information, you want to locate employees who live in Chesterfield. This information may help in setting up the car pool because the people traveling from the city of Maldin pass through Chesterfield on the way to the Landis location.

REMOVING AND DELETING FILTERS

Before creating the new filter, you will remove the current filter and return the table to its full display.

1

● Click ⧩ Toggle Filter in the Sort & Filter group.

Another Method

You also can use ⧩ **Filtered** in the record navigator bar to apply and remove a filter.

Your screen should be similar to **Figure 2.46**

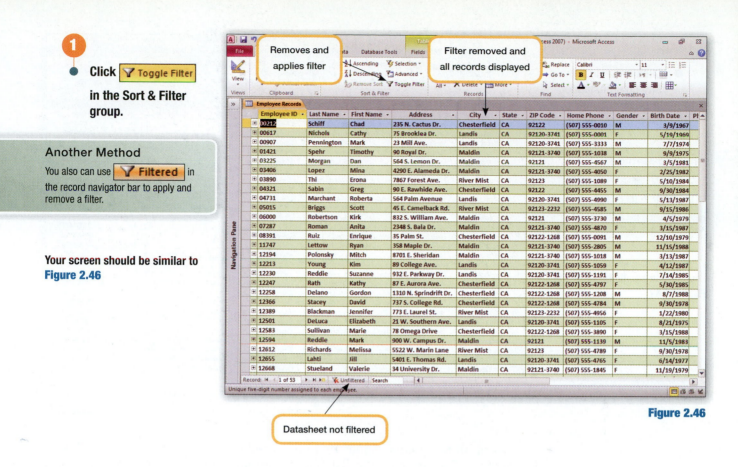

Figure 2.46

The filter is temporarily removed from the field and all the records are displayed again. The status bar displays ⟨K Unfiltered⟩. The filter is still available and can be reapplied quickly by clicking ⧩ Toggle Filter or ⟨K Unfiltered⟩.

You will reapply the filter, and then you will permanently remove these filter settings.

2

● Click ⧩ Toggle Filter to redisplay the filtered datasheet.

● Click ⟨ Advanced ▾⟩ in the Sort & Filter group.

● Choose Clear All Filters.

The filter is removed and all the records are redisplayed. The ⧩ Toggle Filter button is dimmed because the table does not include any filter settings.

FILTERING USING COMMON FILTERS

To filter the employee data by two cities, Chesterfield and Maldin, you can select from a list of several popular filters. Using this list allows you to perform filters on multiple criteria within a single field.

1

- Click on ⏷ in the City column header to open the field's drop-down menu.

Another Method

You also can move to the field to filter on and click in the Sort & Filter group to display the Filter list.

Your screen should be similar to
Figure 2.47

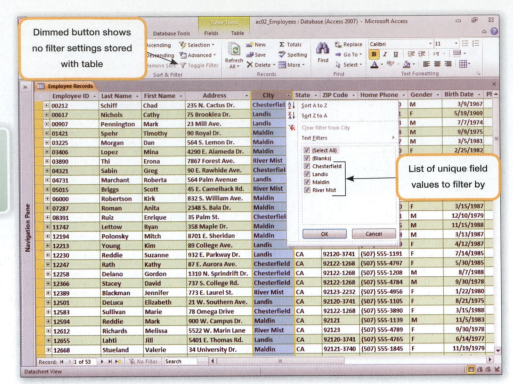

Figure 2.47

A list of all the unique values that are stored in the current field is displayed. Selecting a value from the list filters the table based on the selected value. Depending on the data type of the selected value, you may be able to filter for a range of values by clicking on a value and specifying the appropriate range. In this case, because the field is not filtered, all the values are selected. You will first clear the selection from all values, and then select the names of the two cities you want displayed in the filtered list.

2

- Click the Select All check box to clear the selection from all values.

- Click the Chesterfield and Maldin check boxes to select them.

- Click [OK].

Your screen should be similar to
Figure 2.48

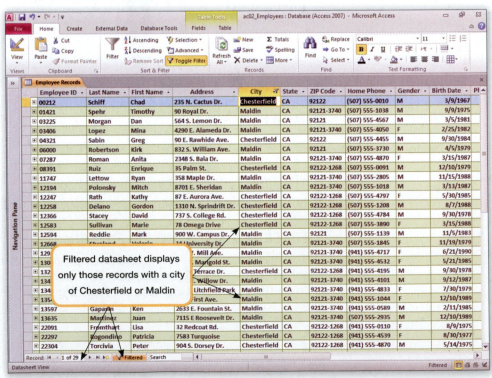

Figure 2.48

The filtered datasheet displays the records for all 29 employees who live in the cities of Chesterfield or Maldin.

FILTERING ON MULTIPLE FIELDS

As you look at the filtered results, you decide to further refine the list by restricting the results to those records that have the same ZIP Code as Juan's ZIP Code of 92121. Although you can only specify one filter per field, you can specify a different filter for each field that is present in the view.

1

- Open the ZIP Code field's drop-down menu to display the field list.

- Clear the checkmark from the 92121-3740 value.

- Click [OK].

Your screen should be similar to Figure 2.49

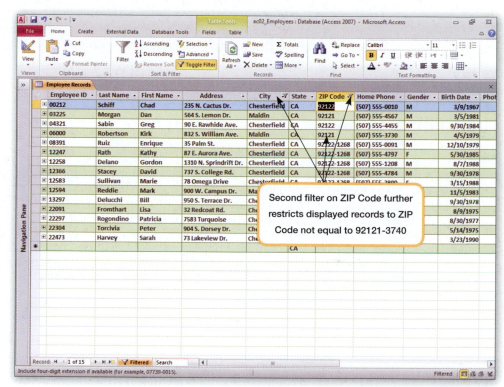

> Second filter on ZIP Code further restricts displayed records to ZIP Code not equal to 92121-3740

Figure 2.49

Now there are only 15 records displayed in the filtered table. Applying the second filter refined the results by removing all records from the filtered list that had a ZIP Code of 92121-3740.

Although you would like to provide a copy of this information to Juan, you realize that it contains more information about each employee than someone would need (or should even have access to) in order to form a car pool. Also, because you are not finished adding records to the employee database, these findings may not be complete.

You will redisplay all the records in the table, but you will not clear the filter settings. If you do not clear the filters, the filter criteria you last specified are stored with the table, and the results can be redisplayed simply by applying the filter again.

2

- Click [🔽 Toggle Filter] to display the unfiltered datasheet.

- Close the table, saving your design changes.

- Redisplay the Navigation pane.

The table is closed and the work area is empty. Next you will learn how to create and use a form in Access.

NOTE If you are ending your session now, close the database file and exit Access. When you begin again, start Access and open the ac02_Employees database file.

Creating a Simple Form

One of your objectives is to make the database easy to use. You know from experience that long hours of viewing large tables can be tiring. Therefore, you want to create an onscreen form to make this table easier to view and use.

Concept 9 Form

A **form** is a database object used primarily to display records onscreen and to make it easier to enter new records and make changes to existing records. Forms can control access to data so that any unnecessary fields or data is not displayed, which makes it easier for people using the database. They enable people to use the data in the tables without having to sift through many lines of data to find the exact record.

Forms are based on an underlying table and can include design elements such as descriptive text, titles, labels, lines, boxes, and pictures. Forms also can use calculations to summarize data that is not listed on the actual table, such as a sales total. The layout and arrangement of information can be customized in a form. Using these features creates a visually attractive form that makes working with the database more enjoyable, more efficient, and less prone to data-entry errors.

You want the onscreen form to be similar to the paper form that is completed by each new employee when hired (shown below). The information from that form is used as the source of input for the new record that will be added to the table for the new employee.

EMPLOYEE DATA

Employee ID _____

First Name _____   Last Name _____

Street _____

City _____   State _____   Zip _____

Phone Number _____

Gender _____

Birth Date _____

There are several different methods you can use to create forms, as described in the following table. The method you use depends on the type of form you want to create.

Method	Use to
Form tool	Create a form containing all the fields in the table.
Split Form tool	Create a form that displays the form and datasheet in a single window
Blank Form tool	Build a form from scratch by adding the fields you select from the table
Datasheet tool	Create a form using all the fields in the table and display it in Datasheet view
Multiple Items tool	Create a form that displays multiple records but is more customizable than a datasheet
Form Wizard	Create a form using a wizard that guides you through the steps to create a complex form that displays selected fields, data groups, sorted records, and data from multiple tables

USING THE FORM TOOL

Using the Form tool is the quickest method to create a simple form. You decide to see if the Form tool will create the form you need.

1

● If necessary, select the Employee Records table in the Navigation pane.

● Open the Create tab.

● Click [Form] in the Forms group.

Your screen should be similar to Figure 2.50

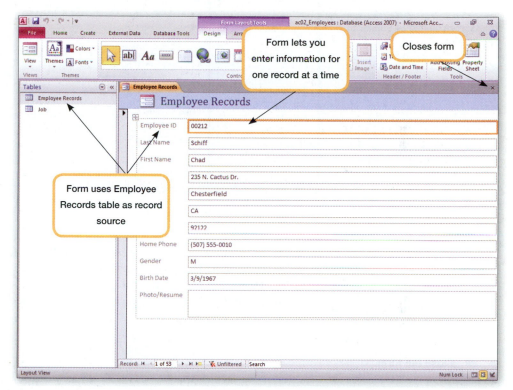

Figure 2.50

A form that allows you to enter data for one record at a time was quickly created. The fields from the Employee Records table were used to create the form because it was the selected object in the Navigation pane. The underlying table that is used to create a form is called the **record source**. The fields are in the same order as in the datasheet.

This form does not quite meet your needs, and you decide to try another method to create the form.

2

● Close the form.

● Click [No] to the prompt to save the form.

USING THE MULTIPLE ITEMS TOOL

Next, you will use the Multiple Items tool to create a form.

1

- If necessary, open the Create tab.

- Click  in the Forms group.

- Choose Multiple Items.

Your screen should be similar to Figure 2.51

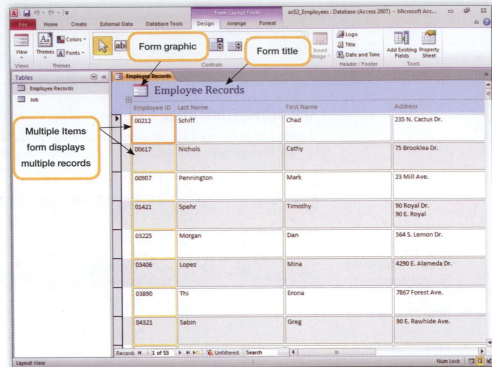

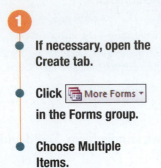

Figure 2.51

A form that displays multiple records at a time was quickly created. Although it looks similar to Datasheet view, it is easier to read and includes a title and graphic. However, this form still does not work and you decide to use the Form Wizard to create a form that is closer to your needs.

2

- Close the form.

- Click **No** to the prompt to save the form.

USING THE FORM WIZARD

The **Form Wizard** will help you create a form that is closer to your needs by guiding you through a series of steps that allow you to specify different form features.

1 ● Open the Create tab and click Form Wizard in the Forms group.

Your screen should be similar to **Figure 2.52**

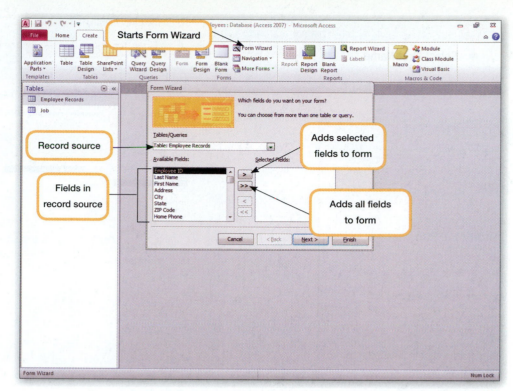

Figure 2.52

The Form Wizard dialog box displays the name of the current table, Employee Records, in the Tables/Queries list box. This is the table that will be used as the record source. If you wanted to use a different table as the record source, you could open the Tables/Queries drop-down list to select the appropriate table.

The fields from the selected table are displayed in the Available Fields list box. You use this box to select the fields you want included on the form, in the order in which you want them to appear. This order is called the **tab order** because it is the order in which the highlight will move through the fields on the form when you press the [Tab ⇆] key during data entry. You decide that you want the fields to be in the same order as they are on the paper form shown in the illustration on page AC2.46.

2

● Select First Name.

● Click **>** Add Field.

Another Method

You also can double-click on each field name in the Available Fields list box to move the field name to the Selected Fields list box.

Additional Information

The **>>** Add All Fields button adds all available fields to the Selected Fields list, in the same order in which they appear in the Available Fields list.

Your screen should be similar to
Figure 2.53

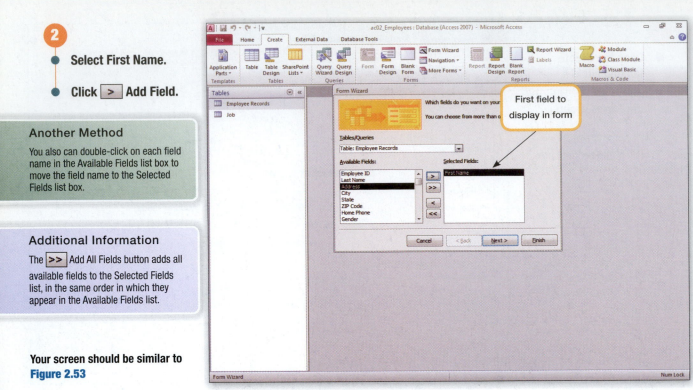

Figure 2.53

The First Name field is removed from the Available Fields list and added to the top of the Selected Fields list box. It will be the first field in the form.

3

● In the same manner, add the following fields to the Selected Fields list in the order shown here:

Last Name
Address
City
State
ZIP Code
Home Phone
Gender
Birth Date
Employee ID

Your screen should be similar to
Figure 2.54

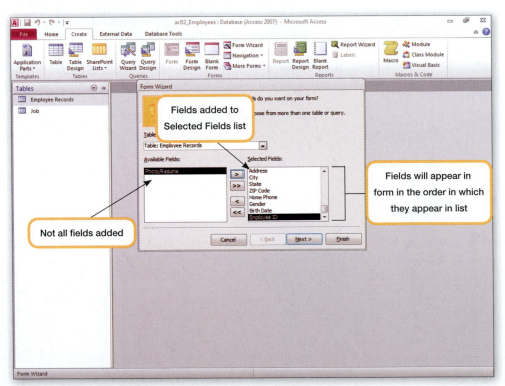

Figure 2.54

When finished, the only remaining field in the Available Fields list box is the Photo/Resume field. The Selected Fields list box contains the fields in the order in which you added them.

You are now ready to move on to the next Form Wizard screen.

4

● **Click** Next > .

Your screen should be similar to Figure 2.55

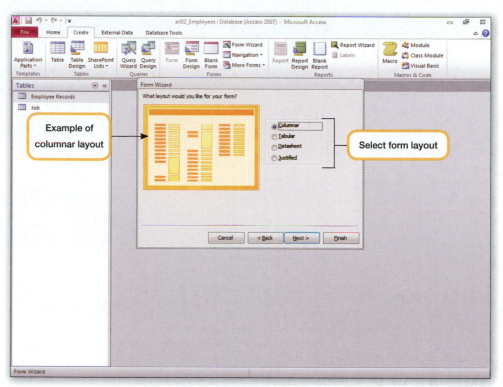

Figure 2.55

In this Form Wizard screen, you are asked to select the control layout for the form. **Layouts** determine how the data is displayed in the form by aligning the items horizontally or vertically to give the form a uniform appearance. Layouts act as a guide for the placement of items on the form.

Layouts are usually configured in a tabular or stacked format. **Tabular formats** arrange the data in rows and columns, with labels across the top. **Stacked formats** arrange data vertically with a field label to the left of the field data. A form can have both types of layouts in different sections.

The four form layouts offered by the Form Wizard are variations of the two basic layouts as described in the following table.

Format		Description
Columnar	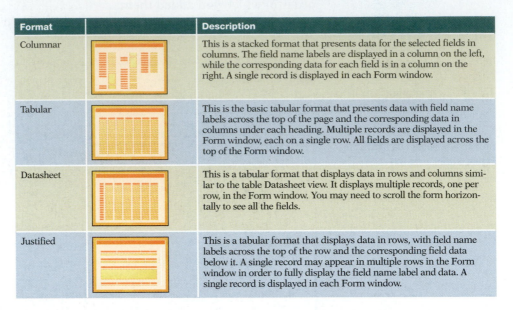	This is a stacked format that presents data for the selected fields in columns. The field name labels are displayed in a column on the left, while the corresponding data for each field is in a column on the right. A single record is displayed in each Form window.
Tabular		This is the basic tabular format that presents data with field name labels across the top of the page and the corresponding data in columns under each heading. Multiple records are displayed in the Form window, each on a single row. All fields are displayed across the top of the Form window.
Datasheet		This is a tabular format that displays data in rows and columns similar to the table Datasheet view. It displays multiple records, one per row, in the Form window. You may need to scroll the form horizontally to see all the fields.
Justified		This is a tabular format that displays data in rows, with field name labels across the top of the row and the corresponding field data below it. A single record may appear in multiple rows in the Form window in order to fully display the field name label and data. A single record is displayed in each Form window.

The columnar format appears most similar to the paper form currently in use by the club, so you decide to use that configuration for your form.

Additional Information

Using 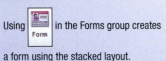 in the Forms group creates a form using the stacked layout.

5

- If necessary, choose Columnar.

- Click Next >.

Your screen should be similar to Figure 2.56

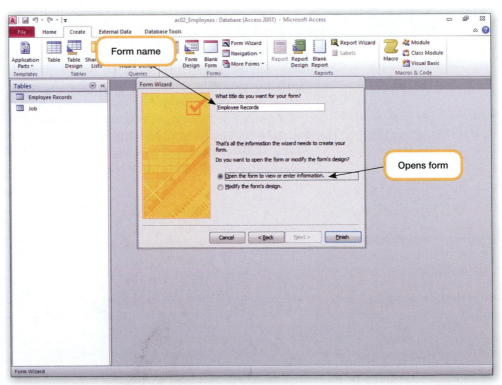

Figure 2.56

In the final Form Wizard dialog box, you can enter a form title to be used as the name of the form, and you can specify whether to open the form or to modify it. The Form Wizard uses the name of the table as the default form title. You will keep the proposed form title and the default of opening the form.

6

● Click  Finish .

Your screen should be similar to
Figure 2.57

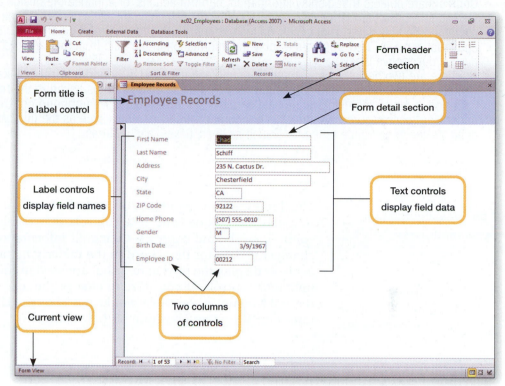

Figure 2.57

The completed form is displayed in the work area in Form view. The form title appears at the top of the form in the form header section. The employee information for Chad Schiff, the first record in the table, is displayed in the form detail section.

The form displays the chosen fields in columnar format with the default form design. The field name labels display in a column on the left, while the data for each corresponding field is displayed in a column on the right.

Each item in the form is a separate object contained in boxes, called controls.

Additional Information

You will learn about changing the form design shortly.

Concept 10 Controls

Controls are objects that display information, perform actions, or enhance the design of a form or report. Access provides controls for many types of objects, including labels, text boxes, check boxes, list boxes, command buttons, lines, rectangles, option buttons, and more. The most common controls are text controls and label controls. **Text controls** display the information in the field from the record source. **Label controls** display descriptive labels.

There are two basic types of controls: bound and unbound. A **bound control** is linked to a field in an underlying table. An example of a bound control is a text control that is linked to the record source (usually a field from a table) and displays the field data in the form or report. An **unbound control** is not connected to an underlying record source. Examples of unbound controls are labels such as the title of a form or elements that enhance the appearance of the form such as lines, boxes, and pictures.

Additional Information

You will learn about reports in Lab 3.

This form contains two types of controls: label controls that display the form title and field names and text controls that display the field data. The text controls are bound controls. Changing information in the text controls will change the data for the record in the underlying table. Even though the label controls display the field names that are used in the underlying table, they are unbound controls. If you were to change the text in the form's label control, the field name in the table would not change. The columnar format determines the layout and position of these controls.

Modifying a Form

Although you are generally satisfied with the look of the form, there are a few changes that you want to make. You see that you accidentally placed the Employee ID field at the bottom of the form. The first change you will make is to move the Employee ID field to the top of the form and size it to more closely fit the data.

You can use Form Layout view or Form Design view to modify the design and layout of a form. As in Datasheet Design view, Form Design view displays the structure of the form, not the data in the form. It is used to make extensive changes to the form. Form Layout view displays the underlying data and allows you to make many basic modifications.

USING FORM LAYOUT VIEW

You will use Form Layout view to make the change to the Employee ID field controls because you want to be able to see the data in the Employee ID field as you adjust the size of the control.

● Click 🔲 **Layout View in the status bar.**

Your screen should be similar to Figure 2.58

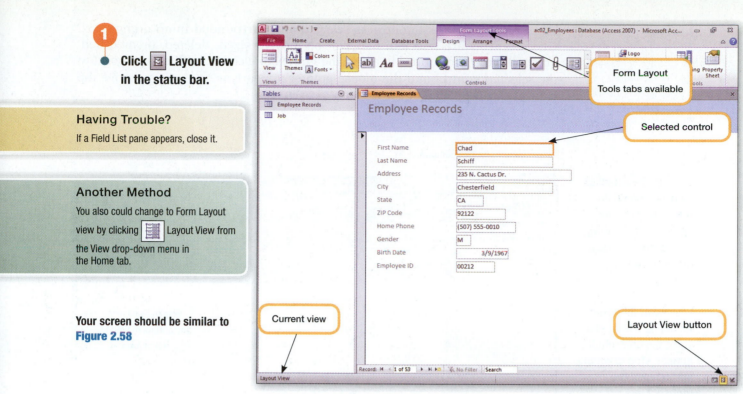

Figure 2.58

The Form Layout Tools Design, Arrange, and Format tabs are now available to help you modify the form design. Currently, the First Name text box control is surrounded with a solid orange box, indicating the control is selected and is the control that will be affected by your actions.

MOVING CONTROLS

First you will select the Employee ID control to move it.

● **Click on the Employee ID text control to select it.**

Your screen should be similar to Figure 2.59

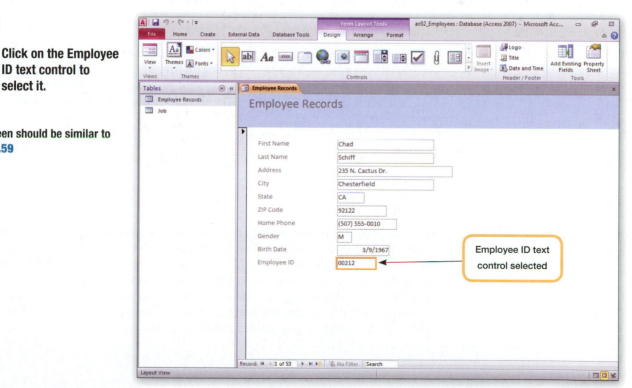

Figure 2.59

Modifying a Form   **AC2.55**

The Employee ID text control is selected and surrounded in an orange box. Once controls are selected, they can be moved, sized, deleted, or modified. You will move the control to above the First Name control. When you point to the selected control and the mouse pointer appears as ⬚, you can move the control by dragging it.

2

- Point to the selected control, and when the mouse pointer appears as ⬚, drag the control up above the First Name text control.

- When you think the mouse is where you want the control to appear, stop dragging and release the mouse.

Your screen should be similar to Figure 2.60

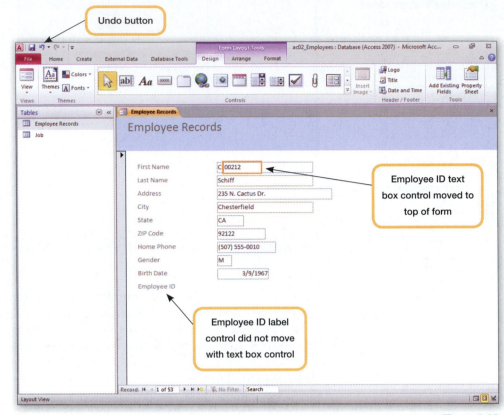

Figure 2.60

When you release the Employee ID control, it probably is on top of the First Name text control and is not aligned with any of the other controls. It also was difficult to know where the control would be placed as you dragged. In addition, the label control, Employee ID, did not move with the text control.

3

- Click ↶ Undo to cancel moving the Employee ID control.

APPLYING A LAYOUT

To make it easier to move and arrange controls, you will group the controls by applying the stacked layout. This will position the controls in a layout consisting of cells arranged in rows and columns, which behave much like a table in Word. When the Wizard created this form, it arranged the controls in a tabular format but did not group the controls in a layout. You want to include all the form controls except the form title in the stacked layout. You first need to select all the controls you want to include in the new layout.

1

- Press Ctrl + A to select all the controls on the form.

- Press Ctrl + click on the Employee Records label in the Form header to deselect it.

- Open the Arrange tab and click 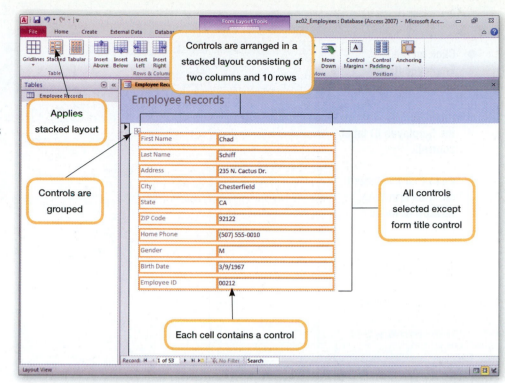 in the Table group.

Your screen should be similar to **Figure 2.61**

Figure 2.61

All controls in the record's detail section of the form are selected and surrounded with a solid orange border. They are grouped and arranged in the basic stacked layout with the label controls in one column to the left of the text controls. The controls in each column are now all the same size. Notice also that the group is surrounded with a dotted border with a ⊞ in the upper left corner. This indicates the controls are grouped in the layout.

Additional Information

You can have more than one layout in a form.

The layout is a guide that helps you align your controls horizontally and vertically. It is similar in appearance to a table, which consists of rows and columns, but the layout differs in that it only allows controls to be placed in the cells. This layout has two columns and 10 rows. Each cell contains a single control.

You will again move the Employee ID control. This time, you also will select the Employee ID label so that both controls will move together. As you move the controls in the layout, a solid orange line will appear showing you where the controls will be placed when you stop dragging.

2

● Click on the
   Employee ID text
   control.

● Press (Shift) + click on
   the Employee ID label
   control.

● Point to the selected
   controls and drag
   upward to move
   them.

Additional Information

Using 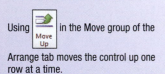 in the Move group of the
Arrange tab moves the control up one
row at a time.

● When the light
   orange line appears
   above the First Name
   control, release the
   mouse button to drop
   the controls in the
   new location.

Your screen should be similar to
Figure 2.62

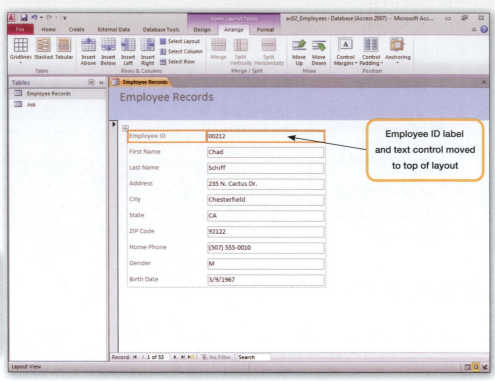

Figure 2.62

The Employee ID label and text controls have moved to the top row of the table and all other controls have moved down one row.

SIZING AND MOVING CONTROLS IN A LAYOUT

Next, you want to reduce the size of the Employee ID text control to match the size of the entry. When you position the mouse pointer on the orange box surrounding the selected control, the pointer changes to ↔ and can be used to size the control. The direction of the arrow indicates in which direction dragging the mouse will alter the shape of the object. This action is similar to sizing a window.

1

● Click on the Employee ID text control to select it.

● Point to the right edge of the control box and, when the mouse pointer is ←→, drag to the left to decrease the size of the control as in Figure 2.63.

Your screen should be similar to Figure 2.63

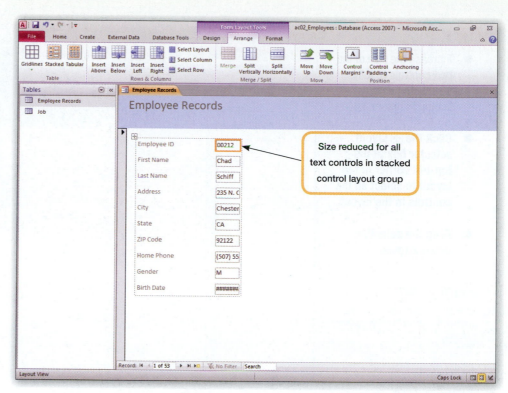

Figure 2.63

Unfortunately, the size of all the text box controls in the column has been reduced. This is because, in order for the stacked control layout to maintain a uniform appearance, it groups the controls so that they size as a unit. To size a control individually, it must be in its own separate column or in a separate layout group. You decide you will move the Employee ID control to a separate layout group so that it stands alone at the top of the form. Then you will size it to fit the contents.

First you resize all the controls in the layout to fully display the information. Then you will make space at the top of the form for the Employee ID controls by moving all the controls in this layout group down.

2

- Increase the size of the text controls to fully display the data as shown in Figure 2.64.

- Click the ⊞ layout selector box at the top-left corner of the layout to select all the controls in the layout.

- Drag the selection down 2 rows.

Having Trouble?

The control layout changes to dark blue as you move it to show the new position of the object.

Your screen should be similar to Figure 2.64

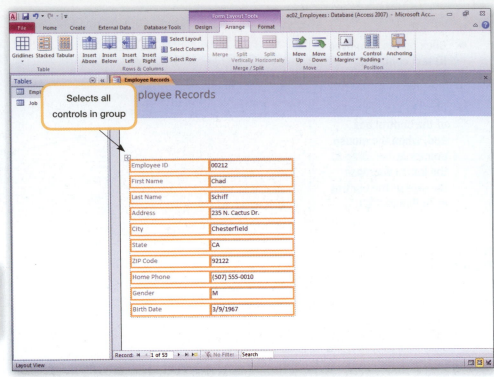

Selects all controls in group

Figure 2.64

Additional Information

You also can remove controls from a layout without placing them in another layout using Layout/Remove Layout on the control's shortcut menu.

SPLITTING A LAYOUT

Now that you have space at the top of the form for the Employee ID information, you will remove the Employee ID control from the layout into a separate stacked layout and then move and size it to fit the contents.

1

- Select the Employee ID text and label controls.

- Click in the Table group of the Arrange tab.

Your screen should be similar to Figure 2.65

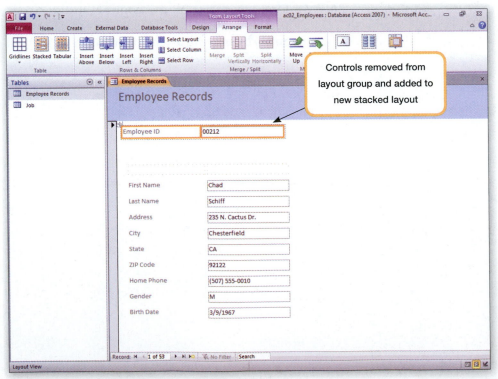

Controls removed from layout group and added to new stacked layout

Figure 2.65

The Employee ID controls have been removed from the original stacked layout and added to a separate stacked layout. There are now two stacked layouts in the form that can be sized individually. You will reposition and size the controls in both layouts next.

2

- Using the ⊞ layout selector, drag the Employee ID object to the position shown in Figure 2.66.

- Reduce the size of the Employee ID text and label controls as in Figure 2.66.

- Click on the First Name label control to select it, and size it to match the size of the Employee ID label control.

Your screen should be similar to Figure 2.66

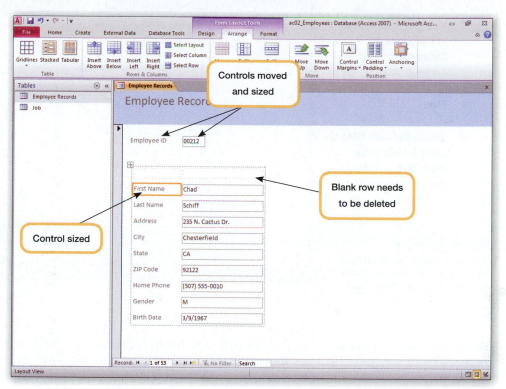

Figure 2.66

The Employee ID is clearly separate from the personal data on the form, and the text control has been sized to fit the data more closely.

REMOVING ROWS FROM A LAYOUT

Notice, however, there is a blank row in the layout where the Employee ID was previously. You will delete the blank row and then move the Last Name controls to the right of the First Name text control, as they appear in the company's paper form.

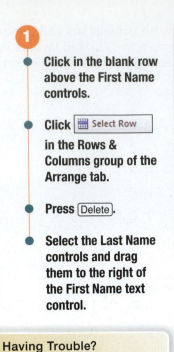

1

- Click in the blank row above the First Name controls.

- Click 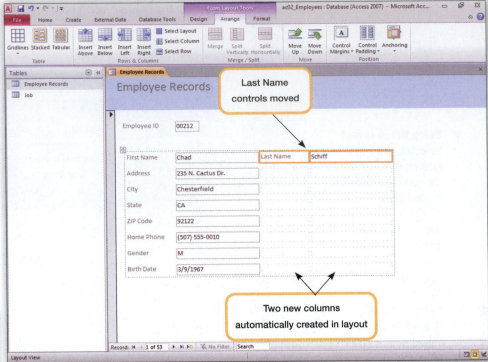 Select Row in the Rows & Columns group of the Arrange tab.

- Press Delete.

- Select the Last Name controls and drag them to the right of the First Name text control.

Having Trouble?

The orange indicator line should be at the right of the First Name text control when you release the mouse.

Figure 2.67

Your screen should be similar to Figure 2.67

Additional Information

You can delete a column by selecting a cell in the column, clicking Select Column, and pressing Delete.

The blank row was deleted and two new columns were added to the layout to accommodate the moved controls. You will continue to arrange the elements on the form so the form appears similar to the paper form the company uses. This will make the process of entering data from the paper form into the database easier for the user.

2

- Select the State controls and move them to the blank cell to the right of City text control.

- Select the ZIP Code controls and move them to the right of the State text control.

- Close the Navigation Pane so you have more room to work.

Your screen should be similar to
Figure 2.68

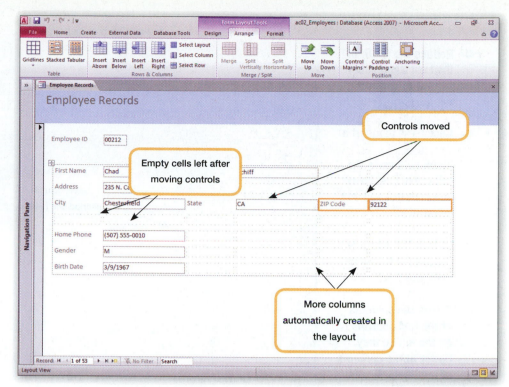

Figure 2.68

The controls are now placed where you want them, but they need to be resized to better fit their contents. Also, you notice the Last Name and State labels are a little close to the boxes on their left and would look better with some space added between them.

INSERTING, MERGING, AND SPLITTING CELLS

Working with layouts also allows you to easily insert columns and rows, and merge and split cells to achieve the design you want for the form. The next change you want to make is to insert a narrow blank column to the left of the Last Name controls to separate the controls.

1

- Reduce the width of the Last Name label control to better fit the label.

- Click  to insert a blank column to the left of the Last Name label control and add separation.

- Reduce the width of the blank column as in Figure 2.69.

- Resize the columns of the text controls on the left so they better fit the contents of the Phone Number control.

Your screen should be similar to Figure 2.69

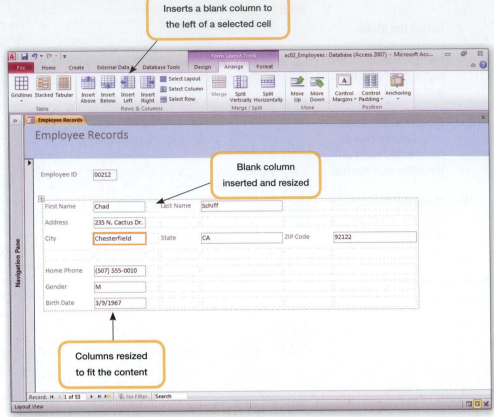

Figure 2.69

The form now has a nice visual separation between the controls on the left and those added on the right.

Now, however, you feel the Address text control could be larger. To fix this, you will merge it with the cells on the right to allow for longer address entries. When you **merge cells** any selected adjacent cells are combined into one big cell spanning the length of the previously selected cells.

You cannot merge cells containing more than one control, because each cell can contain only one control. You can merge any number of empty adjacent cells.

First you must select the cells to be merged.

2

- Select the Address text control.

- Hold down ⬆Shift and click the two empty cells to the right of the Address control.

- Click 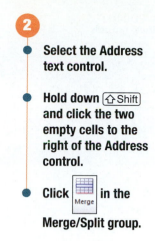 in the Merge/Split group.

Your screen should be similar to Figure 2.70

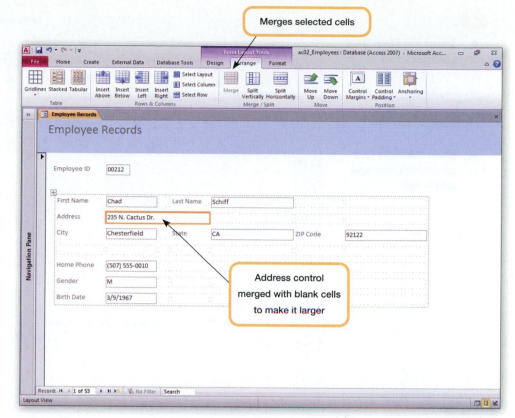

Figure 2.70

The three cells have been combined into one cell that should be large enough to display most addresses. When merging cells, it is better to adjust column sizes as much as possible before merging, as the underlying row and column structure can become complicated and make it difficult to resize just the cells you want.

To further enhance the form, the State and ZIP Code controls could be resized to better fit the text they contain. However, if you resize the State field, it will make the Last Name controls too narrow. Since the State text control only needs to be wide enough for two characters, you think it would fit next to the State label if you could utilize the extra space in the cell. To make one cell into two, you can split the cell.

You can **split cells** horizontally or vertically. Splitting a cell vertically creates a new row and splitting a cell horizontally creates a new column. Splitting can be performed on only one cell at a time. The affected cell can be an empty cell or contain a control. When splitting a cell containing a control, the control is kept in the far left box and an empty cell is created on the right side. You want to split the cell containing the State label.

3

- Select the State label control.

- Click  to split the cell into two.

- Move the State text control into the new empty cell.

Your screen should be similar to Figure 2.71

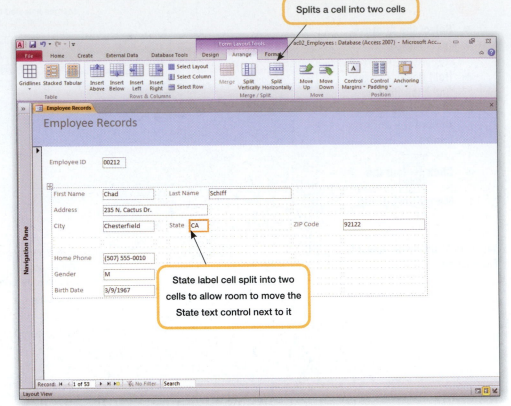

Splits a cell into two cells

State label cell split into two cells to allow room to move the State text control next to it

Figure 2.71

Both State controls now reside within the same column containing the last name label. You notice the Address text control also ends in this column. If you were to try and resize the State or Address text controls, it would affect the entire column, including the cell containing the Last Name label.

Your form has room for the ZIP Code label and text controls to be moved to the right of the State control. You will split the empty cell and move both ZIP Code controls into the new position.

4

● Click the empty cell to the right of the State text control.

● Click 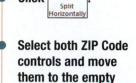.

● Select both ZIP Code controls and move them to the empty cells to the right of the State text control.

● Select the ZIP Code label control, and click ☰ Align Text Right in the Font group of the Format tab.

Your screen should be similar to Figure 2.72

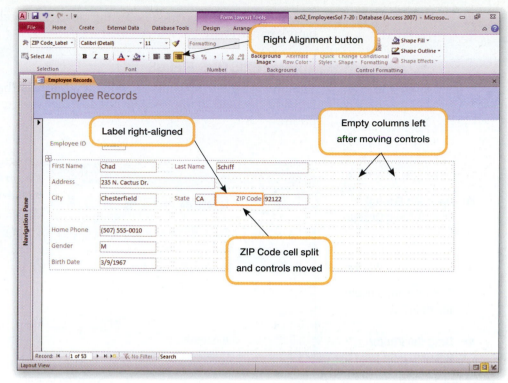

Figure 2.72

Aligning the label to the right gives the appearance of space between the label and the State text control. Now you need to delete the extra columns in the layout and move the last three fields up below the City field. To specify the column to be removed, select any cell in the column and the entire column will be deleted.

5

● Click an empty cell in the column to the right of the Last Name text control.

● Press Delete.

● In the same manner, delete the second empty column.

● Select the label and text controls for the last three fields.

● Drag the selected controls up to the blank cell under the City label.

Your screen should be similar to Figure 2.73

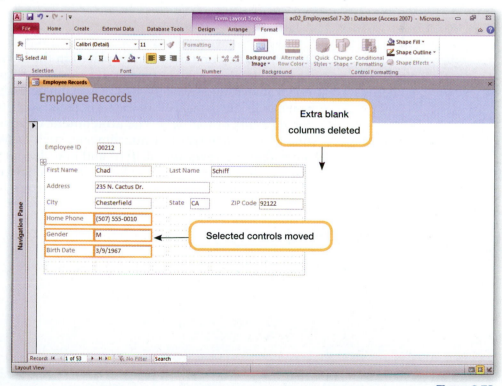

Figure 2.73

The form you have created is getting closer to matching the layout of the company's paper form.

ADDING EXISTING FIELDS

The only element missing on your new form is the Photo/Resume field. You will add the field to the form layout and then merge cells to make room for the photo.

1

- Open the Format Layout Tools Design tab.

- Click [Add Existing Fields] in the Tools group to open the field list.

- Drag the Photo/Resume field from the Field List pane to the empty cell below the Birth Date label.

Your screen should be similar to Figure 2.74

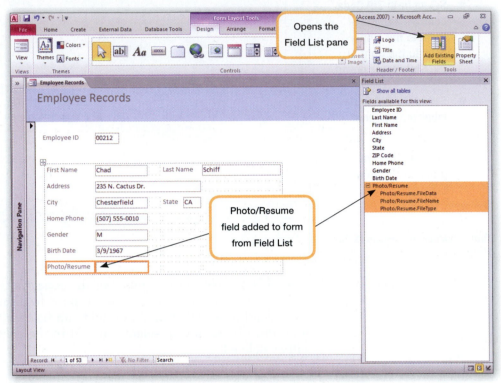

Figure 2.74

The Photo/Resume field is now placed in the layout. The Photo/Resume field has an attachment data type and is a bound control that allows you to add, edit, remove, and save attached files to the field directly from the form, just as you can in the datasheet. In the form, it uses an attachment control to display the contents of the field. The **attachment control** displays image files automatically. Other types of attachments, such as Word documents, appear as icons that represent the file type and must be opened to be viewed. Currently the attachment control that will display the photo is too small to be functional. To enlarge the control, you will insert four rows below it and then merge the new cells for the attachment control.

2

- Click on the Photo/Resume text control.

- Open the Arrange tab and click 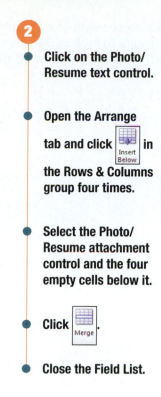 in the Rows & Columns group four times.

- Select the Photo/Resume attachment control and the four empty cells below it.

- Click .

- Close the Field List.

Your screen should be similar to Figure 2.75

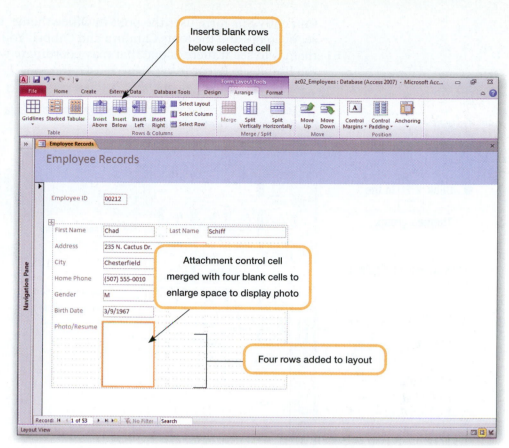

Figure 2.75

Now the Photo/Resume attachment control is large enough to display a photo. The Photo/Resume field's control is currently empty because there are no attachments for this record.

CHANGING THE DESIGN STYLE

Next you want to enhance the form's appearance by making changes to the form colors and fonts. To make it easy to quickly change the appearance of the form you will change the form's design theme.

Concept **11** Theme

A **theme** is a predefined set of formatting choices that can be applied to an entire document in one simple step. Access includes 40 named, built-in themes that can be applied to forms and reports. Each theme includes two subset of themes: colors and fonts. Each color theme consists of 12 colors that are applied to specific elements in the form or report. Each fonts theme includes a set of different body and heading fonts. You also can create your own custom themes by modifying an existing theme and saving it as a custom theme. The blank database file uses the default Office theme for any forms or reports you create.

The same themes also are available in Word 2010, Excel 2010 and PowerPoint 2010. Using themes gives your documents a professional and modern look. Because document themes are shared across 2010 Office applications, all your Office documents can have the same uniform look.

Currently this form uses the built-in Office theme, which consists of a certain set of colors and the fonts Cambria and Calibri. You decide to look at the other themes to see if there is one that may coordinate well with the colors used in the Employee Records table.

● Open the Design tab.

● Click  in the Themes group.

Your screen should be similar to Figure 2.76

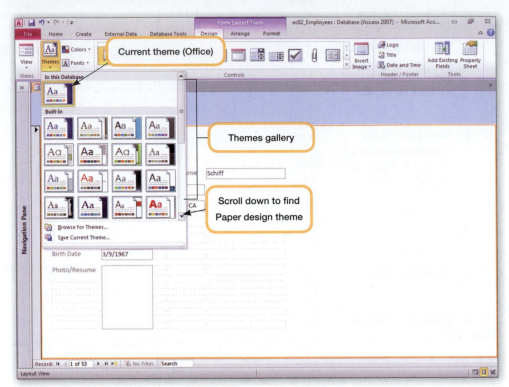

Figure 2.76

A gallery of 40 built-in named themes is displayed. A sample shows the color and font used in each theme. The Office theme is the default theme and is the theme that is used in the form. When you point to each theme, the theme name appears in a ScreenTip and a live preview of how the theme's settings will look is displayed in the form. You think the Paper theme will match the colors you chose for the Employee Records table.

2

- Point to several themes to see the live preview for each.

- Scroll the Themes gallery and choose the Paper theme.

Having Trouble?

The theme names are in alphabetical order in the gallery list.

- Click ![Save] **Save** in the **Quick Access Toolbar** to save the form design changes.

Another Method

You also can use ![Save] **Save** in the Records group of the Home tab.

Additional Information

If you do not save the design changes at this time, you will be prompted to save them before closing the form.

Your screen should be similar to Figure 2.77

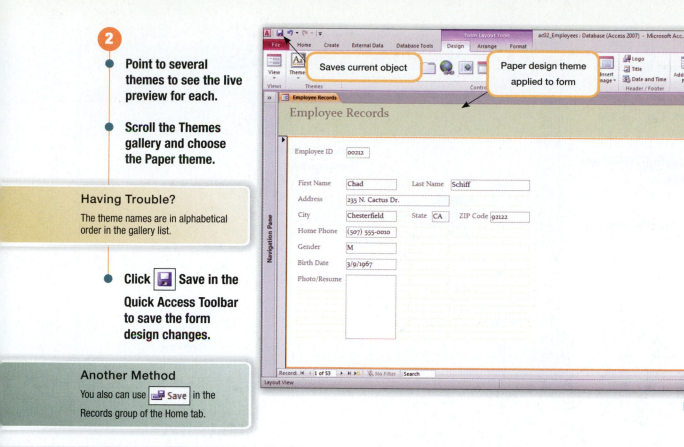

Figure 2.77

The formatting settings associated with the selected theme have been applied to the form. Because themes are available in the other Office applications, you can coordinate the design styles used in documents created in the other applications by choosing the same theme.

Using a Form

Now that you have created the form and enhanced its appearance, you are ready to utilize the form by switching to Form view. Using a form, you can do many of the same things you can do in Datasheet view. For example, you can update and delete records, search for records, and sort and filter the data.

NAVIGATING IN FORM VIEW

You use the same navigation keys in Form view that you used in Datasheet view. You can move between fields in the form by using the (Tab), (←Enter), or (Shift) + (Tab) keys. The → and ← keys are used to move character by character through the entry. You can use (Page Up) and (Page Down), as well as the navigation buttons at the bottom of the form, to move between records.

You will try out several of these navigation keys as you try to locate the record for Roberta Marchant. First, you must switch to Form view.

1

- Change the view to Form View.

- Press `Tab` three times.

- Press `Page Down` two times.

Your screen should be similar to Figure 2.78

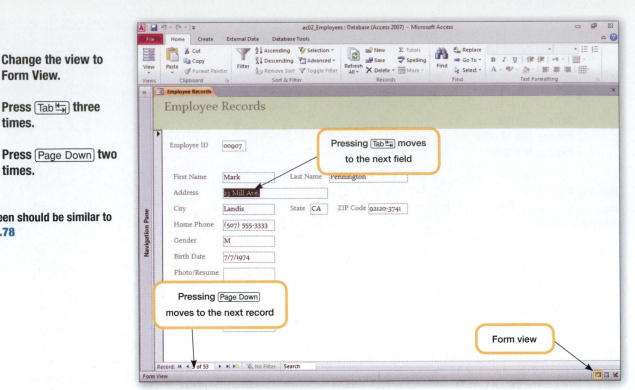

Figure 2.78

First you moved three fields to the Address field in the current record. Then you moved down two records to record three. The field that was selected in the previous record remains the selected field when you move between records.

Searching in Form View

A quicker way to locate a record is to use the Find command or the Search feature. Both features work just as they do in Datasheet view. You will use the Search feature to locate the record for Roberta Marchant by entering the first few characters of her last name in the Search box. As you type the characters, watch how the search advances through the table and highlights matching text.

● Click in the Search
  text box.

● Type **marc**

Your screen should be similar to
Figure 2.79

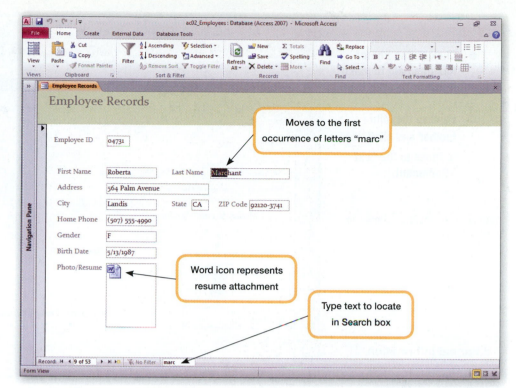

Figure 2.79

The Search feature located Roberta Marchant's record and displays it in the form. The Photo/Resume field displays a Word icon for the resume file. To open the resume file, simply double-click on the Word icon and choose  from the Attachments dialog box. To display the next attachment, click on the Attachment control to make it active. This will display the Mini toolbar, which contains three buttons that are used to work with attachment controls. When the Mini toolbar first displays above the Attachment control, it will appear transparent and may be hard to discern. By pointing to the Mini Toolbar, it will become solid and easier to see. Using the Mini toolbar, you can scroll through attached files using the ⊙ and ⊙ buttons, or you may add or view attachments using 📎 to open the Attachments dialog box. You will use the Mini toolbar to display the photo attachment.

Additional Information

Refer to the Formatting Text section in the Introduction to Microsoft Office 2010 to review the Mini toolbar feature.

2

- Click on the Photo/Resume field to make it active.

- Point to the Mini toolbar and click 🔄 to move to the next attachment.

Your screen should be similar to Figure 2.80

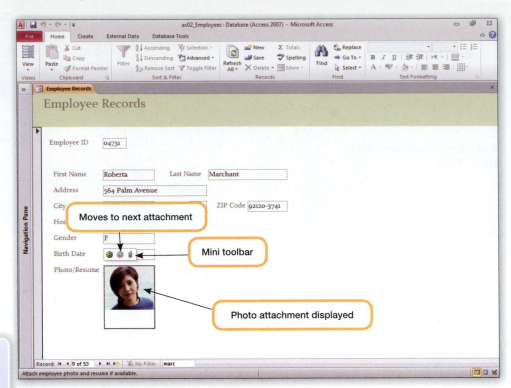

Figure 2.80

Now the photo is displayed in the Photo/Resume field control.

SORTING AND FILTERING DATA IN A FORM

Just as in the table datasheet, you can sort and filter the data that is displayed in a form. You will use these features to sort the records in alphabetical order by last name and display only records for employees who live in River Mist.

1

- Right-click on the Last Name field.

- Choose Sort A to Z.

- Move to any record that displays River Mist and right-click on the City field.

- Choose Equals "River Mist".

- Display the last record.

Your screen should be similar to Figure 2.81

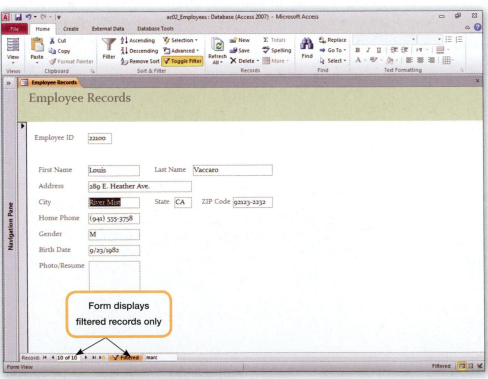

Figure 2.81

The record number indicator tells you that there are only 10 records and the table is filtered. The records are also in sorted order by last name. The sort and filter settings apply only to the object in which they were specified, in this case the form.

ADDING RECORDS USING A FORM

Now you need to add a new employee record to the database whose paper employee record form is shown here. You will add the record while in Form view, using the information on the paper form to input the data into the form's fields. You also will attach a picture to the Photo/Resume field.

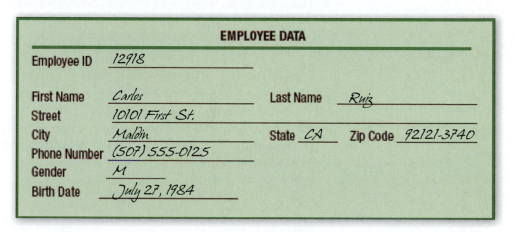

EMPLOYEE DATA

Employee ID   12918

First Name   Carlos   Last Name   Ruiz
Street   10101 First St.
City   Maldin   State CA   Zip Code 92121-3740
Phone Number (507) 555-0125
Gender   M
Birth Date   July 27, 1984

1

● Click ▶✷ New (blank) Record to display a new blank entry form.

Another Method

You also can use 🗃 **New** in the Records group of the Home tab or Ctrl + + to add a new record.

● Enter the data shown in the paper form into the new record.

● Double-click on the Attachment field control.

Another Method

You also could choose Manage Attachments from the shortcut menu or click 📎 Attachments on the Mini toolbar.

● Add the file ac02_ Carlos from your data file location.

Your screen should be similar to Figure 2.82

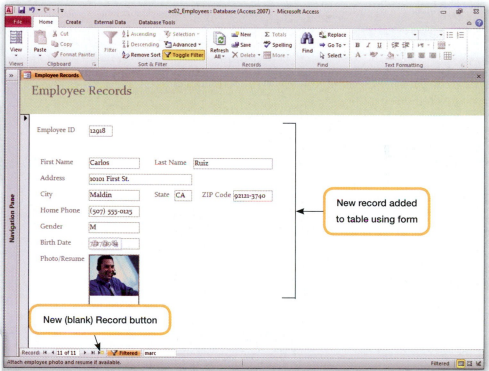

Figure 2.82

Using the form makes entering the new employee data much faster because the fields are in the same order as the information on the paper Employee Data form used by the Personnel department.

Before you end this lab, you will add a record for yourself.

Enter another record using your special Employee ID **99999** and your first and last names. The data in all other fields can be fictitious.

Remove the filter.

Open the Navigation Pane.

The table now contains 55 records. Next, you need to add these two records to the Job table.

Organizing the Navigation Pane

Notice the name of the form does not appear in the Navigation pane. This is because initially the pane is set to display table objects only. To display other objects in the pane, you can change what objects are displayed in the pane and how they are grouped.

Click

    Tables

at the top of the Navigation pane to open the Tables drop-down menu.

Your screen should be similar to **Figure 2.83**

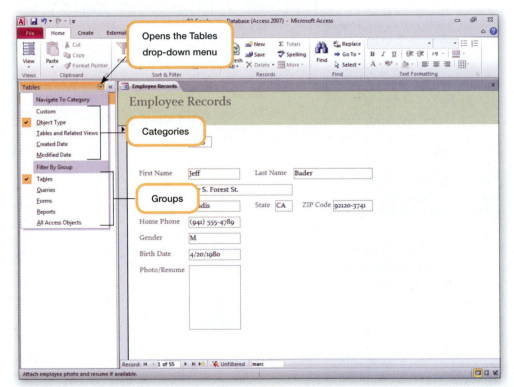

Figure 2.83

The upper section of the menu contains categories, and the lower section contains groups. The groups change as you select different categories. Currently, Object Type is the selected category and Tables is the selected group. You want to keep the category selection as Object Type but want to change the group selection to display all object types in the pane at the same time.

- From the Filter By Group section, choose All Access Objects.

- Double-click the Job table in the Navigation Pane.

Another Method

You also can drag an object from the Navigation pane to the work area to open it.

- Add the information for the two records shown below to the table.

Your screen should be similar to Figure 2.84

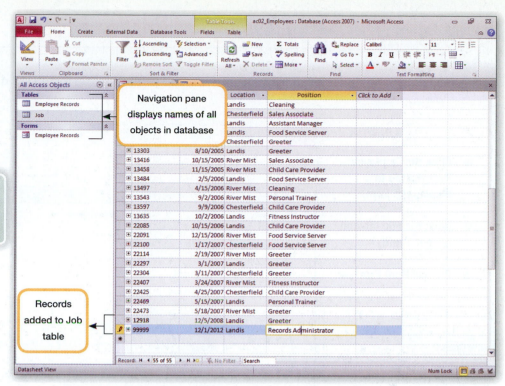

Figure 2.84

Field	Record 54	Record 55
Employee ID	12918	99999
Hire Date	12/5/2008	Today's date
Location	Landis	Landis
Position	Greeter	Records Administrator

Now both tables contain 55 records.

Previewing and Printing a Form

You want to preview and print only the form that displays your record.

1

- Click the Employee Records tab to display the form.

- Open the File tab and choose Print.

- Choose Print Preview.

Having Trouble?

Your form may display fewer records than in Figure 2.85.

Your screen should be similar to
Figure 2.85

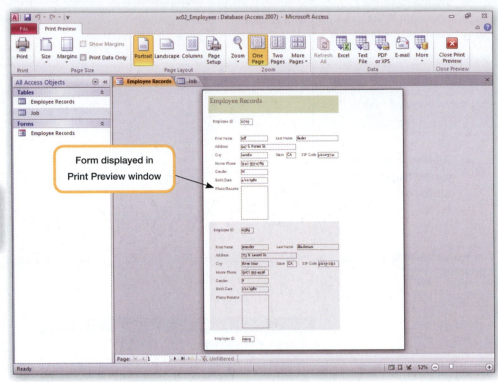

Form displayed in Print Preview window

Figure 2.85

The form object is displayed in the Print Preview window.

PRINTING A SELECTED RECORD

Access prints as many records as can be printed on a page using the Form layout. You want to print only the form displaying your record. To do this, you need to select your record first in Form view.

1

● Click [×] Close Print Preview .

● Display your record in the form.

● Click the Record Selector bar (the blue bar along the left side of the form) to select the entire record.

Another Method

You also can use [Select ▾]/Select in the Find group of the Home tab to select the record.

Your screen should be similar to Figure 2.86

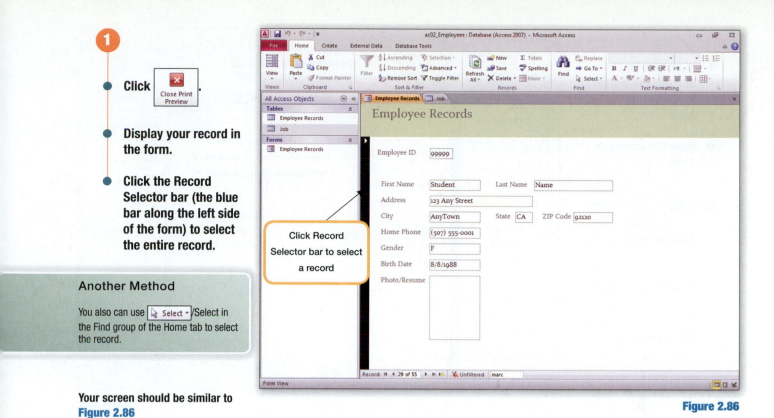

Click Record Selector bar to select a record

Figure 2.86

Now that the record is selected, you can print it.

2

● Open the File tab and choose Print.

● Choose Print.

● Choose the Selected Record(s) option from the Print dialog box.

● If necessary, make sure your printer is on and select the appropriate printer.

● Click [OK].

Identifying Object Dependencies

The form is the third database object that has been added to the file. Many objects that you create in a database have **object dependencies**, meaning they are dependent upon other objects for their content. In this case, the form is dependent upon the Employee Records database table for its content. Sometimes it is helpful to be able to find out what objects an object is dependent on or what depend on it. To help in these situations, you can display the object dependencies.

1

- **Select the Employee Records table object in the Navigation pane.**

- **Open the Database Tools tab.**

- **Click** 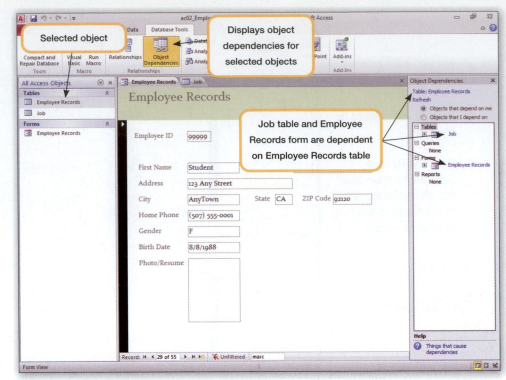 **in the Relationships group.**

- **If necessary, select "Objects that depend on me" from the Object Dependencies task pane.**

Your screen should be similar to
Figure 2.87

Figure 2.87

The Object Dependencies task pane identifies the two objects that are dependent on the table: the Job table and the Employee Records form. Next, you will see which objects depend on the Employee Records form.

2

- **Select Employee Records in the Forms category of the Navigation pane.**

- **Click Refresh in the Object Dependencies task pane.**

Your screen should be similar to
Figure 2.88

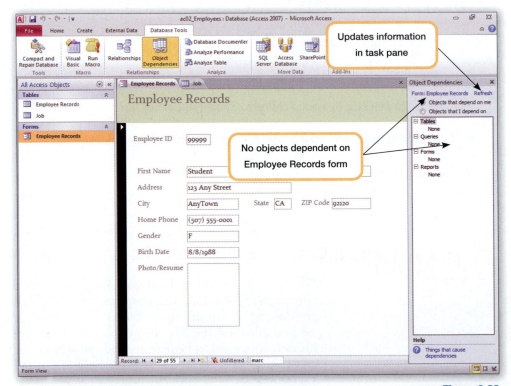

Figure 2.88

You can now see that the Employee Records form object does not have any objects dependent on it.

3
- Choose "Objects that I depend on" from the Object Dependencies task pane.

Your screen should be similar to
Figure 2.89

Figure 2.89

The Object Dependencies task pane identifies that the only object that the form depends on is the Employee Records table.

4

- Close the **Object Dependencies** task pane.

- Close the form and table objects, saving any changes.

- In the database properties, add your name as the author, and in the Comments box, add **This database contains 55 records and is still under construction**.

- Exit Access.

FOCUS ON CAREERS

EXPLORE YOUR CAREER OPTIONS

Administrative Assistant

Administrative assistants are typically responsible for the efficient management of office operations. This position may involve conducting research, training new staff, scheduling meetings, and maintaining databases. As an administrative assistant, you could be responsible for updating an inventory or staffing database. The typical salary range of an administrative assistant is $27,000 to $64,000. Demand for experienced administrative assistants, especially in technology and health fields, is expected to increase through 2018.

Format Property (AC2.7)

The Format property is used to specify the way that numbers, dates, times, and text in a field are displayed and printed.

Default Value Property (AC2.8)

The Default Value property is used to specify a value that is automatically entered in a field when a new record is created.

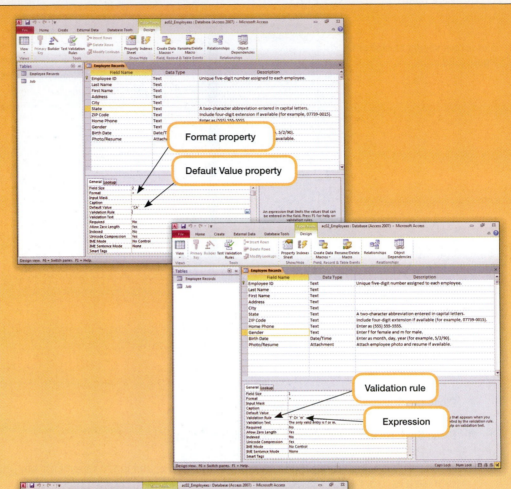

Validation Rule (AC2.11)

Validation rules are used to control the data that can be entered in a field by defining the input values that are valid or allowed.

Expression (AC2.11)

An expression is a formula consisting of a combination of symbols that will produce a single value.

Lookup Field (AC2.18)

A **lookup field** provides a list of values from which the user can choose to make entering data into that field simpler and more accurate.

Find and Replace (AC2.25)

The Find and Replace feature helps you quickly find specific information and automatically replace it with new information.

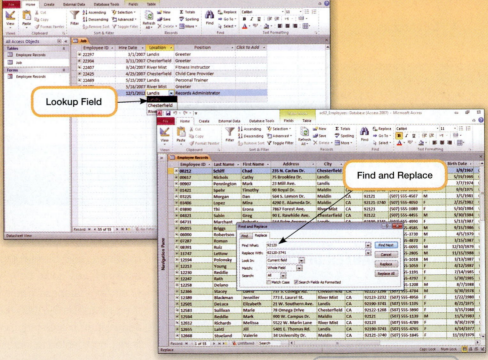

Sorting (AC2.33)

Sorting rearranges the order of the records in a table based on the value in each field.

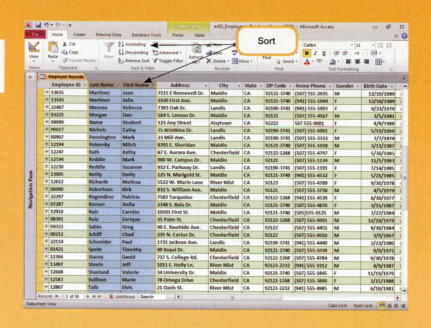

Filter (AC2.40)

A filter is a restriction placed on records in the open table or form to quickly isolate and display a subset of records.

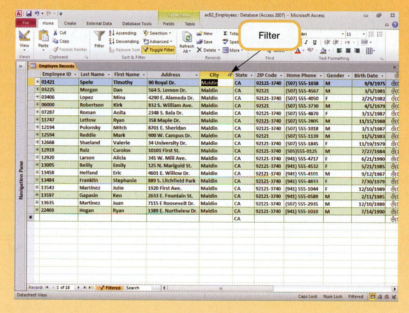

Form (AC2.46)

A form is a database object used primarily to display records onscreen to make it easier to enter new records and to make changes to existing records.

Controls (AC2.54)

Controls are objects that display information, perform actions, or enhance the design of a form or report.

Theme (AC2.69)

A theme is a predefined set of formatting choices that can be applied to an entire document in one simple step.

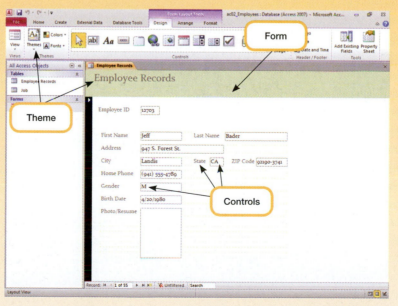

KEY TERMS

argument AC2.11
ascending sort order AC2.33
attachment control AC2.68
bound control AC2.54
character string AC2.8
comparison operator AC2.11
constant AC2.11
control AC2.54
criteria AC2.26
Default Value property AC2.8
descending sort order AC2.33
expression AC2.11
filter AC2.40
Find and Replace AC2.25
form AC2.46
format AC2.7
Format property AC2.7
Form Wizard AC2.48
function AC2.11
identifier AC2.11
IntelliSense AC2.12
label control AC2.54
layout AC2.51
lookup field AC2.18

lookup list AC2.18
Lookup Wizard AC2.18
merge cells AC2.64
object dependencies AC2.79
operator AC2.11
outer sort field AC2.34
record source AC2.47
sorting AC2.33
split cells AC2.65
stacked format AC2.51
tab order AC2.49
tabular format AC2.51
text control AC2.54
theme AC2.68
theme colors AC2.38
unbound control AC2.54
validation rule AC2.11
Validation Rule property AC2.11
validation text AC2.11
Validation Text property AC2.11
value list AC2.18
wildcards AC2.26
wizard AC2.18

COMMAND SUMMARY

Command	Shortcut	Action
Quick Access Toolbar		
↩ Undo	Ctrl + Z	Cancels last action
💾 Save	Ctrl + S	Saves the current object
Home tab		
Views group		
Form View	▣	Changes to Form view
Form Layout View	▤	Changes to Form Layout view
Text Formatting group		
B Bold	Ctrl + B	Applies bold effect to all text in datasheet
A ▾ Font Color		Applies selected color to all text in datasheet
⊞ ▾ Gridlines		Changes the display of gridlines in the datasheet
⊞ ▾ Alternate Row Color		Changes background color of alternate rows in datasheet
Sort & Filter group		
A↓ Ascending		Changes sort order to ascending
Z↓ Descending		Changes sort order to descending
A↕ Remove Sort		Clears all sorts and returns sort order to primary key order
▽ Filter		Used to specify filter settings for selected field
Selection ▾ /Equals		Sets filter to display only those records containing selected value
Advanced ▾ /Clear All Filters		Deletes all filters from table
▽ Toggle Filter		Applies and removes filter from table
Records group		
Save	⇧ Shift + ↵ Enter	Saves changes to object design
New	Ctrl + +	Adds new record
More ▾ /Hide Fields		Hides selected columns in Datasheet view

LAB REVIEW

COMMAND SUMMARY (CONTINUED)

Command	Shortcut	Action
More ▾ /Unhide Fields		Redisplays hidden columns
Find group		
Find	Ctrl + F	Locates specified data
Replace	Ctrl + H	Locates specified data and replaces it with specified replacement text
Go To ▾		Moves to First, Previous, Next, Last, or New record location
Select ▾ /Select		Selects current record
Select ▾ /Select All		Selects all records in database
Create tab		
Tables group		
Table		Creates a new table in Datasheet view
Table Design		Creates a new table in Design view
Forms group		
Form		Creates a new form using all the fields from the underlying table
Blank Form		Displays a blank form to which you add the fields from the table that you want to appear on the form
Form Wizard		Creates a new form by following the steps in the Form Wizard
Database Tools tab		
Relationships group		
Object Dependencies		Shows the objects in the database that use the selected object
Table Tools Design tab		
Tools group		
Insert Rows		Inserts a new field in Table Design view

COMMAND SUMMARY (CONTINUED)

Command	Shortcut	Action
Table Tools Fields tab		
Add & Delete group		
More Fields ▾ / Lookup & Relationship		Creates a lookup field
Form Design Tools Design tab		
Themes group		
Themes		Opens gallery of theme styles
Tools group		
Add Existing Fields		Adds selected existing field to form
Form Design Tools Arrange tab		
Table group		
Stacked		Applies Stacked layout to the controls
Rows & Columns group		
Select Layout		Selects entire layout
Select Column		Selects column in a layout
Select Row		Selects row in a layout
Insert Left		Inserts a blank column to the left of the selected cell in a layout
Insert Below		Inserts a blank row below the selected cell in a layout
Merge/Split group		
Split Horizontally		Divides a layout cell horizontally into two cells
Merge		Combines two or more layout cells into a single cell
Form Design Tools Format tab		
Font group		
Align Text Right		Right aligns contents of cell

LAB EXERCISES

MATCHING

Match the numbered item with the correct lettered description.

1. record source   ____ a. wildcard character
2. form   ____ b. underlying table for a form
3. *   ____ c. locates specified values in a field
4. filter   ____ d. an expression
5. tab order   ____ e. database object used primarily for onscreen display
6. character string   ____ f. order that the selection point moves in a form when Tab ⇆ is used
7. find   ____ g. temporarily displays subset of records
8. >=   ____ h. operator
9. ascending sort   ____ i. a group of characters
10. ="Y" Or "N"   ____ j. rearranges records in A to Z or 0 to 9 order

TRUE/FALSE

Circle the correct answer to the following statements.

1. Values are numbers, dates, or pictures.	True	False
2. An expression is a sequence of characters (letters, numbers, or symbols) that must be handled as text, not as numeric data.	True	False
3. Label controls are bound controls.	True	False
4. A contrast operator is a symbol that allows you to make comparisons between two items.	True	False
5. A validation rule is an expression that defines acceptable data entry values.	True	False
6. Filter results can be saved with the database and quickly redisplayed.	True	False
7. Database objects are not dependent on one another.	True	False
8. The Default Value property determines the value automatically entered into a field of a new record.	True	False
9. Forms are database objects used primarily for viewing data.	True	False
10. Text controls display descriptive labels.	True	False

FILL-IN

Complete the following statements by filling in the blanks with the correct terms.

1. The two basic form layouts are _____ and _____.

2. The _____ property is used to specify a value that is automatically entered in a field when a new record is created.

3. A(n) _____ is a guide that helps you align controls in a form horizontally and vertically.

4. The most common controls are _____ controls and _____ controls.

5. The _____ property changes the way data appears in a field.

6. Format _____ is used to create custom formats that change the way numbers, dates, times, and text display and print.

7. _____ is displayed when an invalid entry is entered.

8. _____ restrict the type of data that can be entered in a field.

9. A(n) _____ is a symbol or word that indicates that an operation is to be performed.

10. The upper section of the Navigation pane contains _____, and the lower section contains_____.

LAB EXERCISES

MULTIPLE CHOICE

Circle the letter of the correct response.

1. A _____ is a feature that guides you step by step through a process.
   a. dialog box
   b. wizard
   c. task pane
   d. gallery

2. _____ properties change the way that data is displayed.
   a. Format
   b. Field
   c. Data
   d. Record

3. The _____ property is commonly used when most of the entries in a field will be the same for the entire table.
   a. AutoNumber
   b. Default Value
   c. Field Data
   d. Best Fit

4. A(n) _____ control is linked to its underlying data source.
   a. bound
   b. label
   c. field
   d. unbound

5. _____ is/are an explanatory message that appears if a user attempts to enter invalid information in a text field.
   a. Validation text
   b. Validation rule
   c. Expressions
   d. Validity checks

6. The _____ is used to specify a value that is automatically entered in a field when a new record is created.
   a. Default Value property
   b. Sort property
   c. field value
   d. Format property

7. _____ layouts arrange data vertically with a field label to the left of the field data.
   a. Datasheet
   b. Justified
   c. Tabular
   d. Stacked

8. A _____ is a temporary restriction placed on a table to display a subset of records.
   a. wildcard
   b. control
   c. filter
   d. sort

9. A form is _____ an underlying table for its content.
   a. independent of
   b. reliant on
   c. contingent on
   d. dependent on

10. _____ control(s) how data is displayed in a form.
    a. Design styles
    b. Controls
    c. Layouts
    d. Tab order

STEP-BY-STEP

NOTE Before you begin, you may want to create a backup copy of each data file by copying and renaming it.

SECOND TIME AROUND INVENTORY DATABASE ★

1. You have already set up an inventory database for the Second Time Around consignment shop. It currently contains fields for the item number, description, price, and consignor last name, and it has records for the inventory currently in stock. The owner of the shop is quite pleased with the database as it stands but has asked you to change the name of the existing Price field to show that it is the original price and to add a new field for the current selling price of the item. Also, she would like you to modify some existing records, create a form to ease data entry, and print a copy of the form. Your completed table and form will be similar to those shown here.

   a. Open the database named ac02_Second Time Around and the table named Antiques Inventory.

   b. Change the Price field name to **Consignment Price**. Change the data type for this field to Currency.

   c. Insert the following field before the Consignor Last Name field:

   Field Name: Sale Price

   Data Type: Currency

   d. Make all fields except Sale Price required. (Hint: Set the Required property to Yes.) Reduce the field size of the Consignor Last Name field to **25**.

   e. Switch to Datasheet view and respond "yes" to all prompts and warnings when saving the design changes. (When the Consignment Price field is converted to the currency data type, the "contact dealer" text will be deleted from the field.)

f. Update the table by entering **0.00** in the Consignment Price field for all records that have a blank entry in this field. (Hint: Use copy and paste.)

g. Enter appropriate values in the Sale Price field for each record. (Generally the sale price is 33 percent more than the consignment price.) Leave the Sale Price field blank for those items with $0.00 in the Consignment Price field.

h. Appropriately size all columns to fully display the data.

i. Find all occurrences of dates that include an apostrophe (1930's) and are preceded with the word circa. Manually delete the 's from each located item.

j. Filter the table to display all records with a consignment price greater than or equal to $4,500. Sort the filtered records in ascending sort order by consignment price.

k. Format the datasheet using alternate row fill colors. Print the filtered table in landscape orientation with normal margins. Close the table object.

l. Use the Form tool to create a simple form for the Antiques Inventory table.

m. Display the form in Layout view. Change the form Theme style to another of your choice. Reduce the size of all the text controls to best fit the contents.

n. Use the new form to enter the following new records:

	Record 1	Record 2
Description	Machine Age Refracting Telescope	Mid Century School House Globe
Consignment Price	$4,800	$1,100
Consignor Last Name	[Your Last Name]	Lewis

o. Print the form for the record containing your name. Close the form, saving it as **Inventory**.

p. Open the table and rerun the filter to display your record in the results. Print the filtered datasheet in landscape orientation using the normal margin setting. Close the table.

q. Display all object types in the Navigation pane.

r. Add your name to the database properties and exit Access.

ENTERPRIZE EMPLOYMENT CLIENT DATABASE ★ ★

2. You work for a private employment agency as an administrative assistant. As part of your responsibilities, you maintain a client database that contains the job candidates' basic contact information: name, address, and phone number. The office manager has asked you to add to the database the date each candidate applied at your office, the date they were placed with an employer, and the employer's name. Also, because the database is getting rather large, you decide to create a form to make it easier to enter and update records. Your completed table and form will be similar to those shown here.

a. Open the database named ac02_ Enterprize Employment Agency and the table named Candidates.

b. Reduce the State field size to **2**. Change the State field Format property to display all entries in uppercase. Make the default value for the State field **FL**.

c. Change the ZIP Code data type to Text with a field size of **10**.

d. Insert the following field after the Application # field.

Field Name:	**Application Date**
Data Type:	Date/Time
Format:	Short Date

e. Add the following two fields to the end of the table:

Field Name:	**Hire Date**
Data Type:	Date/Time
Format:	Short Date
Field Name:	**Employed By**
Data Type:	Text
Description:	**Enter the name of the employer**
Field Size:	**45**

f. Switch to Datasheet view and save the table design changes.

g. All ZIP Codes of 72725 need to be changed to **72725-1016**. Use Find and Replace to make this change in the database. Best Fit the columns.

h. Use the Form Wizard to create a form for the Candidates table. Include all the table fields in their current order. Use the columnar layout and a theme of your choice. Title the form **Candidate Information**.

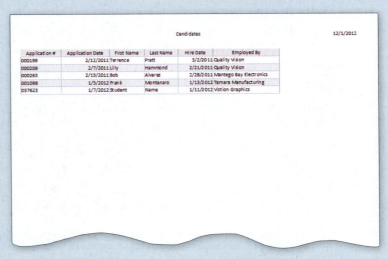

i. In Form Layout view, select the label and text box controls for all the fields except the Application # and Application Date. Apply the stacked layout, then adjust the column widths so they best fit the contents in the form.

j. Insert a column on the right side of the layout. Make the following changes to the placement of the controls:

- Move the Last Name label and control to the right of the First Name field.
- Move the State label and control to the right of the City field.
- Horizontally split the cell containing the State label and then move the State control next to the label.
- Move the ZIP Code field to the right of the State field. Horizontally split the cell containing the ZIP Code; then move the ZIP Code control next to the label.
- Move the Phone label and control underneath the City field.
- Select the Last Name label. Insert a blank row above and a blank column to the left. Adjust the blank column width so that it is about .25″ wide, just enough to give some space between the fields.
- Merge the Address control with the two blank cells on the right.
- Merge the Employed By control with the two blank cells on the right.
- Delete any empty row or column placeholders in the layout, but leave one empty row above the First Name and the Hire Date. Resize all columns to best fit the contents.

k. Use the new form to enter the following records in Form view:

Application #	001098	037623
Application Date	1/5/12	1/7/12
First Name	Frank	Your first name
Last Name	Montanaro	Your last name
Address	124 Beach Front Way	802 Valimara Way
City	Lexington	Palmdale
State	FL	FL
ZIP Code	72724	72725-1016
Phone	(726) 555-4623	(726) 555-0909
Hire Date	1/13/12	1/11/12
Employed By	Tamara Manufacturing	Vistion Graphics

l. Use the Search feature to locate the following records and update their data.

Locate	Application Date	Hire Date	Employed By
Lilly Hammond	2/7/11	2/21/11	Paper Products etc.
Terrence Pratt	2/12/11	3/2/11	Quality Vision
Bob Alvarez	2/15/11	2/28/11	Mantego Bay Electronics

m. Display all object types in the Navigation pane.

n. Print the form for the record containing your name.

o. Filter the Candidates table to display only those records displaying a hire date. Sort the records in ascending order by last name. Hide the Address through Phone columns.

LAB EXERCISES

p. Print the filtered datasheet using the wide margin setting in landscape orientation.

q. Remove the filter and unhide the columns.

r. Add your name to the database properties. Close all objects and exit Access.

ARF TRACKING DATABASE ★★

3. You have created a database for tracking the animals that come into and go out of the Animal Rescue Foundation. Now you need to modify the database structure and customize field properties to control the data entered by the foundation's volunteers who are assigned this task. You also want to create a form to make it easier for the volunteers to enter the necessary information. Your completed datasheet and form will be similar to those shown here.

a. Open the file ac02_ARF Database and the table Rescues in Datasheet view.

b. Use the Replace command to change the Age field from abbreviations to spelled out information. Make Y = Young, A = Adult, and B = Baby.

c. Use Find to locate ID # R-904. Add the adoption date 6/13/2012.

d. Use Search to locate the animal named Spreckels; change the age to B and enter 12/01/2012 as the Foster Date.

e. Create a values lookup field to select Boarded, Foster Care, or Adopted. Place the field before the Arrival Date field, with the following specifications:

Field Name:	**Status**
Description:	**Select Boarded, Foster Care, or Adopted**
Field Size:	**15**

f. Make the following additional changes to the database structure:

- Restrict the entries in the Status field to list items only. Make **Boarded** the default value for Status.

- Add a validation rule and validation text to the Gender field to accept only M or F (male or female). Format the field to display the information in uppercase.

- Change the Age field to a lookup field to accept only the values of Baby, Young, or Adult. Increase the field size to 5. Restrict the entries to items on the list only.

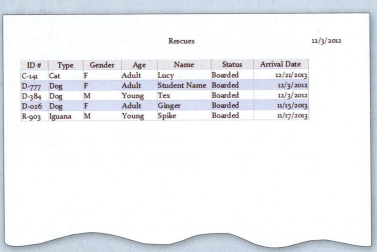

g. In Datasheet view, complete the data for the Status by entering F (if there is a Foster Date only), A (if there is an adoption date), or B (if there is neither a foster nor an adoption date).

h. Add formatting of your choice to the Datasheet. Change the font of the datasheet to Constantia, 12 point.

i. Best Fit all columns.

j. Use the Form Wizard to create a columnar form. Include all the fields except for the Photo attachment field. Add the fields in their current order and title the form **Animals**.

k. Switch to Form Layout view and make the following changes to the form:

- Choose a theme design style of your choice.
- Apply the stacked layout to all the controls except the form title.
- Insert three columns to the right. Move the Name label and control to the right of the ID text control, in the second empty column.
- Add the Photo attachment field under the Name label, on the right side of the form. Select the attachment control box and the four empty cells beneath it. Merge these cells together.
- Adjust the widths of the empty column, labels, and controls to better fit their contents.

l. Search in Form view to locate the animal named Titus and add the picture ac02_WhiteDog to the Attachment field.

m. Add two records using the new form. Use the ID # **D-384** for the first record and attach the picture of ac02_Tex_dog, a young male dog. In the second record you add, use the ID # **D-777** and enter your name in the Name field. Attach the picture of ac02_Lilly_dog, who is an adult female dog, to your record. For both records, use the current date as the arrival date, and make the status Boarded.

n. Save the form and print the record with your name as the animal name.

o. Filter the Rescues datasheet to display only those animals with a status of Boarded. Sort the filtered datasheet by Type. Hide the Foster Date, Adoption Date, and Photo attachment columns. Print the Rescues datasheet in portrait orientation using the wide margin setting.

p. Unhide all columns. Clear all sorts and remove the filter.

q. Display all object types in the Navigation pane.

r. Identify object dependencies.

s. Add your name to the database properties. Close all objects and exit Access.

LAB EXERCISES

PEPPER RIDGE RENTALS DATABASE ★ ★ ★

4. Pepper Ridge Rentals is a property rental business, and you recently put the rental homes into a database to track the rental properties. The database initially began with basic facts about each home, but now you see the need for more detailed information. A database will be useful to look up any information about the rental, including its location, how many bedrooms and bathrooms, square footage, and date available. You decide to make some additional changes to help with inventory control and make data entry even easier. This will help you find rentals within the desired home size and price range of your clients. When you are finished, your printed database table and form should be similar to the ones shown here.

a. Open the database file you created in Lab1, PepperRidgeRentals. Save the file as PepperRidgeRentals2.

b. Open the table Rental Homes.

c. Add a Currency field after the Sq Footage field. Name the new field **Monthly Rent**.

d. Add a Memo field at the end of the table and name it **Comments**.

e. You want to add a new field to show the condition of each home. This field can only contain four possible values: Pets not okay, Pets okay, Horses and pets allowed, or Assistant animals only. Insert a new field after Sq Footage named **Animal Permission**. Use a data type of Lookup and enter the following as list values: **Pets not okay**, **Pets okay**, **Horses and pets allowed**, or **Assistant animals only**. Set the field's default value to **Pets not okay**, and limit entries to the list items.

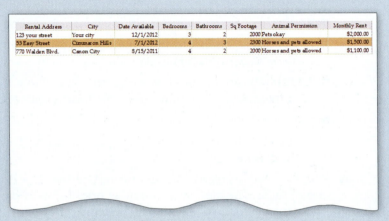

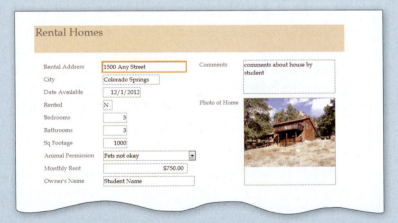

AC2.98   Lab 2: Modifying and Filtering a Table and Creating a Form   WWW.MHHE.COM/OLEARY

Access 2010

f. In Datasheet view, add two new records:

Rental Address:	770 Walden Blvd.	654 Sunset Lane
City:	Canon	Canon
Date Available:	8/15/2011	7/1/2011
Bedrooms:	4	3
Bathrooms:	2	2
Sq Footage:	2000	1500
Animal Permission:	Horses and pets allowed	Assistant animals only
Monthly Rent:	$1100	$850
Owner's Name:	George Mitchel	Gretchen Heinz
Comments:	Beautiful home with horse barn and corrals	Located in the city in a new subdivision with amenities

g. Widen the fields to best fit the data.

h. Hide the Rental ID, Bedrooms, Bathrooms, Sq Footage, Owner's Name, and Photo Attachment fields.

i. Update the other records with information for the new fields (Monthly Rent, Animal Permission, and Comments):

Record	Monthly Rent	Animal Permission	Comments
1500 Sycamore Lane	$1000	Pets not okay	Townhome with homeowners association rules
53 Easy Street	$1500	Horses and pets allowed	Big ranch house with acreage and horse facilities
221 Cedar Street	$650	Pets okay	Older home close to nice parks
Your street	name your price	Pets okay	your comments

j. Unhide all fields.

k. Find all instances of Canon in the City field and replace with **Canon City**.

l. Insert a new field after the Date Available field named **Rented** with a field size of **1**, data type of Text. Add **"Y" or "N"** as a validation rule. Add **Must be Y or N** as the Validation text. Format the field to display in uppercase.

m. Use Search to find the record for 221 Cedar Street. The home has been rented out, so delete the entry in Date Available and type in **Y** for the Rented field. Enter **N** for all other Rented fields.

n. Add formatting of your choice to the datasheet. Change the font of the datasheet to one of your choice. Adjust column widths as needed.

o. Use the Form Wizard to create a form for the Rentals table. Include all of the fields except Rental ID and Photo of Home from the Rentals table, in order. Use the columnar form layout and accept the form name **Rentals**.

p. Switch to Layout view. Select a Theme style. Select the Comments label and text control and apply the stacked layout. Resize the Comments controls so they are the same size as the controls above. Move the Comments stacked control group to the right side of the other fields. Add the Photo of Home form field below the Comments field. Resize the height of the row containing the Photo control so the bottom of the photo box aligns with the bottom of the Owner's Name control. Resize the fields to fit their labels and data.

LAB EXERCISES

q. Use the form to enter another new record with an address of your choice, **Colorado Springs** for the city, and your name as the owner. Include **Pets not okay** for the Animal Permission field, a monthly rent price of **$750**, today's date as the date available, and comments of your choice in the Comments field. Insert the picture **ac02_pine_cottage** for the Photo of Home field.

r. Preview and print the form for your new record in landscape orientation. Save and close the form.

s. Filter the Rental Homes table to display only those records with Rented N, and Pets okay (hint: select both pets okay and pets allowed options). Hide the Rental ID, Rented, Owner Name, Attachments, and Comments fields. Print the filtered datasheet in landscape orientation with narrow margins.

t. Display all object types in the Navigation pane.

u. Add your name to the database properties as the author. Save the database and exit Access.

KODIAK CONSTRUCTION DATABASE ★ ★ ★

5. Although the database you designed for the expanding Kodiak Construction Company was well received, you have been asked to make several additions and improvements to the original design. In addition, they have asked you to create a form to make the process of entering new records in the database easier. Your completed database table and form will be similar to those shown here.

a. Open the file ac02_Kodiak Construction.

b. Open the Clients table and switch to Design view. Insert a new field before the Business Phone field named **Home Phone**. Include a description. Set the field size to **14**.

c. Enter the following Home Phone numbers into the table. Hide the fields between the Last Name and Home Phone fields. Use Find to locate the records. Unhide the columns when you are done.

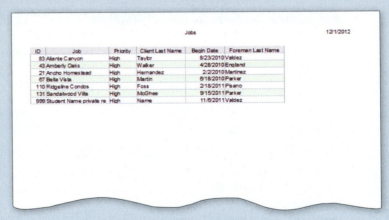

Last Name	Home Phone
Lopez	(303) 555-3772
Miller	(303) 555-0831
Walker	(303) 555-4613
Young	(303) 555-0912

d. Change the City column to a Lookup Field data type. Include the following cities as the lookup list values: Aurora, Denver, Glendale, Lakewood, Littleton, and Parker.

e. Open the City field drop-down list for each record and select a city.

f. Make the default value for the State field **CO**. Change the format to uppercase.

Next, you want to add a field for the job priority to the Jobs table. This field can only contain three possible values: High, Normal, or Low. Instead of typing this information in the field, you will make the field a lookup field.

g. Open the Jobs table in Design view and insert the new field named **Priority** after the Job field. Select the Lookup Wizard from the Data Type list. Select the "I will type in the values that I want." option. In column 1, enter **High** in the first cell, **Normal** in the second cell, and **Low** in the third cell. Accept the field name. Set the field's size to **15** and the default value to **Normal**. Limit entries to values from the list.

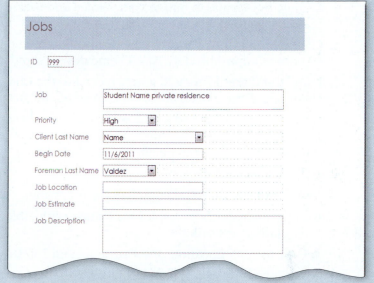

You decide to use the Lookup Wizard for the Client Last Name and Foreman Last Name fields as well because this will save input time and reduce the chance of any entry errors.

h. Create a lookup for the Client Last Name field to obtain its values from the Clients table. Display the Last Name and First Name fields in the lookup. Choose ascending sort order by Last Name. Adjust the column widths for the lookup fields as needed. Use the default name for the label of the lookup field (Client Last Name).

i. In a similar fashion, use the Lookup Wizard to establish the lookup for the Foreman Last Name, using the Foremen table.

j. Switch to Datasheet view, saving your design changes.

k. Open the Priority field drop-down list for each record and select a priority level. Using this same technique, assign clients and foremen to each job.

l. Best Fit the columns.

m. Add formatting of your choice to the Jobs datasheet. Change the font to Arial. Close the table.

n. Enforce referential integrity in the relationships between all tables. Close the Relationships window and save your changes.

o. Use the Form Wizard to create a form for the Jobs table. Include all of the fields from the Jobs table in order. Use the columnar form layout. Accept the default form name (**Jobs**).

p. In Form view, search for the record for R Bar C Ranch. Change the foreman to **Valdez**.

q. In Form Layout view, make the following changes:

- Group the controls in stacked layout, and then move them down about 1".
- Move the ID field outside the layout.
- Add a column to the right side of the main set of stacked fields.
- Horizontally split the cells containing the text controls for Priority and Begin Date.
- Merge the Job Description text control with the cell to the right.
- Merge the Job text control with the cell on the right.
- Appropriately size the label and text controls for all fields.
- Remove the empty row at the top of the stacked layout.

LAB EXERCISES

r. Change the Theme to one of your choice and then change the Font Theme to Austin (Century Gothic).

s. Create similar forms for the Clients and Foremen tables. Keep the default form layout. Size the ID controls appropriately. The Theme design should match the Job table.

t. Using the Client form, add a new record to the Client table using your first and last names as the client name. Save the changes and close the form.

u. Using the Job form, add a new record to the Jobs table with **999** as the ID and **[your last name] private residence** as the job; select your name as the client last name, priority of high, the current date as the begin date, and a foreman of your choice.

v. Print your record in the form.

w. Open the Jobs table and complete the following:

- Filter the records to display only those with a high priority. Sort the filtered records by Job in ascending sort order.
- Hide the Job Location, Job Estimate, and Job Description columns. Print the filtered Jobs datasheet in landscape orientation.
- Unhide all columns. Clear all sorts and remove the filter.

x. Display all object types in the Navigation pane.

y. Add your name to the database properties. Save and close the database.

ON YOUR OWN

ADVENTURE TRAVEL PACKAGES FORM ★

1. You have heard from the employees of Adventure Travel Tours that the database table you created is a bit unwieldy for them to enter the necessary data because it now contains so many fields that it requires scrolling across the screen to locate them. You decide to create a form that will make entering data not only easier, but more attractive as well. Open the ac02_ATT database. Best fit the columns. Change the order of the Length and Description field columns in Design view. Apply formatting of your choice to the datasheet. Sort the table on Destination in ascending order. Use the Form Wizard to create a form called **Travel Packages** for the Packages table. Use the form to enter five new records with tour package information of your choice (use the newspaper travel section or the Web for ideas). Enter your name as the contact in one of the new records. Print the form containing your name. Print the datasheet in landscape orientation.

AMP ACCOUNT TRACKING ★ ★

2. While creating the database table for AMP Enterprises, you learned that some employees have been receiving advances for anticipated expenses (such as for travel). You also have been informed that the CEO wants to start tracking the expenses by department. Open the database file AMP Enterprise (Lab 1, On Your Own 5). Add a new field named **Advanced Amount** with a Currency data type to the Employee Expenses table. Also add a Yes/No field named **Payment Made** to record whether or not the expense has been paid, with a corresponding validation rule and message. In the Employee Info table, add a new field named **Department** for the department's charge code number. Update both tables to include appropriate values in the new fields in the existing records. Apply formatting of your choice to the Employee Expenses datasheet. Sort the Employee Expenses table on the Expense Amount field in descending sort order. Close the table, saving the changes. Use the Form Wizard to create a form named **Expenses** for the Employee Expenses table. Include the form title **Your Name Expenses**. Modify the form in Layout view to make it more attractive and user friendly. To test the form, enter a new expense record using the employee ID number for the record containing your name in the Employee Info table. Select your record in the form and print it.

DENTAL PATIENT DATABASE UPDATE ★ ★

3. The dentist office for which you created a patient database has expanded to include a second dentist and receptionist. The two dentists are Dr. Jones and Dr. Smith. You now need to modify the database to identify required fields and to add a new field that identifies which patient is assigned to which dentist. You also decide that creating a form for the database would make it easier for both you and the other receptionist to enter and locate patient information. Open the Dental Patients database (Lab 1, On Your Own 3) and the Patient Information table. Make the patient identification number, name, and phone number required fields. Add a **Dentist Name** Lookup list field, with the two dentists' names and an appropriate validation rule and message. Update the table to "assign" some of the patients to one of the dentists and some patients to the other dentist. Assign the record containing your name to Dr. Jones. Sort the table by dentist name to see the results of your new assignments. "Reassign" one of the displayed patients and then remove the sort. Filter the table to display only those patients for Dr. Jones. Apply formatting of your choice to the datasheet. Print the filtered datasheet and then remove the filter. Create a form called **Patient Data** for the table using the Form Wizard. Modify the form in Layout view to make it more attractive and user friendly. Enter two new records, one for each of the dentists. Use the Search feature to locate the record that has your name as the patient, and then select and print the displayed record in the form.

LEWIS & LEWIS EMPLOYEE DATABASE ★ ★

4. You work in the Human Resource Management department at Lewis & Lewis, Inc. You recently created a simple database containing information on each employee's department and work telephone extension. Several of your coworkers also want to use the database. You decide to add a field for the employee's job title and enhance the table. You also want to create a form that will make it easier for others to update the information in the database. Open the ac02_Lewis Personnel database and Phone List table and add the **Job Title** field after the Department field. Update the table to include information in the new field for the existing records (hint: use job titles such as Accounts Payable Clerk, Graphic Design Coordinator, Personnel Manager, etc.). Add a new record that

LAB EXERCISES

includes your name and Administrative Assistant for the job title. Apply formatting of your choice to the datasheet. Sort the table by Department and Last Name. Use the Search feature to locate and delete the record for Anna Tai, who has left the company. Print the datasheet in landscape orientation. Remove the sort and close the table, saving the changes. Create a form called **Phone List** for the Phone List table using the Form Wizard. Modify the form using Layout view and place the controls in a more user-friendly order (for example, place the Last Name control to the right of the First Name control.) Enter five new records. Use the Replace command to locate and change the last name for Alexa Hirsch to Alexa **Muirhead**, who has gotten married since you first created the database. Use the Search feature to locate the record form that has your name as the employee. Select and print the displayed record.

TIMELESS TREASURES INVENTORY DATABASE ★ ★ ★

5. You realize that you have left out some very important fields in the Inventory table you created in the Timeless Treasures database (Lab 1, On Your Own 4)—fields that identify the sources where you can obtain the vintage watches your customers are looking for. Repeat your Web search for old watches and note the resources (for example, online shopping services, specialty stores, or individual collectors who are offering these items at online auctions) for the watches in your table. Add a **Source Name** field, a **Source E-mail** field, and a **Source Phone** field to the table. Update the table to include this information in the existing records. Apply formatting of your choice to the datasheet. Sort the records according to the Source Name field and adjust the column widths to accommodate the new information. Print the datasheet. Remove the sort and close the table, saving the changes. Now, to make data entry easier, create a form named **Watches** using the Form Wizard. Modify the arrangement of controls to make the form more visually appealing. Use the form to locate the record with your name as the manufacturer, and then print it.

Objectives

After completing this lab, you will know how to:

1. Evaluate table design.

2. Modify relationships.

3. Enforce referential integrity.

4. Create and modify a simple query.

5. Query two tables.

6. Filter a query.

7. Find unmatched and duplicate records.

8. Create a parameter query.

9. Create reports from tables and queries.

10. Display a Totals row.

11. Modify a report design.

12. Select, move, and size controls.

13. Change page margins.

14. Preview and print a report.

15. Compact and back up a database.

Lifestyle Fitness Club

After modifying the structure of the table of personal data, you have continued to enter many more records. You also have created a second table in the database that contains employee information about location and job titles. Again, the owners are very impressed with the database. They are eager to see how the information in the database can be used.

As you have seen, compiling, storing, and updating information in a database is very useful. The real strength of a database program, however, is its ability to find

the information you need quickly, and to manipulate and analyze it to answer specific questions. You will use the information in the tables to provide the answers to several inquiries about the club's employees. As you learn about the database's analytical features, imagine trying to do the same tasks by hand. How long would it take? Would your results be as accurate or as well presented? In addition, you will create several reports that present the information from the database attractively.

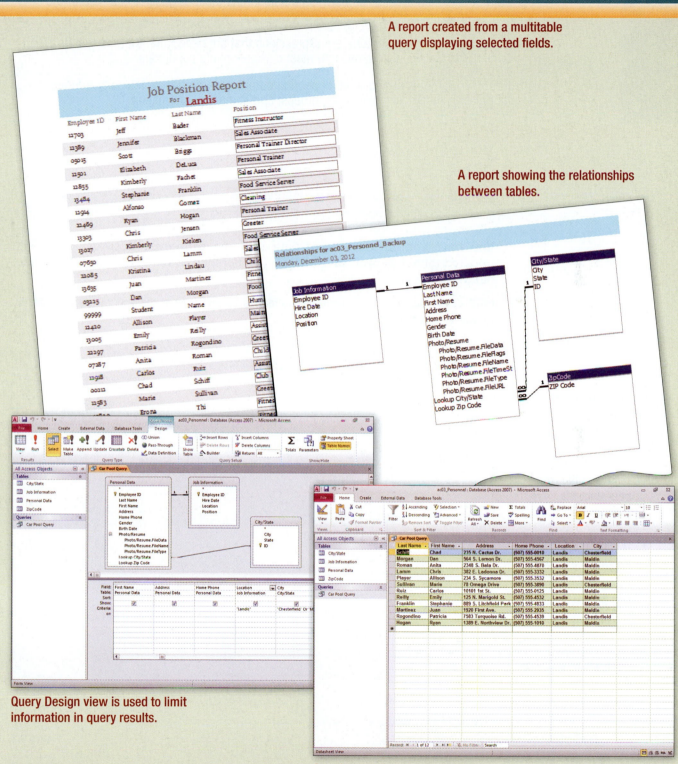

A report created from a multitable query displaying selected fields.

A report showing the relationships between tables.

Query Design view is used to limit information in query results.

Creating queries of data limits the information that is displayed in the results.

The following concepts will be introduced in this lab:

1 Query A query is a request for specific data contained in a database. Queries are used to view data in different ways, to analyze data, and even to change existing data.

2 Join A join is an association between a field in one table or query and a field of the same data type in another table or query.

3 Query Criteria Query criteria are expressions that are used to restrict the results of a query to display only records that meet certain limiting conditions.

4 Report A report is professional-appearing output generated from tables or queries that may include design elements, groups, and summary information.

Refining the Database Design

You have continued to enter data into the Employee Records table. The updated table has been saved for you as Personal Data in the ac03_Personnel database file.

NOTE Before you begin, you may want to create a backup copy of the ac03_Personnel file by copying and renaming it.

1

● Start Microsoft Access 2010.

● Open the ac03_Personnel database file from your data file location.

● If necessary, click

Enable Content

in response to the Security Warning in the message bar.

Your screen should be similar to Figure 3.1

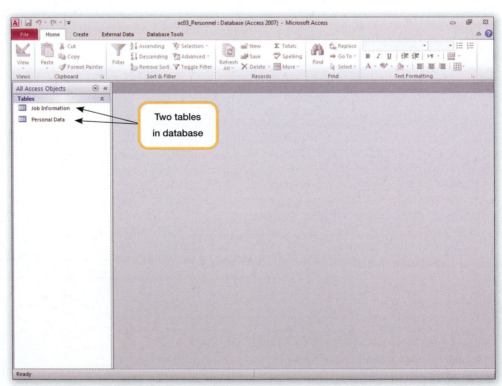

Figure 3.1

The Navigation pane displays the names of two tables in this database: Personal Data and Job Information.

2

- Open the Personal Data table.

- Add your information as record number 70 using your special ID number **99999** and your name. Enter **Maldin** as the city and **92121** as the zip code. Fill in the remaining fields as desired.

- Return to the first field of the first record.

- Hide the Navigation pane.

Your screen should be similar to Figure 3.2

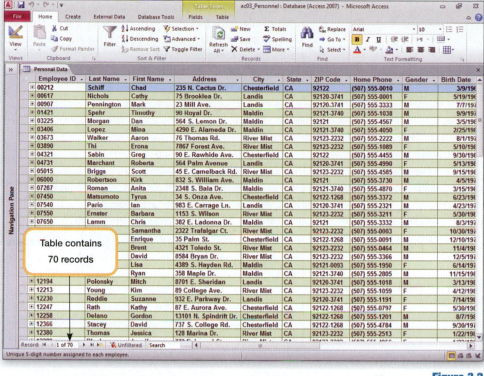

Figure 3.2

EVALUATING TABLE DESIGN

As you continue to use and refine the database, you have noticed that you repeatedly enter the same city, state, and zip code information in the Personal Data table. You decide there may be a better way to organize the table information and will use the Table Analyzer tool to help evaluate the design of the Personal Data table.

1

- Open the Database Tools tab.

- Click Analyze Table in the Analyze group.

Your screen should be similar to Figure 3.3

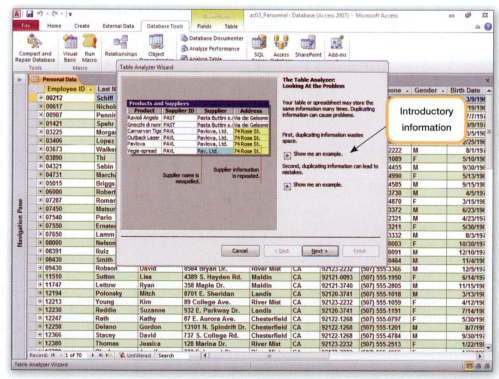

Figure 3.3

Refining the Database Design

AC3.5

The first two windows of Table Analyzer Wizard are introductory pages that review the process that will be used. First, the wizard will analyze the information stored in the table by looking for duplicate information. Then, if duplicates are located, it will split the original table and create new tables to store the information a single time to solve the problem.

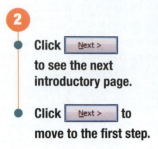

● Click **Next >** to see the next introductory page.

● Click **Next >** to move to the first step.

Your screen should be similar to Figure 3.4

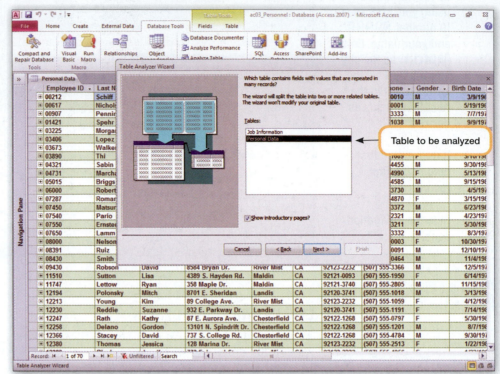

Figure 3.4

In the next two steps, you identify the table you want to evaluate and whether you want the wizard to decide what fields to place in the new table or whether you would rather make that determination yourself.

3

- Click [Next >] to accept analyzing the Personal Data table.

- Click [Next >] to accept letting the wizard decide.

- If the field names in the Table2 and Table3 list boxes are not visible, increase the length and/or width of the box.

Having Trouble?

Drag the top or bottom border to size the object vertically. Drag the right border to change the object's width.

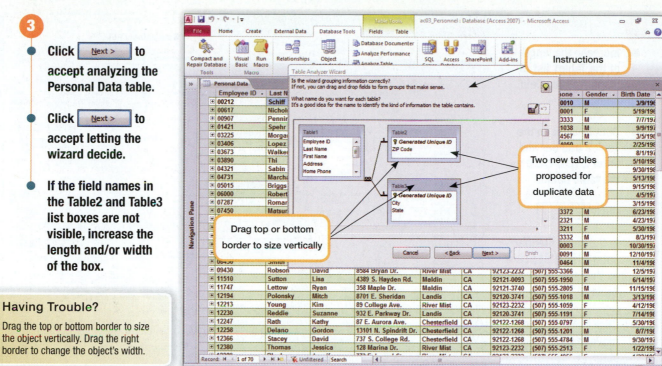

Figure 3.5

Your screen should be similar to
Figure 3.5

The wizard has identified duplicate data in the ZIP Code, City, and State fields and proposes to move these fields into two additional tables—one for ZIP Codes and the other for city and state—where the information would be stored only once. The instructions at the top of the Table Analyzer Wizard box ask you to revise the grouping if needed and to create names for the tables. You agree that creating the two new tables will prevent duplicate data. You will then rename the new tables and move to the next step.

4

- Increase the length of the Table1 list to display all the field names.

- Double-click on the Table2 title bar and enter **ZipCode** as the table name.

- Click ▭ OK ▭.

- In the same manner, enter **City/State** as the table name for Table 3.

- Click ▭ Next > ▭ to move to the next step.

Your screen should be similar to
Figure 3.6

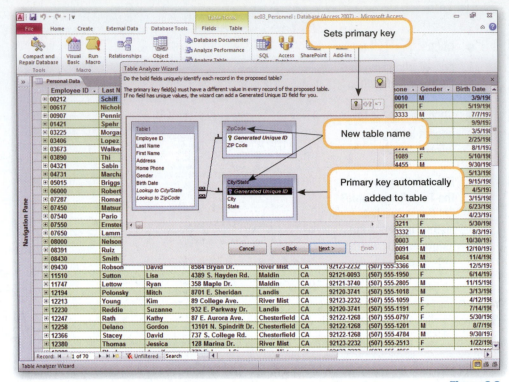

Figure 3.6

This step identifies the fields to use as primary keys in the new tables by bolding the field names. The wizard automatically added a Generated Unique ID field (AutoNumber) to the ZIPCode and City/State tables and defined it as the primary key field. In both tables, this field is unnecessary because the values in the City and ZIP Codes fields are unique and therefore can be used as the primary key fields. You will define the City and ZIP Code fields as the primary key field in each table, which will also remove the Unique ID field.

5

- Select the ZIP Code field and then click ▭.

- In the same manner change the City field to the primary key field.

- Click ▭ Next > ▭ to move to the next step.

Your screen should be similar to
Figure 3.7

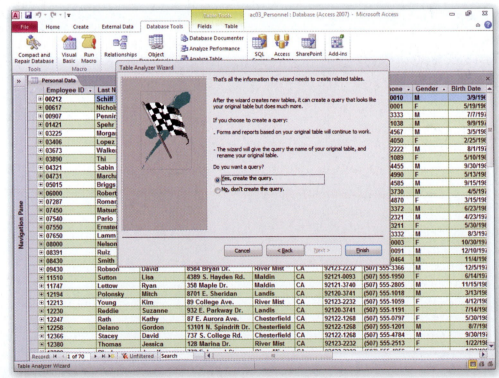

Figure 3.7

The final wizard step asks if you want to create a query. You will be learning about queries shortly, so you will not create a query at this time.

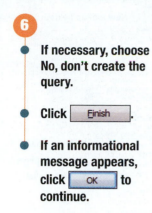

6

● If necessary, choose No, don't create the query.

● Click [Finish].

● If an informational message appears, click [OK] to continue.

Your screen should be similar to Figure 3.8

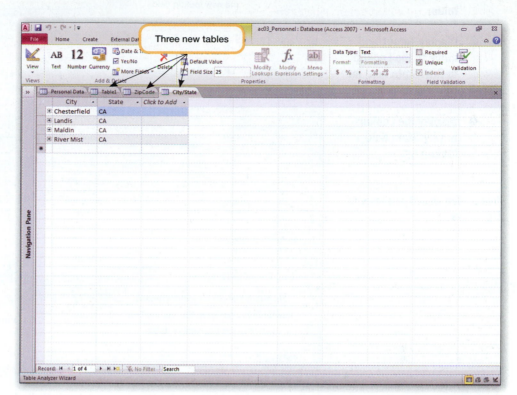

Figure 3.8

There are now three new tables open: City/State, ZipCode, and Table1. Table1 was automatically created by the Table Analyzer Wizard. It is a replica of the Personal Data table but with lookup fields for the City/State and ZipCode tables. The City/State table is currently displayed and consists of two fields, City and State with the City field as the primary key field. You will take a look at the ZipCode table, which only contains the ZIP Code field set as the primary key, and then examine Table1. The primary key fields in the City/State and Zip-Code tables have been associated with the data in the new Table1.

7

- Display the ZipCode table.

- Display Table1 and move to the Lookup to City/State field for the first record.

- Display the Lookup to City/State field lookup list.

Your screen should be similar to Figure 3.9

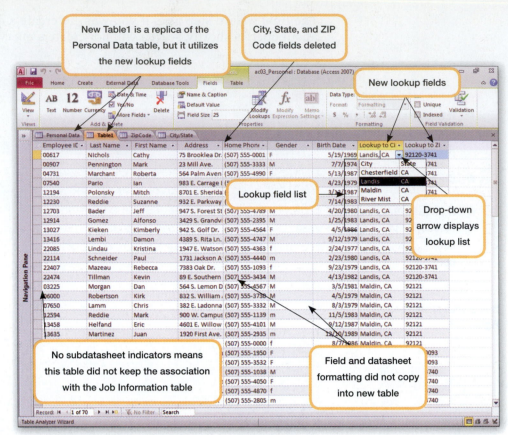

Figure 3.9

Table1 displays the ZIP code, city, and state information as lookup fields with data from their associated tables. Clicking the drop-down arrow in a lookup field displays the list of possible choices from the originating table. The individual fields that stored this information for each record have been deleted from Table1. You can now see how using separate tables to store this data saves space by not repeating the information and also makes data entry easier and more accurate.

CREATING A TABLE LIST LOOKUP FIELD

Now your database contains two tables that hold duplicate data, Table1 and Personal Data, and you need to decide which table to keep. You notice that Table1 did not maintain the association to the Job Information table and the field and datasheet formatting. Rather than make these same changes again to Table1, you decide to modify the Personal Data table by creating lookup fields to the City/State and ZipCode tables.

1

- Display the Personal Data table.

- Scroll to the right to display the last column.

- Open on the *Click to Add* menu and choose Lookup & Relationship.

- Run the Lookup Wizard and specify the following settings:

  - Look up the values in a table or query.

  - Use the City/State table.

  - Add the City and State fields to the Selected Fields list.

  - Specify ascending sort order by City.

  - Clear the checkmark in Hide key column and size the State column to best fit.

  - Choose the City field as the value to store in the database.

  - Enter the field name **Lookup City/State**

- Repeat the steps to add a lookup field for the ZIP Code using the ZipCode table to look up the values and the ZIP Code field in the Selected Fields list. Name the field **Lookup Zip Code**

- Click in the Lookup City/State field for the first record and display the drop-down list.

Your screen should be similar to Figure 3.10

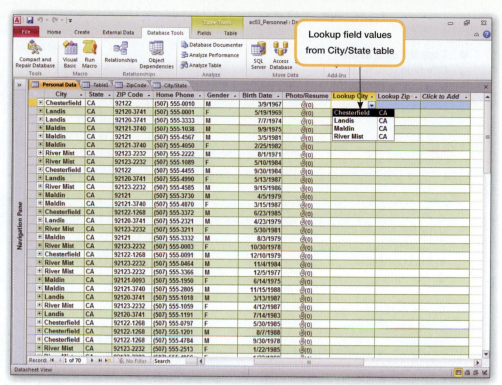

Figure 3.10

You have added two new lookup fields to the table. Now you need to add the data for these fields. Instead of selecting the City and ZIP code for each record, you will copy the data from the existing City and ZIP Code field columns into the new lookup columns. Then, because you will no longer need them, you will delete the original City, State, and ZIP Code fields. Finally, you will move the Lookup field columns after the Address field column.

● Copy the data in the City field column to the Lookup City/State column.

Having Trouble?

Remember: To select an entire column, click on its column heading when the mouse pointer is ↓.

● Copy the data in the ZIP Code field column to the Lookup Zip Code column.

● Delete the City, State, and ZIP Code columns.

● Select both lookup field columns and move them to the right of the Address field.

Having Trouble?

Refer to the Moving a Field topic in Lab 1 to review this feature.

● Add a caption of **City** for the Lookup City/State field.

Having Trouble?

Instead of changing the caption in Design view, use the

[▦ Name & Caption] button in the Fields tab.

● Add the caption of **Zip Code** for the Lookup Zip Code field.

● Best fit the City and Zip Code columns.

Your screen should be similar to **Figure 3.11**

Three fields deleted and replaced by lookup fields

Columns moved and captions added

Figure 3.11

DELETING A TABLE

Now that the Personal Data table is modified, you will delete the duplicate Table1.

1
- Close all tables, saving layout changes when prompted.
- Display the Navigation pane.
- Select Table1 and click ✕ Delete in the Records group of the Home tab.
- Click Yes to confirm the deletion from all groups.

Another Method

You also could press Delete or choose Delete from the object's shortcut menu.

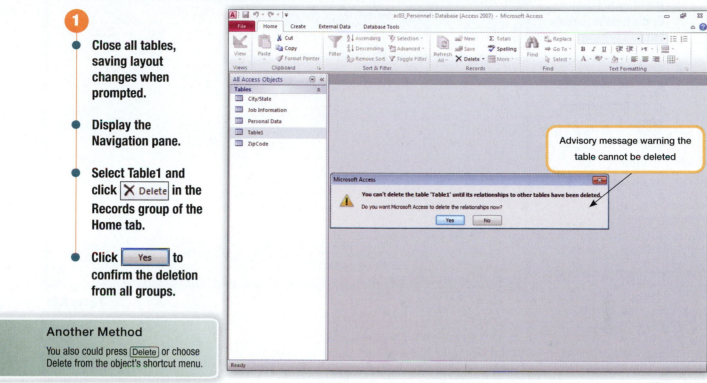

Advisory message warning the table cannot be deleted

Figure 3.12

Your screen should be similar to
Figure 3.12

The advisory message warns that the table cannot be deleted until its relationships to other tables have been deleted. Rather than have the program remove the relationships for you, you will look at the relationships that have been created between all tables first.

2
- Click No.
- Click OK.

Defining and Modifying Relationships

When you create lookup fields, Access automatically establishes relationships between the tables. You will open the Relationships window to edit these relationships.

1

- Click 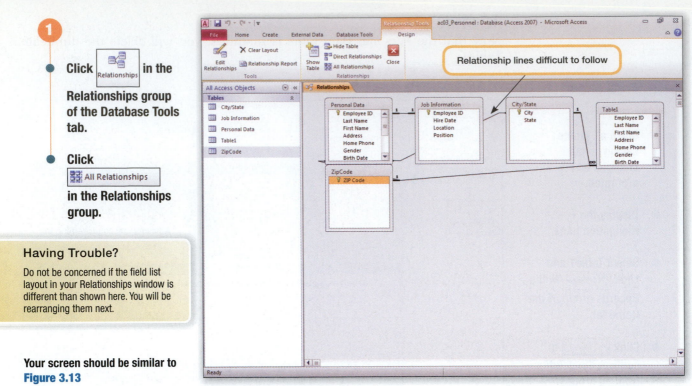 in the **Relationships group of the Database Tools tab.**

- Click ▣▣ **All Relationships** in the Relationships group.

Having Trouble?

Do not be concerned if the field list layout in your Relationships window is different than shown here. You will be rearranging them next.

Your screen should be similar to Figure 3.13

Figure 3.13

When the field lists for each table display, the relationship lines show how the tables are associated. However, the lines may appear tangled and untraceable when the tables first display. To see the relationships better, you will rearrange and size the field lists in the window. The field list can be moved by dragging the title bar and sized by dragging the border.

2

- Click on the Job Information field list title bar, and drag the field list to the left of the Personal Data field list.

- Continue to move the field lists until they are in the locations shown in Figure 3.14.

- Drag the bottom border of the Personal Data field list down so that all fields are displayed.

- Increase the length of the Table1 field list so that all fields are displayed.

Your screen should be similar to Figure 3.14

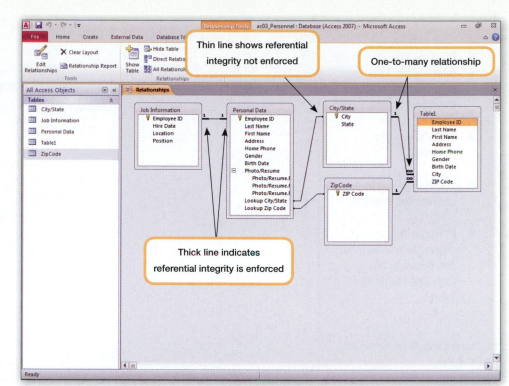

Figure 3.14

Having Trouble?

Refer to the Creating Relationships section of Lab 1 to review this feature.

Now it is easier to follow the relationship lines. The Personal Data and Job Information tables are related by the Employee ID key fields and are connected by a relationship line indicating they have a one-to-one relationship. This relationship was established when you created the Job Information table.

There is also a relationship line between the Lookup Zip Code field in the Personal Data table and the ZIP Code field in the ZipCode table. A thin line between common fields shows that the relationship does not support referential integrity. The third relationship that exists is between the Lookup City/State field and the City field in the City/State table.

Lastly, the ZIP Code field in the ZipCode table and the City field in the City/State table connect to their matching fields in Table1. These lines are thicker at both ends, which indicates referential integrity has been enforced. It also displays a 1 at one end of the line and an infinity symbol (∞) over the other end. This tells you the relationship is a one-to-many type relationship.

DELETING RELATIONSHIPS

The first relationship changes you want to make are to remove the relationships between Table1 and the City/State and ZipCode tables so that you can delete Table1. To edit or delete a relationship, click on the relationship line to select it. It will appear thicker to show it is selected. Then it can be modified.

1

- Click on the relationship line between the ZipCode table and Table1.

- Press Delete to remove it.

- Click Yes to confirm the deletion.

- In the same manner, delete the relationship line between the City/State table and Table1.

Your screen should be similar to Figure 3.15

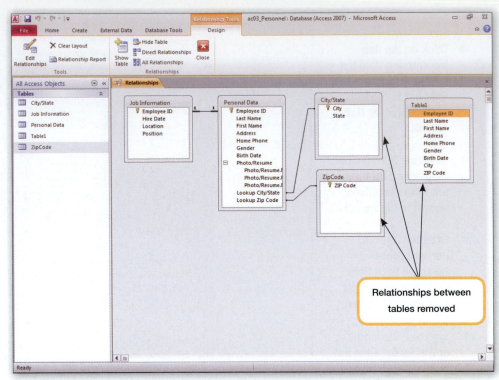

Figure 3.15

The relationship lines have been removed between the tables. Now you can delete the table.

2

- Click on the Table1 field list to select it and then press Delete.

Your screen should be similar to Figure 3.16

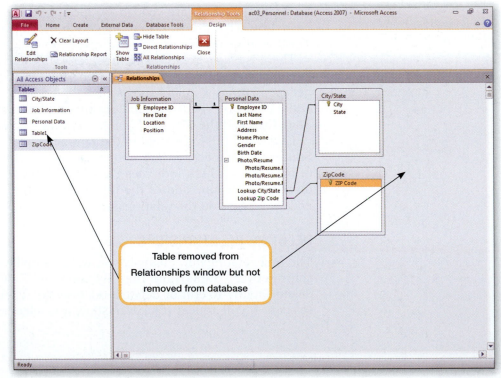

Figure 3.16

The Table1 field list is removed from the Relationships window. However, the Table1 object has not been removed from the Navigation pane, indicating that the table has not been deleted from the database. Now that the relationships have been removed from Table1, you can delete the actual table.

3

- Right-click Table1 in the Navigation Pane.

- Choose Delete from the shortcut menu.

- Click **Yes** to confirm deleting the table.

Your screen should be similar to Figure 3.17

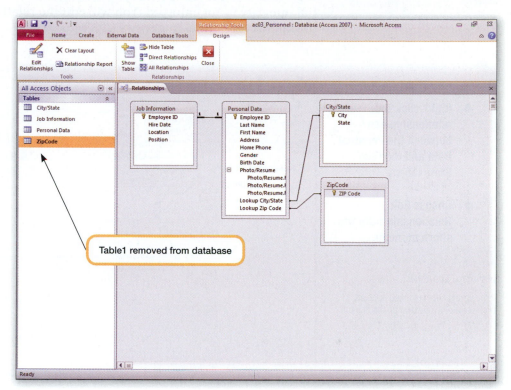

Table1 removed from database

Figure 3.17

Table1 no longer appears in the Tables list in the Navigation Pane, showing that it has been deleted from the database.

EDITING RELATIONSHIPS TO ENFORCE REFERENTIAL INTEGRITY

The next change you want to make is to enforce referential integrity between the tables to ensure that the relationships are valid and that related data is not accidentally changed or deleted. The thin relationship lines connecting the City/State and ZIP Code fields to the Personal Data table indicate that referential integrity is not enforced. You will edit the relationships between the tables to support referential integrity.

Having Trouble?

Refer to the Defining Relationships section of Lab 1 to review referential integrity.

- **Right-click the relationship line between the Personal Data and the City/State tables.**

- **Choose Edit Relationship from the shortcut menu.**

Having Trouble?

If the wrong shortcut menu appears, click on another location on the line to try again.

Another Method

You also can double-click the relationship line or click
Edit Relationships
in the Tools group to open the Edit Relationships dialog box.

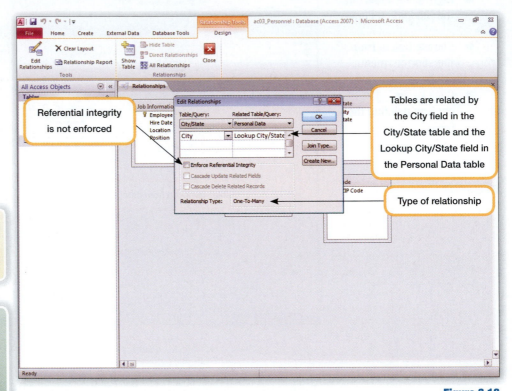

Figure 3.18

Your screen should be similar to Figure 3.18

The Edit Relationships dialog box shows the City field in the City/State table is related to the Lookup City/State field in the Personal Data table. In addition, you can see the relationship type is one-to-many.

You will enforce referential integrity to prevent users from entering a city or ZIP code in the Personal Data table that is not in the associated lookup table. To enter a new city or ZIP code would require that the new city or ZIP code values be entered in the lookup tables first. This prevents cities and ZIP codes that are not in the lookup tables from being used in the Personal Data table and would maintain an accurate lookup field list.

2

● Choose Enforce Referential Integrity.

● Click [OK].

● In a similar manner, edit the relationship line between the Personal Data table and the ZipCode table to enforce referential integrity.

● Click on the ZipCode field list to deselect the relationship line.

Your screen should be similar to Figure 3.19

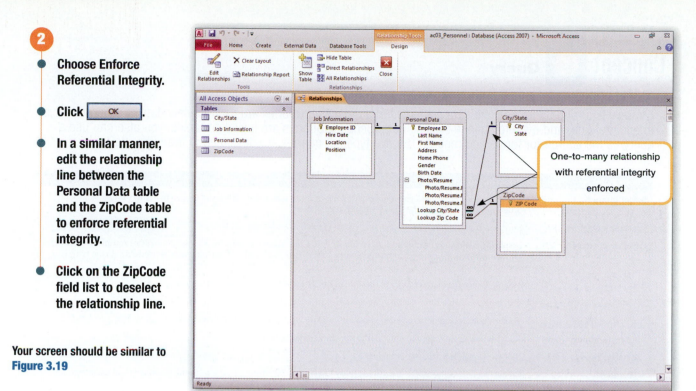

Figure 3.19

Once referential integrity is enforced, the relationship line changes and identifies the type of relationship.

3

● Click 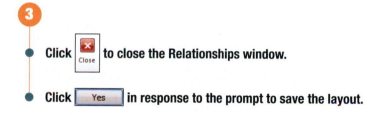 to close the Relationships window.

● Click [Yes] in response to the prompt to save the layout.

The relationship and layout changes are saved. Now that referential integrity is enforced between these tables, a warning message will automatically be displayed if one of the rules is broken while entering or editing data, and you will not be allowed to complete the action you are trying to do.

Creating a Query

You are ready to start gathering information from the database. Your fellow employee, Juan, would like to create a car pool and has enlisted your help as the database expert. In Lab 2, you were able to filter the table to obtain the information needed for the car pool list, but it contained more data about each employee than someone would need, or should have access to. To obtain the exact information you need to give Juan for his car pool, you will use a query.

Concept ① Query

A **query** is a request for specific data contained in a database. Queries are used to view data in different ways, to analyze data, and even to change existing data. Because queries are based on tables, you also can use a query as the source for forms and reports. The five types of queries are described in the following table.

Query Type	Description
Select query	Retrieves the specific data you request from one or more tables, then displays the data in a query datasheet in the order you specify. This is the most common type of query.
Crosstab query	Summarizes large amounts of data in an easy-to-read, row-and-column format.
Parameter query	Displays a dialog box prompting you for information, such as the criteria for locating data. For example, a parameter query might request the beginning and ending dates, then display all records matching dates between the two specified values.
Action query	Makes changes to many records in one operation. There are four types of action queries:
Make-table query	Creates a new table from selected data in one or more tables.
Update query	Makes update changes to records, when, for example, you need to raise salaries of all sales staff by 7 percent.
Append query	Adds records from one or more tables to the end of other tables.
Delete query	Deletes records from a table or tables.
SQL query	Creates a query using SQL (Structured Query Language), an advanced programming language used in Access.

You will create a simple select query to obtain the results for the car pool. Creating a query adds a query object to the database file. It is a named object, just like a form, that can be opened, viewed, and modified at any time.

USING THE QUERY WIZARD

Query Design view or the Query Wizard can be used to create a query. The process is much like creating a table or form. You will first use the Query Wizard to guide you through the steps. Selecting the table object in the Navigation Pane will help start the process in the right direction but is not a required step.

1

● Click the Personal Data table object in the Navigation Pane.

● Open the Create tab and click 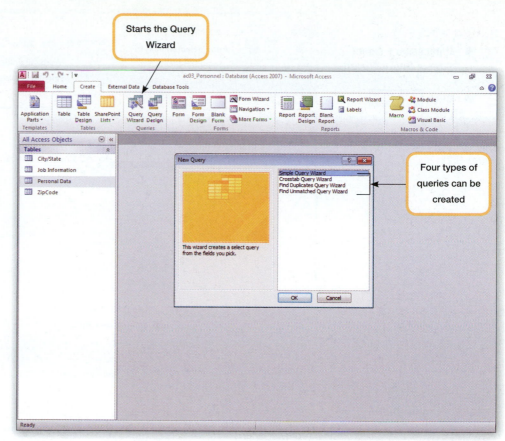 in the Queries group.

Your screen should be similar to Figure 3.20

Figure 3.20

From the New Query dialog box, you select the type of query you want to create using the wizard.

Query Wizard	Type of Query
Simple	Select query.
Crosstab	Crosstab query.
Find Duplicates	Locates all records that contain duplicate values in one or more fields in the specified tables.
Find Unmatched	Locates records in one table that do not have records in another. For example, you could locate all employees in one table who have no hours worked in another table.

You will use the Simple Query Wizard to create a select query to see if it gives you the results you want.

2

- If necessary, select Simple Query Wizard.

- Click **OK**.

Your screen should be similar to Figure 3.21

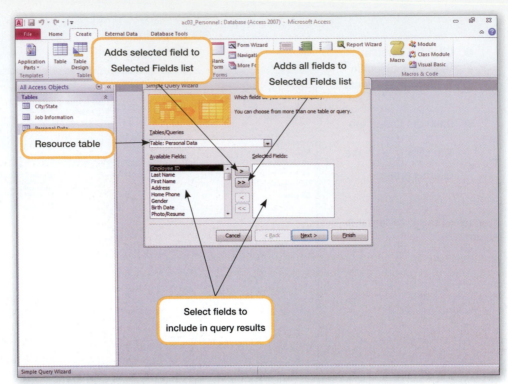

- Adds selected field to Selected Fields list
- Adds all fields to Selected Fields list
- Resource table
- Select fields to include in query results

Figure 3.21

In the first Simple Query Wizard dialog box, you specify the resource table that will be used to supply the data and the fields that you want displayed in the query result, just as you did when creating a form. You will use the Personal Data table as the resource table and select the fields you want displayed in the query output.

3

- If necessary, select the Personal Data table from the Tables/Queries drop-down list.

- Add the Last Name, First Name, Address, Lookup City/State and Home Phone fields to the Selected Fields list in that order.

Additional Information

The quickest way to add a field to the Selected Fields list is to double-click its field name in the Available Fields list.

- Click **Next >**.

Your screen should be similar to Figure 3.22

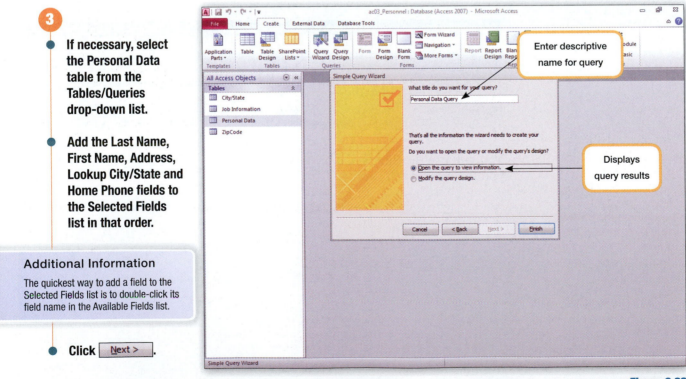

- Enter descriptive name for query
- Displays query results

Figure 3.22

In the last Simple Query Wizard dialog box, you specify a name for your query and whether you want to open it to see the results or modify it in Design view. You also can have Access display Help messages while you are working on your query by clicking the corresponding box at the bottom of this wizard screen. You decide that you just want to display the query results, and you want to give the query a name that will identify it.

4

● Replace the suggested title in the text box with Car Pool Query

● Click **Finish** .

Your screen should be similar to Figure 3.23

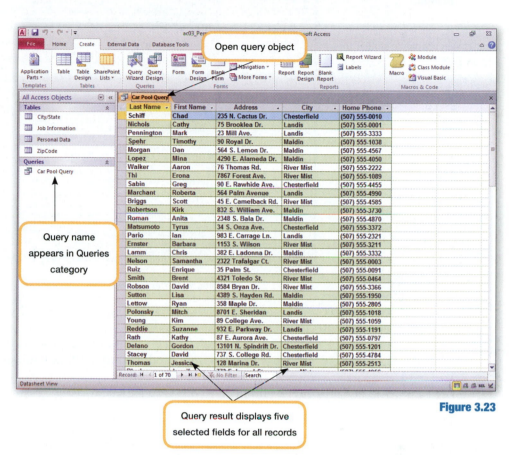

Figure 3.23

The query result displays the five specified fields for all records in the table in a new query datasheet object. The object's tab displays the query name. The Navigation pane also displays the name of the new query object in the Queries category.

FILTERING A QUERY

Having Trouble?

Refer to the Filtering a Table section of Lab 2 to review this feature.

Although the query result displays only the fields you want to see, it includes all the records in the table. To display only those records with the cities needed for the car pool information for Juan, you will filter the query results.

1

Filter the query to display only records with a city name of Chesterfield or Maldin.

Your screen should be similar to Figure 3.24

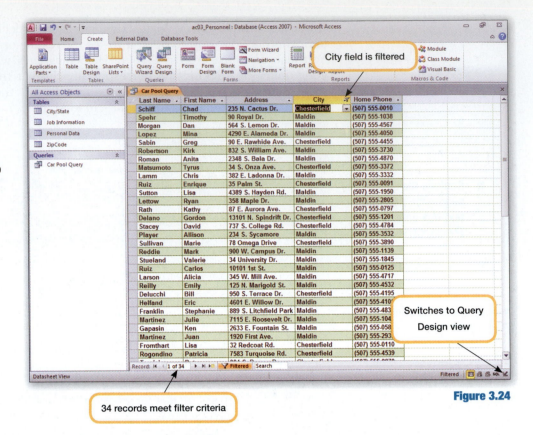

City field is filtered

Switches to Query Design view

34 records meet filter criteria

Figure 3.24

Now the Car Pool Query results display 34 records. Although these results are close to what you need, you are still not satisfied. You want the results to display the work location as well as the city. To make these refinements to the query, you need to use Query Design view.

2

Click [icon] Design View in the status bar to switch to Query Design view.

Your screen should be similar to Figure 3.25

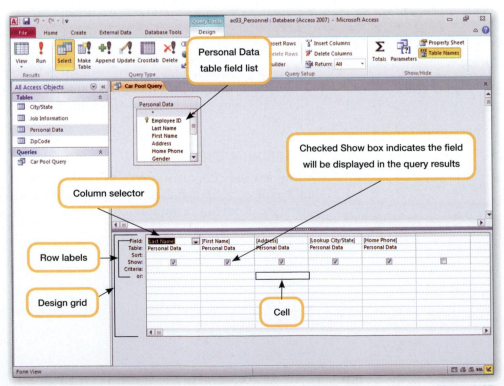

Personal Data table field list

Checked Show box indicates the field will be displayed in the query results

Column selector

Row labels

Design grid

Cell

Figure 3.25

USING QUERY DESIGN VIEW

Query Design view can be used to create a new query as well as modify the structure of an existing query. This view automatically displays the Query Tools Design tab, which contains commands that are used to create, modify, and run queries.

Query Design view is divided into two areas. The upper area displays a list box of all the fields in the selected table. This is called the **field list**. The lower portion of the window displays the **design grid** where you enter the settings that define the query. Each column in the grid holds the information about each field to be included in the query datasheet. The design grid automatically displays the fields that are specified when a query is created using the Query Wizard.

Above the field names is a narrow bar called the **column selector bar**, which is used to select an entire column. Each **row label** identifies the type of information that can be entered. The intersection of a column and row creates a cell where you enter expressions to obtain the query results you need.

The boxes in the Show row are called Show boxes. The **Show box** for a field lets you specify whether you want that field displayed in the query result. A checked box indicates that the field will be displayed; an unchecked box means that it will not.

ADDING A SECOND TABLE TO THE QUERY

To display the work location information for each employee in the query results, you need to add the Job Information table to the query design. A query that uses information from two or more tables to get the results is called a **multitable query**.

1

● Click  in the Query Setup group of the Query Tools Design tab.

● Select the Job Information table.

● Click **Add**.

● Close the Show Table dialog box.

● Increase the length of the Personal Data field list to display all the fields.

Your screen should be similar to Figure 3.26

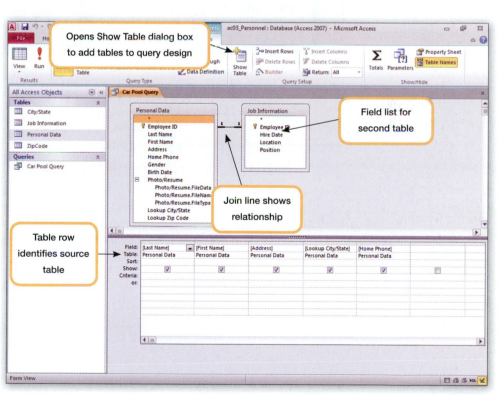

Figure 3.26

The field list for the Job Information table has been added to the Query Design window. When multiple tables are added to a query, Access automatically creates joins between the tables.

Concept 2 Join

A **join** is an association that is created in a query between a field in one table or query and a field of the same data type in another table or query. The join is based on the relationships that have already been defined between tables. A **join line** between the field lists identifies the fields on which the relationship is based.

If a table did not already have a relationship defined, a join would be created between common fields in the tables if one of the common fields is a primary key. If the common fields have different names, however, Access does not automatically create the join. In those cases, you would create the join between the tables using the same procedure that is used to create table relationships.

The difference between a relationship line and a join line in a query is that the join line creates a temporary relationship that establishes rules that the data must match to be included in the query results. Joins also specify that each pair of rows that satisfies the join conditions will be combined in the results to form a single row.

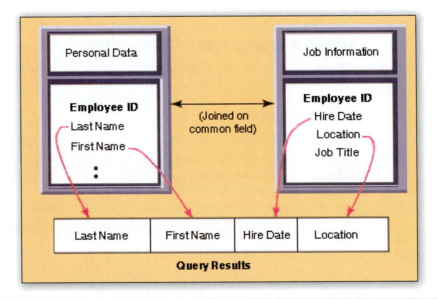

In this case, the join line correctly indicates that the tables are related and that the Employee ID field is the common field. Notice the Table row in the grid. It displays the name of the table from which each field is selected.

Having Trouble?

If the Table row is not displayed, click ![Table Names] in the Show/Hide group.

ADDING FIELDS

You want the query results to display the work location for each record. To do this, you need to add the Location field from the Job Information field list to the design grid. You can use the following methods to add fields to the design grid:

- Select the field name and drag it from the field list to the grid. To select several adjacent fields, press ⇧Shift while you click the field names. To select nonadjacent fields, press Ctrl while clicking the field names. To select all fields, double-click the field list title bar. You can then drag all the selected fields into the grid, and Access will place each field in a separate column.

- Double-click on the field name. The field is added to the next available column in the grid.

- Select the field cell drop-down arrow in the grid, and then choose the field name.

In addition, if you select the asterisk in the field list and add it to the grid, Access displays the table or query name in the field row followed by a period and asterisk. This indicates that all fields in the table will be included in the query results. Also, using this feature will automatically include any new fields that may later be added to the table and will exclude deleted fields. You cannot sort records or specify criteria for fields, however, unless you also add those fields individually to the design grid.

1

Double-click Location in the Job Information field list to add it to the grid.

Your screen should be similar to
Figure 3.27

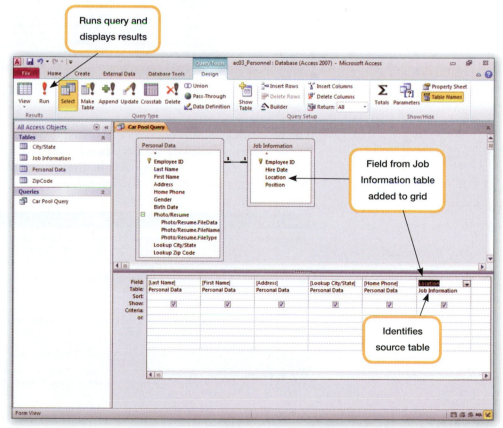

Figure 3.27

Notice the Table row displays the name of the table from which the Location field was drawn. Sometimes when multiple tables are specified in a query, they have fields with the same names. For example, two tables may have fields named Address; however, the address in one table may be a personal address

Creating a Query   **AC3.27**

and the one in the other table may be a business address. It is important to select the appropriate field from a table that contains the data you want to appear in the query. The Table row makes it clear from which table a field was drawn.

Now you want to see the query results. To do this, you run the query.

Click ![Run] **in the Results group of the Query Tools Design tab.**

Your screen should be similar to Figure 3.28

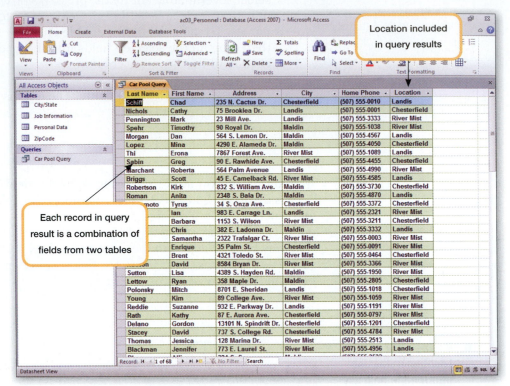

Figure 3.28

The work location for each record is displayed in the results. Now each record in the query results datasheet shows information from both tables. This is because of the type of join used in the query. There are three basic types of joins, as described in the following table.

Join Type	Description
Inner join	Tells a query that rows from one of the joined tables correspond to rows in the other table on the basis of the data in the joined fields. Checks for matching values in the joined fields; when it finds matches, it combines the records and displays them as one record in the query results.
Outer join	Tells a query that although some of the rows on both sides of the join correspond exactly, the query should include all rows from one table even if there is no match in the other table. Each matching record from two tables is combined into one record in the query results. One table contributes all of its records even if the values in its joined field do not match the field values in the other table. Outer joins can be left outer joins or right outer joins. In a query with a left outer join, all rows in the left table are included in the results, and only those rows from the other table where the joining field contains values common to both tables are included. The reverse is true with a right outer join.
Unequal joins	Records to be included in the query results are based on the value in one join field being greater than, less than, not equal to, greater than or equal to, or less than or equal to the value in the other join field.

In a query, the default join type is an inner join. In this case, it checked for matching values in the Employee ID fields, combined matching records, and displayed them as one record in the query result.

Having Trouble?

See Concept 4, Expression, in Lab 2 to review this feature.

SPECIFYING QUERY CRITERIA

You have created a query that displays the employees' names, cities, and work locations. However, you only want to display those with a work location in Landis. You can limit the results of a query by specifying query criteria in the query design grid.

Concept 3 Query Criteria

Query criteria are expressions that are used to restrict the results of a query to display only records that meet certain limiting conditions. In addition to comparison operators that are commonly used in expressions, other commonly used criteria are described in the following table.

Criterion	Description
Is Null	This can be used to find any records where field contents are empty, or "null."
Is Not Null	Returns records only where there is a value in the field.
Not	Return all results *except* those meeting the Not criteria.
DateDiff	Used with Date/Time fields to determine the difference in time between dates.
Like	Returns records where there is a match in content.
Not Like	Returns records that do not contain the text string.

The Criteria row in the query design grid is used to enter the query criteria. Entering the **criteria expression** is similar to using a formula and may contain constants, field names, and/or operators. To instruct the query to locate records meeting multiple criteria, also called **compound criteria**, you use the **AND** or **OR operators**. Using AND narrows the search because a record must meet both conditions to be included. This condition is established by typing the word "and" in a field's Criteria cell as part of its criteria expression. It is also established when you enter criteria in different fields in the design grid. Using OR broadens the search because any record meeting either condition is included in the output. This condition is established by typing the word "or" in a field's Criteria cell or by entering the first criteria expression in the first Criteria cell for the field and the second expression in the Or criteria row cell for the same field.

The following table shows some sample query criteria and their results.

Criteria	Result
DateDiff ("yyyy", [BirthDate], Date()) > 40	Determines the difference between today's year and the BirthDate field. If the difference is greater than 40, the corresponding records will display.
Not Like M*	Returns records for all states whose names start with a character other than "M".
Like "*9.99"	Returns records where the price ends with "9.99", such as $9.99, $19.99, $29.99, and so on.
>= "Canada"	Returns a list of countries starting with Canada and ascending through the rest of the alphabet.
Not "Smith"	Returns all records with names other than Smith.
1 OR 2	Returns all records with either a 1 or a 2 in the selected field.
"Doctor" AND "Denver"	Returns only those records that have the text string of Doctor and Denver within the same record.
"Mi*"	Finds all words starting with the letters "Mi". Example: Michigan, Missouri, Minnesota.
"*Main*"	Finds all records with that contain the text "Main" within it. Example: 590 Main Street, 11233 W. Mainland Dr.

You will enter the query criteria in the Criteria row of the Location column to restrict the query results to only those records where the location is Landis. It is not necessary to enter = (equal to) in the criteria because it is the assumed comparison operator.

1

● Display the query in Design view again.

● Move to the Location Criteria cell.

● Type **Landis**

● Press ←Enter.

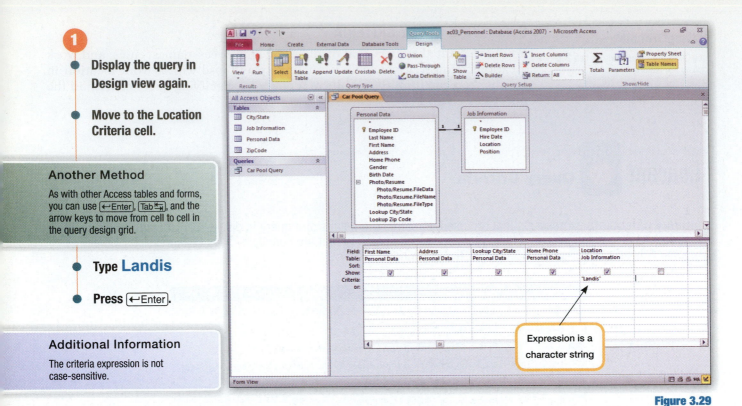

Figure 3.29

Your screen should be similar to **Figure 3.29**

The query criterion is enclosed in quotation marks because it is a character string. To display the query results, you will run the query. Another way to run a query is to change to Datasheet view.

2

● Click  Datasheet View in the status bar.

Your screen should be similar to **Figure 3.30**

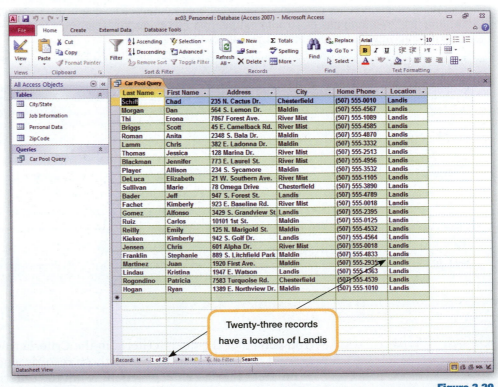

Figure 3.30

Now the query datasheet displays 23 records meeting the location criterion. However, the results do not show only those who reside in Chesterfield or Maldin and commute to the Landis location. You could apply a filter for these cities, but each time you run the query, you would need to reapply the filter. Rather than do this, you decide to specify the criteria in the query design so it will automatically return the results you want each time the query is run.

To include those who live in Chesterfield and Maldin, you will add a second criterion to the City field. Because you want to display the records for employees who live in either city, you will use the OR operator.

Additional Information

The Or criteria row must be used to enter "or" criteria for different fields.

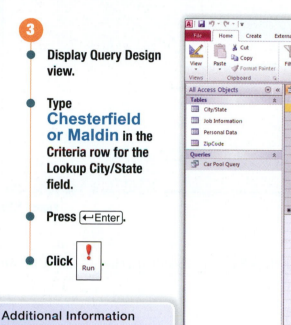

3

- **Display Query Design view.**

- **Type Chesterfield or Maldin in the Criteria row for the Lookup City/State field.**

- **Press** (←Enter).

- **Click** [Run].

Additional Information

If an expression is entered incorrectly, an informational box that indicates the source of the error will be displayed when the query is run.

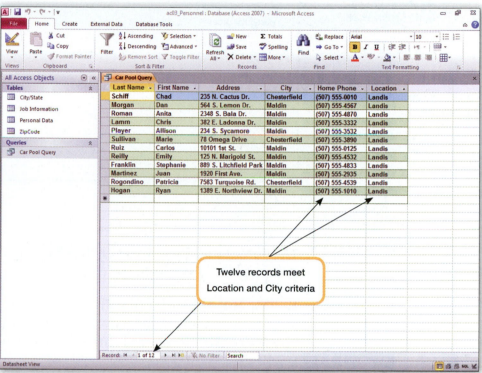

Twelve records meet Location and City criteria

Figure 3.31

Your screen should be similar to Figure 3.31

The results are closer to what you need to create the car pool list. The last step is to exclude those who do not need a car pool because they live close to the Landis work location, in the ZIP code 92121-3740. You will need to add the Lookup ZIP Code field to the query grid and then enter the criteria to exclude the ZIP code of 92121-3740. Then you will run the query.

4

- **Switch to Design view.**

- **Add the Lookup ZIP Code field from the Personal Data field list to the query grid.**

- **Enter <>92121-3740 in the ZIP Code Criteria cell.**

- **Run the query.**

Your screen should be similar to Figure 3.32

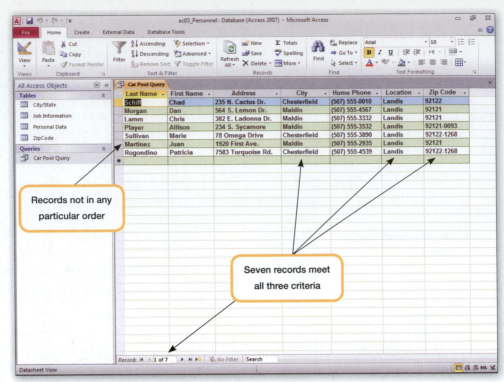

Records not in any particular order

Seven records meet all three criteria

Figure 3.32

The query located seven records that met the specified criteria, and you are pleased with the results so far.

HIDING AND SORTING COLUMNS

However, you still want to make a few additional changes to the query design. You do not want the Zip Code fields displayed in the results and would like the results to be sorted by last name and city.

Switch to Design view.

● **Click the Show box of the Lookup Zip Code field to clear the checkmark.**

● **Click in the Sort row of the Last Name**

Having Trouble?

Scroll the grid to bring field columns into view.

field.

● **Open the Sort drop-down menu and choose Ascending.**

● **Hide the Navigation Pane so you can see all the fields in the query grid.**

Your screen should be similar to Figure 3.33

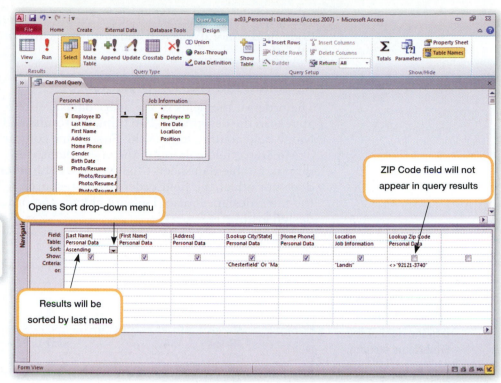

Opens Sort drop-down menu

ZIP Code field will not appear in query results

Results will be sorted by last name

Figure 3.33

Now you can display the results.

Run the query.

Your screen should be similar to Figure 3.34

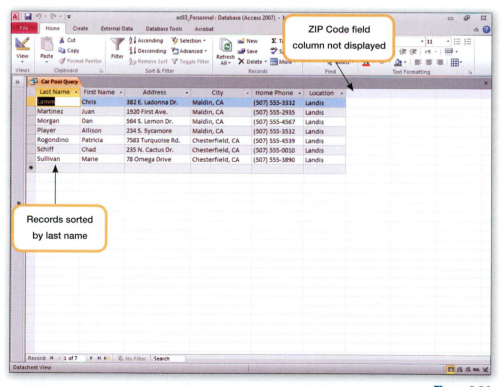

ZIP Code field column not displayed

Records sorted by last name

Figure 3.34

The query result shows that seven employees meet all the criteria. The ZIP Code field is not displayed, and last names are sorted in ascending alphabetical order.

REARRANGING THE QUERY DATASHEET

The order of the fields in the query datasheet reflects the order in which they appear in the design grid. You think the results will be easier to read if the Last Name field column follows the First Name column.

Moving a field column in the query datasheet is the same as moving a column in a table datasheet. Changing the column order in the query datasheet does not affect the field order in the resource table, which is controlled by the table design. It also does not change the order of the fields in the query design grid.

1 Select the Last Name column and move it to the right of the First Name column.

Another Method

You also could move the field columns in the design grid and then run the query to obtain the same results.

Your screen should be similar to **Figure 3.35**

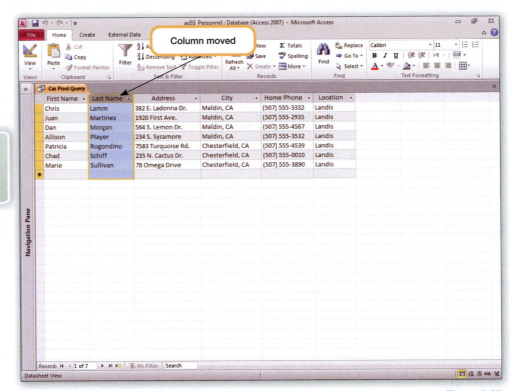

Figure 3.35

This is the information Juan needs to form his car pool. However, as you look at the results, you realize your record should have been included in the list because you live in Maldin and work at the Landis location. You need to determine why your record was not included.

FINDING UNMATCHED RECORDS

When working with a database containing several tables, occasionally a record may be created in one table without any correlating data entered into the corresponding table. This can happen accidentally (for example, when the data entry person forgets to update the related table) or on purpose (when a customer may not have an order pending). The Find Unmatched query is a helpful tool that will locate records in one table that do not have related records in another table. You will use the Find Unmatched query to locate any records that are missing corresponding information in the Job Information table. First, however, you decide to do a manual inspection of the record count in the tables, which will reveal if there are potentially missing records.

1

● **Display the Navigation Pane.**

● **Display the Personal Data table.**

● **Scroll to the bottom of the table to see your record.**

You can see that the Personal Data table has 70 records from the record indicator and that your record is the last record. Now, however, you realize that you did not add your information to the Job Information table.

You will check the Job Information table to see how many records it contains.

2

● **Open the Job Information table.**

Your screen should be similar to Figure 3.36

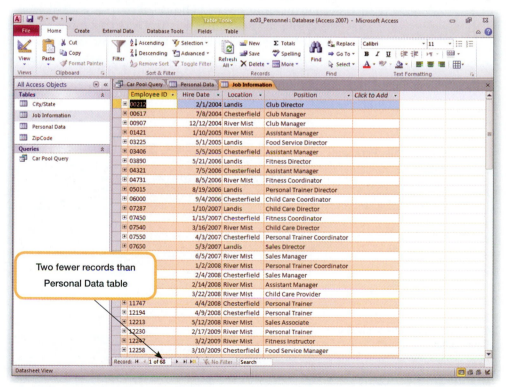

Two fewer records than Personal Data table

Figure 3.36

This table has 68 records, whereas the Personal Data table has 70. You know your record is one of the missing records, but you need to locate the other missing record. You can do this quickly using the Find Unmatched Query Wizard.

3

- Click [Query Wizard] in the Queries group of the Create tab.

- Choose Find Unmatched Query Wizard.

- Click [OK].

Your screen should be similar to Figure 3.37

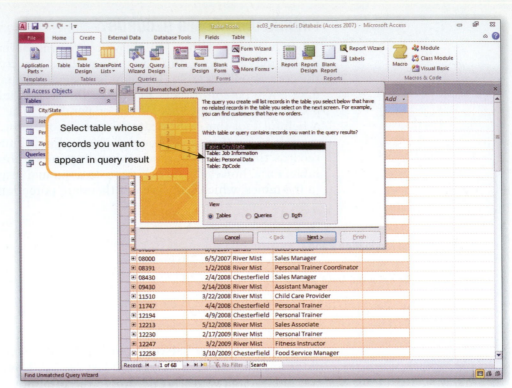

Select table whose records you want to appear in query result

Figure 3.37

In the first wizard dialog box, you select the table that contains records you want to appear in the results. In this case, you will select the Personal Data table first because it is the primary table and has more records than the Job Information table, and these are the records you want to appear in the results. In the second dialog box, you will select the table to compare the first table to. This establishes the join between the tables.

4

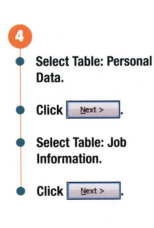

- Select Table: Personal Data.

- Click [Next >].

- Select Table: Job Information.

- Click [Next >].

Your screen should be similar to Figure 3.38

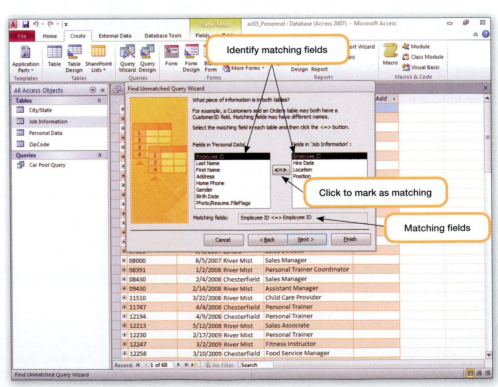

Identify matching fields

Click to mark as matching

Matching fields

Figure 3.38

The third step is to identify the matching (common) fields. The two high-lighted fields, Employee ID, in both tables are already correctly highlighted.

5

● Click <=> to mark these fields as the matching fields.

Additional Information

The field names of the selected matching fields appear in the Matching Fields text box.

● Click Next >.

Your screen should be similar to Figure 3.39

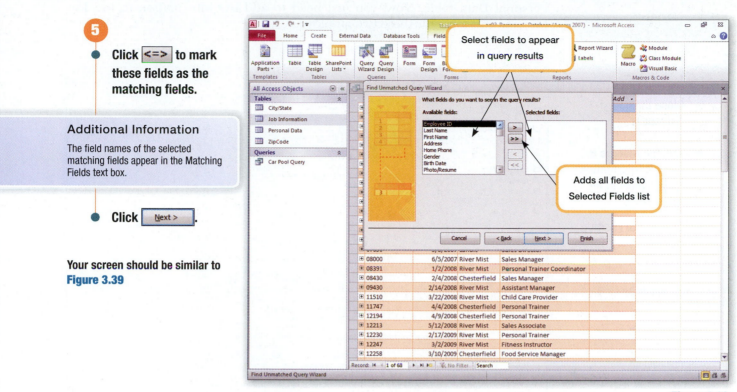

Figure 3.39

Next, you need to identify the fields you want to appear in the query results.

6

● Click >> to add all the fields to the Selected Fields list.

● Click Next >.

● Click Finish.

Your screen should be similar to Figure 3.40

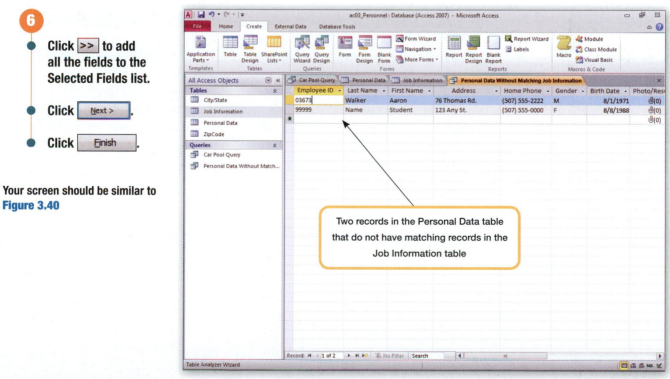

Figure 3.40

The two records in the Personal Data table that do not have matching records in the Job Information table are displayed in the query results. One record is the matching information for your own record that you added earlier to the Personal Data table. Now, you just need to add the information to the Job Information table for these two employees.

7

● Close the query datasheet.

● Add the records to the Job Information table shown in the table below.

● Best fit the Position field.

Your screen should be similar to Figure 3.41

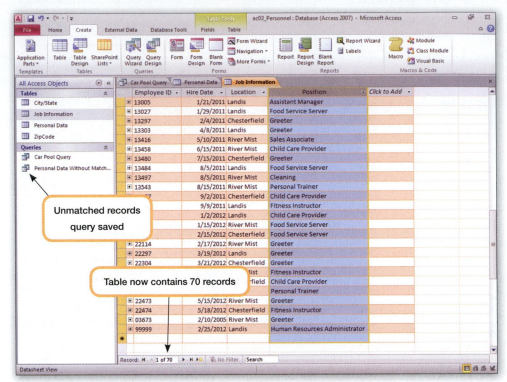

Figure 3.41

Employee ID	Hire Date	Location	Position
03673	2/10/2005	River Mist	Greeter
99999	2/25/2012	Landis	Human Resources Administrator

Both tables now contain 70 records. Notice that the Unmatched Records query was automatically saved and the object is listed in the Queries group of the Navigation pane. If you were to rerun this query, no results would be located because there are no longer any missing records.

Finally, you want to update all objects that use the Location field as the underlying record source to reflect the addition of the new records.

8

- Display the Car Pool Query datasheet.

- Click  in the Records group of the Home tab to refresh the screen image with the change in data.

Your screen should be similar to **Figure 3.42**

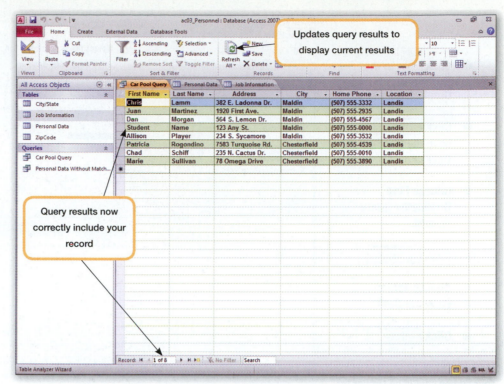

Figure 3.42

The query results list eight records that meet the criteria and now correctly include your record.

FINDING DUPLICATE RECORDS

Next, you want to check the Personal Data table for possible duplicate records. Even though this table uses the Employee ID field as the primary key, it is possible to enter the same record with two different IDs. To check for duplication, you will use the Find Duplicates Query Wizard.

1

- Click  in the Create tab.

- Click [Yes] to save the Car Pool Query.

- Choose Find Duplicates Query Wizard.

- Click [OK].

- Choose Table: Personal Data.

- Click [Next >].

Your screen should be similar to Figure 3.43

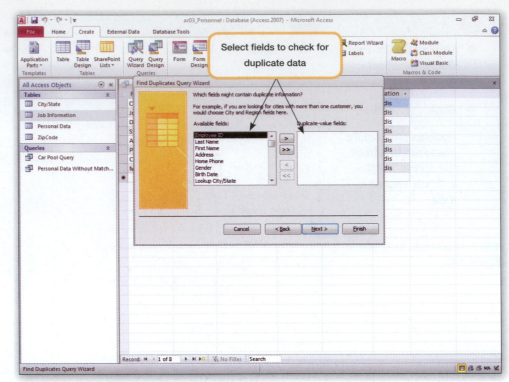

Figure 3.43

In this wizard dialog box, you identify the fields that may contain duplicate data. In this case, you will check the Last Name fields for duplicate values.

2

- Add the Last Name field to the Duplicate-Value Fields list.

- Click [Next >].

Your screen should be similar to Figure 3.44

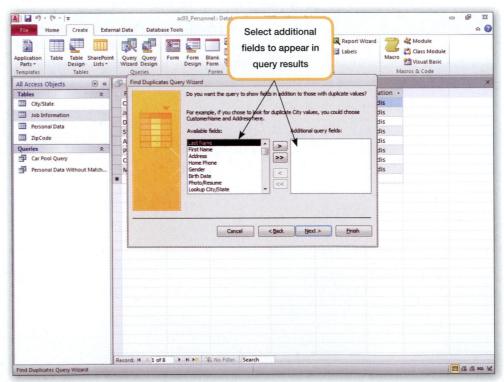

Figure 3.44

Next, you need to identify the additional fields you want to appear in the query results.

3

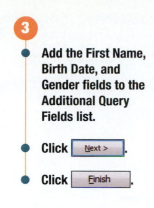

- Add the First Name, Birth Date, and Gender fields to the Additional Query Fields list.

- Click [Next >].

- Click [Finish].

Your screen should be similar to Figure 3.45

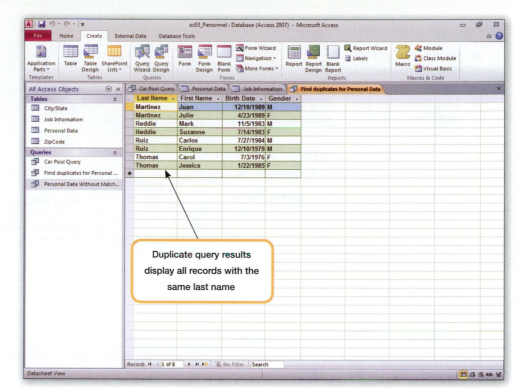

Duplicate query results display all records with the same last name

Figure 3.45

All records with the same last name are listed. These all look like valid records, so you will not make any changes.

CREATING A PARAMETER QUERY

Periodically, the club director wants to know the employee numbers and names of the employees at each club and their job positions. To find this information, you will create a simple query and sort the Location field to group the records.

To create this query, you will modify the existing Car Pool Query design, since it already includes the two tables—Personal Data and Job Information—that you need to use. You will clear the design grid and save the modified query using a new name.

1

- Display the Car Pool Query in Design view.

- Drag across the top of the seven fields in the grid to select them and press Delete.

- Open the File tab and choose Save Object As.

- In the Save 'Car Pool Query' to: text box, enter **Location Query** and click OK.

- Click the Query Tools Design tab to close the Backstage view.

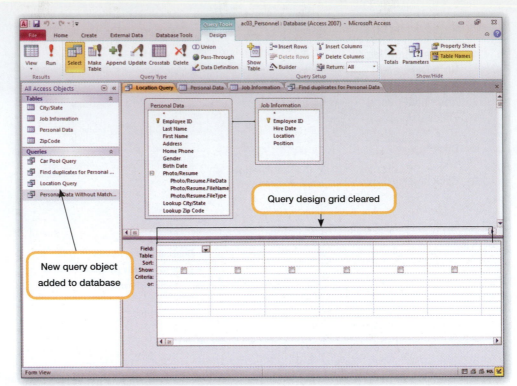

Figure 3.46

Your screen should be similar to Figure 3.46

The query object is added to the Navigation pane and you are ready to define the query. You will add all the fields from the Personal Data table to the grid, along with the Location field from the Job Information table.

2

- Double-click * in the Personal Data field list.

- Double-click Location in the Job Information table.

- Sort the Location field in ascending sort order.

- Run the query.

- Hide the Navigation pane.

- Scroll the window to the right to see the Location field.

Your screen should be similar to **Figure 3.47**

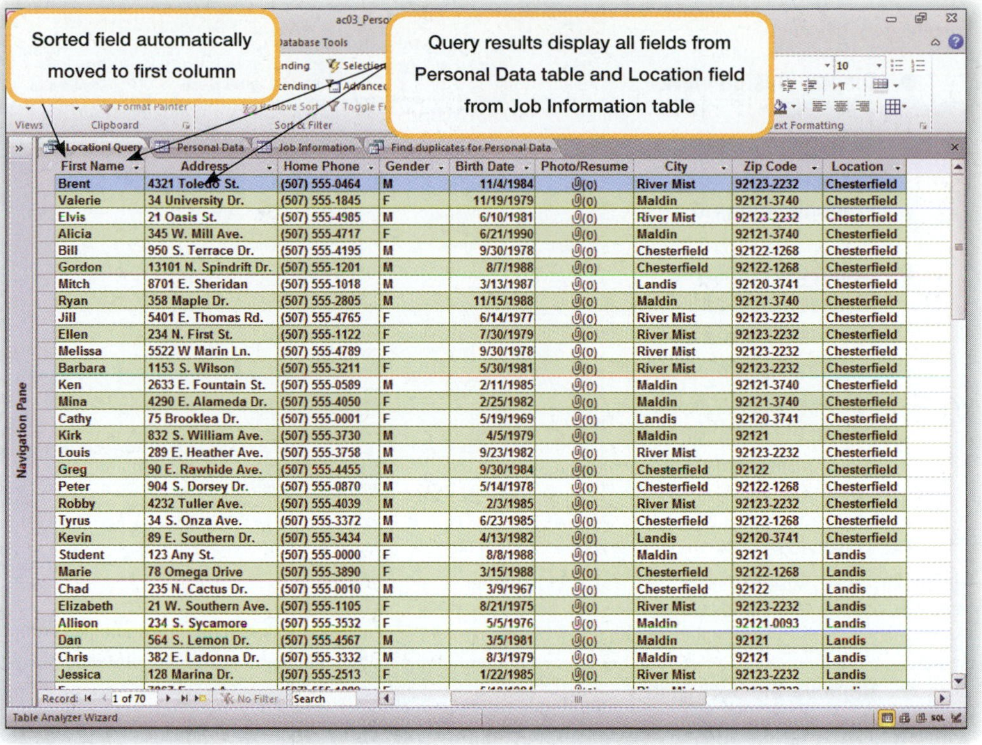

Sorted field automatically moved to first column

Query results display all fields from Personal Data table and Location field from Job Information table

First Name	Address	Home Phone	Gender	Birth Date	Photo/Resume	City	Zip Code	Location
Brent	4321 Toledo St.	(507) 555-0464	M	11/4/1984	(0)	River Mist	92123-2232	Chesterfield
Valerie	34 University Dr.	(507) 555-1845	F	11/19/1979	(0)	Maldin	92121-3740	Chesterfield
Elvis	21 Oasis St.	(507) 555-4985	M	6/10/1981	(0)	River Mist	92123-2232	Chesterfield
Alicia	345 W. Mill Ave.	(507) 555-4717	F	6/21/1990	(0)	Maldin	92121-3740	Chesterfield
Bill	950 S. Terrace Dr.	(507) 555-4195	M	9/30/1978	(0)	Chesterfield	92122-1268	Chesterfield
Gordon	13101 N. Spindrift Dr.	(507) 555-1201	M	8/7/1988	(0)	Chesterfield	92122-1268	Chesterfield
Mitch	8701 E. Sheridan	(507) 555-1018	M	3/13/1987	(0)	Landis	92120-3741	Chesterfield
Ryan	358 Maple Dr.	(507) 555-2805	M	11/15/1988	(0)	Maldin	92121-3740	Chesterfield
Jill	5401 E. Thomas Rd.	(507) 555-4765	F	6/14/1977	(0)	River Mist	92123-2232	Chesterfield
Ellen	234 N. First St.	(507) 555-1122	F	7/30/1979	(0)	River Mist	92123-2232	Chesterfield
Melissa	5522 W Marin Ln.	(507) 555-4789	F	9/30/1978	(0)	River Mist	92123-2232	Chesterfield
Barbara	1153 S. Wilson	(507) 555-3211	F	5/30/1981	(0)	River Mist	92123-2232	Chesterfield
Ken	2633 E. Fountain St.	(507) 555-0589	M	2/11/1985	(0)	Maldin	92121-3740	Chesterfield
Mina	4290 E. Alameda Dr.	(507) 555-4050	F	2/25/1982	(0)	Maldin	92121-3740	Chesterfield
Cathy	75 Brooklea Dr.	(507) 555-0001	F	5/19/1969	(0)	Landis	92120-3741	Chesterfield
Kirk	832 S. William Ave.	(507) 555-3730	M	4/5/1979	(0)	Maldin	92121	Chesterfield
Louis	289 E. Heather Ave.	(507) 555-3758	M	9/23/1982	(0)	River Mist	92123-2232	Chesterfield
Greg	90 E. Rawhide Ave.	(507) 555-4455	M	9/30/1984	(0)	Chesterfield	92122	Chesterfield
Peter	904 S. Dorsey Dr.	(507) 555-0870	M	5/14/1978	(0)	Chesterfield	92122-1268	Chesterfield
Robby	4232 Tuller Ave.	(507) 555-4039	M	2/3/1985	(0)	River Mist	92123-2232	Chesterfield
Tyrus	34 S. Onza Ave.	(507) 555-3372	M	6/23/1985	(0)	Chesterfield	92122-1268	Chesterfield
Kevin	89 E. Southern Dr.	(507) 555-3434	M	4/13/1982	(0)	Landis	92120-3741	Chesterfield
Student	123 Any St.	(507) 555-0000	F	8/8/1988	(0)	Maldin	92121	Landis
Marie	78 Omega Drive	(507) 555-3890	F	3/15/1988	(0)	Chesterfield	92122-1268	Landis
Chad	235 N. Cactus Dr.	(507) 555-0010	M	3/9/1967	(0)	Chesterfield	92122	Landis
Elizabeth	21 W. Southern Ave.	(507) 555-1105	F	8/21/1975	(0)	River Mist	92123-2232	Landis
Allison	234 S. Sycamore	(507) 555-3532	F	5/5/1976	(0)	Maldin	92121-0093	Landis
Dan	564 S. Lemon Dr.	(507) 555-4567	M	3/5/1981	(0)	Maldin	92121	Landis
Chris	382 E. Ladonna Dr.	(507) 555-3332	M	8/3/1979	(0)	Maldin	92121	Landis
Jessica	128 Marina Dr.	(507) 555-2513	F	1/22/1985	(0)	River Mist	92123-2232	Landis

Record: 1 of 70 No Filter Search

Table Analyzer Wizard

Figure 3.47

All the fields from the Personal Data table and the Location field are displayed. The location is in sorted order. However, because the director wants the information for each location on a separate page when printed, sorting the Location field will not work. To display only the records for a single location at a time, you could filter the Location field, or change the criteria in the Location field to provide this information, and then print the results.

Another method, however, is to create a parameter query that will display a dialog box prompting you for location information when the query is run. This saves having to change to Design view and enter the specific criteria or applying a filter. Criteria that are entered in the Criteria cell are **hard-coded criteria**, meaning they are used each time the query is run. In a parameter query, you enter a **parameter value** in the Criteria cell rather than a specific value. The parameter value tells the query to prompt you for the specific criteria you want to use when you run the query.

Additionally, the director does not need all the information from the Personal Data table, so you will change the design to include only the necessary fields. First, you will change the fields in the design grid to display only the Employee ID and the First Name and Last Name fields from the Personal Data table.

- Display Design view.

- Select and delete the Personal Data column in the design grid.

- Select the Employee ID, Last Name, and First Name fields in the Personal Data field list and drag them to before the Location field in the design grid.

Having Trouble?

Hold down ⇧Shift while clicking on each field name to select all three.

- Remove the Sort from the Location field.

- Type **[Enter Location]** in the Location Criteria cell.

Your screen should be similar to Figure 3.48

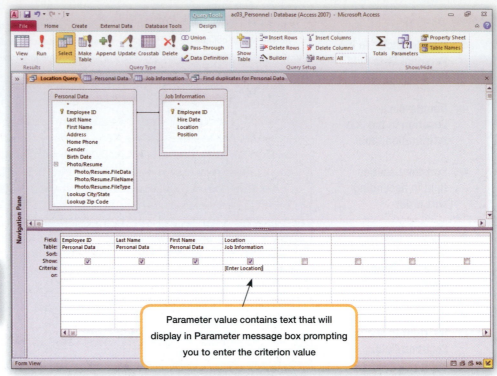

Figure 3.48

The Location criterion you entered is the parameter value. Parameter values are enclosed in square brackets and contain the text you want to appear when the parameter prompt is displayed. The parameter value cannot be a field name because Access will assume you want to use that particular field and will not prompt for input.

4

- Run the query and type **Landis** in the Enter Parameter Value dialog box.

- Click [OK].

Your screen should be similar to Figure 3.49

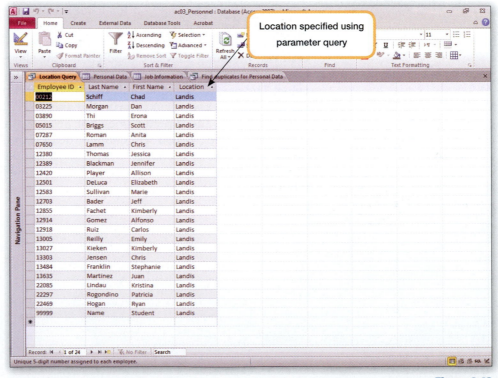

Figure 3.49

Only those records whose location is Landis are displayed. Additionally, only the fields you specified are included in the result. Now, each time you run the query, you simply need to specify the location in the Enter Parameter Value dialog box to obtain results for the different locations.

Displaying a Totals Row

As you look at the query results, you can see the record indicator tells you there are 24 records. The record indicator is a simple count of the total number of records in the table and only appears when you view the datasheet. You decide to display a Totals row in the datasheet that will display this information when you print the datasheet.

In addition to count totals, the Totals row can perform other types of calculations such as averages and sums on a column of data. Calculations that are performed on a range of data are called **aggregate functions**. Because aggregate functions perform calculations, the data type in a column must be a Number, Decimal, or Currency data type. The Personal Data table does not use any of these data types. However, the Count function can be used on all data types.

You will add a Totals row and then use the Count aggregate function to display the record count. The Totals row appears below the star (new record) row in the table and remains fixed on the window as you scroll the table. Clicking in a column of the Totals row selects the field to be calculated. Then you open the drop-down list to select the function you want to use. For Text data types, only the Count function is listed.

Additional Information

Some functions also can use a Date/Time data type.

1

● Click Σ Totals in the Records group of the Home tab.

● Click on the Last Name field in the Totals row.

● Open the drop-down list and choose Count.

Your screen should be similar to Figure 3.50

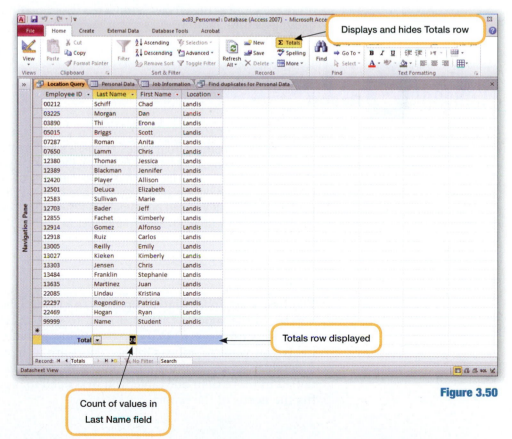

Figure 3.50

Additional Information

If you select a function in the first column of the Totals row, the label is removed and the value is displayed.

The Totals row displays 24 as the number of values in the column. The Totals label in the first column identifies the meaning of this value.

You can turn the display of the Totals row on and off any time by clicking **Σ Totals**. When you redisplay the row, any functions that were selected are displayed again. A Totals row also can be displayed in a table datasheet.

You will print this query datasheet and then close all open objects.

2

- Click 💾 Save in the Quick Access Toolbar to save the query.

- Preview and then print the query datasheet.

- Close the query, saving the layout changes if prompted.

- Close all remaining open objects, saving the layout when prompted.

- Display the Navigation pane.

> **NOTE** If you are running short on time, this is an appropriate place to end your Access session. When you begin again, open the ac03_Personnel database.

Creating Reports

As you know, you can print the table and query datasheets to obtain a simple printout of the data. However, there are many times when you would like the output to look more professional. To do this, you can create custom reports using this information.

Concept 4 Report

A **report** is professional-appearing output generated from tables or queries that may include design elements, groups, and summary information. A report can be a simple listing of all the fields in a table, or it might be a list of selected fields based on a query. Reports generally include design elements such as formatted labels, report titles, and headings, as well as different theme design styles, layouts, and graphics that enhance the display of information. In addition, when creating a report, you can group data to achieve specific results. You can then display summary information such as totals by group to allow the reader to further analyze the data. Creating a report displays the information from your database in a more attractive and meaningful format.

The first step in creating a report is to decide what information you want to appear in the report. Then you need to determine the tables or queries (the report's record source) that can be used to provide this information. If all the fields you want to appear in the report are in a single table, then simply use that table. However, if the information you want to appear in the report is contained in more than one table, you first need to create a query that specifically fits the needs of the report.

There are several different methods you can use to create reports, as described in the following table. The method you use depends on the type of report you need to create.

Report tool	Creates a simple report containing all the fields in the table.
Blank Report tool	Builds a report from scratch in Report Layout view by adding the fields you select from the table.
Report design	Builds a report from scratch in Report Design view by adding the fields you select from the table.
Report Wizard	Guides you through the steps to create a report.

USING THE REPORT TOOL

Although you could give Juan a simple printout of the car pool query results, you decide to create a report of this information. Because the fastest way to create a report is to use the Report tool, you decide to try this method first. This tool uses the selected or displayed table or query object as the report source.

1

● Select the Car Pool Query in the Navigation pane.

● Click [Report] in the Reports group of the Create tab.

● Hide the Navigation pane.

Your screen should be similar to Figure 3.51

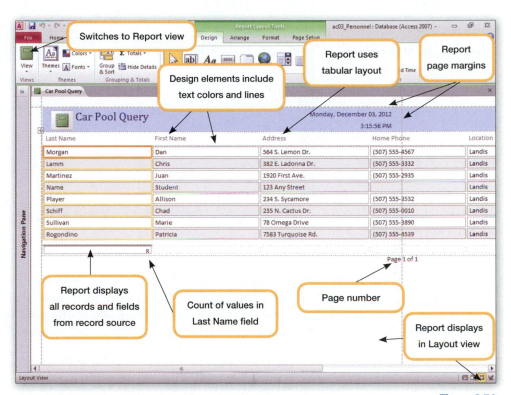

Figure 3.51

The Report tool creates a report that displays all fields and records from the record source in a predesigned report layout and style. It uses a tabular layout in which each field name appears at the top of the column and each record appears in a line, much like in Datasheet view. The fields are displayed in the order in which they appear in the query design. Notice the records are not sorted by last name as they are in the query results. This is because the query sort order is overridden by the report sort order, which is by default unsorted. It also displays the object name as the report title and the current date and time in the title area. The report design elements include blue font color for the report title and field names and blue fill color behind the title. The title is also in a larger text size. The last row displays a total value of the number of records in the report. The dotted lines identify the report page margins and show that the Home Phone field data will be split between two pages.

VIEWING THE REPORT

The report is displayed in Layout view. As in Form Layout view, you could modify the report design if needed in this view. Instead, you will switch to Report view to see how the report will look when printed.

1

● Click 📄 **Report View in the Views group of the Report Layout Tools Design tab.**

● **Scroll to the right to see the last field column.**

Your screen should be similar to
Figure 3.52

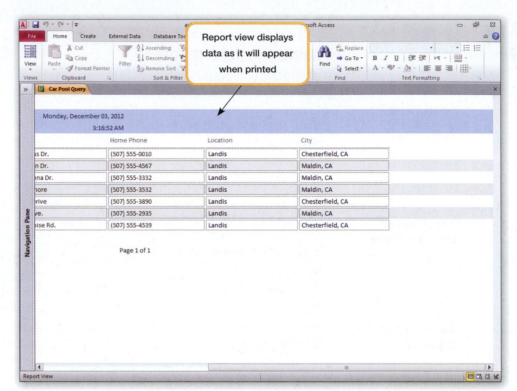

Figure 3.52

Report view displays the data in the report as it will appear when printed. It does not show how the data will fit on a page. This view is useful if you want to copy data from the report and paste it into another document such as a Word file. It also can be used to temporarily change what data is displayed in the report by applying a filter.

The last view you can use is Print Preview. This view will show you exactly how the report will look when printed and can be used to modify the page layout and print-related settings. Another way to display this view is from the object's shortcut menu.

Additional Information

The report date and time will reflect the current date and time on your computer.

2
- Right-click on the report tab or an empty area of the report and choose Print Preview.

Another Method

You also can right-click an object in the Navigation pane to display this shortcut menu.

- Click 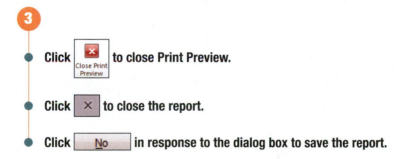 in the Zoom group.

Your screen should be similar to Figure 3.53

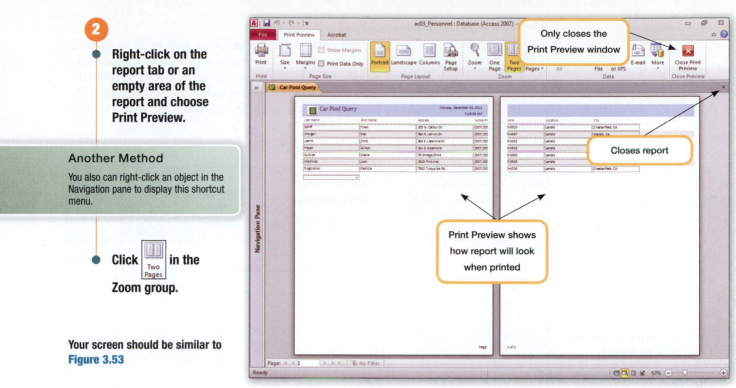

Figure 3.53

It is now easy to see exactly how the report will look when printed. After looking over the report, you decide that although the tabular layout is appropriate for your report, you do not want the report to include all the fields from the query. Rather than modify the report design by removing the unneeded fields, you will close this report without saving it and then use the Report Wizard to create a report that is more appropriate for your needs.

3
- Click [Close Print Preview] to close Print Preview.

- Click [×] to close the report.

- Click [No] in response to the dialog box to save the report.

USING THE REPORT WIZARD

Using the Report Wizard, you can easily specify the fields you want to include in the report. The Report Wizard consists of a series of dialog boxes, much like those in the Form and Query Wizards. In the first dialog box, you specify the table or query to be used in the report and add the fields to be included. The Car Pool Query object is already correctly specified as the object that will be used to create the report.

1

- Click **Report Wizard** in the Reports group of the Create tab.

- Add the First Name field to the Selected Fields list.

- Add all the remaining fields to the list.

- Remove the Location field.

- Click **Next >**.

Your screen should be similar to **Figure 3.54**

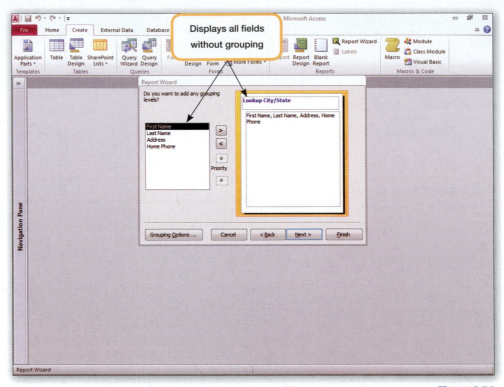

Figure 3.54

In this dialog box, you are asked if you want to add any grouping levels to the report. As suggested, you will group the report by city.

Click Next > .

Your screen should be similar to Figure 3.55

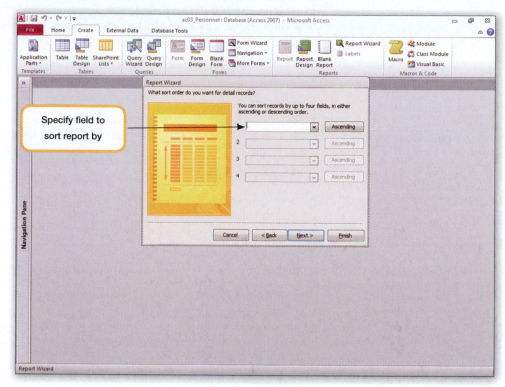

Specify field to sort report by

Figure 3.55

You can specify a sort order for the records in this dialog box. Because you want the last names sorted within each city group, you will specify to sort by last name.

Open the first list box drop-down menu and choose Last Name.

Click Next > .

Your screen should be similar to Figure 3.56

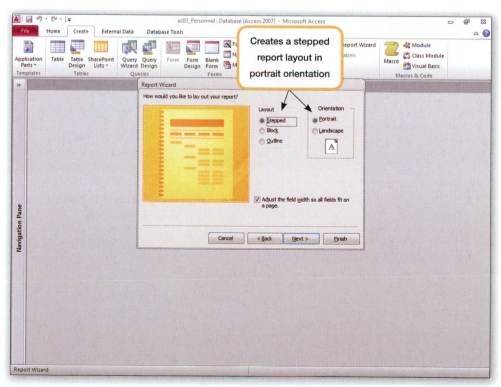

Creates a stepped report layout in portrait orientation

Figure 3.56

Creating Reports **AC3.51**

This dialog box is used to change the report layout and orientation. The default report settings for a grouped report uses a stepped report design layout with portrait orientation. The stepped design displays the report data using a tabular format in which the field labels appear in columns above the rows of data. The data in each group is indented or stepped to clearly identify the groups. In addition, the option to adjust the field width so that all fields fit on one page is selected. The default settings are acceptable.

Click [Next >].

Your screen should be similar to Figure 3.57

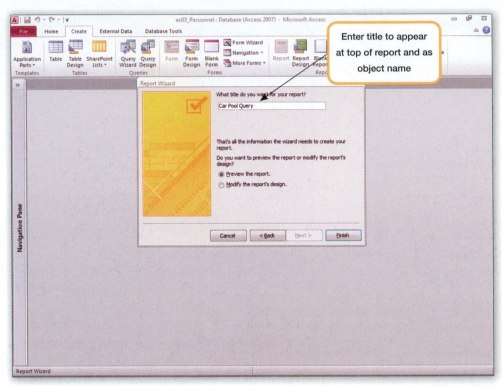

Enter title to appear at top of report and as object name

Figure 3.57

The last Report Wizard dialog box is used to add a title to the report and to specify how the report should be displayed after it is created. The only change you want to make is to replace the query name with a more descriptive report title.

6

- Enter **Car Pool Report: Maldin to Landis** as the title.

- Click [Finish].

Your screen should be similar to Figure 3.58

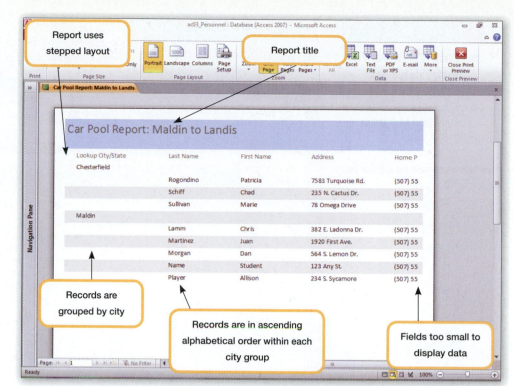

Figure 3.58

In an instant, the completed report with the data from the resource query is displayed in Print Preview. The report appears in the stepped layout, grouped by city. The title reflects the title you specified. The records appear in alphabetical order within each group, as you specified in the Report Wizard.

However, there are a few problems with the report. The most noticeable is that the city field is much larger than it needs to be; consequently, the Home Phone field is truncated. Additionally, you want to change the Lookup City/ State column heading to City and to display the first name field column before the last name.

MODIFYING THE REPORT IN LAYOUT VIEW

To make these changes, you need to modify the report design. You can modify a report in either Design view or Layout view. To make these simple changes, you will use Layout view.

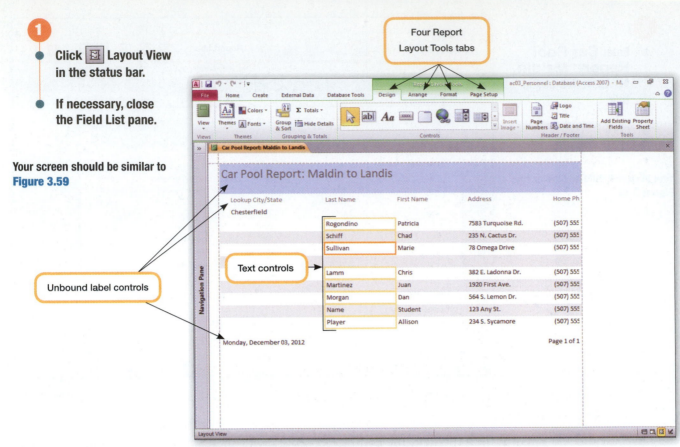

1

● Click ⊞ Layout View in the status bar.

● If necessary, close the Field List pane.

Your screen should be similar to **Figure 3.59**

Four Report Layout Tools tabs

Unbound label controls

Text controls

Figure 3.59

In Layout view, four tabs are available to help you modify the report. The Design tab features are used to add fields, controls, totals, and other elements to the report. The Arrange tab is used to modify the overall layout of the report or of individual elements. The Format tab contains commands to format shapes as well as make text enhancements such as changing the font and font color. The Page Setup tab is used to control the page layout of the report for printing purposes.

Just as in forms, each item in the report is a separate control. The field names are label controls and the field information is a text control. The text controls are bound to the data in the underlying table. The field names and report title are unbound label controls. The stepped report design controls the layout and position of these controls.

The same features you learned when working in Form Layout view are available in Report Layout view. Additionally, just like forms, reports can use a stacked or tabular table layout to make it easier to work with controls. Generally, reports use a tabular layout in which controls are arranged in rows and columns like a spreadsheet, with labels across the top. Currently, although the stepped design you selected in the Report Wizard displays the controls using a tabular design, it did not group the controls in a table layout. You will apply a tabular layout to the report controls so that you can easily modify the report.

Having Trouble?

See Concept 10 in Lab 2 to review controls.

Additional Information

The commands in the Rows & Columns group of the Arrange tab are not available until a table layout has been applied.

2

● Press Ctrl + A to select all the controls on the report.

● Hold down Ctrl while clicking on the title, date, and page # label controls to deselect them.

● Click in the Table group of the Arrange tab to group the selected controls in a tabular layout.

● Double-click on the Lookup City/State label control and change the label to City.

● Click anywhere in the First Name field and click ⊞ Select Column in the Rows & Columns group to select the column.

● Drag the First Name field column to the left of the Last Name field column.

Having Trouble?

When you move a field column, a yellow bar indicates where the column will be placed when you stop dragging.

● Adjust the size of the fields as in Figure 3.60.

Your screen should be similar to **Figure 3.60**

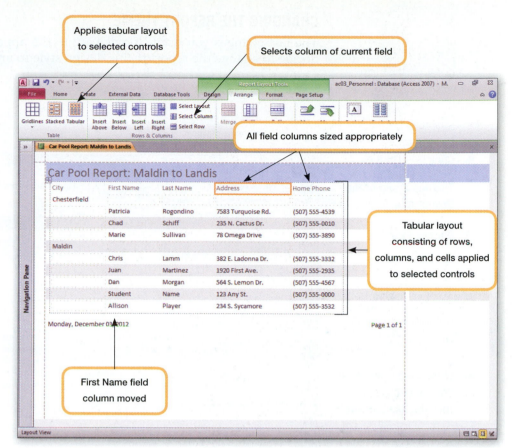

Figure 3.60

Applying the tabular layout made it easy to size and move the controls. Now the report easily fits on a single page and all the fields fully display their contents.

CHANGING THE REPORT THEME

The last changes you want to make are to the appearance of the report. You decide to change the report theme design style to another, more colorful style.

1

● Click [Aa Themes] in the Themes group of the Design tab.

● Choose Flow.

Having Trouble?

The theme names are in alphabetical order and appear in a ScreenTip when you point to the different designs in the Themes gallery.

● Click on the title label control and size it to fully display the text.

Your screen should be similar to Figure 3.61

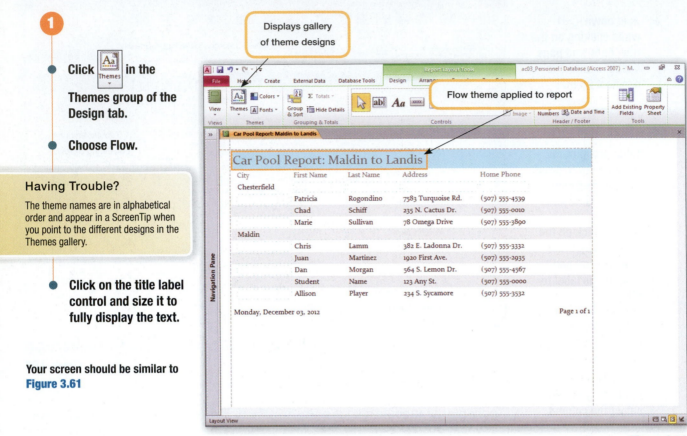

Figure 3.61

The selected theme is applied to the report. It includes brighter colors and different fonts. You are finished making changes to the report and will close and save the report.

2

● Close the report, saving the changes when prompted.

● Display the Navigation pane.

The name of the report you created appears in the Reports category of the Navigation pane.

MODIFYING A REPORT IN DESIGN VIEW

After seeing how easy it was to create a report for the car pool information, you decide to create a custom report for the job position and location information requested by the club director. You will create the report using the Report Wizard. Then you will modify the report in Design view.

1 ● Select the Location Query from the Queries category and click **⬚ Report Wizard** in the Create tab.

● Add all the fields to the report.

● Click **Finish**.

● Enter **River Mist** as the location and click **OK**.

Your screen should be similar to Figure 3.62

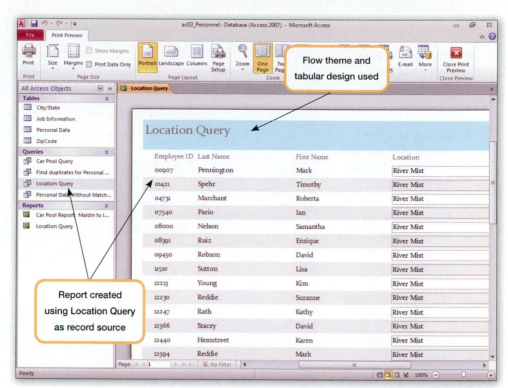

Figure 3.62

Because you knew that you would be using the default or last-used wizard settings, you were able to end the wizard without moving through all the steps. The report displays the specified fields and uses a tabular design and the Flow theme. The tabular design was used because it is the default setting for the Report wizard and the Flow theme was used because it was the last-used theme in the database.

As you look at the report, you realize you forgot to include the Position field. You will modify the query and then add this field in Design view to the report.

- Open the Location Query and enter **River Mist** as the location.

- Change to Query Design view and add the Position field to the design grid.

- Click Save in the Quick Access Toolbar to save the query design changes.

- Display the Location Query report and click  Design View.

- Hide the Navigation pane.

- If the Field List pane is not displayed, click  in the Tools group of the Design tab.

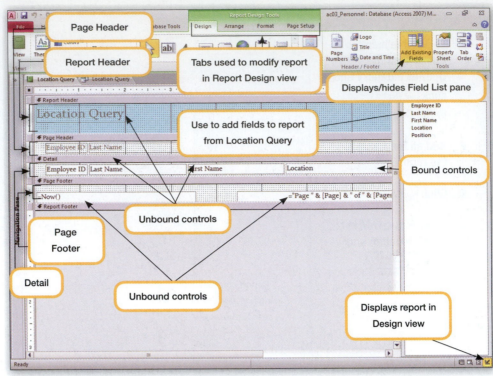

Figure 3.63

Your screen should be similar to Figure 3.63

The report is displayed in Report Design view. This view displays the same four tabs—Design, Arrange, Format, and Page Setup—that were available in Report Layout view.

The Field List task pane displays the field names from the design grid of the Location Query. You will use the Field List task pane shortly to add the missing field to the report.

The Report Design window is divided into five sections: Report Header, Page Header, Detail, Page Footer, and Report Footer. The contents of each section appear below the horizontal bar that contains the name of that section. The sections are described in the following table.

Section	Description
Report Header	Contains information to be printed once at the beginning of the report. The report title is displayed in this section.
Page Header	Contains information to be printed at the top of each page. The column headings are displayed in this section.
Detail	Contains the records of the table. The field column widths are the same as the column widths set in the table design.
Page Footer	Contains information to be printed at the bottom of each page such as the date and page number.
Report Footer	Contains information to be printed at the end of the report. The Report Footer section currently contains no data.

The controls in the Page Header section are unbound label controls whereas those in the Detail section are bound text controls. The control in the Report Header that displays the report title and those in the Page Footers that display the date and page numbers are also unbound label controls.

First, you will group the controls in the Page Header and Detail sections together by applying a tabular layout to the selected fields. Then you will add the missing field to the report.

Click in the ruler area to the left of the fields in the Page Header section to select all the controls in that section.

Additional Information

When positioning the mouse in the ruler, the pointer will appear as a selection arrow ➡ indicating that you can select all fields in the section.

⇧Shift click on the ruler area next to the Detail section to select all the controls in that section as well.

Having Trouble?

You can also select the controls individually by using the ⇧Shift key.

Click  in the Table group of the Arrange tab.

Scroll the window horizontally to view the Location controls and the right edge of the report.

Drag the Position field from the Field List to the right of the Location text control in the Detail section and when a vertical orange bar appears, release the mouse to drop it at that location.

Another Method

You also can double-click on a field in the Field List to move it into the Detail section of the report.

Close the Field List pane.

If necessary, scroll to the left to view all the controls in the report.

Your screen should be similar to Figure 3.64

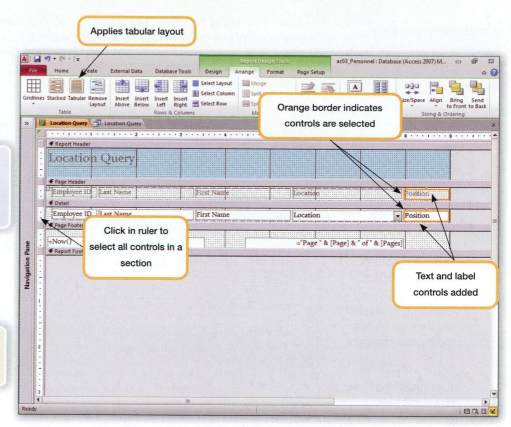

Figure 3.64

The Position field text and label controls have been added to the report. The Position label control was inserted in the Page Header section, and the Position text control was inserted in the Detail section. This is because the controls were inserted into the tabular control layout and comply with the horizontal and vertical alignment settings of the layout. The text control is a bound control that is tied to the Position field data. Both controls are surrounded by an orange border indicating that they are selected.

Additional Information

If you want to move a control out of the control layout, it needs to be removed from the group, as you did when designing the form.

Now you want to move the Last Name controls to the right of the First Name controls. A control can be moved to any location within the control layout by selecting it and then dragging it to the new location. The mouse pointer changes to to indicate that a selected control can be moved.

4

- Select the Last Name label control in the Page Header section.

- Hold down ⇧Shift and click on the Last Name text control in the Detail section.

- Point to the selected controls, and when the pointer changes to ⬚, drag it to the right of the First Name controls.

Another Method

You also can move controls using Ctrl + the directional arrow keys.

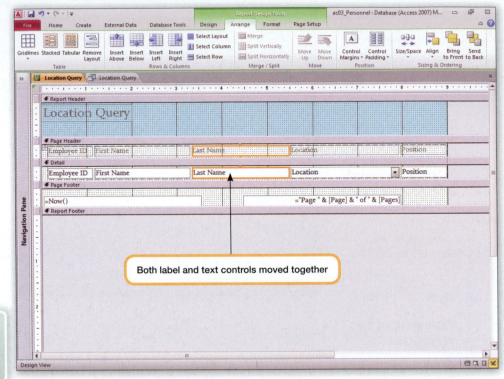

Both label and text controls moved together

Figure 3.65

Your screen should be similar to Figure 3.65

Notice that the Last Name label and text controls moved together because they were both selected. The controls in both the Page Header and Detail sections are horizontally and vertically aligned and spaced an equal distance apart.

FORMATTING CONTROLS

Next, you decide to change the text of the report title and center it over the report. First you will enlarge the title control to extend the width of the report, and then center the text within the control.

1

- Select the report title control.

- Drag the right edge of the control toward the right margin; stop at approximately 8" on the ruler.

- Click  Center in the Font group of the Report Design Tools Format tab.

- Click in the report title control to place the cursor in the text and select the text.

- Type **Job Position Report** and then press ←Enter.

Your screen should be similar to Figure 3.66

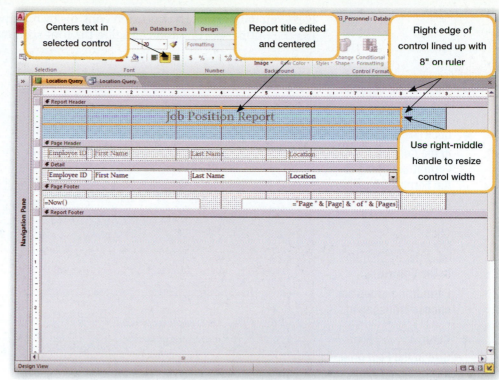

Figure 3.66

The revised title is centered over the report columns. Changing the title text does not change the name of the report object. You also want the work location to be included in the title because the report results could vary depending on what location you entered into the parameter dialog box when the report was opened. To make the title reflect the contents of the report, you will add the Location field to the Report Header area and then use the formatting tools to change its appearance.

2

- Click Add Existing Fields in the Design tab to open the Field List task pane.

- Drag the Location field into the Report Header section, below the title.

- Select and replace the text in the Location label control with **For**

Your screen should be similar to Figure 3.67

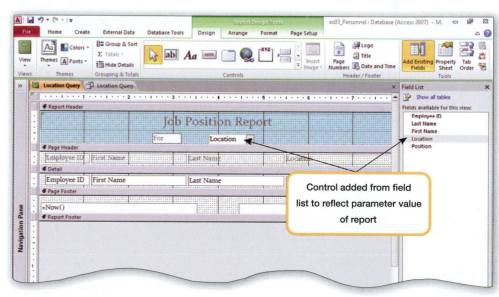

Figure 3.67

Next you will format the Location controls by making them transparent, removing the outline border and changing the font size and color.

3

- Click on the **Location text control**.

- Click [Shape Fill ▾] in the Control Formatting group of the Format tab and choose **Transparent**.

- Click [Shape Outline ▾] in the Control Formatting group and choose **Transparent**.

- Click [11 ▾] **Font Size** in the Font group and choose **18**.

- **Enlarge the Location text control to fully display the text.**

Having Trouble?

In order to grab the corner sizing handles to increase the size of the control, you may need to expand the report header section. Do this by positioning the mouse on the top edge of the Page Header section bar and, when the mouse becomes ✛, drag the bar down slightly.

- Click [A] **Font Color** and choose **Dark Red** from the Standard Colors section of the color gallery (last row, first column).

- **Position and resize both control boxes as shown in Figure 3.68.**

Having Trouble?

Use the large gray handle in the upper-left corner of a control to move each control individually.

- **Close the Field List pane.**

Your screen should be similar to **Figure 3.68**

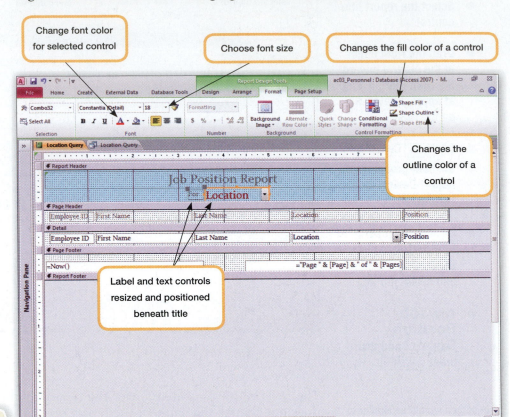

Change font color for selected control

Choose font size

Changes the fill color of a control

Changes the outline color of a control

Label and text controls resized and positioned beneath title

Figure 3.68

When you were attempting to position the Location text and label controls, you may have noticed how they moved together. When the controls are associated and act as one when moved, they are called **compound controls**.

Now you want to see the effects of your changes. You will be prompted to enter the location. This time, you will enter Landis as the location, and the report title now will update to include the location information.

- Switch to Layout view.

- Enter the location of **Landis**

Your screen should be similar to **Figure 3.69**

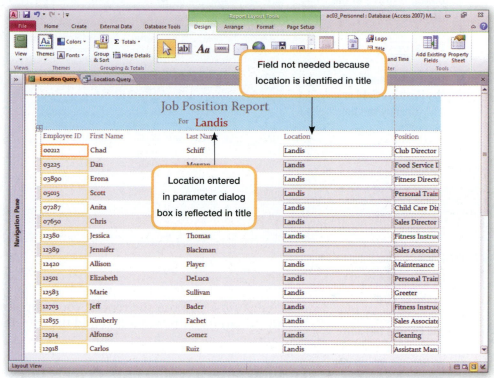

Figure 3.69

The report is really shaping up. However, there are still a few changes you need to make. You want to remove the Location field because the report title now identifies the location. Then you will adjust the sizes of the fields to make the report fill more of the width of the page.

DELETING A FIELD

You will delete the Location field and make adjustments to the other fields in Layout view so you can see the field content and layout while working with them.

1

- Click in the Location field.

- Click ▦ Select Column in the Rows & Columns group of the Arrange tab.

- Press Delete.

- Increase the size of the Position field to fully display the field contents.

Having Trouble?

Scroll to the end of the report to make sure that the largest text entry in the Position field is fully displayed.

- Click

  ✏ Shape Outline ▾

  in the Control Formatting group of the Format tab and choose Transparent to remove the border around the Position field.

- Decrease the width of the First Name and Last Name columns to better fit the text.

- Increase the size of the Employee ID field slightly.

Your screen should be similar to Figure 3.70

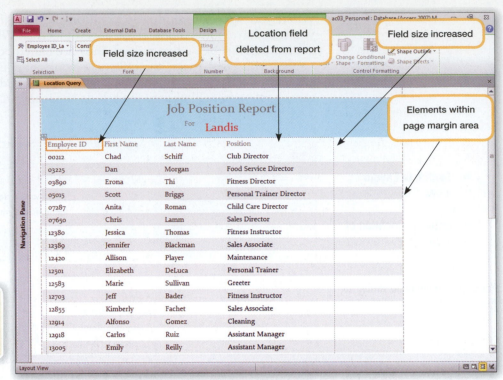

Figure 3.70

Now, each time you run the report, you simply need to enter the location in the query parameter message box and the title and report contents will reflect your input.

SORTING AND FILTERING DATA IN A REPORT

You also notice that the records in the report are in order by employee ID. This is because a sort order was not specified in the query or the report when they were created. Just as in a table datasheet, query, or form, you can sort and filter the data that is displayed in a report. You will use these features to sort the records in alphabetical order by last name and display only the records for employees whose job is fitness instructor.

1

- **Right-click on the Last Name field of any record.**

- **Choose Sort A to Z.**

- **Right-click on the Position field of any record that displays Fitness Instructor.**

- **Choose Equals "Fitness Instructor".**

Your screen should be similar to Figure 3.71

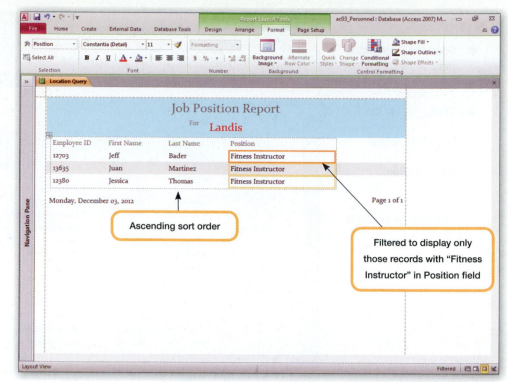

Figure 3.71

Only the three records meeting the filter requirements are displayed in the report. They are in alphabetical order by last name. You will remove the filter but maintain the sorted record order.

2

- **Right-click on the Position field of any record.**

- **Choose Clear filter from Position.**

Additional Information

You also can click **⌄ Toggle Filter** in the Home tab to remove the filter.

All the records are redisplayed again.

Preparing Reports for Printing

You can print the report from any view or even when the report is closed. However, unless you are sure the page settings are correct, it is a good idea to check how its elements are arranged in Layout view or Print Preview before printing. The advantage to Layout view is that you can instantly see how any changes made to the page layout will affect the printed report and you can make any needed adjustments.

MODIFYING THE PAGE SETUP

Additional Information

The default margin setting is Narrow, which sets all margins to 0.25 inch.

As you look at the layout of the report on the page, you see the report is not centered horizontally on the page and there is a lot of empty space to the right of the Position column. To fix this, you will increase the size of the margins, which will push the columns to the right and better center the elements on the page. Then you will readjust the column widths.

1

- Open the Page Setup tab.

- Click 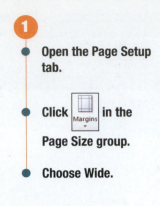 in the Page Size group.

- Choose Wide.

Your screen should be similar to Figure 3.72

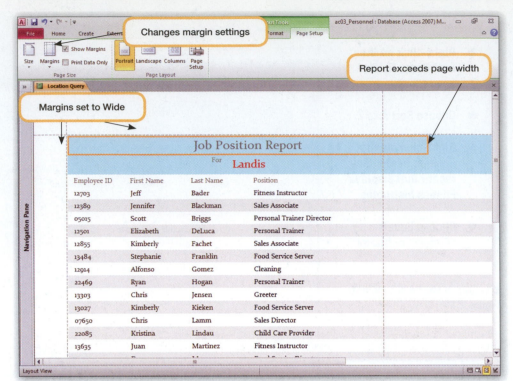

Figure 3.72

The Wide margin option increases the left and right margins to 0.75 inch. The columns now begin at 0.75 inch, and the report appears more balanced on the page; however, now the report width exceeds a single page. This is because some of the controls in the report exceed the new page margins. Additionally, the title is no longer centered because the control is wider than the new page width. These problems can be quickly fixed by reducing the size of the controls that are causing the problem. You decide to increase the margins to 1 inch and then make the adjustments to the controls to fit the new page width. To do this, you will set custom left and right margins.

- Click  in the Page Layout group.

- Enter **1** in the Left and Right Margin text boxes.

- Click **OK**.

- Size the title control to fit the new page width.

- Click on the Landis Location control in the title area, then ⟨⇧Shift⟩ click on the For label control.

- Move the controls so they are once again centered under the Job Position Report title.

- Scroll to the bottom of the report and click on the Page Number control in the footer.

- Reduce the Page Number control size (from the right edge) until it is inside the right margin line.

- If the report still exceeds the margins, further adjust the sizes of the field columns until the report fits within the margins.

- Scroll to the top of the report.

Your screen should be similar to
Figure 3.73

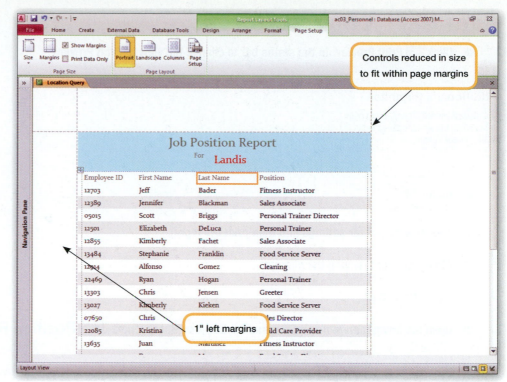

Figure 3.73

Now the columns are spaced attractively across the page. The page layout settings you specify are saved with the report, so unless you make changes to the report design, you only need to set them once.

PREVIEWING AND PRINTING REPORTS

Although you believe the report is ready to print, you will preview it first and then print it.

1

Click 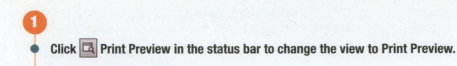 Print Preview in the status bar to change the view to Print Preview.

Additional Information

You also can specify margins and page setup using the same features in the Print Preview ribbon.

● Click [Print].

● Specify your printer settings and then print the report.

● Close the report, saving the changes.

● Close the query.

● Open the Navigation pane and rename the Location Query report **Job Position Report**

Your printed report should look like the one shown in the case study at the beginning of the lab.

PRINTING A RELATIONSHIPS REPORT

Before exiting Access, you want to print a report that shows the relationships between the tables in your database.

1

● Open the Database Tools tab.

● Click [Relationships].

● If necessary, click [All Relationships] to show all table relationships.

● Click [Relationship Report] in the Tools group.

● Print the report.

Your screen should be similar to **Figure 3.74**

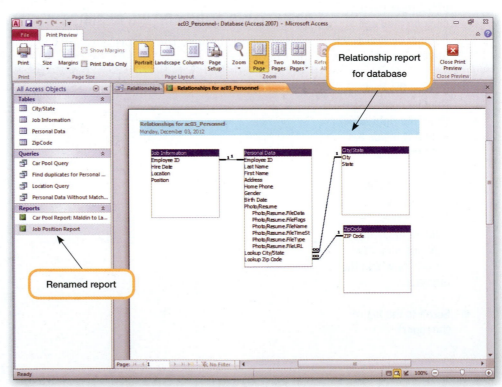

Figure 3.74

A preview of how the report will look when printed is displayed on the screen. The database name and creation date are automatically used as the report header. You can print this report as well as save it for future reference.

2

● Close the relationship report without saving it.

● Close the Relationships window.

Compacting and Backing Up the Database

As you modify a database, the changes are saved to your disk. When you delete data or objects, the database file can become fragmented and use disk space inefficiently. To make the database perform optimally, you should **compact** the database on a regular basis. Compacting makes a copy of the file and rearranges the way that the file is stored on your disk.

1

● Open the File tab and if necessary, choose Info.

● Click to compact and repair the database.

Although it appears that nothing has happened, the database file has been compacted and repaired as needed. It is also a good idea to back up your databases periodically. This will ensure that you have a copy of each database in case of a power outage or other system failure while you are working on a file, or in case you need to access a previous version of a database that you have changed.

2

● Open the File tab and choose Save & Publish.

● Double-click Back Up Database.

Your screen should be similar to Figure 3.75

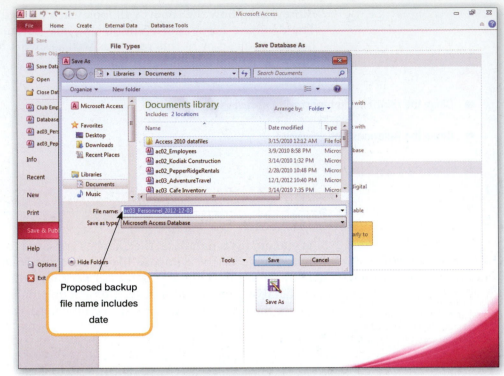

Proposed backup file name includes date

Figure 3.75

The Save As dialog box displays your database name (which in this case is ac03_Personnel) with the current date appended to it. This is a good way to keep track of when you performed the backup on the database, so you will not change this file name.

3

● If necessary, change to the location where you save your solution files.

● Click [Save].

● Close the database and exit Access.

The backup database file has been saved to your solution file location. If you need to restore a backed-up database, you just change the name of the backup file (so it does not conflict with another file of the same name that you may have created since the backup) and then open it in Access.

FOCUS ON CAREERS

EXPLORE YOUR CAREER OPTIONS

Database Administrator

Database administrators are responsible for organizing and maintaining an organization's information resources by working with database management software to implement, analyze, and organize the presentation and use of the data. The administrator usually controls user access, tests new objects, backs up the data, and trains new users to use the database.

As a database administrator, your position also would include safeguarding the system from threats, whether internal or via the Internet. The typical salary range of a database administrator is $40,000 to $65,000, but with years of experience an administrator can earn as much as $100,000. A bachelor's degree in computer science is typically preferred in addition to practical experience. Demand for skilled database administrators is expected to make this one of the fastest-growing occupations.

Query (AC3.20)

A query is a request for specific data contained in a database. Queries are used to view data in different ways, to analyze data, and even to change existing data.

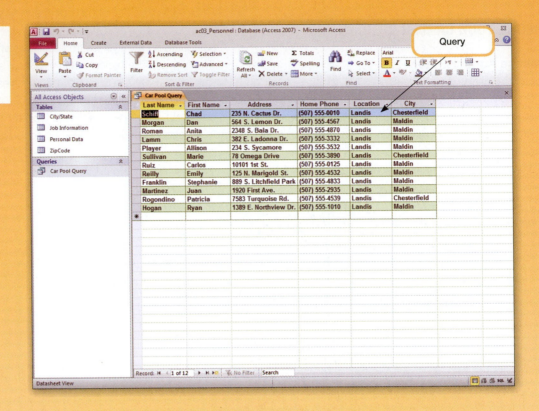

Join (AC3.26)

A join is an association that is created in a query between a field in one table or query and a field of the same data type in another table or query.

Query Criteria (AC3.29)

Query criteria are expressions that are used to restrict the results of a query to display only records that meet certain limiting conditions.

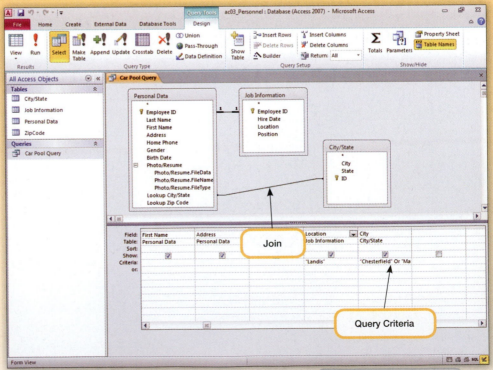

Report (AC3.46)

A report is professional-appearing output generated from tables or queries that may include design elements, groups, and summary information.

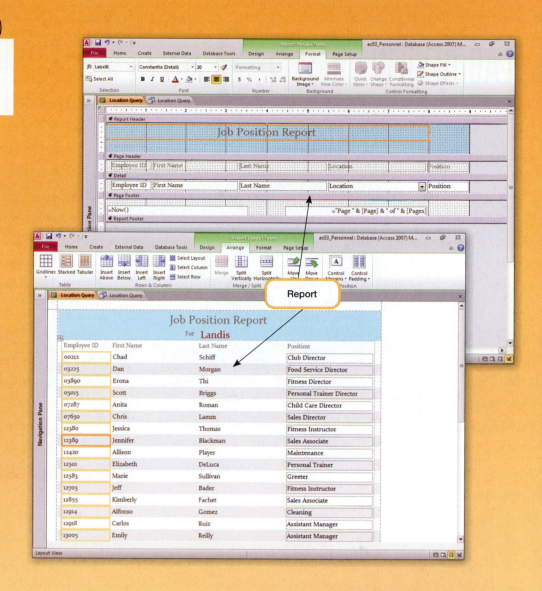

KEY TERMS

action query AC3.20
aggregate functions AC3.45
AND operator AC3.29
append query AC3.20
column selector bar AC3.25
compact AC3.69
compound control AC3.63
compound criteria AC3.29
criteria expression AC3.29
crosstab query AC3.20
delete query AC3.20
design grid AC3.25
field list AC3.25
hard-coded criteria AC3.43
inner join AC3.28
join AC3.26
join line AC3.26

make-table query AC3.20
multitable query AC3.25
OR operator AC3.29
orphaned records AC3.18
outer join AC3.28
parameter query AC3.20
parameter value AC3.43
query AC3.20
query criteria AC3.29
report AC3.18
row label AC3.25
select query AC3.20
Show box AC3.25
SQL query AC3.20
unequal join AC3.28
update query AC3.20

COMMAND SUMMARY

Command	Shortcut	Action
File Tab		
Save Database As		Saves database object with a new file name
Save & Publish>Back Up Database		Backs up database
Info> [Compact & Repair Database]		Compacts and repairs database file
Home tab		
Views group		
Report View		Displays report in Report view
Report Layout View		Displays report in Layout view
Records group		
Refresh All		Updates selected object
Σ Totals		Displays/hides Totals row
Create tab		
Queries group		
Query Wizard		Creates a query using the Query Wizard
Query Design		Creates a query using Query Design view
Reports group		
Report		Creates a report using all fields in current table
Report Design		Creates a report using Report Design view
Report Wizard		Creates a report using the Report Wizard

LAB REVIEW

COMMAND SUMMARY (CONTINUED)

Command	Shortcut	Action
Database Tools tab		
Relationships group		
Relationships		Defines how the data in tables is related
Analyze group		
Analyze Table		Evaluates table design
Query Tools Design tab		
Results group		
Run		Displays query results in Query Datasheet view
Query Setup group		
Show Table		Displays/hides Show Table dialog box
Show/Hide group		
Table Names		Displays/hides the Table row
Report Layout Tools Arrange tab		
Tabular		Arranges controls in a stacked tabular arrangement
Select Column		Selects column
Report Layout Tools Format tab		
Font group		
Align Text Left		Aligns text at left edge of control
Center		Centers text in selected control
11		Used to change the font size of text
Font color		Changes color of text

COMMAND SUMMARY (CONTINUED)

Command	Shortcut	Action
Controls Formatting group		
Shape Fill ▾		Changes the color fill inside a control
Shape Outline ▾		Opens menu to change the border color and line thickness
Report Layout Tools Design tab		
Tools group		
Add Existing Fields		Displays/hides Add Existing Fields task pane
Themes		Applies predesigned theme styles to report
Report Layout Tools Page Setup tab		
Page Size group		
Margins		Sets margins of printed report
Page Layout group		
Page Setup		Sets features related to the page layout of printed report
Relationship Tools Design tab		
Tools group		
Relationship Report		Creates a report of the displayed relationships
Print Preview tab		
Page Size group		
Margins		Adjusts margins in printed output

LAB EXERCISES

MATCHING

Match the numbered item with the correct lettered description.

1. select query   _____ a. query that uses data from more than one table

2. ![Run]   _____ b. used to ask questions about database tables

3. cell   _____ c. the most common type of query

4. query   _____ d. makes a copy of the file and rearranges the way that the file is stored on your disk

5. aggregate functions   _____ e. records that do not have a matching primary key record in the associated table

6. multitable query   _____ f. runs a query and displays a query datasheet

7. compact   _____ g. calculations that are performed on a range of data

8. orphaned   _____ h. intersection of a column and row

9. parameter value   _____ i. prompts you for the specific criteria you want to use when you run the query

10. query criteria   _____ j. set of limiting conditions

TRUE/FALSE

Circle the correct answer to the following statements.

1. A compound control consists of two controls that are associated.	True	False
2. A query can be created with information from more than one table.	True	False
3. Reports can be generated from tables only.	True	False
4. Queries are used to view data in different ways, to analyze data, and to change existing data.	True	False
5. Values that tell Access how to filter the criteria in a query are called filter expressions.	True	False
6. Hard-coded criteria are used each time the query is run.	True	False
7. A delete query is the most common type of query.	True	False
8. A compound criterion is created using the AND operator.	True	False
9. A field cannot be added to a report without using the Report Wizard.	True	False
10. A join line shows how different tables are related.	True	False

FILL-IN

Complete the following statements by filling in the blanks with the correct terms.

1. Aggregate functions perform _____.

2. A(n) _____ is used to display the results of a query.

3. A(n) _____ is a request for specific data contained in a database.

4. A(n) _____ control is used to enter multiple criteria.

5. The _____ operator narrows the search for records that meet both conditions.

6. The Page Setup tab is used to control the page layout of the report for _____ purposes.

7. To be joined, tables must have at least one _____ field.

8. _____ are the set of limiting conditions used in filters and queries.

9. In a report, a(n) _____ is not connected to a field.

10. The _____ is where you enter the settings that define the query.

LAB EXERCISES

MULTIPLE CHOICE

Circle the letter of the correct response.

1. Bound and unbound are types of _____.
   a. buttons
   b. forms
   c. properties
   d. controls

2. The operator that broadens the filter, because any record meeting either condition is included in the output, is _____.
   a. AND
   b. OR
   c. MOST
   d. ALL

3. _____ view can be used to view the data in a report and modify the report design and layout.
   a. Layout
   b. Design
   c. Print Preview
   d. Datasheet

4. When a file is _____, it uses disk space inefficiently.
   a. broken
   b. fragmented
   c. compacted
   d. repaired

5. _____ view is used to create and modify the structure of a query.
   a. Design
   b. Update
   c. Layout
   d. Datasheet

6. A(n) _____ query prompts you for the specific criteria you want to use when you run the query.
   a. parameter
   b. SQL
   c. update
   d. append

7. A report title is a(n) _____ control because it is not connected to a field.
   a. bound
   b. associated
   c. unbound
   d. text

8. The _____ operator is assumed when you enter criteria in multiple fields.
   a. OR
   b. AND
   c. BETWEEN
   d. EQUAL TO

9. The query _____ is where you enter the settings that define the query.
   a. field list
   b. Show box
   c. design grid
   d. object

10. A join line creates a _____ relationship that establishes rules that the data must match to be included in the query results.
    a. permanent
    b. partial
    c. temporary
    d. complete

RATING SYSTEM

★	Easy
★ ★	Moderate
★ ★ ★	Difficult

PEPPER RIDGE RENTALS ★

1. As your property rental business has grown, you've noticed that potential renters usually want to search by price and date availability. You decide to create a query to determine inventory according to these parameters. Your completed query will be similar to that shown here.

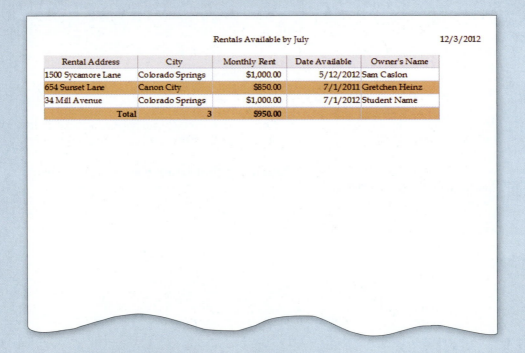

Rentals Available by July				12/3/2012
Rental Address	City	Monthly Rent	Date Available	Owner's Name
1500 Sycamore Lane	Colorado Springs	$1,000.00	5/12/2012	Sam Caslon
654 Sunset Lane	Canon City	$850.00	7/1/2011	Gretchen Heinz
34 Mill Avenue	Colorado Springs	$1,000.00	7/1/2012	Student Name
Total	3	$950.00		

a. Open the PepperRidgeRentals2 database you modified in Lab 2, Step-by-Step Exercise 4, and save as PepperRidgeRentals3.

b. Open the Rental form and add the following two new records:

Rental Address:	901 W. Sunnyslope	34 Mill Avenue
City:	Cimmaron Hills	Colorado Springs
Rented:	Y	N
Date Available:	6/15/2012	7/1/2012
Bedrooms/Baths:	3/2	2/2
Sq Footage:	1400	1300
Monthly Rent:	$750	$1000
Owner's Name:	Kim Ming	Your name

c. Create a query based on the Rentals table. Include, in this order, the Rental Address, City, Monthly Rent, Date Available, Rented, and Owner's Name fields. Save the query as **Rentals Available by July**. Use the criteria of **<=July 1, 2012** for the available date and **<=1000** for the price.

d. Filter the query to show only the records for the homes that are not currently rented. Best fit the query datasheet columns. Display a Totals row with a count in the City column and an Average in the Monthly Rent column. Print the query results.

e. Close all objects. Compact and repair the database. Exit Access.

SCENSATIONS SPA DATABASE ★★

2. The Scensations Salon and Day Spa offers hair and spa treatments exclusively for women. The owner of the spa is offering a new spa package that would include various anti-aging skin treatments and massages. She wants to send an announcement about this package to her clients who are over the age of 45. You will get this information for her from the client information that is stored in an Access 2010 database file. Your printed report will be similar to that shown here.

a. Open the database file named ac03_Scensations Spa and the table named Clients.

b. Find and delete any duplicate records using the Last Name field as the field to check for duplicate data. Delete the record with the higher Client ID#.

c. Use the Table Analyzer Wizard to create a second table containing the city, state, and zip code information. Name the new table **City/State/Zip**. Make the Zip Code field the primary key in this table.

d. Delete the Clients table. Rename Table1 **Clients**. Move the Lookup field after the Address field. Best fit all the fields in the table.

e. Query the Clients table to display the First Name, Last Name, and Address fields for those records with a birth date before **1/1/65**. Add all the fields from the City/State/Zip table. Move the Birth Date field to the first position in the datasheet. Run the query. If you get an error message, click OK as necessary.

Clients 45+ Report

Last Name	First Name	Address	City	State/Province	ZIP/Postal Code
Anderson	Lisa	7428 S. Hill	Yerington	NV	89447
Arnold	Beatrice	369 N. Main	Yerington	NV	89447
Austin	Alma	560 E. Hickory	Smith Valley	NV	89430
Chavez	Kristen	861 S. Tenth	Smith Valley	NV	89430
Cook	Gloria	224 E. Laurel	Dayton	NV	89403
Foster	Phyllis	27984 W. Dogwood	Fernley	NV	89408
Hayes	Robin	861 N. Fourth	Fernley	NV	89408
Henderson	Andrea	8666 N. 9th	Dayton	NV	89403
Jones	Barbara	738 N. Eighth	Smith Valley	NV	89430
Kelley	Elsie	1008 W. 11th	Silver City	NV	89428
Matthews	Erica	738 E. Sixth	Yerington	NV	89447
Myers	Peggy	492 S. Lincoln	Fernley	NV	89408
Name	Student	123 Any Street	Smith Valley	NV	89430
Peters	Sue	1238 E. Fourth	Silver City	NV	89428
Reed	Doris	10494 N. Forest	Dayton	NV	89403
Sims	Vanessa	784 N. Cherry	Smith Valley	NV	89430
Sullivan	Dawn	369 E. 8th	Fernley	NV	89408
Taylor	Dorothy	1238 E. Fifth	Smith Valley	NV	89430
Williams	Linda	495 W. Cherry	Smith Valley	NV	89430

Saturday, December 01, 2012   Page 1 of 1

LAB EXERCISES

f. Display a Totals row showing a count of the Last Name field. Save the query as **Clients 45+**. Print the query results.

g. Use the Report Wizard to create a report with the client names and addresses, based on the Clients 45+ query. Choose landscape orientation and tabular layout. Save the report as **Clients 45+ Report**.

h. Change the report margins to Normal. Apply tabular layout to the controls and then adjust the controls to fit the report on a single page widthwise.

i. Add a new record to the Clients table that includes your name in the First Name and Last Name fields and a birth date of **2/11/62**.

j. Refresh the query and report to update them.

k. Print the report.

l. Compact and repair the database. Back up the database.

m. Close the database, saving as needed, and exit Access.

DOWNTOWN INTERNET CAFÉ INVENTORY ★★

3. The Inventory database you created for the Downtown Internet Café (Lab 1, Step-by-Step Exercise 4) has been in use several weeks now and is working well. During this time, you have modified the table design and added more information to the table. Evan, the owner, has asked you to submit a daily report on all low-quantity items so he can place the necessary orders. You will use the database to monitor inventory levels and respond to Evan's request. First, you decide to run a query to find the low-stock items, and then you can generate the requested report from the query. Your completed report should look similar to the report below.

a. Open the database file named ac03_Cafe Inventory. Open the Stock table to view its contents. In the Suppliers table, replace the contact for Cuppa Jo (Joseph Tan) with your name.

b. Use the Query Wizard to create a query based on the Stock table. Include all fields, except Item, in their current order. Name the query **Low Stock**.

c. In Query Design view, enter the criteria to display only those records with an In Stock value less than **30**, and run the query.

d. Upon reviewing the query results, you realize that the query needs to include the contact names, phone numbers, and e-mail addresses for Evan to use when he places orders. Add these fields from the Suppliers table to the query design, then run and save the query.

e. Use the Report Wizard to create a report based on the Low Stock query. Include all the fields in the order listed. Select Supplier as the only sort field. Select the tabular layout and landscape orientation. Name the report **Low Stock Report**.

f. In Design view, select the label and text box controls in both the Page Header and Detail sections. Apply the tabular layout arrangement. In Report Layout view, change the theme design for the report to Essential. Resize the control box for the title, and then change the title font color to a color of your choice. Make the shape outline for the Supplier control transparent. Adjust the field column widths as needed to appropriately display the data. Center the data in the Special Order column. Change the margin setting to Normal, and resize or move any controls that cause the report to overlap to a second page.

g. Preview and print the report. Close the Report window, saving the changes.

h. Compact and repair the database.

i. Back up the database. Exit Access.

ADVENTURE TRAVEL TOURS ★★

4. You have continued working on the database you created for Adventure Travel in Lab 2, On Your Own Exercise 1. Although you are pleased with it, it still needs some revisions to make booking trips easier, as well as a price sheet for selected packages to give to potential customers. Your finished report will appear similar to that shown below.

a. Open ac03_AdventureTravel and then open the Clients table. Add a new record with your name as Client **99999**, and fill out the remaining information for your client record.

Adventure Travel Selected Destinations

For Client	Name	
Price	$2,000.00	
Destination	Caribbean	
Length	8 days	
Description	Cruise ship traveling Caribbean islands	
Accommodations	Balcony Cabin, Cruise Ship	

b. Create a new table named **Trip Sales**. In Design view, enter **Sale #** as an AutoNumber ID field and set it as the primary key. Create a lookup field called **Client**, based on the Client table, and use the last name and first name fields sorted in ascending order. Create a lookup field called **Package**, using the Package table. Include the Destination and Length fields, and sort in ascending order by destination. Lastly, create a lookup field called **Agent**, based on the Agent table, and use the agent's last and first name, sorted in ascending order. For the Package field, look up the Destination and Length fields, and sort by destination. Adjust all column widths in the lookup as needed.

c. Switch to Datasheet view and assign trips to these customers:

Client	Package	Agent
Your Name	Caribbean	Mary Cook
Frank Cider	Hawaii	Mark Milligan
Torri Dun	Atlantic City	Lynn Sims
Scott Berco	Lake Tahoe	Mary Cook

d. Create relationships for the four tables. Enforce referential integrity for all relationships. Print the relationships report.

LAB EXERCISES

e. Create a parameter query named **Destination Query** that displays all fields from the Packages table and the Client field from the Trip Sales table. Enter **[Enter Destination]** for the criteria. Run and test the query using the destination of **Caribbean**.

f. Using the Report Wizard, create a report using the Destination Query. Include the Destination, Length, Description, Accommodations, and Price fields. Sort by price in ascending order. Use columnar layout. Save the report as **Adventure Travel Selected Destinations**.

g. Change the font size for the Price text box control to 14 point, and align the text to the left. Add the Client field to the report header, under the Adventure Travel Selected Destinations title. In the Client label, type in the word **For** to the left of Client. In Layout view, apply tabular layout to the labels and text controls before adjusting the width of any controls as needed. Print the report.

h. Add your name as the author to the database properties.

i. Compact and repair the database. Save any changes and exit Access.

ARF REPORTS ★★★

5. The Animal Rescue Foundation volunteers are successfully using the database you created in Lab 2, Step-by-Step Exercise 3, to enter information for all the rescued animals. Meanwhile, you created another table containing information about the foster homes (including names, addresses, and phone numbers). The Animal Rescue Foundation management has now asked you for a report, shown below, of all animals placed in foster homes in the past year (2011), and the names and addresses of those providing foster care, so the appropriate thank-you notes can be sent. Your completed report will be similar to the report shown here.

a. Open the database file named ac03_ARF3. Open both tables to review their content.

b. In the Rescues table, search for the dog named Tasha, update the information for Foster Date to **4/15/2011**, and attach the photo ac03_Tasha. Update her Current Status to reflect that she is now being fostered.

c. Find and delete any duplicate records in the Fosters table using the Last Name field as the field to check for duplicate data. Delete the duplicate records that have the highest Foster ID number.

d. Add your name as a new foster parent with the ID number **999** with the city of **Tempe**. Close the Fosters table.

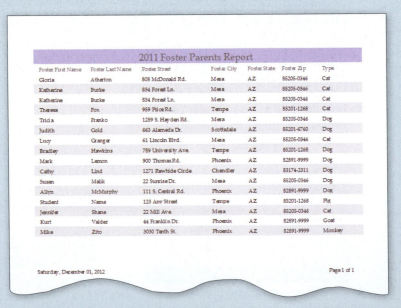

e. To generate the requested information, you need to add a new field to the Rescues table that identifies the foster person that was assigned to the animal. Instead of checking the Fosters table to find the number and then entering the number in the Rescues table, you will make the new field a lookup field that will display values from the Fosters table.

In Design view, add the **Foster ID#** field after the Foster Date field of the Rescues table. Select Lookup Wizard from the Data Type list. Select the following options from the Lookup Wizard:

- Look up values in a table.
- Use the Fosters table.
- Display the Foster ID#, Foster Last Name, and Foster First Name fields.
- Sort by the last and first names.
- Clear the Hide key column option, and then adjust the widths as needed.
- Select Foster ID# as the value to store.
- Use the Foster ID# field name.

f. Switch to Datasheet view. Now you need to enter the Foster ID# for all animals that have been in a foster home. Create a query to display only the pets that have had a foster in 2011. Display the animal's Name, Current Status, Foster Date, and Foster ID# columns only. Type in **>=#1/1/2011#** for the Foster Date criteria. Name the query **Fosters for 2011**. When you run the query, only the pets with a foster in 2011 should display. From the Foster ID# drop-down list, select a foster name for each record (the foster list is quite long, and you can scroll to choose more names). Select your name as the foster parent for the last animal.

g. Next you will modify the query to display the information you need in the report. Add the Fosters table to the query design and resize both table field lists to fully display their information. Delete the Foster ID# field from the grid. Add the following fields from the tables specified in the order listed below.

Rescues table

- Type

Fosters table

- Foster First Name
- Foster Last Name
- Foster Street
- Foster City
- Foster State
- Foster Zip

h. Sort the Foster Last Name column in ascending order. Run the query and review the resulting datasheet. Hide the Current Status field. Save the query again as **2011 Foster Parents**.

LAB EXERCISES

i. Use the Report Wizard to create a report based on the 2011 Foster Parents query you just saved. Include the following fields in the order listed below:

- Foster First Name
- Foster Last Name
- Foster Street
- Foster City
- Foster State
- Foster Zip
- Type

j. Group the data by Rescues; use the tabular layout and landscape orientation. Name the report **2011 Foster Parents Report**.

k. Change the page margin setting to Wide. Center the Report Header control at the top of the page. Change the theme to one of your choice. Apply the tabular table layout to all the controls in the Page Header and Detail sections. Size the controls as needed to enhance the report appearance and fit the entire report on a single page.

l. Preview and then print the report. Close the report window, saving the changes you made.

m. Compact and repair the database.

n. Back up the database and exit Access.

ON YOUR OWN

TIMELESS TREASURES REPORT ★

1. The owners of Timeless Treasures have decided to expand their offerings to include vintage clocks as well as watches. Open the database file Timeless Treasures that you worked on in Lab 2, On Your Own Exercise 5. Revisit the Web to obtain information on vintage clocks. Create a second table in the database with the same fields as the Watches table to use for maintaining the clock inventory. Name this table **Clocks**. Enter 10 records in the new table. Create an inventory report called **Timeless Treasures Watches Inventory** that displays the Identification Number, Description, Price, and Quantity on Hand fields of information. Use a layout and theme design style of your choice. Modify the report design as needed to improve its appearance. Create the same report for the Clocks table and name it **Timeless Treasures Clocks Inventory**. Preview and print both reports. Compact and back up the database.

DENTAL OFFICE CAR POOL LIST ★

2. As the office manager at Jones & Smith Dentistry, you see a need to arrange carpooling for the employees. Open the Dental Patients database you worked with in Lab 2, On Your Own Exercise 3. Create a table named **Employees** that includes fields for the employee ID number, first and last names, and home contact information (street, city, state, zip code, and phone). Enter eight records in the table. For the employee's city, choose from these three cities: **Williams**, **Flagstaff**, and **Munds Park**. Include your name as the employee name in one of the records. Then use this table to create a query that includes only the employee first and last names and home address fields of information. Sort the query by city. Enter the criteria of Williams OR Munds Park for the city. Save the query as **Employees Outside of Flagstaff**. Create a report named **Employee Car Pool List** using the query as the record source. Use tabular layout and a theme design style of your choice. Modify the report design as needed to improve its appearance. Compact and back up the database.

LEARNSOFT DEVELOPERS ★ ★

3. Learnsoft Inc. develops computer-based curricula for grades K–8. The company uses a database to track which software titles have been worked on by the project managers. The program manager for Learnsoft wants a report of this information so he can use it for employee reviews the following week. Open the database file ac03_Learnsoft and the table named Software. Add a new field named **Project Manager** before the Release Date field to include the name of the project manager for each title. Make this field a lookup list field that will look up the names of the five project managers. (Use names of your choice, but include your name as one of the project managers.) Complete the data for this field by selecting a project manager for each record. Assign your name as project manager to one of the records with a release date in 2012. Create a report named **Project Manager Report** that shows the titles, subject, and project manager names for the years 2010 through 2012. Use a theme design style and layout of your choice. Modify the report design as needed to improve its appearance. Compact and back up the database.

AMP EXPENSE ACCOUNT REPORT ★ ★

4. One of the department managers at AMP Enterprises has requested a report showing who in her department has submitted an expense reimbursement request but has not yet been paid. You decide this would be a good report to generate for all departments. In the AMP Enterprises database, open the Employee Expenses table you updated in Lab 2, On Your Own Exercise 2. Create a one-to-many relationship between the Employee Info table and the Employee Expenses table based on the Employee ID fields. Enforce referential integrity and select the Cascade Update option. Create a query that displays all fields from both tables, sorted by department. View the query results. Modify the query to not show the Employee ID field and to display only those employees who have not been paid. Apply an ascending sort to the Submission Date field. Save the query as **Pending Payment**. Use the Report Wizard to create a report named **Open Expense Requests** based on the Pending Payment query. Use a theme design style and layout of your choice. Modify the report design as needed to improve its appearance. Preview and print the report. Compact and back up the database.

LAB EXERCISES

KODIAK CONSTRUCTION REPORTS ★ ★ ★

5. The database you created for Kodiak Construction has been very well received. A few requests for changes to the database have been made, so you will create a query and a report to fulfill these requests. Open the database file named ac02_Kodiak Construction that you modified in Lab 2, Step-by-Step Exercise 5. Create a parameter query named **Priority** that displays the ID, Job, Priority, Client Last Name, and Begin Date from the Jobs table and the Foreman Last Name from the Foremen table. For the Priority field criteria, type in the parameter question **[Enter priority level]**. Create a report using the Priority query for jobs with a high priority. Include the ID, Job, Priority, Begin Date, and Foreman Last Name fields. Sort the report by begin date. Use the tabular layout in portrait orientation. Name the report **Job Priority Report**. Change the page margins to Wide. Adjust the size of the report controls in Layout view to appropriately display the data on one page. Use the Flow theme style. Preview and print the report. Create and print a relationships report. Compact and repair the database.

CASE STUDY

Lifestyle Fitness Club

Periodically, the club director wants to know the names of the employees at each club and their job positions. You created a parameter query to obtain this information and a custom report to display it professionally. Now you want to provide this information to the director.

You will learn about exporting Access data to Excel and Word using the Export Wizard. Then you will learn how to copy and paste objects and selections between Access and Word to create a memo to the director.

Your memo containing a copy of the query results and the report generated by Access will look like the one shown here.

NOTE This tutorial assumes that you already know how to use Word 2010 and that you have completed Lab 3 of Access 2010.

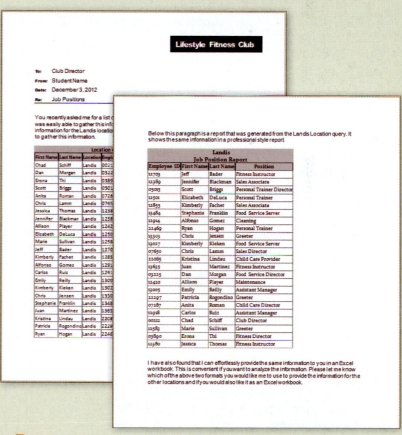

Exporting Data

There are often circumstances when you will want to provide data from an Access database for use in another program or method of presentation. The process of copying this information to a file outside the database is called

exporting. There are a variety of methods you can use, depending upon the type of output needed. The most common export types are described below:

Export to	Description
Excel	Creates a copy of the selected data, table, query, or form object and stores the copy in an Excel worksheet.
Word	Creates a copy of the selected data, table, query, form, or report, including formatting, in a new rich text file (*.rtf) that can be utilized in Word.
Access database	Creates a copy of the table definition and data or just the table definition in another Access database.
Text file	Creates a copy of the selected data, table, query, form, or report, approximating formatting if possible, in a new text file (*.txt) document.
SharePoint site	Creates a copy of a table or query and stores it on a SharePoint site as a list.

The Export Wizard is used for all types of exports. In addition, in some cases, you can copy and paste an object in another application. The file that you export from is the **source file** and the file that is created is the **destination file**.

EXPORTING TO EXCEL 2010

The director does not have Access 2010 installed on his computer, so you need to export the data to either Word 2010 or Excel 2010 format. You will try both methods to see what the output in each application looks like.

When exporting to Excel, the database file you want to copy from must be open in Access. Then you select the object you want to export. The Export Wizard can copy selected data, a table, a query, or a form object, but it cannot export a report to Excel. Because you cannot export a report, you will export the Job Positions query instead.

Additional Information

If you want to export a selection, you need to open the object and select the records you want to export.

Additional Information

Only one object can be exported at a time.

1

- Start Access 2010 and open the database file acwt1_ Personnel from your data file location.

- If necessary, respond appropriately to the Security Warning.

- Select Location Query in the Navigation pane.

- Click [Excel] in the Export group of the External Data tab.

Your screen should be similar to Figure 1

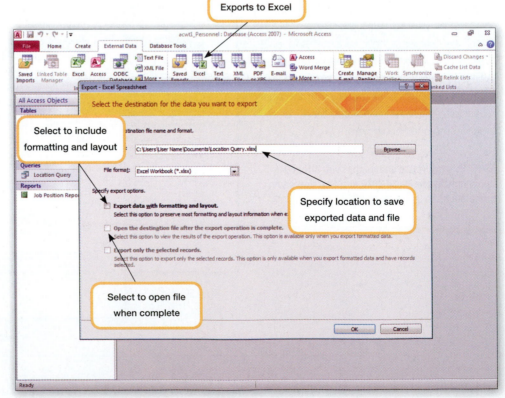

Figure 1

In the first Export-Excel Spreadsheet wizard dialog box, you specify the name of the destination file and the file format. The default file format of an Excel 2010 workbook file (.xlsx) is acceptable; however, you need to change the file location and name. In addition, you want to include the formatting from the query object and see the new Excel workbook file after it is created. Because the query is a parameter query, you also will be asked to enter which fitness club location you want the exported query results to display.

2

- Click **Browse...** and specify the location to save the file.

- In the File Save dialog box, enter the file name **Landis Job Positions** and click **Save**.

- Choose Export data with formatting and layout.

- Choose Open the destination file after the export operation is complete.

- Click **OK**.

- Type **Landis** in the Enter Parameter Value dialog box.

- Click **OK**.

- If necessary, maximize the Excel application window.

Your screen should be similar to **Figure 2**

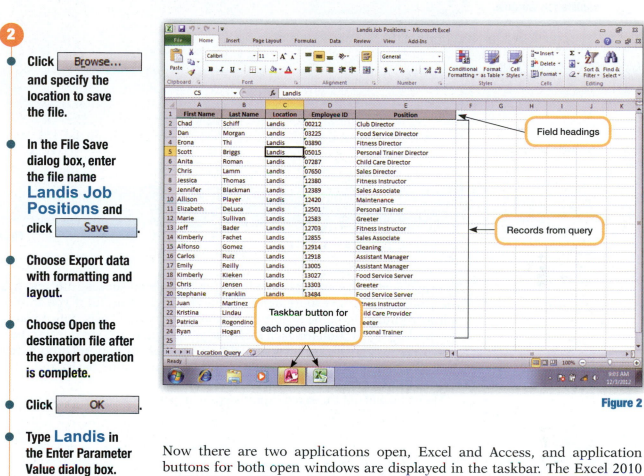

Figure 2

Now there are two applications open, Excel and Access, and application buttons for both open windows are displayed in the taskbar. The Excel 2010 application window is displayed, and the exported data has been copied into a worksheet of the new workbook file. The field headings appear formatted in the first row of the worksheet, and each row that follows is a record from the query datasheet. Notice that the Microsoft Access button in the taskbar is flashing. This is to tell you that the wizard is not yet done.

3
● Click on the ![A] Microsoft Access button in the taskbar to switch to the Access application window.

Having Trouble?

If your taskbar is hidden, point to the thin line at the bottom of the screen to redisplay it.

Your screen should be similar to Figure 3

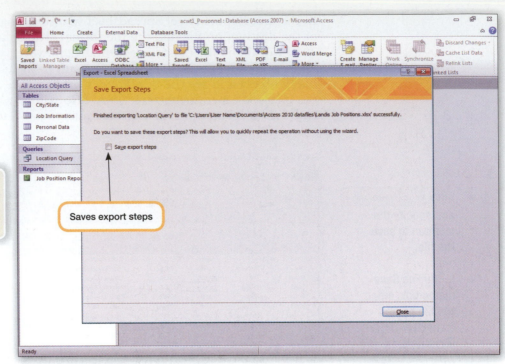

Saves export steps

Figure 3

The final step tells you the export has been completed successfully and asks if you want to save the export steps. Saving the steps is useful if you think you will be running the same export operation on a routine basis. Since you need to repeat this operation for each location, you will save the steps using the suggested name. The wizard also can add a reminder for you in Outlook to run the export if you need to generate the results on a routine basis. You will not include this feature at this time.

Then you will use the saved export steps to export the River Mist location data.

Choose Save Export Steps.

Click ⬚ Save Export ⬚.

Click  **in the Export group to start the next export process.**

Your screen should be similar to Figure 4

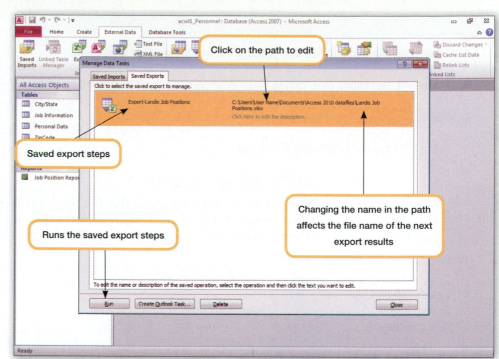

Figure 4

The Saved Exports dialog box contains options for running export steps that have been previously executed and saved. The only change you will make to the saved export is to edit the file name that is used to save the exported data in Excel to reflect the River Mist location.

5

Click on the path, select Landis in the file name, and change it to River Mist

Press ⬚←Enter⬚ **to complete the change.**

Click ⬚ Run ⬚.

In the Enter Parameter Value dialog box, type River Mist as the location.

Click ⬚ OK ⬚.

Your screen should be similar to Figure 5

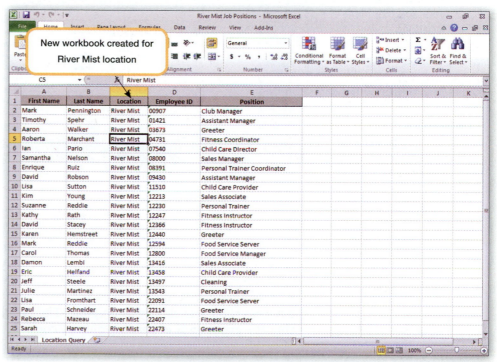

Figure 5

A separate workbook file was created and contains the data for the River Mist location. Now all the Excel features can be used to analyze the data in the worksheets. After exporting each location to a workbook, you could combine the workbooks by copying the worksheet data from each worksheet into one workbook file.

6

- Enter your name in cell A26 and print the River Mist location worksheet.

- Close both workbook files, saving when prompted, and exit the Excel application.

- Click [OK] to acknowledge that the export is finished.

- Close the Manage Data Tasks dialog box.

EXPORTING TO WORD 2010

Next, you will try exporting the Job Position Report to a Word document. When you use the Export Wizard to do this, a copy of the object's data is inserted into a Microsoft Word Rich Text Format file (.rtf).

1

- Select Job Position Report in the Navigation pane.

- Click  More in the Export group, and then choose

  Word
  Export the selected object to Rich Text

- If necessary, change the file location to your solution file location.

Having Trouble?

The report will be saved using the default file name of Job Position Report.

- Choose Open the destination file after the export operation is complete.

- Click [OK].

- Type Landis in the Enter Parameter Value dialog box and click [OK].

Your screen should be similar to Figure 6

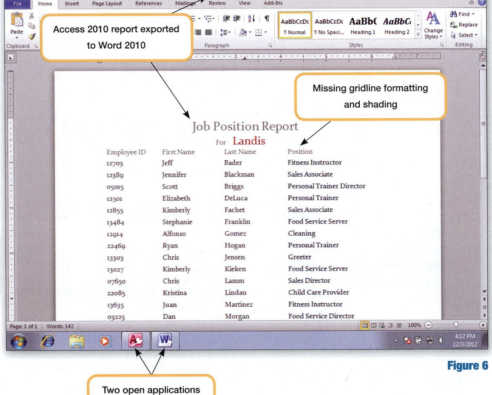

Figure 6

Now there are two applications open, Word 2010 and Access 2010, and application buttons for both open windows are displayed in the taskbar. The Word 2010 application window is displayed, and the exported data has been copied into a document file and saved as Job Position Report. The report resembles the Access report as closely as possible. The problem with the exported report is that the gridlines and shading did not copy.

Having Trouble?

If WordPad is the open application, this is because your system has associated .rtf file types with this application. You could close WordPad and open the document in Word 2010.

Again, the Microsoft Access button in the taskbar is flashing. This time you will not save the steps.

2

- Switch to the Access application window.

- Click [Close] to close the Export Wizard.

COPYING A QUERY OBJECT TO WORD 2010

Finally, you decide to try copying an Access object to an existing Word document without using the Export Wizard. To do this, you can use the Copy and Paste commands or drag and drop to copy a database object between the Access and Word applications.

You have already started a memo to the club director about the Job Position query and report you created.

1

- Switch to the Word application window and close the Job Position Report document.

- Open the document acwt1_Job Positions from your data file location.

- In the memo header, replace Student Name with your name.

Your screen should be similar to Figure 7

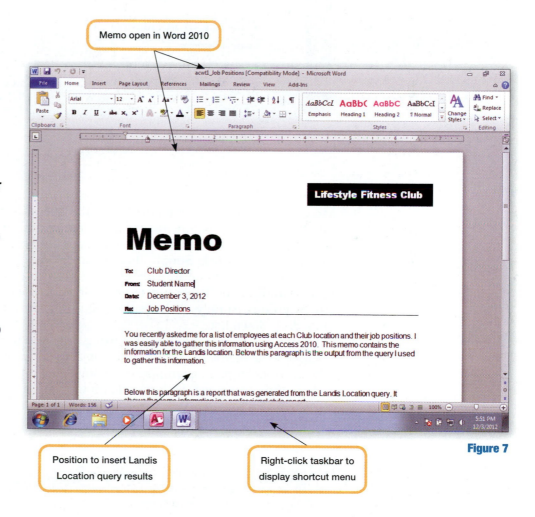

Memo open in Word 2010

Position to insert Landis Location query results

Right-click taskbar to display shortcut menu

Figure 7

This document contains the text of the memo to the director. Below the first paragraph, you want to copy the output from the Landis Location query results using drag and drop. To do this, both applications must be open and visible, which you will do by displaying the application windows side by side.

2

- Right-click on a blank area of the taskbar to open the shortcut menu.

- Choose Show Windows Side by Side.

- Click in the Word application window to make it the active window.

Your screen should be similar to
Figure 8

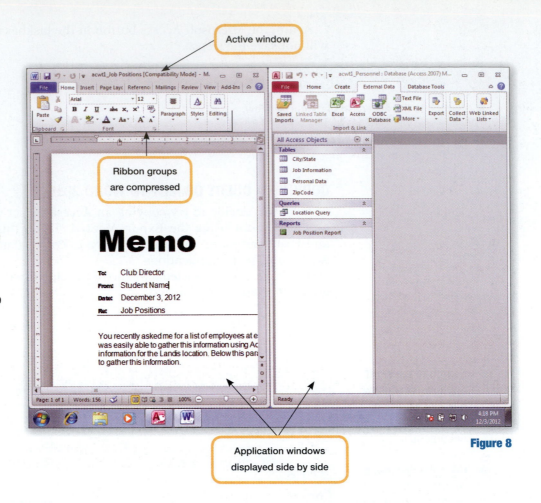

Active window

Ribbon groups are compressed

Application windows displayed side by side

Figure 8

You can now see the contents of both the Access and Word applications. The Word document contains the insertion point, and the window title bar text is not dimmed, which indicates that it is the **active window**, or the window in which you can work. Simply clicking on the other document makes it active. Because the windows are side by side and there is less horizontal space in each window, the Ribbon groups are compressed. To access commands in these groups, simply click on the group button and the commands appear in a drop-down list.

You will copy the query results using drag and drop to below the first paragraph of the memo. As you drag the object you want to copy from Access into the Word document, a temporary cursor ⌶ shows the location in the document where the content will be inserted and the mouse pointer appears as ⊡.

3

- Select Location Query in the Access Navigation pane.

- Drag the selected object to the blank line below the first paragraph of the memo.

- Enter Landis as the Location parameter and click OK .

- Click in the Word document to deselect the table.

- Scroll the document to see the table.

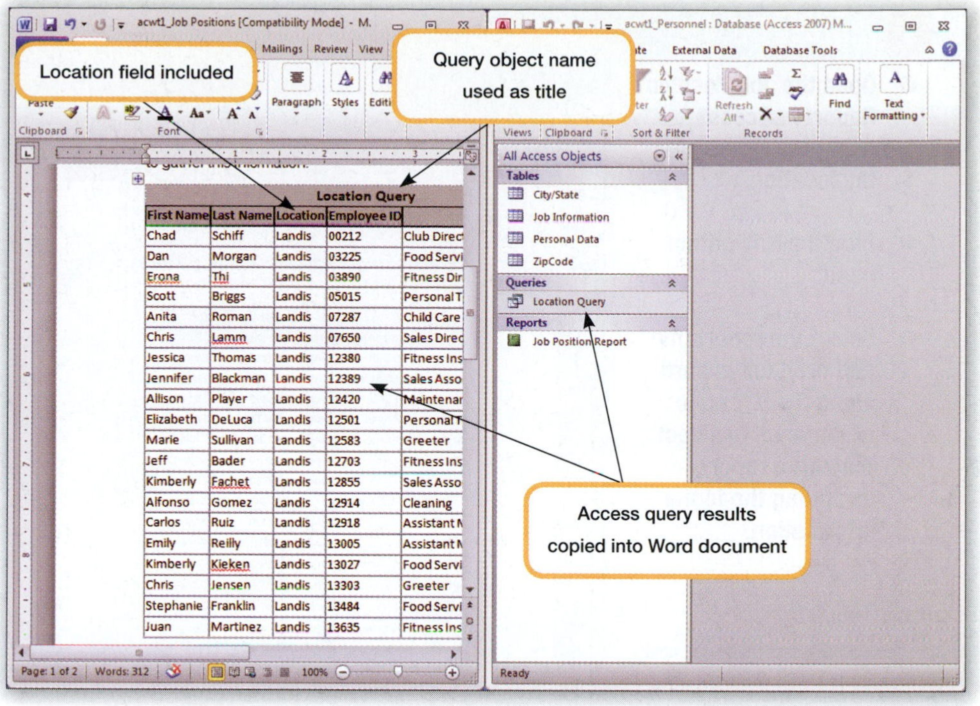

Your screen should be similar to Figure 9

Location field included

Query object name used as title

Location Query

First Name	Last Name	Location	Employee ID	
Chad	Schiff	Landis	00212	Club Direc
Dan	Morgan	Landis	03225	Food Servi
Erona	Thi	Landis	03890	Fitness Dir
Scott	Briggs	Landis	05015	Personal T
Anita	Roman	Landis	07287	Child Care
Chris	Lamm	Landis	07650	Sales Direc
Jessica	Thomas	Landis	12380	Fitness Ins
Jennifer	Blackman	Landis	12389	Sales Asso
Allison	Player	Landis	12420	Maintenar
Elizabeth	DeLuca	Landis	12501	Personal T
Marie	Sullivan	Landis	12583	Greeter
Jeff	Bader	Landis	12703	Fitness Ins
Kimberly	Fachet	Landis	12855	Sales Asso
Alfonso	Gomez	Landis	12914	Cleaning
Carlos	Ruiz	Landis	12918	Assistant M
Emily	Reilly	Landis	13005	Assistant M
Kimberly	Kieken	Landis	13027	Food Servi
Chris	Jensen	Landis	13303	Greeter
Stephanie	Franklin	Landis	13484	Food Servi
Juan	Martinez	Landis	13635	Fitness Ins

All Access Objects
Tables
- City/State
- Job Information
- Personal Data
- ZipCode
Queries
- Location Query
Reports
- Job Position Report

Access query results copied into Word document

Page: 1 of 2   Words: 312   100%   Ready

Figure 9

The query results have been copied into the Word document as a table that can be edited and manipulated within Word. The formatting associated with the copied object also is included. However, the title is the same as the query name and the Location field is displayed. To change this, you could edit the title and then delete the table column using Word 2010.

COPYING A REPORT

Next, you will copy the report into the memo to show how it will look. To copy report data, you run the report in Access and then use the Copy and Paste commands to copy the contents to a Word document.

1

- Open the Job Position Report in Access using **Landis** as the location.

- Hide the Navigation pane.

- Select the report title and drag downward along the left edge of the rows to select the entire report, excluding the footer information.

Having Trouble?

If you accidentally select the footer, hold down ⇧Shift and click to the left of the last record to remove the selection from the footer.

- Open the Home tab and click 🗐 **Copy** in the Clipboard group.

Your screen should be similar to
Figure 10

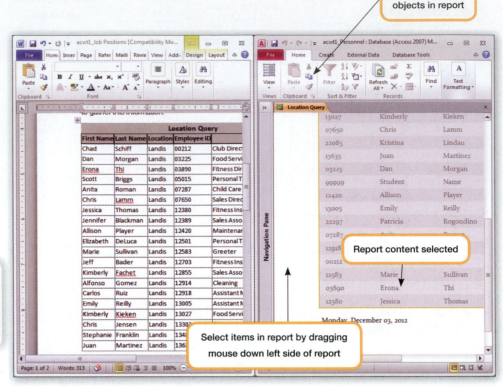

Copies selected objects in report

Report content selected

Select items in report by dragging mouse down left side of report

Figure 10

Next, you need to select the location in the memo where you want the copied data inserted.

2

- Scroll the Word document and click on the blank line between the second and third paragraphs.

- Click 📋 **Paste** in the Home tab.

- Scroll the document up to see the top of the report.

Your screen should be similar to
Figure 11

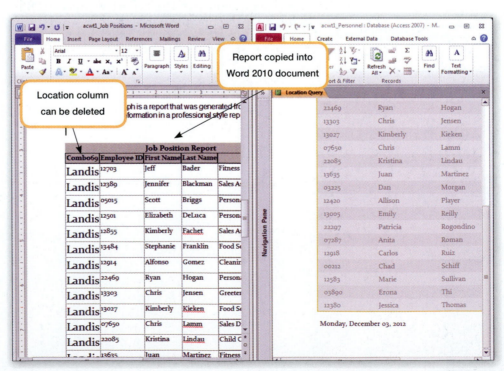

Location column can be deleted

Report copied into Word 2010 document

Figure 11

The copied report is similar to the copied query. The location is displayed in a column in the Word document, even though it was not displayed in the report. You will remove the column and add the location to the report title.

3

- Select the cells in the column containing the heading Combo69 and the Landis text.

Having Trouble?

You will have to scroll up to the previous page to select the column heading at the beginning of the table.

- Right-click the selection and choose Delete Cells.

- Click [OK] to shift the cells left.

- Click in front of the Job Position Report title.

- Type **Landis** and press ⏎Enter.

Your screen should be similar to Figure 12

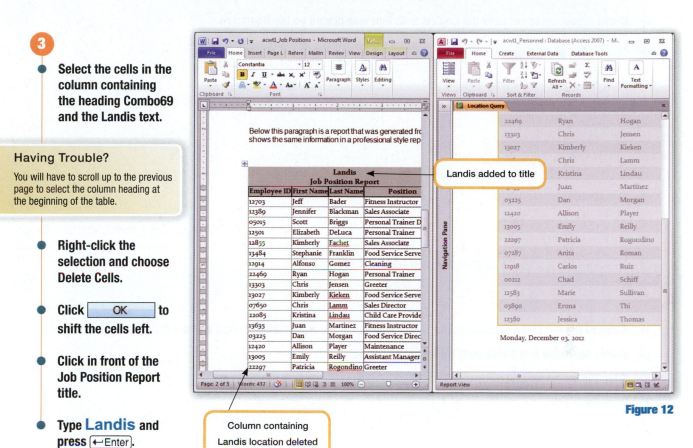

Column containing Landis location deleted

Landis added to title

Figure 12

The Location column has been removed and the table title is now descriptive of the table contents.

4

- Switch to Access and close the report.

- Click [No] to not save the copied data that was placed on the Clipboard.

- Display the Navigation pane.

- Undo the side-by-side windows.

Having Trouble?

Choose Undo Show Side by Side from the taskbar shortcut menu.

- Exit Access.

Currently the Word document is three pages long and the Location Query table is split between pages. To correct this, you will remove the MEMO heading at the top of the document.

5

- Move to the top of the document and select and delete the word "MEMO". Add a blank line at that location.

- Delete the blank line above both tables in the memo.

- Save the memo as **Landis Job Positions** to your solution file location.

- Print the memo.

- Exit Word.

Deleting the MEMO heading allowed enough room for each table to fit on its own page. Your printed memo should now be only two pages long and look similar to the one shown in the case study at the beginning of this lab.

KEY TERMS

active window ACWT1.8
destination file ACWT1.2

export ACWT1.2
source file ACWT1.2

COMMAND SUMMARY

Command	Shortcut	Action
Home tab		
Clipboard group		
Copy	Ctrl + C	Copies selection to Clipboard
Paste	Ctrl + V	Pastes selection into document at insertion point
External Data tab		
Export group		
Saved Exports		Views and runs saved exports
Excel		Exports selected object to an Excel workbook
More — Word Export the selected object to Rich Text		Exports selected object to a Rich Text Format (*.rtf) file

STEP-BY-STEP

SPA MARKETING MEMO ★

1. The Scensations Salon and Day Spa database has been used extensively. The owner asked you for a list of clients who are over the age of 45 to get an idea of how much interest there would be in an anti-aging spa package she is considering offering. You already filtered the Clients table to locate this information and now want to include the results in a memo to Latisha. The first page of the memo is shown here.

   a. Open the ac03_Scensations Spa database file and the Clients table that you modified in Lab 3, Step-by-Step Exercise 2. Display the results of the Clients 45+ query.

   b. Start Word 2010 and enter the following text in a new document.

   To: **Latisha Pine**
   From: **[Your Name]**
   Date: **[current date]**

   Here is the information you requested on the clients who are over the age of 45:

   c. Select the Clients 45+ query results and copy them into the Word document.

   d. Save the memo as **45+ Spa Clients**. Print the memo.

   e. Close the document and exit Word.

   f. Close the table and database.

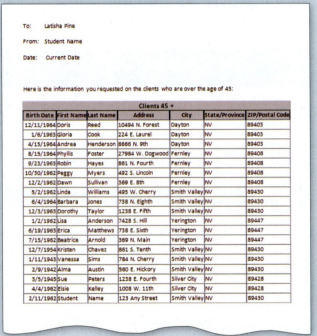

To: Latisha Pine

From: Student Name

Date: Current Date

Here is the information you requested on the clients who are over the age of 45:

Clients 45 +					
Birth Date	First Name	Last Name	Address	City	State/Province	ZIP/Postal Code
12/11/1964	Doris	Reed	10494 N. Forest	Dayton	NV	89403
1/6/1963	Gloria	Cook	224 E. Laurel	Dayton	NV	89403
4/15/1964	Andrea	Henderson	8666 N. 9th	Dayton	NV	89403
8/15/1964	Phyllis	Foster	27984 W. Dogwood	Fernley	NV	89408
9/23/1963	Robin	Hayes	861 N. Fourth	Fernley	NV	89408
10/30/1962	Peggy	Myers	492 S. Lincoln	Fernley	NV	89408
12/2/1962	Dawn	Sullivan	369 E. 8th	Fernley	NV	89408
5/2/1962	Linda	Williams	495 W. Cherry	Smith Valley	NV	89430
6/4/1964	Barbara	Jones	738 N. Eighth	Smith Valley	NV	89430
12/3/1963	Dorothy	Taylor	1238 E. Fifth	Smith Valley	NV	89430
1/2/1962	Lisa	Anderson	7428 S. Hill	Yerington	NV	89447
6/19/1963	Erica	Matthews	738 E. Sixth	Yerington	NV	89447
7/15/1962	Beatrice	Arnold	369 N. Main	Yerington	NV	89447
12/7/1954	Kristen	Chavez	861 S. Tenth	Smith Valley	NV	89430
1/11/1943	Vanessa	Sims	784 N. Cherry	Smith Valley	NV	89430
2/9/1942	Alma	Austin	560 E. Hickory	Smith Valley	NV	89430
3/5/1945	Sue	Peters	1238 E. Fourth	Silver City	NV	89428
4/4/1962	Elsie	Kelley	1008 W. 11th	Silver City	NV	89428
2/11/1962	Student	Name	123 Any Street	Smith Valley	NV	89430

LOW STOCK ANALYSIS ★ ★

2. Evan, the owner of the Downtown Internet Café, continues to be impressed with the café's inventory database (Lab 3, Step-by-Step Exercise 3). He has asked you for a list of all special-order items and how many of these items are currently in stock. He wants this information as an Excel 2010 worksheet so that he can further analyze the data. You will provide this information by exporting the data from Access 2010 to Excel 2010. Your completed worksheet of this data should be similar to that shown here.

Item	Description	In Stock	Special Order?	Supplier
121	Powdered cream	31	Y	ABC Restaurant Supply
131	T-Shirts	10	Y	By Design
171	Decaf Viennese	33	Y	Pure Processing
172	Decaf Sumatra	35	Y	Pure Processing
200	Business cards	43	Y	Pro Printing
257	Coffee mints	30	Y	Sweet Stuff
273	French Roast	47	Y	Café Ole
753	Guatamala coffee	45	Y	Cuppa Jo
754	Java coffee	46	Y	Cuppa Jo
755	Arabian coffee	47	Y	Cuppa Jo
759	Espresso	11	Y	Cuppa Jo
859	Darjeeling Tea	13	Y	Tea and Toast Inc.

   a. Open the ac03_Cafe Inventory database that you modified in Lab 3, Step-by-Step Exercise 3.

   b. Create a new query named **Special Orders** that will display items with Y in the Special Order? field, and include the Description, In Stock, Special Order?, and Supplier fields (in that order). Run the query, then save it.

   c. Export the data to Excel using the file name **Special Orders**. Include formatting but do not choose Open to view the file. Close the workbook file.

   d. Save the export steps.

   e. In Access, with the query still open, change the InStock for t-shirts to **10** and coffee mints to **30**. Rerun the export using the saved steps, replacing the Special Orders file.

   f. Print the worksheet and exit Excel.

   g. Save the query. Close the table and database.

LAB EXERCISES

FOSTER PARENTS MEMO ★★

3. The Foster Parents Report you created for the Animal Rescue Foundation needs to be sent to management. (See Lab 3, Step-by-Step Exercise 5.) You want to include a brief note with the report and decide to export the report to a memo you create using Word. Your completed memo should be similar to that shown here.

    a. Open the ac03_ARF3 database that you created in Lab 3, Step-by-Step Exercise 5. Save the database as acWT1_ARF. Modify the 2011 Foster Parents query to show only the Name, Foster Date, Foster First Name, and Foster Last Name fields. Leave the criteria for the foster date at >=#1/1/2011#. Save the query as **2011 Foster Names**.

    b. Export the 2011 Foster Names query results to a Word document named **ARF Foster Parents**.

    c. Enter the following text appropriately spaced above the table in the document.

To:	**ARF Management**
From:	**[Your Name]**
Date:	**[current date]**
Re:	**Foster Parents for 2011**

As you requested, here is a list of foster parents and pets for the year 2011.

    d. Apply formatting of your choice to the table. Size and center the table appropriately.

    e. Save the memo. Print the document.

    f. Close the document and database.

ACCESS 2010 COMMAND SUMMARY

COMMAND	SHORTCUT	ACTION
Quick Access Toolbar		
Save	Ctrl + S	Saves the current object
Undo	Ctrl + Z	Cancels last action
File Tab		
Save	Ctrl + S	Saves database object
Save Database As		Saves database object with a new file name
Open	Ctrl + O	Opens an existing database
Close Database		Closes open window
Info> Compact & Repair Database		Compacts and repairs database file
New		Opens a new blank database
Print/Print	Ctrl + P	Specifies print settings and prints current database object
Print/Print Preview		Displays file as it will appear when printed
Save & Publish > Back Up Database		Backs up database
Exit		Closes Access
Home Tab		
Views Group		
Datasheet View		Displays object in Datasheet view
Design View		Displays object in Design view
Form View		Changes to Form view
Form Layout View		Changes to Form Layout view
Report View		Displays report in Report view
Report Layout View		Displays report in Layout view
Clipboard Group		
Paste	Ctrl + V	Inserts copy of item from the Clipboard
Cut	Ctrl + X	Removes selected item and copies it to the Clipboard
Copy	Ctrl + C	Duplicates selected item and copies to the Clipboard

ACCESS 2010 COMMAND SUMMARY

COMMAND	SHORTCUT	ACTION
Sort & Filter Group		
Filter		Specifies filter settings for selected field
A↓ Ascending		Changes sort order to ascending
Z↓ Descending		Changes sort order to descending
Remove Sort		Clears all sorts and returns sort order to primary key order
Selection ▾ /Equals		Sets filter to display only those records containing selected value
Advanced ▾ /Clear All Filters		Removes all filters from table
Toggle Filter		Applies and removes filter from table
Records Group		
Refresh All ▾		Updates selected object
New	Ctrl + +	Adds new record
Save	⇧Shift + ↵Enter	Saves changes to object design
✕ Delete	Delete	Deletes current record
Σ Totals		Displays/hides Totals row
More ▾ /Hide Fields		Hides selected columns in Datasheet view
More ▾ /Unhide Fields		Redisplays hidden columns
More ▾ /Field Width		Adjusts width of selected column
Find Group		
Find	Ctrl + F	Locates specified data
Replace	Ctrl + H	Locates specified data and replaces it with specified replacement text
Go To ▾		Moves to First, Previous, Next, Last, or New record location
Select ▾ /Select		Selects current record

ACCESS 2010 COMMAND SUMMARY

COMMAND	SHORTCUT	ACTION
Select ▾ /Select All		Selects all records in database
Text Formatting Group		
B Bold	Ctrl + B	Applies bold effect to all text in datasheet
A ▾ Font Color		Applies selected color to all text in datasheet
▾ Alternate Row Color		Changes background color of datasheet
▾ Gridlines		Changes display of gridlines in the datasheet
Create Tab		
Tables Group		
Table		Creates a new table in Datasheet view
Table Design		Creates a new table in Design view
Queries Group		
Query Wizard		Creates a query using the Query Wizard
Query Design		Creates a query using Query Design view
Forms Group		
Form		Creates a new form using all the fields from the underlying table
Blank Form		Displays a blank form to which you add the fields from the table that you want to appear on the form
Form Wizard		Creates a new form by following the steps in the Form Wizard
Reports Group		
Report		Creates a report using all fields in current table
Report Design		Creates a report using Report Design view
Report Wizard		Creates a report using the Report Wizard

ACCESS 2010 COMMAND SUMMARY

COMMAND	SHORTCUT	ACTION
External Data Tab		
Export Group		
Saved Exports		Views and runs saved exports
Excel		Exports selected object to an Excel workbook
More ▾		Displays more export choices
More ▾ / Word — Export the selected object to Rich Text		Exports selected object to a Rich Text Format (*.rtf) file
Database Tools Tab		
Relationships Group		
Relationships		Opens relationships window
Object Dependencies		Shows the objects in the database that use the selected object
Analyze Group		
Analyze Table		Evaluates table design
Table Tools Fields Tab		
Views Group		
Datasheet View		Displays table in Datasheet view
Design View		Displays table in Design view
Add & Delete Group		
AB Text		Inserts a new text field
Date & Time		Inserts a new Date/time field
More Fields ▾		Creates more fields
More Fields ▾ / Lookup & Relationship		Creates a lookup field

WWW.MHHE.COM/OLEARY

COMMAND	SHORTCUT	ACTION
Delete	Delete	Removes selected field column
Properties Group		
Name & Caption		Renames selected field
Formatting Group		
Data Type: Text		Changes the data type for current field
Format:		Sets the display format of the selected field

Table Tools Design Tab

COMMAND	SHORTCUT	ACTION
Views Group		
Datasheet View		Displays table in Datasheet view
Design View		Displays table in Design view
Tools Group		
Primary Key		Makes current field a primary key field
Insert Rows		Inserts a new field in Table Design view
Delete Rows	Delete	Deletes selected field row

Query Tools Design Tab

COMMAND	SHORTCUT	ACTION
Results Group		
Run		Displays query results in Query Datasheet view
Query Setup Group		
Show Table		Displays/hides Show Table dialog box
Show/Hide Group		
Table Names		Displays/hides the Table row

Relationship Tools Design Tab

COMMAND	SHORTCUT	ACTION
Tools Group		
Relationship Report		Creates a report of the displayed relationships

COMMAND	SHORTCUT	ACTION
Report Layout Tools Design Tab		
Themes Group		
Themes		Applies predesigned theme styles to report
Tools Group		
Add Existing Fields		Displays/hides Add Existing Fields task pane
Report Layout Tools Arrange tab		
Tabular		Arranges controls in a stacked tabular arrangement
Select Column		Selects column
Report Layout Tools Format Tab		
Font Group		
Font color		Changes color of text
Align Text Left		Aligns text at left edge of control
Center		Centers text in selected control
11		Used to change the font size of text
Control Formatting Group		
Shape Fill		Changes the color fill inside a control
Shape Outline		Opens menu to change the border color and line thickness of a selected control
Report Layout Tools Page Setup Tab		
Page Size Group		
Margins		Sets margins of printed report
Page Layout Group		
Page Setup		Sets features related to the page layout of printed report
Form Design Tools Tab		
Themes Group		
Themes		Opens gallery of theme styles

ACCESS 2010 COMMAND SUMMARY

COMMAND	SHORTCUT	ACTION
Tools Group		
Add Existing Fields		Adds selected existing field to form
Font Group		
≡		Right aligns contents of cell
Form Design Tools Arrange Tab		
Table Group		
Stacked		Applies Stacked layout to the controls
Rows and Columns Group		
Insert Below		Inserts a blank row below the selected cell
Insert Left		Inserts a blank column to the left of the selected cell
Select Layout		Selects entire layout
Select Column		Selects column in a layout
Select Row		Selects row in a layout
Merge/Split Group		
Merge		Merges two or more layout cells into a single cell
Split Horizontally		Splits a layout cell horizontally into two cells
Print Preview Tab		
Print Group		
Print	Ctrl + P	Prints displayed object
Page Size Group		
Margins		Adjusts margins in printed output

ACCESS 2010 COMMAND SUMMARY

COMMAND	SHORTCUT	ACTION
Page Layout Group		
Portrait		Changes print orientation to portrait
Landscape		Changes print orientation to landscape
Zoom Group		
One Page		Displays one entire page in Print Preview
Two Pages		Displays two entire pages in Print Preview
Close Preview Group		
Close Print Preview		Closes Print Preview window

b

Backstage view: Contains commands that allow you to work with your document, unlike the Ribbon that allows you to work in your document; contains commands that apply to the entire document.

Buttons: Graphical elements that perform the associated action when you click on them using the mouse.

c

Clipboard: Where a selection is stored when it is cut or copied.

Commands: Options that carry out a selected action.

Context menu: Also called a shortcut menu; opened by right-clicking on an item on the screen.

Contextual tabs: Also called on-demand tabs; tabs that are displayed only as needed. For example, when you are working with a picture, the Picture Tools tab appears.

Cursor: The blinking vertical bar that marks your location in the document and indicates where text you type will appear; also called the insertion point.

d

Database: A collection of related data.

Default: The standard options used by Office 2010.

Destination: The new location into which a selection that is moved from its original location is inserted.

Dialog box launcher: A button that is displayed in the lower-right corner of a tab group if more commands are available; clicking opens a dialog box or task pane of additional options.

Document window: The large center area of the program window where open application files are displayed.

e

Edit: To revise a document by changing the parts that need to be modified.

Enhanced ScreenTip: Displayed by pointing to a button in the Ribbon; shows the name of the button and the keyboard shortcut.

f

Field: The smallest unit of information about a record; a column in a table.

Font: Type style; also called typeface.

Font size: Size of typeface, given in points.

Format: The appearance of a document.

g

Groups: Part of a tab that contains related items.

h

Hyperlink: Connection to information located in a separate location, such as on a Web site.

i

Insertion point: Also called the cursor; the blinking vertical bar that marks your location in a document and indicates where text you type will appear.

k

Keyboard shortcut: A combination of keys that can be used to execute a command in place of clicking a button.

Keyword: A descriptive word that is associated with the file and can be used to locate a file using a search.

l

Live Preview: A feature that shows you how selected text in a document will appear if a formatting option is chosen.

m

Metadata: Details about the document that describe or identify it, such as title, author name, subject, and keywords; also called document properties.

Mini toolbar: Appears automatically when you select text; displays command buttons for often-used commands from the Font and Paragraph groups that are used to format a document.

o

Office Clipboard: Can store up to 24 items that have been cut or copied.

On-demand tabs: Also called contextual tabs; tabs that are displayed only as needed.

p

Paste Preview: Shows how a Paste Option will affect a selection.

Properties: Shown in a panel along the right side of the Info tab, divided into four groups; information such as author, keywords, document size, number of words, and number of pages.

q

Quick Access Toolbar: Located to the right of the Window button; provides quick access to frequently used commands such as Save, Undo, and Redo.

r

Records: The information about one person, thing, or place; contained in a row of a table.

Ribbon: Below the title bar; provides a centralized location of commands that are used to work in your document.

s

ScreenTip: Also called a tooltip; appears with the command name and the keyboard shortcut.

Scroll bar: Horizontal or vertical, it is used with a mouse to bring additional information into view in a window.

Selection cursor: Cursor that allows you to select an object.

Shortcut menu: A context-sensitive menu, meaning it displays only those commands relevant to the item or screen location; also called a context menu, it is opened by right-clicking on an item on the screen.

Slide: An individual page of a presentation.

Slide shows: Onscreen electronic presentations.

Source: The original location of a selection that is inserted in a new location.

Status bar: At the bottom of the application window; displays information about the open file and features that help you view the file.

t

Tables: A database object consisting of columns and rows.

Tabs: Used to divide the Ribbon into major activity areas.

Tag: A descriptive word that is associated with the file and can be used to locate a file using a search; also called a keyword.

Task pane: A list of additional options opened by clicking the dialog box launcher; also called a dialog box.

Text effects: Enhancements such as bold, italic, and color that are applied to selected text.

Tooltip: Also called a ScreenTip; appears displaying a command name and the keyboard shortcut.

Typeface: A set of characters with a specific design; also commonly referred to as a font.

u

User interface: A set of graphical elements that are designed to help you interact with the program and provide instructions for the actions you want to perform.

v

View buttons: Used to change how the information in the document window is displayed.

w

Worksheet: An electronic spreadsheet, or worksheet, that is used to organize, manipulate, and graph numeric data.

z

Zoom slider: Located at the far right end of the status bar; used to change the amount of information displayed in the document window by "zooming in" to get a close-up view or "zooming out" to see more of the document at a reduced view.

a

Action query: Used to make changes to many records in one operation. There are four types of action queries.

Active window: The window in which you can work.

Aggregate functions: Calculations that are performed on a range of data; to use, the data type in the column must be a number, decimal, or currency.

Allow Zero Length property: Specifies whether an entry containing no characters is valid. This property is used to indicate that you know no value exists for a field. A zero-length string is entered as "" with no space between the quotation marks.

AND operator: Instructs the query to locate records meeting multiple criteria, narrowing the search because any record must meet both conditions included in the output.

Append query: Adds records from one or more tables to the end of other tables.

Argument: Specifies the data the function should use; enclosed in parentheses.

Ascending sort order: Data arranged A to Z or 0 to 9.

Attachment control: A bound control that allows you to add, edit, remove, and save attached files to the field directly from the form, just as you can in the datasheet.

Attachment data type: Used to add multiple files of different types to a field.

AutoNumber data type: Automatically assigns a number to each record as it is added to a table; useful for maintaining record order.

b

Best Fit feature: Automatically adjusts the column widths of all selected columns to accommodate the longest entry or column heading in each of the selected columns.

Bound control: A control linked to a field in an underlying table, such as a text control that is linked to the record source and displays the field data in the form or report.

c

Calculated data type: Use to create a calculated field in a table.

Caption: The text that displays in the column heading while in Datasheet view. It is used when you want the label to be different from the actual field name.

Caption property: Specifies a field label other than the field name that is used in queries, forms, and reports.

Cell: The intersection of the row and column.

Character string: Constants such as "F" or "M"; enclosed in quotation marks.

Clipboard: A temporary storage area in memory.

Column selector bar: A narrow bar above the field names in Query Design view; used to select an entire column.

Column width: Adjusts to change the appearance of the datasheet.

Common field: A field shared between two tables.

Compact: Makes a copy of the database file and rearranges the way that the file is stored on your disk.

Comparison operator: A symbol that allows you to make comparisons between two items.

Composite key: A primary key that uses more than one field.

Compound controls: The controls are associated, and the two controls will act as one when moved, indicated by both controls being surrounded by an orange border.

Compound criteria: Using more than one type of criteria in a query.

Control: Objects that display information, perform actions, or enhance the design of a form or report.

Criteria: Expressions that are used to restrict the results of a query to display only records that meet certain limiting conditions.

Criteria expression: Defines the query criteria in the query design grid; similar to using a formula and may contain constants, field names, and/or operators.

Crosstab query: Summarizes large amounts of data in an easy-to-read, row-and-column format.

Currency data type: Use in number fields that are monetary values or that you do not want rounded. Numbers are formatted to display decimal places and a currency symbol.

Current field: The selected field.

Current record: The record containing the insertion point.

d

Data type: Defines the type of data the field will contain. Access uses the data type to ensure that the right kind of data is entered in a field.

Database: An organized collection of related information.

Datasheet view: Provides a row-and-column view of the data in tables or query results.

Date/Time data type: Used in fields that will contain dates and times; checks all dates for validity. Even though dates and times are formatted to appear as a date or time, they are stored as serial values so that they can be used in calculations.

Default Value property: Used to specify a value that is automatically entered in a field when a new record is created.

Delete query: Deletes records from a table or tables.

Descending sort order: Data arranged Z to A or 9 to 0.

Design grid: In Query Design view, the lower portion of the window where you enter the settings that define the query.

Design view: Used to create a table, form, query, or report. Displays the underlying design structure, not the data.

Destination: The location where you paste the copied data from the Clipboard.

Destination file: The file that is created by exporting information from a database.

Drawing object: A graphic consisting of shapes such as lines and boxes that can be created using a drawing program such as Paint.

e

Export: The process of copying information to a file outside of a database.

Expression: A formula consisting of a combination of symbols that will produce a single value.

f

Field: Information that appears in a column about the subject recorded in the table.

Field list: List of fields contained in a table.

Field model: A predefined field or set of fields that includes a field name, a data type, and other settings that control the appearance and behavior of the field.

Field name: Displayed in the header row at the top of the datasheet in Datasheet view.

Field property: A characteristic that helps define the appearance and behavior of a field.

Field Size property: The maximum number of characters that can be entered in the field.

Filter: A restriction placed on records in the open datasheet or form to quickly isolate and display a subset of records.

Find and Replace: A feature that helps you quickly find specific information and automatically replace it with new information

Foreign key: A field in one table that refers to the primary key field in another table and indicates how the tables are related.

Form: A database object used primarily to display records onscreen to make it easier to enter new records and to make changes to existing records.

Form view: Displays the records in a form.

Form Wizard: Guides you through the steps to create a complex form that displays selected fields, data groups, sorted records, and data from multiple tables.

Format: The way the data is displayed.

Format property: Used to specify the way that numbers, dates, times, and text in a field are displayed and printed.

Function: Built-in formulas that perform certain types of calculations automatically.

g

Graphic: A nontext element or object, such as a picture or shape.

h

Hard-coded criteria: Criteria that are entered in the criteria cell; they are used each time the query is run.

Header row: The row at the top of the datasheet where field names are displayed.

Hyperlink data type: Used when you want the field to store a link to an object, document, Web page, or other destinations.

i

Identifier: An element that refers to the value of a field, a graphical object, or a property.

Indexed property: Sets a field as an index field (a field that controls the order of records).

Inner join: Tells a query that rows from one of the joined tables corresponds to rows in the other table on the basis of the data in the joined fields. Checks for matching values in the joined fields; when it finds matches, it combines the records and displays them as one record in the query results.

Input Mask property: Controls the data that is required in a field and the way the data is to be displayed.

IntelliSense: The context-sensitive menu that appears anytime you can enter an expression; suggests identifiers and functions that could be used.

j

Join: An association that is created in a query between a field in one table or query and a field of the same data type in another table or query.

Join line: Identifies the fields on which the relationship is based.

l

Label control: Displays descriptive labels in a form or report.

Layout: Determines how the data is displayed in a form by aligning the items horizontally or vertically to a uniform appearance.

Layout view: Displays the object's data while in the process of designing the object.

Lookup field: Provides a list of values from which you can choose to make entering data into a field simpler and more accurate.

Lookup list: A lookup field that uses another table as the source for values.

Lookup Wizard: A feature that guides you step by step through creating a lookup field that will allow you to select from a list of values.

m

Make-table query: Creates a new table from selected data in one or more tables.

Margin: The blank space around the edge of a page.

Memo data type: Field entry consisting of a long block of text, such as a product description.

Merging cells: Combines any selected adjacent cells into one big cell spanning the length of the previously selected cells.

Mini toolbar: Appears when the attachment control is made active; contains three buttons that are used to work with attachment controls.

Multitable query: A query that uses information from two or more tables to get results.

n

Navigation buttons: Found on the bottom of the work area on both sides of the record number; used to move through records with a mouse.

Navigation pane: Located along the left edge of the work area; displays all the objects in the database and is used to open and manage the objects.

Normal form: A set of constraints that must be satisfied. There are five sequential normal form levels; the third level, commonly called 3NF, is the level that is required for most database designs. This level requires that every nonkey column be dependent on the primary key and that nonkey columns be independent of each other.

Normalization: A design technique that identifies and eliminates redundancy by applying a set of rules to your tables to confirm that they are structured properly.

Number data type: Field entry consisting of numbers only; this data type drops any leading zeros.

o

Object: Items that make up a database, such as a table or report, consisting of many elements. An object can be created, selected, and manipulated as a unit.

OLE Object data type: Used in fields to store an object from other Microsoft Windows programs, such as a document or graph; the object is converted to a bitmap image and displayed in the table field, form, or report.

One-to-many: An association between two tables in which the primary key field value in each record in the primary table corresponds to the value in the matching field or fields of many records in the related table.

One-to-one: An association between two tables in which each record in the first table contains a field value that corresponds to (matches) the field value of one record in the other table.

Operator: A symbol or word that indicates that an operation is to be performed.

OR operator: Instructs the query to locate records meeting multiple criteria, broadening the search because any record meeting either condition is included in the output.

Orientation: Refers to the direction that text prints on a page.

Orphaned records: Records that do not have a matching primary key record in the associated table.

Outer join: Tells a query that although some of the rows on both sides of the join correspond exactly, the query should include all rows from one table even if there is no match in the other table.

Outer sort field: The primary field in a sort; must be to the left of the inner sort field.

p

Parameter query: Displays a dialog box prompting you for information, such as the criteria for locating data.

Parameter value: Tells the query to prompt you for the specific criteria you want to use when you run the query.

Picture: A graphic such as a scanned photograph.

Primary key: A field that uniquely identifies each record and is used to associate data from multiple tables.

Print Preview: Displays a form, report, table, or query as it will appear when printed.

q

Query: Finds and displays specific data contained in a database.

Query criteria: Expressions that are used to restrict the results of a query in order to display only records that meet certain limiting conditions.

r

Record: All the information about one person, thing, or place.

Record number indicator: Shows the number of the current record as well as the total number of records in the table.

Record source: The underlying table that is used to create a form.

Referential integrity: Ensures that relationships between tables are valid and that related data is not accidentally changed or deleted.

Relational database: Databases containing multiple tables that can be linked to produce combined output from all tables.

Relationship: Establishes the association between common fields in two tables.

Report: A professional-appearing output generated from tables or queries that may include design elements, groups, and summary information; analyzes and displays data in a specific layout.

Report view: Displays the table data in a report layout.

Required property: The data that is required in a field.

Row label: Identifies the type of information that can be entered in the fields of a query design grid.

S

Search: Finds any character(s) anywhere in the database.

Select query: Retrieves the specific data you request from one or more tables, then displays the data in a query datasheet in the order you specify.

Select Record button: The square to the left of each row in Datasheet view; used to select an entire record.

Serial value: Data stored as sequential numbers, such as dates and times.

Show box: The box in the row label of a query design grid; lets you specify whether you want a field displayed in the query result.

Source: The original information.

Source file: The database file from which you export information.

Splitting cells: Divides a cell into two or more adjacent cells.

SQL query: A query created using SQL (Structured Query Language), an advanced programming language used in Access.

Stacked layout: Arranges data vertically with a field label to the left of the field data.

Subdatasheet: A data table nested in another data table that contains data related or joined to the table where it resides.

t

Tab order: The order in which the highlight will move through fields on a form when you press the [Tab ⇆] key during data entry.

Table: Organized collection of information, consisting of vertical columns and horizontal rows.

Tabular layout: Arranges the data in rows and columns, with labels across the top.

Template: Document model provided by Microsoft; generally includes the data structure, tables, queries, forms, and reports for the selected type of database.

Text control: Displays the information in a field from a record source.

Text data type: Field designation for text and special numbers. It allows other characters, such as the parentheses or hyphens in a telephone number, to be included in the entry. Also, by specifying the type as Text, leading zeros will be preserved.

Theme: A predefined set of font and color formats that can be applied to an entire document in one simple step.

Theme colors: A set of 12 colors that are applied to specific elements in a document.

U

Unbound control: A text control that is not connected to an underlying record source.

Unequal join: Records to be included in query results that are based on the value in one join field being greater than, less than, not equal to, greater than or equal to, or less than or equal to the value in the other join field.

Update query: Makes update changes to records.

V

Validation rule: Limits data entered in a field to values that meet certain requirements.

Validation Rule property: Specifies a validation rule, which limits the values that can be entered in the field to those that meet certain requirements.

Validation text: An explanatory message that appears if a user attempts to enter invalid information in a text field for which there is a validity check.

Validation Text property: The message to be displayed when the associated validation rule is not satisfied.

Value: Data entered in a field.

Value list: A list of options for a drop-down list.

View: Window formats that are used to display and work with the objects in a database.

W

Wildcards: Symbols that are used to represent characters. The * symbol represents any collection of characters; the ? symbol represents any individual character.

Wizard: A feature that guides you step by step through the process to perform a task.

Y

Yes/No data type: Use when the field contents can only be a Yes/No, True/False, or On/Off value. A Yes value is stored as a 1 and a No value is stored as a 0 so that they can be used in expressions.

&, AC2.7
*, AC2.11, AC2.26
+, AC2.11
=, AC2.11
?, AC2.26
@, AC2.7
-, AC2.11
/, AC2.11
<, AC2.7, AC2.11
<=, AC2.11
>, AC2.7, AC2.11
>=, AC2.11

a

.accdb, AC1.7, IO.54
Access 2010, IO.7–IO.9
Access window, AC1.8, AC1.9
Accuracy of data, AC1.35–AC1.37
Action query, AC3.20
Active table, AC1.63
Active window, ACWT1.8
Add and Delete group, AC1.88, AC2.87, ACCS.4
Adding records (form), AC2.75–AC2.76
Administrative assistant, AC2.81
Admitting nurse, AC1.83
Aggregate function, AC3.45
Allow Zero Length property, AC1.22
Alternate Background Color drop-down menu, AC2.37
Analyze group, AC3.76, ACCS.4
AND operator, AC3.29
Append query, AC3.20
Application programs (overview)
    Access 2010, IO.7–IO.9
    Excel 2010, IO.5–IO.6
    other programs, IO.2
    PowerPoint 2010, IO.10–IO.11
    Word 2010, IO.2–IO.4
Argument, AC2.11
Ascending sort order, AC2.33
Attaching files to records, AC1.39–AC1.44
Attachment control, AC2.68, AC2.69
Attachment data type, AC1.15, AC1.34
Attachments dialog box, AC1.40, AC2.73
Author, IO.51, IO.52
AutoCorrect, AC1.37–AC1.39
AutoCorrect Options button, AC1.37, AC1.38
AutoNumber data type, AC1.15
AutoRecover, IO.53

b

Back up, AC3.69–AC3.70
Background and gridline color, AC2.36–AC2.39
Backspace key, IO.36
Backstage view, IO.25, AC1.7
Best Fit feature, AC1.49
Blank Database template, AC1.7
Blank Form tool, AC2.47
Blank Report tool, AC3.47

Bound control, AC2.54
Buttons, IO.15

c

Calculated data type, AC1.15
Caption, AC1.27
Caption property, AC1.22
Careers
    administrative assistant, AC2.81
    admitting nurse, AC1.83
    database administrator, AC3.71
Cascade Delete, AC1.69, AC3.18
Cascade Update, AC1.69, AC3.18
Categories, IO.51
Cell, AC1.11
Changing data type, AC1.26
Character string, AC2.8
Clipboard, IO.45, IO.47, AC1.64
Clipboard group, IO.67, AC1.87, ACWT1.13, ACCS.1
Close, IO.60
    database, AC1.73
    table, AC1.67
Close button, IO.14
Close Preview group, AC1.89, ACCS.7
Color
    background and gridline, AC2.36–AC2.39
    standard, AC2.37, AC2.38
    text, AC2.39–AC2.40
    theme, AC2.37, AC2.38
Color theme, AC2.69
Column selector bar, AC3.25
Column width, AC1.35, AC1.47–AC1.52
Columnar format, AC2.51, AC2.52
Command buttons, IO.19, IO.21–IO.22
Command summary, IO.66–IO.67, AC1.87–AC1.89, AC2.85–AC2.87, AC3.75–AC3.77, ACWT1.13, ACCS.1–ACCS.7
Commands, IO.18–IO.19
Comments, IO.51
Common filters, AC2.43–AC2.45
Compacting, AC3.69
Comparison operator, AC2.11
Compatibility, IO.55
Composite key, AC1.28
Compound criteria, AC3.29
Concept
    controls, AC2.54
    data type, AC1.15
    database, AC1.4
    default value property, AC2.8
    expression, AC2.11
    field property, AC1.22
    filter, AC2.40
    find and replace, AC2.25
    form, AC2.46
    format property, AC2.7
    join, AC3.26
    lookup field, AC2.18
    object, AC1.9
    primary key, AC1.28

Concept—*Cont.*
  query, AC3.20
  query criteria, AC3.29
  relationship, AC1.66
  report, AC3.46
  sorting, AC2.33
  subdatasheet, AC1.71
  theme, AC2.69
  validation rule, AC2.11
Constant, AC2.11
Context menu, IO.17, IO.43
Contextual tabs, IO.20
Control Formatting group, ACCS.6
Controls, AC2.54
Controls Formatting group, AC3.76
Copy, IO.45–IO.46
  field content, AC1.63–AC1.65
  formats, IO.49–IO.50
  Paste, and, AC1.53
  query object to Word, ACWT1.7–ACWT1.9
  report, ACWT1.9–ACWT1.12
Copy and Paste, AC1.53
Count function, AC3.45
Create
  attachment field, AC1.34
  database, AC1.7
  field (design view), AC1.31–AC1.34
  form, AC2.46–AC2.51
  lookup field, AC2.17–AC2.23, AC3.10–AC3.12
  query, AC3.19–AC3.45
  relationship, AC1.65–AC1.66
  report, AC3.46–AC3.65
  table, AC1.10–AC1.21, AC1.58–AC1.59
  table list lookup field, AC3.10–AC3.12
Create tab, AC2.86, AC3.75, ACCS.3
Criteria, AC2.26, AC3.43
Criteria expression, AC3.29
Crosstab query, AC3.20
Currency data type, AC1.15
Current field, AC1.24
Current record, AC1.11
Current view, AC1.8
Cursor, IO.14, IO.15
Customize Quick Access toolbar, IO.16
Customizing fields, AC2.4–AC2.14
  default values, AC2.7–AC2.10
  display formats, AC2.6–AC2.7
  validation rules, AC2.10–AC2.14
Cut, IO.47–IO.48

d

Data accuracy and validity, AC1.35–AC1.37
Data type, AC1.14–AC1.17, AC1.26
Data Type Quick Add menu, AC1.17, AC1.18
Database
  back up, AC3.69–AC3.70
  close, AC1.73
  compacting, AC3.69
  create, AC1.7
  defined, AC1.4
  open, AC1.73–AC1.75
  properties, AC1.75–AC1.77
  relational, AC1.4
Database administrator, AC3.71
Database design process, AC1.5
Database properties, AC1.75–AC1.77
Database template, AC1.7
Database Tools tab, AC2.86, AC3.76, ACCS.4

Datasheet format, AC2.52. *See also* Formatting the
    datasheet
Datasheet Formatting dialog box, AC2.37, AC2.38
Datasheet tool, AC2.47
Datasheet view, AC1.11
Date serial values, AC1.15
Date/Time data type, AC1.15
Date/Time formats, AC1.33
DateDiff, AC3.29
Default join type, AC3.28
Default Value property, AC1.22, AC2.8
Default values, AC2.7–AC2.10
Defining relationships, AC1.69–AC1.70
Delete
  columns, AC2.67
  field (datasheet view), AC1.21
  field (design view), AC1.31
  field (report), AC3.63–AC3.64
  filter, AC2.42–AC2.43
  records, AC1.57–AC1.58
  relationship, AC3.15–AC3.17
  table, AC3.13, AC3.17
Delete key, IO.36
Delete query, AC3.20
Descending sort order, AC2.33
Design, AC1.5
Design grid, AC3.25
Design style, AC2.69–AC2.71
Design view, AC1.11
Designing a new database, AC1.4–AC1.6
Destination, IO.45, AC1.64
Destination file, ACWT1.2
Detail, AC3.58
Develop, AC1.5
Dialog box launcher, IO.23
Display formats, AC2.6–AC2.7
.doc, IO.54
.docm, IO.54
Document properties, IO.27, IO.51–IO.52
Document window, IO.14–IO.15
Documenting a table object, AC1.77–AC1.78
.docx, IO.54
.dotx, IO.54
Drag and drop, IO.49
Drawing object, AC1.39
Duplicate information, AC1.5
Duplicate records, AC3.39–AC3.41

e

Edit Relationships dialog box, AC1.69, AC3.18
Editing field names, AC1.27–AC1.28
Editing text, IO.36, IO.37
Enhanced ScreenTips, IO.20–IO.21
Enter
  field data, AC1.12–AC1.13
  field description, AC1.29–AC1.30
Entering text, IO.34–IO.35
Evaluating table design, AC3.5–AC3.10
Excel
  copy query object, ACWT1.7–ACWT1.9
  export to, ACWT1.2–ACWT1.6
Excel 2010, IO.5–IO.6
Exit, AC1.83, IO.65
Expand/minimize ribbon, IO.24
Export
  Excel, to, ACWT1.2–ACWT1.6
  Word, to, ACWT1.6–ACWT1.7
Export group, ACCS.4, ACWT1.13

Expression, AC2.11, AC2.12
External Data tab, ACCS.4, ACWT1.13

f

Favorite Links list, IO.29
Field, AC1.11, AC1.12
  add (forms), AC2.68–AC2.69
  add (query), AC3.27–AC3.28
  copy field content, AC1.63–AC1.65
  customize. *See* Customizing fields
  defined, AC1.4
  delete (datasheet view), AC1.21
  delete (design view), AC1.31
  delete (report), AC3.63–AC3.64
  hide, AC2.14–AC2.17
  insert, AC1.59–AC1.61
  move, AC1.61–AC1.63
  naming convention, AC1.13
  redisplay, AC2.16–AC2.17
  zoom, AC1.45–AC.47
Field data type, AC1.14–AC1.17
Field description, AC1.29–AC1.30
Field list, AC3.25
Field List pane, AC2.68
Field List task pane, AC3.58
Field model, AC1.18–AC1.19
Field name, AC1.13, AC1.14, AC1.27–AC1.28
Field property, AC1.22
Field Size property, AC1.22
File extension, IO.54, AC1.7
File menu, IO.25–IO.27, AC3.75
File tab, IO.67, AC1.87, ACCS.1
Filter, AC2.40. *See also* Filtering
Filter by selection, AC2.41–AC2.42
Filtering
  common filters, AC2.43–AC2.45
  filter by selection, AC2.41–AC2.42
  form, AC2.74–AC2.75
  multiple fields, AC2.45–AC2.46
  overview, AC2.40
  query, AC3.23–AC3.24
  remove/delete filter, AC2.42–AC2.43
  report, AC3.64–AC3.65
  table, AC2.40–AC2.46
Find, AC2.25–AC2.30
Find and Replace, AC2.25–AC2.32
Find and Replace dialog box, AC2.26–AC2.31
Find Duplicates query, AC3.21
Find Duplicates Query Wizard, AC3.40
Find group, AC1.87, AC2.86, ACCS.2–ACCS.3
Find Unmatched query, AC3.21, AC3.35
Find Unmatched Query Wizard, AC3.36, AC3.37
Font, IO.40, IO.41
Font group, IO.67, AC3.76, ACCS.6
Font size, IO.40, IO.41
Fonts theme, AC2.69
Foreign key, AC1.69
Form, AC2.46–AC2.76
  add existing fields, AC2.68–AC2.69
  adding records, AC2.75–AC2.76
  attachment control, AC2.68, AC2.69
  create, AC2.46–AC2.51
  delete columns, AC2.67
  design style, AC2.69–AC2.71
  filtering, AC2.74–AC2.75
  insert columns, AC2.63–AC2.64
  layout. *See* Layout
  merging cells, AC2.64–AC2.65
  moving controls, AC2.55–AC2.56
  navigating, AC2.71–AC2.72
  overview, AC2.46
  preview/print, AC2.78–AC2.79
  searching, AC2.72–AC2.74
  sizing and moving controls (layout), AC2.58–AC2.59
  sorting, AC2.74–AC2.75
  splitting cells, AC2.65–AC2.66
  theme, AC2.69–AC2.71
Form Design view, AC2.54
Form layout. *See* Layout
Form Layout Tools Arrange tab, AC2.87, ACCS.6–ACCS.7
Form Layout Tools Design tab, AC2.87, ACCS.6
Form Layout Tools tabs, AC2.55–AC2.71
Form Layout view, AC2.54
Form name, AC2.52, AC2.53
Form object, AC1.9
Form tool, AC2.47
Form view, AC1.11
Form Wizard, AC2.47, AC2.48–AC2.53
Form Wizard dialog box, AC2.49–AC2.53
Format Painter, IO.49, IO.50
Format property, AC1.22, AC2.7
Formatting group, AC1.88, ACCS.5
Formatting text, IO.40–IO.43
Formatting the datasheet
  background and gridline color, AC2.36–AC2.39
  text color, AC2.39–AC2.40
Forms group, AC2.86, ACCS.3
Function, AC2.11

g

Glossary, ACG.1–ACG.4
Graphic, AC1.39
Grayed-out arrow, AC1.82
Gridline color, AC2.36–AC2.39
Groups, IO.18, IO.19

h

Hard-coded criteria, AC3.43
Header row, AC1.11
Help, IO.60–IO.65
Help table of contents, IO.63
Hide
  column (query), AC3.32–AC3.34
  field, AC2.14–AC2.17
Home tab, AC1.87, AC2.85, AC3.75, ACWT1.13, IO.67, ACCS.1–ACCS.3
Hyperlink data type, AC1.15

i

ID field, AC1.12
Identifier, AC2.11
Implement, AC1.5
Index property, AC1.22
Infinity symbol, AC3.19
InfoPath 2010, IO.2
Inner join, AC3.28
Inner sort field, AC2.34
Input Mask property, AC1.22
Insert
  column, AC2.63–AC2.64
  field, AC1.59–AC1.61
Insertion point (cursor), IO.14, IO.15
Instructional conventions, IO.12–IO.13

IntelliSense, AC2.12
Interface features, IO.14–IO.15
Is Not Null, AC3.29
Is Null, AC3.29

j

Join, AC3.26, AC3.28
Join line, AC3.26
Justified format, AC2.52

k

Keyboard directional keys, IO.31, IO.35
Keyboard shortcuts, IO.16
Keyword, IO.51

l

Label controls, AC2.54
Layout, AC2.51. *See also* Form
    apply, AC2.56–AC2.58
    formats, AC2.51, AC2.52
    remove rows, AC2.61–AC2.63
    size/move controls, AC2.58–AC2.59
    split, AC2.60–AC2.61
Layout view, AC1.11
Left outer join, AC3.28
Like, AC3.29
List
    field, AC3.25
    lookup, AC2.18
    value, AC2.18
Live preview, IO.40
Lookup field, AC2.17–AC2.23, AC3.10–AC3.12
Lookup list, AC2.18
Lookup tab, AC2.21
Lookup Wizard, AC2.18
Lookup Wizard dialog box, AC2.19, AC2.20

m

Magnification, IO.33, AC1.82
Major concepts. *See* Concept
Make-table query, AC3.20
Many-to-many relationship, AC1.66
Margin, AC1.82
.mdb, IO.54
Memo, copy report to, ACWT1.9–ACWT1.12
Memo data type, AC1.15
Merge/Split group, AC2.87, ACCS.7
Merging cells, AC2.64–AC2.65
Metadata, IO.51
Microsoft Help system, IO.60–IO.65
Mini toolbar, IO.39, IO.41–IO.43, AC2.73
Minimize button, IO.14
Minimize/expand ribbon, IO.24
Mouse actions, IO.31, IO.37
Mouse pointer, IO.14, AC1.8, AC1.9
Move, IO.47–IO.48
    control, AC2.55–AC2.56
    field, AC1.61–AC1.63
    between fields, AC1.44–AC1.45
    keyboard, AC1.54–AC1.55
    navigation buttons, AC1.55–AC1.56
    navigation keys, AC1.44, AC1.54
    specific record, to, AC1.56–AC1.57

Multiple Items tool, AC2.47
Multitable query, AC3.25

n

Naming conventions
    field name, AC1.13
    form name, AC2.53
    table name, AC1.23
Navigation buttons, AC1.10, AC1.11, AC1.55–AC1.56
Navigation keys, IO.31, IO.35, AC1.44, AC1.54
Navigation pane, AC1.8, AC1.10, AC2.76–AC2.77
New Query dialog box, AC3.21
New (blank) Record button, AC2.9
New tab, IO.26
Normal form, AC1.72
Normalization, AC1.72
Not, AC3.29
Not Like, AC3.29
Number data type, AC1.15

o

Object, AC1.9
Object dependencies, AC2.79–AC2.81
Object Dependencies task pane, AC2.80, AC2.81
Office 2010 programs, IO.2
Office clipboard, IO.45
Office help, IO.60–IO.65
OLE Object data type, AC1.15
OLE server program, AC1.15
On-demand tabs, IO.20
One-to-many relationship, AC1.66, AC3.15, AC3.19
One-to-one relationship, AC1.66, AC3.15
OneNote 2010, IO.2
Open
    database, AC1.71–AC1.73
    file, IO.28–IO.30
    table, AC1.70, AC1.71
Open dialog box, IO.28
Open options, IO.29
Operator, AC2.11
OR operator, AC3.29
Orange, AC1.35
Orientation, AC1.81, AC1.82
Orphaned records, AC3.18
Outer join, AC3.28
Outer sort field, AC2.34
Outlook 2010, IO.2
Overview (application programs). *See* Application
    programs (overview)

p

Page Footer, AC3.58
Page Header, AC3.58
Page Layout group, AC1.89, AC3.77, ACCS.6, ACCS.7
Page margin, AC1.82
Page orientation, AC1.81, AC1.82
Page setup, AC3.65–AC3.67
Page Size group, AC3.77, ACCS.6, ACCS.7
Paragraph dialog box, IO.23
Parameter query, AC3.20, AC3.41–AC3.45
Parameter value, AC3.43, AC3.44
Paste, IO.45, IO.46, IO.48
Paste Options, IO.46
Paste Preview, IO.46
Pencil symbol, AC1.36

Picture, AC1.39
Plan, AC1.5
.potm, IO.54
.potx, IO.54
Power failure, IO.53
PowerPoint 2010, IO.10–IO.11
.ppam, IO.54
.ppsm, IO.54
.ppsx, IO.54
.ppt, IO.54
.pptm, IO.54
.pptx, IO.54
Previewing a table, AC1.78–AC1.79
Print, IO.56–IO.59
    form, AC2.78–AC2.79
    relationship report, AC3.68–AC3.69
    report, AC3.65–AC3.69
    selected record, AC2.78–AC2.79
    table, AC1.80
Print dialog box, AC1.80
Print group, AC1.88, ACCS.7
Print Preview, IO.58, IO.59, AC1.11, AC2.78, AC3.48
Print Preview tab, AC1.88–AC1.89, AC3.77, ACCS.7
Print Preview window, AC1.79
Print settings, IO.57, IO.58
Project 2010, IO.2
Properties, IO.27, IO.51–IO.52
Properties dialog box, AC1.76
Properties group, ACCS.5
Properties panel, IO.52
Property Update Options button, AC1.30
Protect Document drop-down menu, IO.27
Publisher 2010, IO.2

q

Queries group, ACCS.3
Query, AC3.19–AC3.45
    adding fields, AC3.27–AC3.28
    duplicate records, AC3.39–AC3.41
    filtering, AC3.23–AC3.24
    hiding/sorting columns, AC3.32–AC3.34
    join, AC3.26, AC3.28
    multitable, AC3.25
    overview, AC3.20
    parameter, AC3.41–AC3.45
    Query Wizard, AC3.20–AC3.23
    rearrange datasheet, AC3.34
    second table, AC3.25–AC3.26
    sort, AC3.33
    specifying criteria, AC3.29–AC3.32
    types, AC3.20
    unmatched records, AC3.35–AC3.39
Query criteria, AC3.29–AC3.32
Query Design view, AC3.25
Query object, AC1.9
Query Setup group, AC3.76, ACCS.5
Query Tools Design tab, AC3.25, AC3.76, ACCS.5
Query Wizard, AC3.20–AC3.23
Quick Access toolbar, IO.14–IO.18, IO.66, AC2.85, ACCS.1
Quick add feature, AC1.17–AC1.18
Quick Add shortcut menu, AC1.19

r

Recent Databases window, AC1.74
Recent tab, IO.25
Record, AC1.4

Record indicator, AC3.45
Record number indicator, AC1.10, AC1.11
Record source, AC2.47
Records group, AC1.87, AC2.85, AC3.75, ACCS.2
Redisplaying hidden fields, AC2.16–AC2.17
Redo button, IO.45
Redundant data, AC1.5
Referential integrity, AC3.15, AC3.18–AC3.19
Refine and review, AC1.5
Relational database, AC1.4
Relationship, AC3.13–AC3.19
    define, AC1.69–AC1.70
    delete, AC3.15–AC3.17
    overview, AC1.66
    print report, AC3.68–AC3.69
    referential integrity, AC3.18–AC3.19
    types, AC1.66
    view, AC1.67–AC1.69
Relationship report, AC3.68–AC3.69
Relationship Tools Design tab, AC3.77, ACCS.5
Relationships group, AC2.86, AC3.76, ACCS.4
Repeat button, IO.43
Replace, AC2.30–AC2.32
Report, AC3.46. *See also* Report writing
Report design, AC3.47
Report Design view, AC3.58
Report Design window, AC3.58
Report Footer, AC3.58
Report Header, AC3.58
Report Layout Tools Design tab, AC3.77,
    ACCS.5–ACCS.6
Report Layout Tools Format tab, AC3.76
Report Layout Tools Page Setup tab, AC3.77
Report Layout Tools tabs, AC3.54–AC3.67
Report object, AC1.9
Report theme, AC3.56
Report tool, AC3.47–AC3.48
Report view, AC1.11, AC3.48
Report Wizard, AC3.49–AC3.53
Report writing, AC3.46–AC3.68
    copy report, ACWT9–ACWT1.12
    creation, methods of, AC3.47
    deleting a field, AC3.63–AC3.64
    filtering, AC3.64–AC3.65
    formatting controls, AC3.60–AC3.63
    modify report (design view), AC3.56–AC3.60
    modify report (layout view), AC3.53–AC3.55
    overview, AC3.46
    page setup, AC3.65–AC3.67
    preview, AC3.67–AC3.68
    print, AC3.65–AC3.69
    relationship report, AC3.68–AC3.69
    report theme, AC3.56
    Report tool, AC3.47–AC3.48
    Report Wizard, AC3.49–AC3.53
    sections (design window), AC3.58
    sort, AC3.64–AC3.65
    viewing the report, AC3.48–AC3.49
Reports group, AC3.75, ACCS.3
Required property, AC1.22
Restore button, IO.14
Results group, AC3.76, ACCS.5
Ribbon, IO.14, IO.15, IO.18–IO.20, IO.24, AC1.8
Right outer join, AC3.28
Row label, AC3.25
Row Source property box, AC2.21
Rows and Columns group, AC2.87, ACCS.6–ACCS.7
Rules of referential integrity, AC1.66, AC3.15,
    AC3.18–AC3.19

S

Save, IO.52–IO.55
Save as, IO.53, IO.54
Save As dialog box, IO.54, AC3.70
Saved Exports dialog box, ACWT1.5
ScreenTips, IO.15–IO.16, IO.20–IO.21
Scrolling the document window, IO.30–IO.33
Search, AC2.23–AC2.25
Search box, AC2.23
Select All button, AC1.10
Select query, AC3.20
Select Record button, AC1.10, AC1.11
Selecting text, IO.37–IO.40
Selection keys, IO.37
Serial value, AC1.15
Setting database and object properties, AC1.75–AC1.78
SharePoint Designer 2010, IO.2
Shortcut keys, IO.66, IO.67
Shortcut menu, IO.17
Show box, AC3.25
Show/Hide group, AC3.76, ACCS.5
Show Table dialog box, AC1.68
Shutter Bar close button, AC1.10
Simple Query Wizard dialog box, AC3.22, AC3.23
Sizing
    controls, AC2.58–AC2.59
    resize a column, AC1.48
Sort, AC2.35–AC2.36
    form, AC2.74
    multiple fields, AC2.34–AC2.36
    overview, AC2.33
    query, AC3.33
    report, AC3.64–AC3.65
    single field, AC2.33–AC2.34
Sort & Filter group, AC2.85–AC2.86, ACCS.2
Source, AC1.64, IO.45
Source file, ACWT1.2
Split
    cells, AC2.64–AC2.65
    layout, AC2.60–AC2.61
Split Form tool, AC2.47
SQL query, AC3.20
Stacked format, AC2.51
Standard colors, AC2.37, AC2.38
Starting an Office 2010 application, IO.14–IO.15
Status bar, IO.14, IO.15, AC1.8
Subdatasheet, AC1.71–AC1.72
Switching views, AC1.22–AC1.24
System clipboard, IO.45, IO.47

T

Tab order, AC2.49
Table, AC1.4
    active, AC1.63
    close, AC1.67
    create, AC1.10–AC1.21, AC1.58–AC1.59
    delete, AC3.13, AC3.17
    documentation, AC1.77–AC1.78
    evaluate design, AC3.5–AC3.10
    open, AC1.70, AC1.71
    preview, AC1.78–AC1.79
    print, AC1.80
    switching between, AC1.63

Table Analyzer Wizard, AC3.5–AC3.8
Table fields, AC1.11, AC1.12
Table group, AC2.87, ACCS.6
Table list lookup field, AC3.10–AC3.12
Table name, AC1.23, AC1.24
Table object, AC1.9
Table tab, AC1.9
Table Tools Datasheet tab, AC2.87, ACCS.5
Table Tools Design tab, AC1.24, AC1.88, AC2.86
Table Tools Field Tab, AC1.9, AC1.88, ACCS.4–ACCS.5
Tables drop-down menu, AC2.76
Tables group, AC2.86, ACCS.3
Tabs, IO.18, IO.19–IO.20
Tabular format, AC2.51, AC2.52
Tag, IO.51
Task pane, IO.24
Template, AC1.7
Terminology. *See* Concept; Glossary
Text
    edit, IO.36, IO.37
    enter, IO.34–IO.35
    format, IO.40–IO.43
    select, IO.37–IO.40
Text color, AC2.39–AC2.40
Text controls, AC2.54
Text data type, AC1.15
Text effects, IO.40
Text Formatting group, AC2.85, ACCS.3
Text length, AC1.24–AC1.26
Theme, AC2.69–AC2.71, AC3.56
Theme colors, AC2.37, AC2.38
Themes gallery, AC2.70
Themes group, AC2.87, ACCS.5
.thmx, IO.54
3NF, AC1.72
Title, IO.51
Title bar, IO.14
Tools group, AC1.88, AC2.86, AC3.77, ACCS.5, ACCS.6
Tooltip, IO.16
Totals row, AC3.45–AC3.46
Typeface, IO.40

U

Unbound control, AC2.54
Undo, IO.43–IO.45
Undo drop-down menu, IO.44
Unequal join, AC3.28
Unhide Columns dialog box, AC2.16
Unmatched records, AC3.35–AC3.39
Update query, AC3.20

V

Validation rule expression, AC2.12
Validation Rule property, AC1.22
Validation rules, AC2.10–AC2.14
Validation text, AC2.11
Validation Text property, AC1.22
Value list, AC2.18
Verifying data accuracy and validity, AC1.35–AC1.37
Version compatibility, IO.55
View
    basic views, listed, AC1.11
    relationship, AC1.67–AC1.69

report, AC3.48–AC3.49
  subdatasheet, AC1.71–AC1.72
  switching, AC1.22–AC1.24
View buttons, IO.15, AC1.8
View drop-down menu, AC1.23
View selector, IO.14
View tab, IO.67
Views group, AC1.87, AC1.88, AC2.85, AC3.75, ACCS.1,
  ACCS.4, ACCS.5
Visio 2010, IO.2

W

Wildcard, AC2.26
Window, IO.14–IO.15, AC1.8, AC1.9
Window button, IO.14
Windows Photo Viewer, AC1.42
Wizard, AC2.18
Word 2010, IO.2–IO.4
  copy query object to, ACWT1.7–ACWT1.9
  export to, ACWT1.6–ACWT1.7

X

.xls, IO.54
.xlsm, IO.54
.xlsx, IO.54
.xltx, IO.54
.xps, IO.54

Y

Yes/No data type, AC1.15

Z

Zoom, IO.33–IO.34
Zoom dialog box, IO.33, IO.34, AC1.46
Zoom group, IO.67, AC1.89, ACCS.7
Zoom slider, IO.14, IO.15, IO.33
Zooming a field, AC1.45–AC.47

Credits

AC1.2   Ryan Mcvay/Getty Images

AC2.2   Jupiterimages

AC3.2   Corbis Super R/Alamy

Notes

Notes

Notes

Notes

Notes

Notes

Notes

Notes